Judaism Before Jesus

THE IDEAS AND EVENTS THAT SHAPED THE NEW TESTAMENT WORLD

ANTHONY J. TOMASINO

InterVarsity Press
Downers Grove, Illinois
Leicester, England

InterVarsity Press, USA
P.O. Box 1400, Downers Grove, IL 60515-1426, USA
World Wide Web: www.ivpress.com
E-mail: mail@ivpress.com

Inter-Varsity Press, England
38 De Montfort Street, Leicester LE1 7GP, England
World Wide Web: www.ivpbooks.com
E-mail: ivp@uccf.org.uk

InterVarsity Press®, U.S.A., is the book-publishing division of InterVarsity Christian Fellowship/USA®, a student
movement active on campus at hundreds of universities, colleges and schools of nursing in the United States of America,
and a member movement of the International Fellowship of Evangelical Students. For information about local
and regional activities, write Public Relations Dept., InterVarsity Christian Fellowship/USA, 6400 Schroeder Rd.,
P.O. Box 7895, Madison, WI 53707-7895, or visit the IVCF website at <www.ivcf.org>.

Inter-Varsity Press, England, is the book-publishing division of the Universities and Colleges Christian Fellowship
(formerly the Inter-Varsity Fellowship), a student movement linking Christian Unions in universities and
colleges throughout the United Kingdom and the Republic of Ireland, and a member movement of the International
Fellowship of Evangelical Students. For information about local and national activities write to UCCF, 38 De Montfort Street,
Leicester LE1 7GP.

Scripture quotations, unless otherwise noted, are from the New Revised Standard Version of the Bible,
copyright 1989 by the Division of Christian Education of the National Council of the Churches of Christ in the USA.
Used by permission. All rights reserved.

Cover design: Kathleen Lay Burrows

Cover image: SEF/Art Resource

USA ISBN 0-8308-2730-7
UK ISBN 0-85111-787-2

Printed in the United States of America ∞

Library of Congress Cataloging-in-Publication Data

Tomasino, Anthony J., 1961-
   Judaism before Jesus: the events & ideas that shaped the New
Testament world/ Anthony J. Tomasino.
    p. cm.
Includes bibliographical references and indexes.
   ISNB 0-8308-2730-7 (bpk.: alk. paper)
   1. Bible. O.T.—History of Biblical events. 2. Jews—History—To 70
A.D. 3. Judaism—History—To 70 A.D. 4. Bible. N.T.—Relation to the
Old Testament. I. Title.
   BS 1197.T63 2003
   296'.09'014—dc22
                         2003016151

British Library Cataloguing in Publication Data

A catalogue record for this book is available from the British Library.

P	20	19	18	17	16	15	14	13	12	11	10	9	8	7	6	5	4	3	2	1
Y	19	18	17	16	15	14	13	12	11	10	09	08	07	06	05	04	03			

Contents

List of Figures

Preface

It's customary to begin a work of this sort by explaining why the author felt the need to write the book. With so many excellent texts on early Judaism available, why have I felt compelled to field yet another contestant? And almost all of those who undertake projects like this one defend their work by saying, "But this one's different!" And so, you won't be surprised when I make the same claim. But the fact is, I conceived this project from the start to be something unique: an introduction that assumes almost no prior knowledge of the subject matter. This book has been written for readers who wouldn't know an apocalypse from an apostrophe, or a Hyrcanus from a hurricane. It's an introduction for the uninitiated.

Of course, there are other texts on the market that claim to require no prior knowledge of the material. But in my experience, the standard texts are pretty daunting to beginning students. When I was teaching public education courses for the University of Chicago, students often asked if I could recommend a good, general overview of the Second Temple Period for their personal studies. I gave them the names of several introductory texts, good books written by top-notch scholars. And invariably the students were back a couple weeks later, asking, "Can you recommend anything else?" Their complaint was almost always that the authors assumed too much background knowledge. Often written for students in seminaries or biblical studies programs, the books were above the heads of the typical layperson. The works are impressive and useful, but they're not very accessible to the general public or the average churchgoer.

My perception of the need for a different kind of introduction grew while I was serving as a pastor. I would sometimes give lectures on the Dead Sea Scrolls and intertestamental Judaism in the congregations I served, and sometimes these lectures attracted crowds from a variety of churches. I often heard comments like, "I always wondered why the Old Testament was written in Hebrew and the New Testament was written in Greek!" And I often had people ask me whether I'd consider writing a book for the person in the pew, telling them in plain language what happened, why it happened and what it means for our Christian faith.

It's on this last issue that the standard introductions often fail. Some of these texts have been written or edited by multifaith teams, and they're careful to avoid the appearance of "confessional bias." Several good texts have been produced by Jewish scholars that deal very competently with questions of interest to those of their own faith, but not so well with questions buzzing around in the minds of New Testament readers. And even books produced by Christian scholars often avoid dealing with faith issues because they anticipate their texts being used in secular classrooms. It seemed to me that I could fill a niche by writing a readable introduction to the period that was designed specifically for Christian lay readers: a book that assumes readers with a conservative view of the Scriptures and anticipates the "cognitive dissonance" that such readers feel when they're introduced to academic studies of the Bible and biblical history; one that would be user friendly to a Bible school student, a seminarian or a Sunday school teacher who, for example, just wants to know why the Sadducees didn't believe in the resurrection of the dead.

I originally planned this book as a short, breezy overview of the historical and theological developments of the intertestamental period, directed solely at a lay audience. But Dan Reid of InterVarsity Press saw the manuscript's potential as a supplemental text for classroom use (thanks, Dan— I think). So we've expanded the text, added numerous textboxes and beefed up the documentation. Hopefully, these features will make the book more useful to students, and maybe even some biblical scholars will find it a profitable read. Because this text is an introduction, I've tried to stick to the scholarly consensus on points of uncertainty, whenever possible. Of course, there are cases where I believe the consensus is wrong, and I've tried to keep a clear distinction between the general opinion and my own conclusions. I realize that I don't argue my case here to the satisfaction of scholars. But technical arguments would lose my general readers and would require me to spend precious pages documenting quotations, opinions and other such minutiae. No doubt some passages in this book will be a little controversial. But in a field fraught with so much uncertainty, a little controversy is unavoidable.

I'd like to express my thanks to Dan Reid and the other good people at IVP who read the text. Thanks for catching a good many infelicities, some indiscretions and maybe a few actual mistakes. Any errors that remain are, I suppose, my own responsibility (although I'd rather blame them on Belial). I'd also like to thank my wife, Cordelia, for putting up with me while I labored over the manuscript and she labored over the delivery of our third child. And finally, I have to say a special word of thanks to my father, Robert Tomasino, who read the entire manuscript before it went to the editors. He's just the kind of person that I wrote this book for—an armchair biblical scholar. It was he who first introduced me to Josephus, probably before I was in my teens. I'm sure neither of us imagined at the time just how close Josephus and I would one day become.

Abbreviations

Flavius Josephus

Ant.	*Antiquities of the Jews*
Life	*The Life of Flavius Josephus*
War	*The Jewish War*

Rabbinic Literature

M.	Mishnah
T.	Tosephta
B. Tal.	Babylonian Talmud *(Talmud Bavli)*
Y. Tal.	Jerusalem Talmud *(Talmud Yerushalmi)*

Apocrypha

1 Macc	1 Maccabees
2 Macc	2 Maccabees
Sir	Sirach (Ecclesiasticus)
Wis	Wisdom of Solomon

Biblical Books

Gen	1 Sam
Ex	2 Sam
Lev	1 Kings
Num	2 Kings
Deut	1 Chron
Josh	2 Chron
Judg	Ezra
Ruth	Neh

Esther	Lk
Job	Jn
Ps	Acts
Prov	Rom
Eccles	1 Cor
Song	2 Cor
Is	Gal
Jer	Eph
Lam	Phil
Ezek	Col
Dan	1 Thess
Hos	2 Thess
Joel	1 Tim
Amos	2 Tim
Obad	Tit
Jon	Philem
Mic	Heb
Nahum	Jas
Hab	1 Pet
Zeph	2 Pet
Hag	1 Jn
Zech	2 Jn
Mal	3 Jn
Mt	Jude
Mk	Rev

I

Putting Together the Past

Imagine you're sitting in your living room engrossed in an old-fashioned mystery movie. The tension mounts as characters are introduced and then creatively "dispatched." The clues point to several possible suspects. For about an hour you've been sitting on the edge of your seat, eagerly anticipating each new development. And then the phone rings. You reluctantly pull yourself away from the TV and rush to the receiver, planning to make a quick apology and get back to your flick. But when you recognize your boss's voice on the other end of the line, you know the movie's going to have to wait. You listen dutifully for the next half hour as your manager outlines the strategy for the sales meeting next Tuesday. But as soon as he says, "I'll see you tomorrow," you pop the handset into its cradle, and you're back to the tube like a flash, eager to see what has transpired.

You're just in time to catch the end of the flick. The detective has gathered all the suspects in the old mansion's parlor—but you don't recognize half of their faces. The characters recount crimes and clues that you've never heard of. Disappointed and irritated, you discover that *you're* the one who's clueless. After missing the middle of the movie, the climax doesn't make a lot of sense.

Frustrating? No doubt. But it's not much unlike the experience of trying to piece together Jewish history by reading through the Old and New Testaments in the Protestant Bible. The Old Testament chronicles the epic story of the rise and fall of Israel. This story begins about two thousand years before the time of Christ, when God chose an insignificant Semitic people to become his special instrument in the world. It tells of Israel's rise to power and its collapse under the weight of its sin. It closes with the account of how the Persians restored the Jews to their land and incorporated them into the Persian Empire. When the Old Testament historical narrative ends, the Jews are still the insignificant subjects of the mighty Persians. We enter into the period that some Protestants have called "the Four Hundred Silent Years."

When the New Testament story begins, the world is entirely different. The Persians have vanished from the picture, and the Romans rule over God's chosen people. The common language is no longer Hebrew, nor (as one might expect) is it now Latin—it's Greek. The geography also has changed. Jesus comes from the town of Nazareth in the obscure region called Galilee, rarely mentioned in the Old Testament. The Jews have become a cosmopolitan people, present it seems in every province and city of the Roman Empire. New social groups and religious ideas confront us in every Gospel story. We read about Pharisees, Sadducees and Herodians. There's frequent talk of the devil and demons; of eternal suffering in hell and eternal life in heaven—concepts never discussed much in the Old Testament. Astute Bible students might be able to trace the connections from some of these New Testament ideas back to their Old Testament roots, but the task won't be an easy one. They're missing several hundred years of Jewish political and religious history. That's like trying to figure out the plot of a two-hour movie after missing a half hour in the middle—and one of the most eventful half hours at that.

We can certainly understand most of the New Testament without a knowledge of the "intertestamental period"—the time between the Testaments. We can understand the Old Testament too. But we can't fully appreciate the way these two bodies of literature relate to one another without knowing something of what the Jews experienced between the time of the prophet Malachi and the time of Jesus. As we study the intertestamental literature, we'll come to see how Jewish and Christian ideas about the devil and his minions arose from early Israelite concepts of evil. We also see that the Jewish sects so prominent in the New Testament didn't just spring out of the earth. And we can see that Jesus' ministry, while probably not what most of the Jews would have hoped for from their Messiah, fit well into the mosaic of Jewish expectations during the time in which he lived. A basic knowledge of intertestamental Judaism will give our New Testament study a greater richness. The words, the ideas and the people will take on new depth as we look at them in the light of four hundred years of Jewish struggle, suffering and theological speculation.

This is an exciting time for the study of intertestamental Judaism. The 1947 discovery of the Dead Sea Scrolls, ancient Jewish manuscripts dating to the time of Jesus, has opened up a rich vein of new information on Judaism in Jesus' day. Other recently discovered ancient texts as well as new archaeological methods have also given us a great deal of useful data. What has long been hidden can now be revealed and profitably applied to the study of the Scriptures by any interested minister or layperson. The new land is ready to be spied out; its fruit waits to be savored.

Archaeological Sources for Reconstructing Jewish History

How do we go about giving a voice to the so-called silent years? One source historians use for reconstructing the distant past is archaeological findings. Most of us have a general idea about what archaeologists do. We imagine them using pick and spade to uncover ancient artifacts and pry open doorways into the past. The excavations of important biblical sites have thrown important light on the past and forced us to reassess our understandings of some aspects of Israelite and Judean history. But not all the archaeologists' efforts are devoted to digging in ancient settlements, recovering broken pots or spearheads, or reconstructing ruined buildings. Archaeologists also devote many hours to digging in professional journals and museum collections. They work in interdisciplinary teams, sharing knowledge to interpret the significance of their findings. Modern archaeology draws on insights from many fields, such as geology, anthropology and even botany. And if they're especially fortunate, archaeologists may have opportunities to work with philologists in deciphering ancient inscriptions, texts or coins from bygone days. But such informative artifacts are rarely discovered from biblical-era Palestine.

Serious archaeologists aren't like the romantic movie heroes, racing all over the world in search of new discoveries. They specialize in a specific area and might devote many years—or even their entire career—to excavating and interpreting the history of a single site. They may produce profiles of various historical conditions, such as the population density of a region or the habitation and abandonment of a city. They can give us important information about the origins and culture of an ancient people. For instance, the earliest Philistine pots and decorations bear some striking resemblance to ancient Mycenaean pots, giving us a pretty good basis for concluding that the Philistines were of Mycenaean descent. Archaeologists

might also be able to tell us who was trading with whom: Egyptian artifacts found in Bronze Age (c. 2000 B.C.) Canaanite cities reveal the extensive trade occurring between the Egyptians and Canaanites during that
era. Sometimes excavators dig up telling clues about the rise and fall of ancient settlements. The ruins at Khirbet Qumran, near the caves where the
Dead Sea Scrolls were discovered, have yielded informative artifacts: a
devastated wall and a layer of rubble riddled with Roman arrowheads and
other imperial paraphernalia speak volumes about the circumstances under which the settlement was destroyed.

These examples demonstrate worthwhile and appropriate uses of archaeology. Some archaeologists might go further still and attempt to create
detailed reconstructions of past events on the basis of archaeological data
alone. Such hypotheses are notoriously unreliable. The history of archaeology is littered with the relics of ambitious reconstructions that had to be
abandoned when new evidence came to light.

Archaeology, for all its marvelous progress, is still an inexact science
and probably always will be. It can't give us a complete picture of what
people did, why they did it or what they might have said. It generally can't
tell us what anyone was thinking at a given time. It usually can't tell us
when major events happened, except within a few years or decades. And
many important events, like a bloodless coup or the ministry of a great individual, might leave no evidence in the archaeological record at all. And
as any honest archaeologist will admit, the absence of evidence can hardly
be taken as evidence at all. So, for example, there's no *archaeological* evidence that a man named Moses ever existed. But that lack of evidence can't
be the basis for concluding that Moses is a myth, as some scholars have argued. Negative evidence, as it's called, can't be the basis for a solid argument. A number of biblical "reconstructionists" (scholars who contend
that most of the Old Testament history is myth) are currently wiping egg
off their faces because they had insisted that King David was pure fabrica-
tion. Since no archaeological evidence of David's empire had been found,
these scholars argued that the whole United Monarchy was dreamed up
somewhere between the fifth and second centuries B.C. But just recently an
inscription was found at Tel Dan in northern Israel that mentions the
"house of David" and "king of Israel." The inscription has been dated to
the ninth century B.C.—well before the time that the reconstructionists argue the biblical stories about David originated. At the very least the inscription demonstrates the antiquity of the David tradition, and it serves

as strong external evidence to the fact that David really did exist. In this case negative evidence has been disproved by the simple turn of a spade.

Even when archaeologists have many well-preserved artifacts to study, it can still be difficult to interpret their meaning. Different archaeologists looking at the same material will often come to very different conclusions. The site known as Khirbet Qumran is an excellent example. When Father Roland DeVaux was given the assignment of excavating the site in the 1950s, he believed that the Dead Sea Scrolls were written at that very location. He interpreted his findings in light of descriptions of communal life found in some of the Scrolls. DeVaux identified a large water reservoir as a pool for ritual bathing. One large room was reconstructed as a communal dining hall. Another room identified as a scriptorium, where brothers of the Community leaned over tables to copy their scrolls. Most scholars basically accept DeVaux's interpretation of the site, but not everyone is in agreement. Other archaeologists have argued that Khirbet Qumran was a military fortress, and some have even claimed it was a palatial villa. Qualified investigators can interpret the same data in very different ways. Archaeological reconstructions of the past must always be regarded as tentative, subject to further review and the discovery of new evidence.

Textual Sources for Reconstructing Jewish History

So if archaeological evidence can be imprecise and unreliable, how do we go about reconstructing ancient history? Our primary sources will always be ancient texts. For ancient Israel, our major textual source of historical information is the Old Testament itself. Except for a few scattered inscriptions and references in other ancient texts, the Bible tells us almost everything we know about biblical-era Israel. Once we push out into the intertestamental era there's a good deal more archaeological data, from ruins to coins to funerary inscriptions. But even so, historians still depend primarily on the vast wealth of textual witnesses that derive from this most creative and productive period. It's clear now that these years were anything but "silent"—it was a time of great literary creativity and theological reflection among the Jews. Some might argue that God's voice had been stilled during this time, but his people certainly continued to speak, and they spoke volumes.

Biblical Texts. Most of the intertestamental age falls into the time that scholars call the Second Temple Period (515 B.C. to A.D. 70)—aptly named because it was the time when the Jews' second temple stood in Jerusalem (the first temple—Solomon's—was destroyed in 586 B.C.). Because it forms such a well-defined unit, we'll consider the entire Second Temple Period in this study, and not the intertestamental period alone. For the beginning of this period the biblical books of Ezra, Nehemiah, Haggai and Zechariah are our most important sources of information. Archaeologists have discovered other ancient texts that supplement our knowledge of the period, but they can't begin to match the significance of these biblical documents.

Once we move beyond the century or so covered by these texts, our sources become much more diverse. We no longer have a nicely edited biblical narrative on which we may rely for information. Only one book of the Protestant Bible really deals with the era in any depth: the book of Daniel. According to the stories in the opening chapters of the book, Daniel, a Jewish seer, was taken away to live in Babylon after the siege of Jerusalem in 598 B.C. There, he rose to a high position in the Babylonian court, due to his ability to interpret dreams (a position he held under the Persians, as well). He was also given symbolic visions whereby God revealed future events. Tradition holds that Daniel wrote the entire book that bears his name, and some scholars believe the tradition is reliable. Most scholars, however, believe that the final form of the book comes from the time around 167 B.C., when the Jews in Palestine were being persecuted by a Greek tyrant named Antiochus Epiphanes.[1] And yet, whether we date the composition of Daniel earlier or later, almost all students of the book agree that the later chapters, and especially chapter 11, speak of the time when the Greeks dominated the East, explicitly recounting major political events from the time when Alexander the Great conquered Palestine (332 B.C.) up to the time of Antiochus Epiphanes. And so the book of Daniel provides us with some significant historical data about the era when the Greeks ruled the Jews. It also gives us insights into the development of Jewish religious ideas in the Second Temple Period.

---

[1]Daniel 11 describes how the "king of the Greeks" (Alexander the Great) would conquer the king of Persia, an event that occurred in 331 B.C. The chapter continues to outline the political history of Greek rule in the East up to the time of King Antiochus Epiphanes in 167 B.C., describing how he would declare himself a god and persecute the Jews. From that point on the author seems to have no specific knowledge of events—only a general idea that God would intervene and save his people. And so, say many scholars, the book of Daniel seems to have been published during the time of the Antiochan persecution to provide encouragement for the suffering Jews. The greatest difficulty with this theory is an ethical one: wouldn't it have been deceptive and dishonest to issue a book in the name of a long-dead figure and present it as a prophecy? We will discuss this issue more when we consider the nature of pseudepigrapha, literary works issued in the names of dead saints.

The Apocrypha. In the Protestant Bible the book of Daniel is the only source of historical information for the four hundred silent years. But Catholic and Orthodox Bibles preserve a great deal of literature from this period, in the collection known as the Apocrypha (from the Greek word meaning "hidden") or deuterocanonical books ("second canon"). These books originated in different places and at different times—from the third century B.C. to almost A.D. 100. They were originally written in Hebrew, Aramaic (the official language of the Babylonian and Persian empires) and Greek. Some were written in Palestine, others in Babylon, and some were written by Jews living in Egypt. They represent a variety of points of view and experiences.

The reason these books don't appear in the Protestant or Jewish Bibles arises from the circumstances in which Christianity and rabbinic Judaism developed. The first Christians were all Jewish, and their Bible was the Hebrew Bible of the Jews—what we now call the Old Testament. At the time of Jesus there was still some disagreement among the Jews about which books should be considered holy Scripture. Different versions of the Bible circulated among groups like the Pharisees, the Sadducees, the Dead Sea Scrolls community and the Jews who lived outside of Palestine. There was broad agreement on the basics: all Jews accepted the books of Moses and probably the Prophets as divine Scripture. Most accepted the Psalms, but there was some disagreement about which Psalms were actually inspired by God. Both the Dead Sea Scrolls and some ancient translations of the Old Testament contain significantly different versions of the Psalms than those that were included in the collection eventually accepted by the Jews (and Christians). There also seems to have been debate around books like Ecclesiastes and the Song of Songs, and maybe Esther as well. It was once widely believed that the precise contents of the Old Testament *canon*—the authoritative list of books in the Bible—were fixed in A.D. 90 by a rabbinic council meeting in a town called Jamnia. According to Jewish tradition this council established the "closed canon," determining that only books produced before the time of Ezra would be regarded as Holy Scripture. Most modern scholars are skeptical about the tradition, but it may have some basis in history. The precise contents of the canon were still apparently in question at the time when the Dead Sea Scrolls and New Testament were written, and through most of the first century A.D., but around the end of the first century A.D. the Jewish historian Josephus states emphatically that

BOOKS OF THE APOCRYPHA

Listed by similarities.

Prayer of Manasseh: Included in some Orthodox Bibles, but not Catholic editions. The apostate king offers a prayer of repentance. Of uncertain date, but probably pre-Christian.

Tobit: The story of how a Jewish man overcomes a demon with divine assistance. Written about 180 B.C.

Judith: The story of a woman who uses her charm and beauty to save her people from an Assyrian oppressor. Written around 150 B.C.

1 Esdras (or 3 Ezra): Found only in the Orthodox Bible. The story of the Old Testament figure Ezra is rewritten with an emphasis on his priestly role. Composed sometime between 150 and 100 B.C.

2 Esdras (or 4 Ezra): Only in some Orthodox Bibles. Records visions purportedly given to Ezra about the destruction of the Temple and the coming of the Messiah. Written around A.D. 100 and very reminiscent of the book of Revelation in the New Testament.

Additions to Esther: A collection of prayers, letters and so forth inserted at various points in Greek versions of Esther, which make the text more explicitly "religious." Probably pre-Christian but of uncertain date.

Psalm 151: Orthodox canon only. A synopsis of the story of David. Written in Hebrew in perhaps the third century B.C.

Wisdom of Solomon: A collection of proverbs ascribed to Solomon, heavily influenced by Greek thought. Composed originally in Greek, probably in the first century B.C.

Wisdom of Jesus ben Sirach (Ecclesiasticus): A collection of proverbs and anecdotes from a Jewish world traveler. Originally written in Hebrew about 200 B.C. and then translated into Greek by the author's grandson.

Baruch: A composite text including prayers, psalms and proverbs ascribed to Baruch, Jeremiah's scribe. Written in Hebrew in the first or second century B.C.

Epistle of Jeremiah: A letter admonishing the Jews not to worship idols. Written sometime around 300 B.C. but later attached to Baruch as a sixth chapter.

Additions to Daniel: Prayers and songs attributed to the three Hebrew youths in the furnace, and two stories demonstrating Daniel's wisdom and the folly of idolatry. Written between 165 and 100 B.C.

First Maccabees: Account of the Jewish revolt against Antiochus Epiphanes. Styled after biblical chronicles. Written sometime around 100 B.C. in Hebrew or Aramaic.

Second Maccabees: Another account of the Jewish revolt, written in Greek, with more colorful digressions. Also written around 100 B.C.

Third Maccabees: Found in the Orthodox canon only. A prequel to the Maccabees, it tells of the Egyptian Jews' escape from persecution by an angry king. Written in Greek around 100 B.C.

Fourth Maccabees: Included as an appendix in some Orthodox Bibles. An expansion of the martyrdom stories from 2 Maccabees, with heavy influence from Greek thought. Written in the first century A.D.

the contents of the Jews' Bible were immutably set at a fixed number.[2] So at the end of the first century we can be pretty sure that the "mainstream" Jews considered their canon to be closed—no more books could be added to the Hebrew Bible.

But before the time when the Jews had decided on the contents of their canon, Christianity had already experienced a great deal of growth outside Judea, among people of non-Jewish backgrounds (the Gentiles). These new converts weren't able to read the Bible in the Hebrew language. Since Greek—for reasons that will become clear later—was the common language of the day, the church came to use as its Old Testament a Greek translation of the Hebrew Bible known as the Septuagint. This name comes from a Greek word meaning "seventy," based on a legend that the translation was the work of seventy-two (or, in some versions, seventy) scholars.[3]

Where did this translation come from? It arose from simple necessity. Long before the time of Jesus, many Jews had settled outside of Palestine, dispersed throughout Egypt, Babylon, Asia Minor and even in Greece and Rome. For most of these far-flung people of this so-called Diaspora, Hebrew was no longer a living language. They spoke, wrote and thought in Greek, the lingua franca of the Mediterranean world. And so in order that these children of Abraham could continue to study the Scriptures with understanding, a Greek translation (or translations) was produced and read in the Jewish synagogues throughout the realm. This translation differed significantly from the Hebrew Bible text that the rabbis chose as their canon. Every translation is to some extent an interpretation, and the translators of the Septuagint often interpreted Scripture passages according to their own interests or biases. But there were other differences as well. For one thing the books were arranged differently. The traditional Hebrew text is arranged with Law (books of Moses) first, Prophets (including Judges through 2 Kings, called the "former prophets") second, and the various Writings (Psalms, Proverbs, Job, Song of Solomon, Ruth, Lamentations,

---

[2]Josephus *Against Apion* 1.8. There's been much discussion about whether or not Josephus's number can be made to correspond to the actual contents of the canon, but the point here is that he claims the Jews held the contents of the Bible to be fixed, not whether or not there was universal agreement on the canon's contents.

[3]The legend is first found in the so-called *Letter of Aristeas*. It probably has little basis in fact. The Septuagint is most likely a composite work containing several styles of Greek and representing different translation philosophies. It came into being over many years, as need arose for various Bible books in Greek.

Ecclesiastes, Esther, Daniel, Ezra, Nehemiah, 1-2 Chronicles) third.[4] Probably the arrangement reflected the level of "holiness" attached to the books, or perhaps the "Writings" were simply composed later than the other texts. In any event the Septuagint arranged the books differently: Law first, historical books next, then the poetic and "wise sayings" books, and last the prophets (major prophets first, then the minor prophets, in their supposed order of composition).[5]

That wasn't the only difference, however. Somehow the Septuagint came to have several books included in it that the traditional Hebrew text lacked—the books of the Apocrypha. There's some mystery surrounding how that addition occurred. Philo of Alexandria, a Jewish philosopher of the first century B.C. to the first century A.D., never quotes from these books as Scripture, though he must have been aware of their contents. The earliest evidence of the apocryphal works treated as Scripture comes from ancient Christian codices (plural of codex, the precursors to modern books), which bound these books together with the Septuagint translation of the Old Testament. Based on this evidence some have argued that the Apocrypha was a Christian invention. Perhaps so, but there's no reason to doubt that some Jews were reading at least parts of the Septuagint as Scripture. At any rate it's clear that for early Christians who used the Septuagint, the intertestamental period wasn't a time of silence. It was part of God's salvation history. Even after most of the Jews had adopted the rabbis' canon, the Christians continued to use their beloved Septuagint, with its apocryphal additions.

After many years of Roman rule Latin displaced Greek as the language of the people. Now the church felt the need for a new Bible in the common language. In the 4th century A.D. Jerome undertook a translation of the Bible from Greek to Latin, using both a Hebrew text and the Septuagint as the basis of his Old Testament. He decreed the books that existed in the Septuagint, but not in the Hebrew canon, to be "apocryphal," and he didn't include them in his edition of the Old Testament. Not long after his time, however, the church restored them to the text in Latin translation. This edition became known as the Vulgate (Latin for "common") Bible, and it was used in the Catholic Church up through the Middle Ages. The

---

[4]The historical books of the Old Testament were believed to have been written by prophets, so they were considered part of the prophetic corpus.

[5]How this arrangement came about is uncertain. It may even have been a Christian invention, reflecting the church's belief that Christ is the fulfillment of prophecy.

THE NEW TESTAMENT CANON

Unlike the Old Testament, the history of the New Testament canon can be traced with relative ease. In the decades after Jesus the Christians began to collect various documents that expressed the essentials of the faith. These included sayings of Jesus that had been passed on orally among his followers and later committed to writing. Eventually they were incorporated into some of the Gospels.

Other authoritative texts included letters from apostles written to various churches. In 2 Peter 3:16 the letters of Paul are grouped together with "the rest of the Scriptures." To the author of this letter they were Scripture—just like the books of the Septuagint.

By the mid-second century A.D. there was a wide consensus in the church about what texts were authoritative, but there was no New Testament canon as such. The first canon list was produced by a heretic named Marcion in A.D. 150. This collection comprised some genuine and some fake letters of Paul, and a truncated version of the Gospel according to Luke. Other heretics soon followed suit and produced New Testaments of their own.

The orthodox church responded by producing its own lists of authentic New Testament texts and official repudiations of texts that were considered spurious. The chief criteria for whether or not a book was canonical was apostolic authorship. A text either had to have been written by an apostle or a close associate of the apostles (like Luke). The collective wisdom of the church took a couple of centuries to come to a firm conclusion on which books were true and which were false, but the consensus was remarkable. The earliest orthodox canon list was the so-called Muratorian canon, dated to A.D. 180. It contained twenty-two of our current twenty-seven books of the New Testament, omitting Hebrews, James, 1-2 Peter and 3 John. It also consciously repudiated the popular Shepherd of Hermas text because it was "written too recently" to be considered Scripture.

Several more canon lists were produced in the next two centuries, agreeing on most of the books in our current New Testament. The four Gospels and the letters of Paul were universally accepted. Unlike some modern scholars, the early church had no problem discerning between authentic Gospel traditions and spurious works like the so-called "Gospel of Thomas." The books subject to the most dispute were 2 Peter, 2-3 John and Revelation.

There were two developments that necessitated the church's agreement on a "closed" canon. One was the development of the codex in second century A.D. A codex could only contain so many pages, and there was a tendency for those reading the codex to attribute great authority to its contents. The church councils had to reach an agreement on which books should be bound together.

Another significant event was the persecution initiated by Emperor Diocletian in A.D. 303. Anyone who owned a copy of the New Testament could be executed. It was essential that the church come to a consensus so none of its members would be martyred for anything but the true Word of God. After several more decades of debate on a few disputed books, the New Testament canon was officially closed at the Council of Carthage in A.D. 397.

Church came to regard the Vulgate with what can be called superstitious awe, considering the translation itself to be inspired and authoritative. Even after Latin ceased to be a living language, the Vulgate was still used in the Church. By the Middle Ages only scholars could understand the words of the Christian Scriptures.

By the fifteenth century, however, many reformers felt it was time for new Bibles in the languages of the people, so they could study the Scriptures for themselves. The first of these modern-language Bibles were simply translations of the Vulgate into English. But eventually, the Protestant scholars began to produce translations that were based not on the Latin translation but on texts in the original biblical languages: Hebrew, Aramaic and Greek. Like Jerome they used the Hebrew Bible of the Jews as the basis for their Old Testament. They also rejected the books of the Septuagint that weren't found in the Jewish Bible. (In part their reasons for rejecting these books were theological. Some books of the Apocrypha had been used to support Catholic doctrines with which the Protestants disagreed.) Martin Luther separated the Greek additions from the other biblical books and placed them under the heading "Apocrypha." While he commended these books as profitable, he cautioned that they weren't to be considered authoritative. In most Protestant circles the apocryphal books eventually came to be regarded as uninspired and unedifying reading. This was how, for most Protestants, the intertestamental period became a time of darkness and silence, as if both God and his people had lost their voices for several centuries.

Fortunately, translations of the Apocrypha are now easily available to all Christians, whether Protestant or Catholic. They provide us with a marvelous cross section of the kinds of prose and poetry that were being produced by Second Temple Period Jews. Most of the apocryphal texts aren't all that useful for reconstructing the history of the Jews per se. But two of these books, 1 and 2 Maccabees, have been vitally important to historians. It's not really accurate to call them "first" and "second," because we really don't know for sure which was written first. Nor should we think of them as first and second, like 1-2 Kings in the Old Testament. For while 1-2 Kings record earlier and later events, respectively, 1-2 Maccabees record essentially the same events: those leading up to the Jewish revolt against the Greek king Antiochus Epiphanes in 167 B.C. and the establishment of a new Jewish dynasty. But in spite of the fact that the two works have basically the same story line, they're very different in character. First Maccabees was written in Judea, in Aramaic or possibly Hebrew. The original, however, has perished and now exists only in Greek translation. This book was consciously patterned after the Old Testament royal chronicles (1-2 Kings; 1-2 Chronicles). It's clearly designed to demonstrate that the Maccabees (more accurately the "Hasmonaeans," as we will see later) should be regarded as the legitimate monarchs of the Jews. Second Maccabees is an abbreviated edition of a much longer work written by Jason, a Jew living in Cyrene (North Africa). We don't know who edited the text. The original work was written in Greek for Jews living outside Palestine, among the Diaspora communities (Jews living in Gentile lands). It's shorter than 1 Maccabees and covers a smaller span of time. This work is written more along the line of a Greek history, like the work of Herodotus. It has the pace of an adventure story and includes many legendary and gruesome stories that make it a fascinating read. First and Second Maccabees also differ in theological point of view. In 1 Maccabees there seems to be an assumption that our only hope of an "afterlife" is in gaining glory and a good name, so that our descendants will sing our praises. There's little in this book about angels or divine intervention. Its outlook seems similar to the one associated with the Sadducees in the New Testament. In 2 Maccabees, on the other hand, there's a strong emphasis on the resurrection of the dead and eternal rewards. There's also more interest in supernatural phenomenon, like the appearance of angelic beings. The second book of Maccabees tends more toward what would become the Pharisees' theology—and Christians' as well.

The pseudepigrapha and apocalypses. Another large body of important texts from this period is that group we know as the "pseudepigrapha" (singular "pseudepigraphon"). The word *pseudepigrapha* means "false inscriptions." It refers to works issued under a false name, usually of some famous person, often one who's long dead by the time of the writing. Some pseudepigrapha, like the Wisdom of Solomon (written about 100 B.C.), capitalize on the reputation of an ancient saint to present an updated message for the author's time. The book of *Jubilees*, written about 150 B.C., is a very important pseudepigraphon written in the name of Moses. This work retells the stories of Genesis and Exodus, but the author puts a "spin" on the stories that clearly reveals his own biases and concerns. He is especially concerned about ritual purity (i.e., proper washings), mixed marriages between Jews and Gentiles, and fixing the proper dates for various Jewish holidays. This text receives its name from the fact that it divides history into periods of forty-nine years, the biblical "jubilee."[6]

Many pseudepigrapha claim to record prophetic visions of ancient seers—visions that describe the very events occurring at the time when the pseudepigrapha were written. The *Fourth Book of Ezra,* for example, claims to record visions given to Ezra the scribe, who lived over four hundred years before the time of Jesus. But actually the book was quite clearly written during the days of the Roman Empire. The vision "foretells" the rise of Rome, its oppression of the Jews and the destruction of the temple in Jerusalem—an event that occurred in A.D. 70. It continues on to predict the imminent coming of the Messiah, who would bring an end to the Roman tyranny.

This pseudepigraphon and many others are what we call "apocalypses" (from the Greek word meaning "to uncover"). When we use the word *apocalypse* in Jewish studies, we're referring to a category of literary works that share several characteristics. First, most apocalypses are pseudepigraphic. That is, they're usually written in the name of a famous person from the author's past. In the apocalypse the hero may travel to heaven or hell to receive a revelation; or he may see a symbolic vision that predicts and explains significant events. An angel usually accompanies the seer to explain the meaning of the scenes or symbols revealed in the vision. In most cases the visions describe events that are actually occurring during the author's time, and they promise that God will dramatically intervene in world affairs. In the Bible there are two major apocalypses: Daniel 7—12 and the Revelation of John. Outside the Bible there were a great many apocalypses written by both Jews and Christians. It was a very popular genre of literature.

One figure who was the subject of several apocalypses was Enoch, the early descendant of Adam who was so pious that God took him to heaven without requiring him to experience death (Gen 5:24). Many Jewish writers speculated about the wonders that Enoch must have seen on his trip to heaven—and any other trips he might have taken before the final journey. The text called *1 Enoch* is actually a collection of several independent works that have been edited together into a single book. Its sections include (among others) the "Astronomical Book," written before 200 B.C., recording Enoch's vision of the heavenly bodies; the "Animal Apocalypse," c. 165 B.C., which symbolically "predicts" the Jewish revolt against the

---

[6]See Lev 25:8-17, 29-34, 47-55; 27:22-24.

Greeks; and the "Similitudes," c. 100 B.C., which speaks of the coming of a supernatural Messiah, who will judge all of creation.

One of the troubling aspects of pseudepigraphic literature is that it seems deliberately deceptive. Were the authors of these texts dishonest people, attempting to bamboozle the naive masses with their trickery? But if they were deliberately attempting to deceive, what did they hope to gain by it? No one made any money writing pseudepigrapha, and they certainly didn't intend to become famous through their efforts. Quite the opposite, in fact: if they had done their work well, no one would ever know they were responsible for these texts. It seems safe to rule out self-interest as the motive for writing works such as these. Could zealotry be a more likely motive? After all, fanatics can often justify less-than-honest methods to further a cause that they consider just. But would scrupulously pious Jews be comfortable using deliberate deception, even in the service of a good cause? It hardly seems likely that they could rail against dishonesty and deceit while they themselves were being willfully dishonest in their method of presentation.

These problems have led some people to suggest that the authors wrote the pseudepigrapha knowing that their readers would recognize them for what they are: pious frauds. But that explanation doesn't hold water either. When the author of the book of Jude quotes from the *Similitudes of Enoch,* he leaves no doubt that he's attributing the work to the old patriarch himself (Jude 14-15). Of course, in the two hundred years or so between the composition of the *Similitudes* and the composition of Jude, the Jews may well have forgotten when the text actually appeared. But what about a case like *4 Ezra*? This interesting apocalypse was clearly written sometime around A.D. 90, after the destruction of Jerusalem by the Romans, but it claims to record a revelation given to the fifth-century B.C. scribe Ezra. When the text suddenly appeared in A.D. 90, did the Jews credulously accept it as a long-lost biblical text? We know that *4 Ezra* was widely read and may even have been treated as Scripture by some Jews. Did no one wonder where the text had been hiding for the last five hundred years?

There seems to have been a shared understanding between the authors of these texts and their readers that *some* contemporary writers could speak for long-dead saints. Possibly, pseudepigraphic writing was considered a form of prophecy—inspired communication that proclaimed a God-given message. Perhaps the audience believed that its modern author was completely subsumed in the ancient character whose name he appro-

SOME IMPORTANT JEWISH PSEUDEPIGRAPHA
OF THE SECOND TEMPLE PERIOD

1 Enoch

A composite work whose various sections date from the third century
B.C. to at least the first century A.D. It purports to record revelations given
to Enoch, the Old Testament figure who was "translated" to heaven (Gen
5:21-25). Sections include "The Book of Watchers," expanding on the
story of the fallen angels from Genesis 6; the "Book of Similitudes,"
where Enoch sees a vision of the heavenly Son of Man; the "Animal
Apocalypse," a symbolic account of the Maccabean Revolt and the coming kingdom of God; the "Astronomical Book," a collection of astronomical observations; and the "Apocalypse of Weeks," an account of biblical
history. The best manuscript of the text is preserved in Ethiopic, a Semitic
language still used by Ethiopian Christians.

Testaments of the Twelve Patriarchs

A collection of texts purporting to be the last wills or "testaments" of the
patriarchs to their sons. As it now exists the Testament is a Christian work,
but portions of the work may have been composed in the Second Temple
Period by Jewish authors. A fragmentary *Testament of Levi* was found
among the Dead Sea Scrolls (4Q213) that apparently underlies our existing
Greek version. A fragmentary *Testament of Naphtali* also was found among
the Scrolls, but its relationship with the Greek version is unclear.

Jubilees

A text purporting to be an account of biblical history told to Moses on Mt.
Sinai. It essentially retells the biblical narrative of Genesis and Exodus,
dividing the history in periods of forty-nine-year "jubilees." The text emphasizes purity laws and separation from non-Jews. It was probably
composed before the Hasmonean Revolt, early in the second century B.C.
Fragments of the original Hebrew text have been found among the Dead
Sea Scrolls, but the only complete manuscripts are in Ethiopic translation.

Letter of Aristeas

An important Jewish text composed in Greek, purporting to be the letter of an Alexandrian Jew named Aristeas to his brother Philocrates recounting the translation of the Jewish Scriptures (actually, just the books of Moses) into Greek. The account is certainly legendary, but details of Jewish life and the priesthood recorded here are very enlightening. The text probably originated between 150-100 B.C.

Sybilline Oracles

Sibylline prophecies were widely known and very popular in ancient Mediterranean society. Supposedly, these were oracles uttered by women of great antiquity, undying prophetesses who predicted future events. In Jewish tradition the Sybil was identified as a daughter-in-law of Noah. The twelve books of *Sibylline Oracles* were preserved as a Christian collection, but some of the texts were undoubtedly Jewish compositions (later retouched by Christian editors). They date from various times, the earliest being composed probably in the second century B.C.

Psalms of Solomon

These eighteen texts were composed in the name of Solomon, but they probably date to the first century B.C. Their main theme is Judea's subjugation to Rome and God's imminent deliverance of his people through his Messiah. The texts were originally composed in Hebrew and later translated into Greek.

Testament of Moses

A text that purports to be Moses' final words to Joshua. It retells biblical history and extends into the Second Temple Period. Its current form comes from the first century A.D., but it may have originally been composed in an earlier period and supplemented with later additions. An important section of the text speaks of a certain "Taxo," whose voluntary martyrdom may have been expected to usher in God's kingdom.

2 Baruch

Also called the *Apocalypse of Baruch*. This text is written in the name of Jeremiah's secretary Baruch. It contains prayers, hymns, didactic (teaching) passages and visions of the future. It was probably written in the first quarter of the second century A.D. in Palestine, and it reflects on the destruction of the second temple.

priated. So even though a text might have been created by an unknown first-century A.D. Jewish sage, his creation might have been considered the actual words of Moses or Daniel or Ezra. The author intended no fraud, and the audience—as a general rule—made no such charge.

The pseudepigrapha, though, weren't automatically accepted as legitimate. Like prophecies and other religious works, they had to prove their worth. Some of these texts, like *Jubilees* and *1 Enoch*, were widely accepted as legitimate expressions of the voice of God, but not so authoritative as to be included in the Bible when the sages set the contents of the canon. Others seem to have enjoyed a good deal of popularity in a restricted circle. Some of the Dead Sea Scrolls, for example, fall into this category. They circulated in numerous copies, but never seem to have been read by anyone but the members of the sect that produced them. Still other pseudepigrapha were probably rejected right from the beginning as frauds.

The pseudepigrapha are exceptionally important texts for a couple of reasons. First, they can tell us a good deal about events taking place at the time they were written. The ancient saints in whose names the texts are written sometimes speak in detail about the political circumstances of the time when the texts were actually written. The "Animal Apocalypse" of *1 Enoch*, for instance, gives us a detailed allegorical account of the Maccabean Revolt (167 B.C.); *4 Ezra* (A.D. 90) writes symbolically about the destruction of Jerusalem in A.D. 70. Furthermore, these texts provide us with important information about the development of Jewish religious thought. The book of *Jubilees* (c. 200-175 B.C.), which claims to be a revelation given to Moses, tells us a good deal about the beliefs of the strictly observant Jew who wrote this text. The fact that the text circulated widely demonstrates that many other Jews resonated with its author's opinions. Some of the Dead Sea Scrolls base their teachings on this very text. Since many of the pseudepigrapha can be dated pretty precisely (because of the historical events they mention), we can use them to fill out our understanding of when and how various ideas came into Judaism. Ideas about the Messiah or the resurrection of the dead are just two important notions that figure prominently in a number of the pseudepigrapha.

The Dead Sea Scrolls. Since I've already mentioned the Dead Sea Scrolls several times, a brief explanation of these texts is in order. An Arab shepherd discovered the first of the Dead Sea Scrolls in a cave near the Dead Sea in 1947. Subsequently, many other texts were discovered in other caves in the region. A few of the scrolls were very well preserved, but most were broken into small pieces, with much of their content lost through the ages. About 30,000 fragments of scrolls were discovered, which fully assembled would yield 800 or 900 different texts. Initial suggestions that the texts were copied or composed in the centuries just before and after Jesus' day have been confirmed by carbon-14 dating. In fact, the earliest of the scrolls may have been written around 200 B.C., while the latest probably come from the second half of the first century A.D.

About one third of the texts are ancient copies of books of the Bible. Fragments of every Old Testament book but Esther have been found by the Dead Sea. Some researchers have argued that a tiny fragment written in Greek is a portion of the Gospel of Mark, but the identification is very dubious. (No other New Testament manuscripts were found among the Scrolls.) The biblical scrolls from the Dead Sea are the oldest Old Testament manuscripts in existence. They're fully a thousand years older than any previously known biblical manuscripts. These texts help us understand the "textual history" of the Bible (i.e., how certain biblical books circulated in different versions), and they give us important insights into the formation of the biblical canon.

The remaining two-thirds are nonbiblical texts, the vast majority of which are religious compositions. Some of these texts were previously known, but they existed only in translations from the Middle Ages: copies of the book of *Jubilees,* older sections of the book of *Enoch* and sections of the Wisdom of Ben Sirach, all in their original languages, have been found in the caves by the Dead Sea. Many others are religious compositions that were never before known, including texts that originate with a group that called itself the *Yahad,* or "Community." It's probably safe to assume that members of this Community (or its descendants) were responsible for writing or copying many of the Scrolls; they may have acquired others that were incorporated into their library. The Community members were probably involved in hiding the collection in the caves around Qumran, as well.

One of the first Dead Sea Scrolls discovered (1JQS) was a rule for ordering the Community, describing requirements for entrance, rules for purity, conduct at meals and so forth. One of its early investigators called this text the *Manual of Discipline* because it reminded him of the Methodist *Manual of Discipline.* A similar text, the *Damascus Document*, includes both rules for conduct—sometimes differing substantially from those of the *Community Rule*—and some cryptic history behind the group's formation.

THE DEAD SEA SCROLLS

There are between eight and nine hundred different texts represented among the thirty thousand fragments of the Dead Sea Scrolls. Scholars identify the Scrolls with codes that indicate the cave in which they were discovered and the reference number assigned to the manuscript by its investigators. So 11Q13 indicates that the manuscript was found in Qumran ("Q") Cave 11, and it was assigned the number 13. Many texts have been assigned names as well. 11Q13 is also known as 11Q Melchizedek (11QMelch), since its main theme is the ministry of the priest-king Melchizedek (see chap. ten). Several manuscript fragments, identified by the numbers 4Q394-399, are known collectively as 4QMMT, or 4Q*Miqsat Ma'aseh Torah*, "Some of the Deeds of the Law." In this case a single text exists in several fragmentary manuscripts.

The following categories are somewhat arbitrary because it's not always possible to distinguish between different kinds of texts. The examples following in parentheses are representative, not exhaustive. This list is primarily meant to illustrate the variety of materials found among the Dead Sea Scrolls, not to list all their contents.

Biblical Texts: At least one fragmentary copy of every book of the Old Testament, except Esther

Books from the Apocrypha: Portions of Ben Sirach (Ecclesiasticus) in Hebrew; portions of Tobit in Aramaic

Previously Known Pseudepigrapha: Portions of *1 Enoch* and *Jubilees*

Sectarian "Rules": Texts for ordering the life of the Community. For example, several copies of the *Community Rule,* or *Manual of Discipline* (1QS, for *serekh,* "order"); the *Damascus Document* (CD [a manuscript of this text was first discovered in "C"airo, Egypt, and later among the Dead Sea Scrolls]; 4QDam); the *War Scroll* (1QM, for *milchamah,* "war")

Liturgical Texts: Texts used in worship. For example, hymn collections (1Q "Psalms"; 4Q and 11Q *Songs of the Sabbath Sacrifice);*

blessings and prayers (1QSb; 4Q503); liturgies for various services (4Q409; 4Q414); calendrical texts (describing when various rituals would be performed, or when different groups of priests would serve in the temple; 4Q327-4Q330; 4Q334)

Legal Texts: For example, texts concerning laws of purity and conduct (4QHalakhah-A; 4QMMT; 4Q228); commentaries on biblical laws (4Q251); records of discipline for Community members who violated the rules (4Q477)

Biblical Commentaries: Including both verse-by-verse commentaries and "Rewritten Bible," or biblical stories retold and expanded. These include 1Q *Genesis Apocryphon*, recounting and expanding on some events from the book of Genesis; 4Q *Prayer of Nabonidus*, a prayer of the penitent king; 11Q *Temple Scroll*, which gives descriptions and regulations of an ideal temple; testaments and soliloquies of Old Testament figures *(Testament of Levi; Words of Naphtali)*; commentaries on biblical prophecies (the *pesharim*; e.g., the *Habakkuk Pesher* [1QpHab]; the Melchizedek scroll [11QMelch])

Apocalyptic and Messianic Texts: Eschatological (i.e., "end of the world") visions often attributed to various ancient seers. E.g., 4Q243, a pseudo-Daniel text; 4Q246, which speaks of a figure who'll be called "the son of God"; 4Q552-3, which includes a vision of four world kingdoms similar to those of Daniel 2 and 7

Wisdom texts: Collections of proverbs and insights. For example, *Songs of the Sage* (4Q510); lists of proverbial admonitions (4Q416, 418)

Court Tales: Tales set in the court of a foreign king (e.g., the tale of Bagasraw [4Q550])

"Magic" Texts: Physiognomies, which relate people's physical features to their character (4Q186); brontologia, which interpret the significance of celestial phenomena (4Q318); exorcism rituals (4Q560)

Miscellaneous Documents: The *Copper Scroll* (3Q15), a record inscribed on copper that tells where various treasuries have been buried; a few deeds, bills of sale, etc. (4Q342-358)

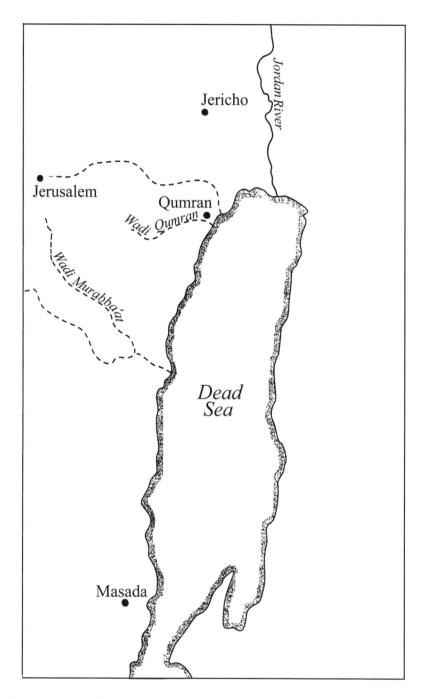

Figure 1. Location of Qumran

It tells how an evil priest persecuted the group's leader, the Teacher of Righteousness. The group was forced to flee to Damascus and set up its community there. Another text, *Miqsat Ma'aseh Hattorah* ("Some of the Matters of the Law," abbreviated 4QMMT) is written in the form of a letter to a Judean authority, outlining the Community's specific grievances against the religious establishment in Jerusalem. (We'll discuss some of these grievances in a later chapter.) An interesting text called the *War Scroll* foretells an imminent battle with Rome. It includes prophecies, instructions, hymns and prayers, all assuring the "righteous" Jews of their total victory over the "forces of darkness." Other texts include commentaries on biblical laws, retellings of biblical stories, poetry books, apocalypses and pseudepigrapha. It's not always possible to determine which of these texts were composed by Community members and which were not.

A group of very enlightening texts includes commentaries on prophetic books of the Bible. Scholars call these texts *pesharim* (Hebrew for "interpretations"), a word that figures prominently in these manuscripts. The *pesharim* interpret the ancient biblical prophecies as predictions of specific events occurring in the interpreter's time. The typical form begins with a biblical quotation, as in this example from the *Habakkuk Pesher*: "For see, I am raising up the Chaldeans [Babylonians], a bitter, hasty people" (Hab 1:6). The author interprets the verse in this manner: "Its interpretation *(pesher)* is this: it refers to the Kittim [Romans], who are swift and mighty in battle, destroying multitudes. . . ." The commentator applied Habakkuk's prophecy about the Babylonians to the enemies that existed in his own day. Such commentaries exist for portions of Isaiah, Nahum, Habakkuk, Psalms (which both the Community members and the New Testament treat as prophecy) and even scattered references from Numbers, Deuteronomy and other books. The theological assumption behind this method—that prophecies aren't bound to a specific historical context but can have multiple fulfillments—seems to underlie some New Testament biblical interpretation as well. Often in the Gospels, Old Testament prophecies that already had been fulfilled in antiquity are reinterpreted as having a greater fulfillment in the ministry of Jesus Christ.[7]

---

[7]For example, Mt 1:22-23, where Isaiah's prophecy about a miraculous birth that will signal the downfall of Samaria and Damascus (Is 7:1-16) is reinterpreted as a prediction of the virgin birth. So too Mt 2:15, where Hos 11:1, "Out of Egypt I called my son," is interpreted as a prediction of Mary and Joseph's flight to Egypt. The prophecy originally spoke of the Exodus. See further the text box on "Interpreting Prophecy" in chapter two.

The nonbiblical Scrolls give us some cryptic references to historical events, but their value for reconstructing Jewish history is rather small. Their greatest benefit to us is what they tell us about Jewish religious beliefs around the time of Jesus. From the Scrolls we learn that the religious scenery in early Judaism was more complicated than we had imagined. Power struggles, separatism, asceticism and militancy are all revealed among the Dead Sea Scrolls.

Flavius Josephus. All the texts that we've discussed so far form parts of a historical mosaic. They give us significant glimpses into the development of Jewish culture and religious thought during the time between the Testaments. But by far the most important source of information for the latter part of this era is the Jewish historian Flavius Josephus. Josephus was born about A.D. 37, and did his historical writing around the end of the first century and the beginning of the second. His work was comprehensive, surveying the history of his people from Abraham through to his own day. For the Old Testament period, it appears that his sole source of information was the Old Testament itself—interpreted at times with his own "unique" perspective. But for the intertestamental period, he obviously had access to sources that no longer exist today. Some of his reports are clearly legendary; some a mix of legend and history; but most—bearing in mind their author's purpose—seem to be largely reliable. For the New Testament era, his detailed reports on Jewish politics and religion are unparalleled in value.

Josephus was himself one of the true characters of history. We know a good deal about him because one of Josephus's favorite subjects was Josephus himself. He wrote an autobiography called *The Life of Flavius Josephus* (or the *Vita*, referenced in the notes as *Life*) and also detailed many of his activities in his account of the Jewish revolt against Rome (titled *The War of the Jews*, or *Bellum*, referenced in the notes as *War*). In these sources we're told that Josephus was a child prodigy who (like Jesus) dazzled the teachers of the law with his brilliance. As a young man he investigated several different Jewish sects, but he eventually aligned himself with the Pharisees. He became involved in the Jewish revolt against Rome in A.D. 67 and claims to have been the general of the Jewish militia in Galilee, north of Judea. It would have been a tremendous responsibility for a young man: Galilee was the Jews' first line of defense against the Roman army. And if you take Josephus's account seriously, it sounds like he discharged his responsibility admirably, considering the underequipped and poorly trained troops that he had to work with. In fact, the way Josephus tells the story, it appears that he would have made a noble stand if not for the duplicity and incompetence of those around him. But Josephus wants us to know that in spite of his impressive military maneuvers it was never actually his expectation to defeat Rome. Rather, he recognized that revolt was hopeless, and he fought only to spare his country from utter destruction at the hands of the vastly superior Roman forces. He presents his position as an ambivalent one, torn between the desire to keep the peace and the desire to discharge his duties to the best of his ability.

Josephus tells us in detail about how he recruited and trained the Galilean militia. He seems to have been proud of his troops. But unfortunately at the first encounter with the Romans, his army scattered. Josephus led his remaining soldiers to the city of Jotapata, which they fortified to withstand a lengthy Roman siege.[8] But when the city fell before General Vespasian's army, Josephus and forty of his soldiers slipped away and hid in a nearby cave. Realizing the hopelessness of their situation, they formed a suicide pact. Josephus reports that he strongly opposed the idea of suicide, but his comrades were determined to die. Josephus persuaded them, however, that it was better to die by the hand of another than to die by their own hands. So the soldiers drew lots, intending that the person who drew number one would be killed by number two, number two then killed by number three, until the last would kill himself. And as "fate" would have it, Josephus drew the final position.

The Jewish soldiers began to dispatch each other in order. One after another they fell. Finally, only Josephus and one other remained. Now Josephus saw his chance. He persuaded his partner that a Jew shouldn't stain his hands with the blood of a fellow Jew and that their deaths would accomplish nothing. Instead, they should surrender to Vespasian and attempt to help their people by bringing a quick end to the war. The partner agreed. So Josephus presented himself to the Roman general. We have no idea what happened to the partner—he simply disappears from the scene. But Josephus intimated to the general that he himself was no ordinary captive. Not only did he have great insights into the motives and tactics of the Jewish rebels, he also had the power to tell the future! Josephus informed Vespasian that God revealed to him that the Roman general would one

---

[8]The story of the Jotapata affair is found in *War* 3.7.1—8.9 (340-408). See the "Further Reading" section for an explanation of the reference numbers.

day become the emperor. At the time it would have seemed an unlikely development. Vespasian wasn't related to Emperor Nero, and he was far from Rome, fighting in an obscure province against a troublesome but unimportant people. Nonetheless Vespasian agreed to put Josephus to the test. If he did indeed become emperor, Josephus would receive a pardon and the favor of the emperor. If he didn't, Josephus would be executed.

As the war progressed, Josephus aided the Romans in their efforts to put down the rebellion. He tells us of his pain as he stood outside the walls of Jerusalem and pleaded with his fellow Jews to give up their mad resistance. And then in A.D. 69 Emperor Nero died, leaving no heir. In the struggle that ensued one candidate was put forth as emperor and then assassinated; then another was installed, and the same fate befell him. Finally, Vespasian's legions took it upon themselves to install their general as emperor. Josephus was vindicated, and when the Jewish Revolt was done, he returned with Vespasian's army to Rome. There, living in luxury on a government pension, he began his writing career. He published numerous works, several of which have survived to our own day. In addition to his autobiography and an account of the Great Revolt, which were mentioned above, he also published *The Antiquities of the Jews* (*Antiquitates Judaicae*, referenced in the notes as *Ant.*), recounting the history of Judaism from Abraham to Josephus's day, and an apologetic work, *Against Apion* (*Contra Apionem*), defending Judaism from its detractors.

Throughout history Christians have found much value in Josephus's writings. His works were copied and studied by Christian scholars, occasionally being retouched by them to make Josephus sound more well-disposed toward Christianity than he actually was. Jews, understandably enough, considered Josephus a traitor, and until the last century or so paid little attention to his writings. Now, however, we all acknowledge the great debt history owes to this self-styled prophet and collaborator. Are his writings completely reliable? Of course not. As noted earlier his history of Old Testament Israel comes almost exclusively from the Old Testament itself, distorted at times to serve his own purposes. For example, Josephus retells the stories from the era after Judah was conquered by Babylon in ways that make the Jews seem like the ideal subjects of foreign monarchs—just what he'd have the Romans believe about his people. There's no doubt too that Josephus's accounts of the Jewish revolt are designed to place the blame for the war on low-bred hotheads, while he casts himself and other members of the Jewish elite in the best possible light. Some stories, most scholars would agree, are outright fiction. The whole episode of the suicide pact at Jotapata seems especially suspect.

On the other hand, Josephus's historiography shouldn't be judged too harshly. He didn't write solely to vindicate himself or to portray himself as a great hero. He also had some more noble motives. He wanted to make the Jewish people known to the world. He wanted to demonstrate to the nations that Israel had a long and proud history—an important consideration, seeing that the dominant worldview of Josephus's day considered "old" and "good" to be almost synonymous. And most of all he wrote to soften the hearts of the Gentiles so that Roman retribution wouldn't be too terrible. His writings are both history and propaganda, to be sure. But when read with a critical eye, their historical value far outweighs that of any other surviving sources.

Philo Judeus and other sources. Another important writer from this era is Philo of Alexandria, or Philo Judeus. Philo was probably born sometime around 20 B.C., and he lived until sometime after A.D. 40. He was an aristocratic Jew from the cosmopolitan Egyptian city of Alexandria. This jewel of the ancient world was a center of learning and trade, and a variety of ethnic groups made their homes there—including a large number of Jews. Philo, like other members of his family, was a well-known statesman who held positions of considerable authority. However, Philo's importance to us doesn't derive from his political accomplishments but his literary work. He wrote volumes on philosophy, biblical interpretation, and history, many of which have survived to this day.

Philo's philosophy merged Jewish ideas with gleanings from several Greek philosophers. Aspects of Neo-Platonism, Stoicism and other systems illuminated his thinking. Christians found great value in his theories about the *logos*, or Word of God, as a person separate from God but equally divine. It seemed that he anticipated the sentiments expressed by John at the beginning of his Gospel. Some early church fathers (especially Origen) adopted Philo's method of interpreting Old Testament stories as allegories, seeing each character or event as a symbol of a deep theological truth. But most important for our purposes are his descriptions of Jewish customs, beliefs and groups that existed in his day. He also wrote accounts of some important political events of the first century A.D. that affected Jewish life in both Egypt and Palestine.

There were other ancient historians who showed some interest in the Jews. The Greek historians Herodotus (born about 480 B.C.) and Thucy-

RABBINIC LITERATURE

The phrase "rabbinic literature" is used rather loosely to designate texts produced by Jewish rabbis from about the second through the twelfth centuries A.D. Some of the most important of these texts include:

Mishnah ("second [law]"?)—A collection of rabbinic legal discussions and other traditions dating from about the first two centuries A.D. It is divided into six orders, or major sections: "Seeds," "Appointed Times," "Women," "Damages," "Holy Things" and "Purifications." These orders are subdivided into sixty-three tractates covering areas of law under the general headings (e.g., the tractate "Sabbath" is found in the order "Appointed Times"). Tradition holds that Rabbi Judah the Prince compiled the text early in the third century from the discussions of the Tannaim, rabbinic scholars of the first two centuries A.D. The Mishnah is written in a late form of Hebrew. Orthodox Jews consider the Mishnah to be an authoritative document, second to the Scriptures. In references the Mishnah is designated "M.", followed by the tractate name, then chapter and verse reference number, e.g., *M. Sanhedrin* 2.3.

Tosephta ("addition")—A collection of Tannaitic traditions, mostly halakhic (i.e., legal), not included in the Mishnah. The Jews don't consider the Tosephta to be authoritative in the same way that the Mishnah is regarded. In this study, references to the Tosephta are designated "T.", followed by the tractate and reference number.

Talmud ("teaching")—An expansion of the Mishnah. It includes the Mishnah and an extensive Aramaic (or sometimes Hebrew) commentary called the *gemara* ("tradition"), written by later rabbis. The *gemara* sometimes delves further into legal issues, but more often it offers a homiletical or devotional commentary. Two editions of the Talmud were produced. One, called the "Jerusalem Talmud," was composed in Palestine, probably in the fifth century A.D. The other was written in Babylon, probably in the sixth century A.D. Both are divided into orders and tractates, following those of the Mishnah. Jewish tradition regards the Babylonian Talmud to be more authoritative. The Babylonian Talmud is referenced here as *B. Tal.*, and the Palestinian as *Y. Tal.* (for "Yerushalmi," meaning "of Jerusalem"), followed by standard reference numbers.

Midrashim (singular Midrash, "exposition")—Rabbinic biblical commentaries. Some midrashim contain comments from a variety of authors, while others are attributed to a single rabbi. Some of these texts emphasize legal matters (called *halakhah* by the rabbis), while others are more devotional (called *haggadah*). The earliest of the midrashim may have been written before the end of the second century A.D., and they were produced well into the Middle Ages. Midrashim are cited by their titles and reference numbers in standard editions.

Targumin (singular Targum, "translation")—An Aramaic translation of the Old Testament. Like the Septuagint, which was produced for use in the Greek synagogues, the targumin were probably produced for use in the Aramaic-speaking communities of Palestine and the Diaspora. Several different Targumin exist. They often incorporate interesting midrashim, or commentaries, into the text. Targumin are cited by name, book, chapter and verse.

dides (born around 460 B.C.) provide helpful background information for
the times in which they lived, but they tell us little about the Jews per se.
A later Greek writer, Strabo (born c. 64 B.C.), gives us some information
(and a little misinformation) about Jewish life and lands in the decades before the time of Jesus. The Roman historians Tacitus (born about A.D. 56)
and Suetonius (born mid-first century A.D.) devote some attention to the
Jews, but their testimonies are highly unflattering. These authors are far
more important to us for what they say about Roman government in the
New Testament era. The Christian historian Eusebius, writing in the
fourth century A.D., tells us some interesting tidbits concerning Jewish history and culture in the days after Christ. He also preserves some fragmentary testimonies about the Jews from classical authors.

Jewish rabbinic literature, written in the first few centuries of the time
after Christ, also records traditions (some more reliable than others) about
Jewish beliefs and culture in intertestamental times. The Mishnah (abbreviated *M.*), Tosephta (abbreviated *T.*), the Babylonian Talmud (*B. Tal.*), and
the Palestinian Talmud (or *Talmud Yerushalmi, Y. Tal.*) are the most significant Jewish texts of this era. One first-century A.D. Jewish text, the "Scroll
of Fasting" *(Megillat Ta'anith)*, has proven useful to historians. It's a list of
days when it was forbidden to fast because those days were anniversaries
of some joyous occasion. It helps us to fix the chronology of some major
occurrences in Jewish history.

Telling the Story

The history of Second Temple Judaism must be recounted in terms of
events and ideas. It's the events that form the framework of history, and
the ideas that comprise its substance. Events often inspire ideas, and ideas
can lead to great deeds. So in the chapters that follow you'll read of significant achievements, heroic actions and great ideas. But you'll also read of
tragedies, evil deeds and notions that sometimes seem to fly in the face of
both reason and revelation. Be charitable in your judgments—after all, the
people of ancient Judah weren't privileged to the two thousand years of
reflection and continued revelations that modern Christians enjoy.

At the end of this book you'll find a table that summarizes the biblical
and postbiblical story from the days of Abraham up to the end of the Second Temple Period. This broad outline will help you to orient yourself as
you navigate through the unfamiliar territory of the time between the
Testaments.

For Further Reading

Here are some general treatments of intertestamental literature and history, and some useful collections of texts and studies. The introductory surveys are offered here so the reader can compare a variety of perspectives. Some of these works will be noted in the "For Further Reading" sections at the end of each chapter.

Texts

Brenton, Lancelot. *The Septuagint with Apocrypha*. Peabody, Mass.: Hendrickson, 1986. A useful Greek version with English translation, but no critical apparatus.

Charles, R. H. *Apocrypha and Pseudepigrapha of the Old Testament*. 2 vols. Oxford: Clarendon Press, 1913. Textual anthology in English translation.

Charlesworth, James, ed., *The Old Testament Pseudepigrapha*. 2 vols. Garden City, N.Y.: Doubleday, 1983, 1985. A modern anthology which expands on Charles's classic work.

Danby, Herbert. *The Mishnah*. Oxford: Oxford University Press, 1933. References to the Mishnah are designated "M.," followed by the tractate and reference number.

García Martínez, Florentino. *The Dead Sea Scrolls Translated*. 2nd ed. New York: E. J. Brill; Grand Rapids: Eerdmans, 1996. Generally regarded as an academic standard.

Schiffman, Lawrence H. *Texts and Traditions: A Source Reader for the Study of Second Temple and Rabbinic Judaism*. Hoboken, N.J.: Ktav, 1998.

Thackeray, H. St. John; R. Marcus; A. Wikgren; and L. H. Feldman. *Josephus*. Loeb Classical Library, 9 vols. Cambridge: Harvard University Press, 1926-1965. Greek text with English translation. See Whiston below for an explanation of reference numbers.

Vermes, Geza. *The Complete Dead Sea Scrolls in English*. New York: Penguin, 1997. An inexpensive and generally accurate translation.

Whiston, William, trans. *The Works of Flavius Josephus*. Grand Rapids: Kregel, 1998. Standard popular translation. In this book, I include both the Whiston and Loeb reference numbers in the following format: book number. Whiston chapter number. Whiston paragraph number (Loeb paragraph number). So *Antiquities*, book 2, chapter 4, paragraph 1, is cited thus: *Ant.* 2.4.1 (39-40), where "39-40" refers to the Loeb numbering system.

Wise, Michael O., Edward Cook, and Martin G. Abegg Jr., *The Dead Sea Scrolls: A New Translation*. San Francisco: Harper, 1996. Very readable translation with useful commentary.

General Studies of Intertestamental Judaism

Cohen, Shaye J. D. *From the Maccabees to the Mishnah*. Philadelphia: Fortress, 1989. Generally topical approach by a respected Jewish scholar.

Grabbe, Lester. *Judaism from Cyrus to Hadrian*. 2 vols. Minneapolis: Fortress, 1992. A comprehensive and authoritative treatment.

Hayes, J. H., and J. M. Miller, eds. *Israelite and Judaean History*. London: SCM Press, 1977. Pertinent chapters cover the Persian period.

Helyer, Larry R. *Exploring Jewish Literature of the Second Temple Period: A Guide for New Testament Students*. Downers Grove, Ill.: InterVarsity Press, 2002. Good text-based overview of the latter half of the period.

Horbury, William, W. D. Davies, Louis Finkelstein, and John Sturdy. *The Cambridge History of Judaism*. Vols. 1-3. Cambridge: Cambridge University Press, 1984-1999. Collected essays on various periods and topics.

Kraft, Robert A., and George W. E. Nickelsburg, eds. *Early Judaism and Its Modern Interpreters*. Atlanta: Scholars Press, 1986. Synopses of important studies and overviews of the state of the research in the late 1980s.

Murphy, Frederick J. *Early Judaism: The Exile to the Time of Jesus*. Peabody, Mass.: Hendrickson, 2002. Designed as a textbook for college use.

Schürer, Emil. *A History of the Jewish People in the Age of Jesus Christ*. Edited by Geza Vermes, Fergus Millar and Matthew Black. 4 vols. Edinburgh: T & T Clark, 1973-1987. A scholarly classic recently revised.

Stone, Michael, ed. *Jewish Writings of the Second Temple Period: Apocrypha, Pseudepigrapha, Qumran Sectarian Writings, Philo, Josephus*. Philadelphia: Fortress, 1984. Collection of essays giving overviews of the contents of the ancient texts.

VanderKam, James. *An Introduction to Early Judaism*. Grand Rapids: Eerdmans, 2000. Recent study is especially useful for its synopses of Jewish literature.

Apocalyptic and Pseudepigrapha

Collins, John J. *The Apocalyptic Imagination*. New York: Crossroad, 1984. Excellent introduction by a respected scholar.

Hellholm, D., ed. *Apocalypticism in the Mediterranean World and the Near*

East. Tübingen: J. C. B. Mohr, 1983. Collection of academic essays covering various regions.

Russell, D. S. *The Method and Message of Jewish Apocalyptic.* Philadelphia: Westminster Press, 1964. Classic work still frequently cited.

Apocrypha

deSilva, David. *Introducing the Apocrypha: Message, Context, and Significance.* Grand Rapids: Baker, 2002. A recent, worthwhile contribution to a difficult field.

Metzger, Bruce. *An Introduction to the Apocrypha.* Oxford: Oxford University Press, 1957. Classic overview of the contents and importance of the Apocrypha.

Biblical History, Historiography and Archaeology

Bright, John. *A History of Israel.* 4th ed. Philadelphia: Westminster John Knox, 1999. A standard text with a moderately critical approach to Old Testament history.

Dever, William G. *What Did the Biblical Writers Know and When Did They Know It?* Grand Rapids: Eerdmans, 2001. Though hardly conservative, Dever argues for a balanced integration of archaeology and biblical studies.

Hoerth, Alfred. *Archaeology and the Old Testament.* Grand Rapids: Baker, 1998. Conservative work discusses the benefits and limits of archaeology and its relevance for biblical studies.

Merrill, Eugene. *Kingdom of Priests: A History of Old Testament Israel.* Grand Rapids: Baker, 1996. A very conservative overview of biblical history.

2

Returning and Rebuilding

U sually, it's not our triumphs but our tragedies that most profoundly shape our character. In times of disaster we're forced to look within ourselves and take stock of our beliefs. We reassess our priorities. We reach out to our neighbors and link arms with our brothers and sisters. We resolve to meet the future with a deeper commitment to the things that truly matter—our core values. Our victories may be invigorating, but our tragedies can be transforming.

Such was the case for ancient Judah. Throughout the salad days of the Judean monarchy, it seemed the nation was constantly struggling against apostasy. Baal, the storm god of the Syrians and Canaanites, or Molech, the king of the underworld, were frequently drawing the Israelites and Judeans away from Yahweh, God of their fathers. Exclusive Yahwists— people who worshiped Yahweh alone—were probably always a minority in the time of the Judean monarchy. In order to change the Judeans' hearts and fix their affections on the Lord, it took a tragedy of inconceivable magnitude: the destruction of the Judean state. In 586 B.C. the Lord brought the Babylonians down on Jerusalem. The city was besieged and conquered. Its walls were demolished, its buildings destroyed, its glorious temple—the temple of Solomon—was burned to the ground. The Judean royal household was carried away to Babylon as exiles along with most of the country's scholars, priests and other people of influence.

In that alien land the foundations were laid for a new Judean religion and a new Jewish people. Yahwism (the religion of ancient Israel), with its emphasis on sacrifices in the temple and national destiny, was being replaced by Judaism, with its emphasis on personal destiny and obedience to God's law. This process began at the exile and continued throughout the intertestamental period, reaching its completion well after the time when the New Testament ends.

The story of the Second Temple Period begins in the latest books of the Old Testament. The final chapters of 2 Chronicles, the books of Ezra and Nehemiah, and a number of passages from the "minor" prophets chronicle a new phase in Judean history, during which the Jewish people experienced dramatic changes in their social, religious and political life. They also record the appearance of a new power that will play a very significant role in intertestamental events: the Persian Empire. And so it's with these events, actually recorded in the Old Testament, that our survey of Second Temple Jewish history will commence.

Liberation by Cyrus

The Bible reports that the Jews were not unwilling exiles for long.[1] The prophet Jeremiah had predicted that the nations would be subject to Babylon for seventy years (Jer 25:11)—a typological number representing a biblical "lifespan."[2] Ezekiel had prophesied that the Jews would have to languish in captivity for forty years to pay for their sins—a biblical generation (Ezek 4:6). And indeed, it was about a generation after the fall of Jerusalem that God raised up a most unlikely deliverer for his chosen people: Cyrus the Great, emperor of Persia.

Cyrus was a man of exceptional talents and ambitions. When he ascended to the throne of his kingdom, Persia was an important vassal of the Median Empire (centered in what is now Iran). The king of Media respected Cyrus's abilities and gave him his daughter in marriage. But being included in the imperial family wasn't enough to satisfy a man like Cyrus. He soon campaigned against his own father-in-law, conquering Media and taking control of its considerable territories. Cyrus then began extending his realm, first to the west and then to the east, from Turkey to the borders of India. A benevolent tyrant, he won over native populations with propaganda, favors and pious demonstrations at the local shrines. Cyrus fashioned himself as a great liberator who would remove unjust kings from their thrones and carry out the will of the native gods. In a few short

---

[1] Primary sources for this section are 2 Chron 36:22-23; Ezra 1.

[2] The number is approximately equal to the period from the rise of Nebuchadnezzar (605 B.C.) to the fall of Babylon (538 B.C.).

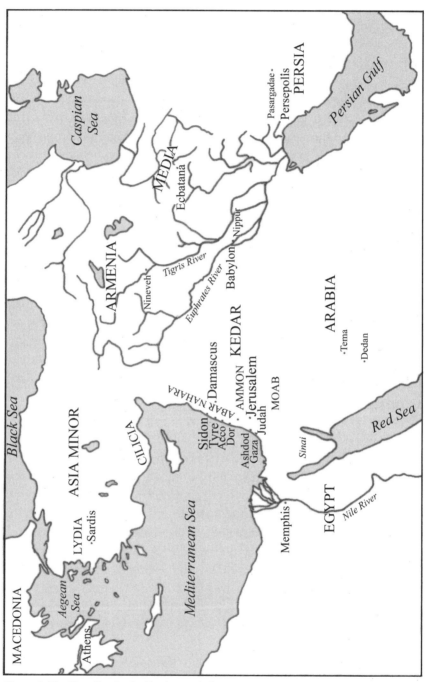

Figure 2. The Near East in the Persian period

years, through the conquests of Iran, Asia Minor and eastern regions, he forged the largest empire the world had ever seen. And he wasn't done yet. Once the region north of the Tigris River was firmly in his grasp, he set his heart on the greatest prize of all: Babylon and all her vassals. Cyrus let it be known to the people of Babylon that the god Marduk, traditional chief of the Babylonian pantheon, appeared to him in a dream. Cyrus had been summoned to come and remove the impious King Nabonidus from the Babylonian throne. (Nabonidus had neglected Marduk and given his primary allegiance to the moon goddess Sin, causing something of a scandal among Babylon's religious conservatives.) The peoples of the Middle East were astir with the anticipation of Babylon's downfall. Even the Jews looked to Cyrus as the Lord's anointed deliverer, one who would initiate a new exodus from their foreign bondage (Is 44:24—45:13).

Cyrus's seemingly irrepressible success plunged the Babylonian leaders into a state of near panic. In a desperate move Nabonidus had idols taken from their shrines in holy sites around the empire and brought to the capital city, hoping that the concentration of "divinity" would protect Babylon from defeat. But actually the move only further alienated his subjects, who didn't appreciate being left without gods of their own. Even Babylon's soldiers seemed reluctant to go to war against Cyrus, and many defected to the Persians. The first major encounter between a huge Babylonian army and a smaller Persian host ended in a resounding rout for the Babylonians. It was now apparent to everyone that the gods had placed their blessings on Cyrus, and whatever will there had been to resist collapsed. Nabonidus fled his capital, and in 539 B.C. Babylon surrendered to Cyrus's general without a fight. Babylon and its vassals thus became part of the Persian Empire—a kingdom that now spread from India to the border of Egypt.

Cyrus extended his goodwill policies to the people of Babylon, restoring the idols to their shrines and giving lavish gifts to the temples and public buildings. The Jews also benefited from his generous spirit. It seems strange that a king ruling over so vast an empire would take notice of such an insignificant portion of his realm. But Cyrus knew how to win friends, and he certainly wanted to keep on the good side of all the local deities. And so in 538 B.C. he issued a decree that any Jewish exiles who wished to return to Jerusalem could go and set to work rebuilding their temple. The vessels taken from the temple were restored to the Jews, and Cyrus bestowed gifts on them to aid them in the project. The great king appointed

Sheshbazzar, a "prince of Judah,"[3] as their governor and leader. The repatriates left behind the comforts of Babylon for a long and difficult trek through Mesopotamia, Syria and Palestine.

Sheshbazzar's group probably wasn't large. Cyrus's decree stated only that those who would be rebuilding the temple were permitted to return to Judah. The group probably consisted of little more than the necessary craftsmen and their families. The book of Ezra says that about fifty thousand Jews eventually immigrated from Babylon to Judah, but that number very likely represents the total number of Jews in both the first return and in the second wave that occurred twenty years later, and perhaps other repatriates as well.[4] And in spite of Cyrus's official sanction the small group faced some stiff opposition. Nearby countries remembered well the days when Judah extended its control over its environs. Samaria, in particular, bore a grudge against Judah dating from the days of King Josiah (640-609 B.C.), when the Jewish king imposed his rule—and his religious sensibilities—on the people of that realm. Then there were the "people of the land," the Jews who remained in Judah when Nebuchadnezzar had taken many Jews into exile. Many of these people had moved into Jerusalem as "squatters," and they probably weren't pleased to see a wave of settlers coming in to dispossess them of the lands they had taken over as their own. Sheshbazzar and his crew had a difficult task before them.

The Situation in Jerusalem

What remained of Jerusalem was but a shadow of the former glory. Nebuchadnezzar had reduced the city walls to useless heaps. Most of the large public structures and private homes were razed to the ground. Anything that had been spared the torch was plundered by looters. But the greatest tragedy was the condition of the site where Solomon's temple once stood. The great edifice, a wonder of the ancient world, was reduced to blackened rubble. In the place where thousands of priests had performed their rituals, where the singers and musicians had declared the praises of the Lord, there stood now a simple shrine to which local priests made pilgrimage.

---

[3]Sheshbazzar was probably the grandson of King Jehoiakim. See 1 Chron 3:17-18, where one "Shenazzar"—a variant of the same name—is listed as a son of Jeconiah.

[4]Ezra 2:64-65. The book of Ezra conflates the careers of Sheshbazzar and his successor Zerubbabel, so it is difficult to determine where Sheshbazzar's work ended and Zerubbabel's began. Combining the stories of people with similar accomplishments was a common practice in ancient historiographical writing.

TEMPLE WORSHIP

The Jerusalem temple was the center of Israelite religion from the days of King Solomon (c. 950 B.C.). Prior to Solomon's day sacrifices had been performed at the site of the tabernacle, a movable shrine stationed in Jerusalem that housed the Ark of the Covenant. But sacrifices were also performed at various shrines—"high places"—scattered throughout the land. The high places were frequented by the priests of the Lord, but pagan deities were often honored in these local shrines as well. Solomon built the temple to replace the tabernacle. It housed the Ark and was the site of the nation's most important acts of worship. The high places, however, continued in operation until the days of King Josiah (c. 640 B.C.), who centralized all worship in Jerusalem and required the priests to work only in the holy city.

Temple worship was an elaborate affair conducted by hundreds of priests and helpers, all members of the tribe of Levi. There were many altars located in the temple courts, but the most sacred altar was located outside the holy of holies, the innermost temple court where the Ark was housed. Each morning, priests presented sacrifices to the Lord as a sign of Israel's devotion. Also, any Israelite could bring a "peace offering," designed to express thankfulness to God, to fulfill a vow or simply to curry God's favor. These could be animal or vegetable gifts. An Israelite who unwittingly sinned was required to present a "sin offering" to remove his or her guilt. These offerings had to be animals. (The priests would retain a portion of each sacrifice for their livelihood.) Once a year on the Day of Atonement, the high priest would offer a sacrifice to remove the collective guilt of the entire nation.

While any Israelite could bring offerings to the temple, only the priests were allowed to perform the sacrifices. Traditionally the priests were all descended from the sons of Moses' brother Aaron. The high priesthood was passed on from generation to generation, with the eldest son succeeding the father to the post. In the days of Solomon the high priesthood was conferred on a priest named Zadok and his descendants. The Zadokites retained the high priesthood until the second century B.C.

For the Jews, the loss of the temple meant that the heart was ripped out of their religion. The daily sacrifices that expressed praise to God, the guilt offerings that covered the transgressions of the people, the Day of Atonement—when the sins of the entire nation were carried away, giving the children of Israel a "clean slate" before the Lord—none of these could continue as they had before, when the temple stood intact. King Nebuchadnezzar had forced the Jews to consider what religion without an elaborate sacrificial cult might mean. A new theology was coming into being, based on ideas that were already present in preexilic Yahwism.[5] This theology stressed good works rather than animal sacrifices as a means of atoning for sins. But it would be a long time before the Jews would be ready to entertain the notion of religion without a sacrificial cult. For now, rebuilding the temple was vital.

Sheshbazzar apparently laid the foundations for a new house of God in Jerusalem, but his work proceeded no further. We don't know why Sheshbazzar never made much progress on the job that he had traveled so far to accomplish. Perhaps he died. Maybe it was the death of King Cyrus in 530 B.C. that brought the whole project to a screeching halt. The Jews had enemies around them who wouldn't have favored the restoration of such an important building—one that could become the focus for Jewish nationalism. People like the Edomites and Ammonites to the south once lived under the thrall of Judah, and they had no interest in seeing the nation rise to power again. And there were the unfriendly Samaritans to the north, and the "people of the land" in the confines of the city itself. Few stood to benefit from the rebuilding of the temple, and since Cambyses, the new emperor, apparently didn't share his father's desire to curry the favor of all gods, the restoration work ceased.

Besides, Persia had much bigger things to worry about than the restoration of a temple. Cambyses had a great ambition: to add Egypt to the Persian Empire. His armies marched to the south, bent on the conquest of that ancient land. He accomplished this goal in 525 B.C. with the help of native tribes sympathetic to the Persians. But while Cambyses was still celebrating in Egypt, a revolt broke out back in Persia. In 522 B.C. a usurper named Smerdis seized power, claiming to be a son of Cyrus. Cambyses set off at once for home, but he took ill on the way and died. A struggle ensued for the Persian throne, and the empire erupted in revolts. Kingdoms that

---

[5]See Ps 51:16-17; Mic 6:6-8.

had willingly accepted the yoke of Cyrus now tried to assert their independence. But before the year's end Darius I, a royal cousin, secured the throne for himself. He quickly put down the rebellions and set to work creating a more stable and efficient system of government.

Cyrus had been a remarkable visionary and motivator, but Darius I was a remarkable administrator. He organized the empire into twenty "satrapies," or provinces, each of which was administered by a governor called a "satrap." Judah belonged to the satrapy called "Abar-Nahara," an Aramaic phrase meaning "across the river" (i.e., the Euphrates). In order to maintain communication with even the most distant provinces, he developed a sophisticated system of roads and an efficient postal system. He initiated a new system of taxation and lent his name to a standard coin—the "daric"—that could be used throughout the empire. Darius also undertook a reform of the legal system: native peoples were allowed to live by their own "ancestral laws" so long as these laws didn't conflict with the laws of the Persian Empire. Darius required that the native laws be codified and standardized so justice would be administered fairly. In spite of all this administrative activity Darius still managed to expand the empire even further to the east and north, adding parts of India and eastern Europe to a kingdom that was already far larger than any the world had ever seen.

The Second Return

It was during the reign of Darius I that the issue of the Jerusalem temple arose once again.[6] And though it might seem odd that an emperor with so much on his plate would undertake so "minor" a matter as the rebuilding of the temple for a small group of Jews, such actions were quite typical of him. He was a pious man who undertook similar projects in Egypt, rebuilding a religious establishment called the House of Life and aiding the construction of a temple to the sun god Amon-Re. He also ordered the renovation of other temples throughout his realm. But considering the opposition that the Jerusalem project faced, the work on the temple would probably have proceeded slowly if not for the vigorous efforts of several remarkable people. The prophets Haggai and Zechariah informed the people that God wanted them to rebuild the temple at once and not to wait for special signs or an improvement of the political situation. Zechariah even

---

[6]Primary sources in this section are Ezra 3—6.

implied that the restoration of the temple would initiate a glorious new age for Judah and that the coming of a messianic prince wouldn't be far behind.[7] The high priest Joshua, too, was an important figure of the time. Haggai holds him up as a strong leader, addressing him and the governor of Judah as coleaders (Hag 1:1, 12, 14; 2:2, 4). Zechariah seems to have held him in even higher regard, predicting that he would take away all the shame of Judah and using him—rather than the governor—as a symbol of the king who would come and restore the nation's fortunes (Zech 3; 6:10-15). But it was surely the governor of Judah, Zerubbabel, who deserves the lion's share of credit for getting the rebuilding project underway. While Joshua may have had the hearts of the people, Zerubbabel had the ear of the satrap (his Persian overlord). When he arrived in around 520 B.C. with a large group of immigrants, he brought a new resolve to the reconstruction efforts. Haggai predicted that God would do great things for Zerubbabel, granting him heavenly assistance to complete the temple (Hag 2:4-9, 21-23). Zechariah prophesied that God would make the mountains into plains before Zerubbabel, and the Holy Spirit would empower him to finish the building project (Zech 4:6-10).

Outside of Haggai's and Zechariah's prophecies and the Chronicler's records, we know very little about Zerubbabel. He was the son of someone named Shealtiel, a man of royal blood (1 Chron 3:17-24). Perhaps Haggai believed that Zerubbabel could restore the Judean monarchy. He wrote that the Lord had "chosen" Zerubbabel and that God would make him his "signet ring" (Hag 2:23). Neither phrase necessarily has any messianic significance (that is, neither was used by the prophets as a technical term for the long-awaited king who would restore the nation's glory), but they clearly anticipate great things for the governor. Even so, neither Haggai nor Zechariah went so far as to predict that Zerubbabel would become king of Judah—in spite of the fact that Zechariah seems to have expected the restoration of the Judean kingdom soon after the temple was completed (see Zech 6:12-13).

Zerubbabel brought great determination to the temple project. The Samaritans and their governor, Rehum, did everything in their power to subvert the effort. They actually wrote a letter to Tattenai, the Persian satrap of Abar-Na-

---

[7]See Zech 6:12-15. The title the "Branch" comes from Is 4:2, where it refers to a coming messianic king. Theologically, we might understand Zechariah's prophecy to have been fulfilled in the coming of Jesus, who spoke of himself as the temple of God. In him a new temple and the anointed kingship were combined.

hara, accusing the Jews of plotting treachery. "Look into their history," they advised. "These Jews are a rebellious people, and if you allow them to rebuild their temple, who knows what mischief will follow!" (see Ezra 4:12-16). (There was, indeed, some substance to the charges. The Jews *had* rebelled against both the Assyrians and the Babylonians, and Zechariah's rhetoric implied that a new rebellion might not be long coming.) Tattenai questioned the

INTERPRETING BIBLICAL PROPHECY

Modern Bible readers sometimes interpret prophecies as if they have but one fulfillment. In ancient times, however, there was no such assumption. A prophecy could be understood to refer to several different events. Frequently an oracle that was fulfilled soon after it was given was reinterpreted with a "deeper" meaning by later readers. The prophecy wasn't bound to a specific historical setting. This understanding of prophecy is often demonstrated in the Dead Sea Scrolls, where many biblical prophecies are given new significance in light of the interpreters' experience and expectations. The rabbis, too, often gave several interpretations for the same prophecy. The New Testament writers reinterpret some Old Testament prophecies and find their greater fulfillment in the ministry of Jesus. One of the most famous examples is Matthew 2:17-18, where Jeremiah 31:15, "A voice is heard in Ramah, / lamentation and bitter weeping," is interpreted as a prediction of Herod's "slaughter of the innocents." The original prophecy clearly refers to the Babylonians' destruction of Jerusalem. The ancient interpreters assumed that God's word wasn't necessarily bound to specific times and circumstances.

When reading biblical prophecies, then, we should bear in mind that they might have several layers of significance: an immediate fulfillment for the age in which they were given; an eschatological significance for the time of the consummation of God's salvation story; and an ongoing fulfillment, an ethical or theological significance for God's people of any time and place.

Jews, and they informed him that the rebuilding order had been issued by King Cyrus himself. So Tattenai referred the matter to King Darius, who commissioned a search of the royal archives. And when it was discovered that Cyrus had, indeed, ordered the construction, King Darius gave his approval to the project. Tattenai ordered the Samaritans not to interfere.

The work proceeded according to plan. But sometime during the course of the rebuilding, Zerubbabel left the scene. Like Sheshbazzar, he simply vanishes. When the completed temple was dedicated in 515 B.C., Zerubbabel was nowhere to be found. Where did he disappear to? The Bible gives us few clues. But considering the nationalistic hopes that seemed to be attached to the governor, it's quite possible that the Persians viewed him as a threat and removed him from his post. It's even been suggested that he was assassinated by some of the "people of the land" who opposed his rebuilding efforts. Some scholars have suggested that when the book of Zechariah records, "When they look on the one whom they have pierced, they shall mourn for him" (Zech 12:10), the prophet was originally talking about the murder of Zerubbabel![8] Whatever the reason, the glories and the conquests that Zechariah predicted didn't materialize during the days of Zerubbabel. The country remained a vassal of the Persians. However, the important work of temple building was eventually completed.

The temple of the Lord was rededicated on the third day of the Hebrew month of Adar (mid-March), in 515 B.C. Almost four years had been spent on the project. Captured items from the old temple were restored to their rightful places, and the Persian monarchs themselves made donations to the project. But still the new temple was a mere shadow of the old. Judah no longer had the kind of resources it had in Solomon's day that could be lavished on its central shrine. Yet the completion of the temple was a cause for great joy and celebration, and the new structure was dedicated with the blood of hundreds of sacrificial animals. The Second Temple Period had begun.

The Work of Ezra and Nehemiah

The next sixty years or so of Jewish history are passed over in silence. The next—and final—events recorded in the biblical chronicles are the minis-

---

[8]Jn 19:37 sees the ultimate fulfillment of this prophecy in the crucifixion of Jesus Christ. John's method of prophetic interpretation is similar to a method used in the Dead Sea Scrolls, which was discussed in chapter one.

tries of Ezra and Nehemiah.[9] These two men may have done more to shape the character of the Jewish faith than anyone since Moses. The figure of Ezra looms particularly large in Jewish tradition. Indeed, the Talmud (the holy book of rabbinic Judaism) states that if Moses hadn't written the Law, Ezra would have.[10] And in some sense, it might almost be said that he *did* write the Law—or rather, that he was its editor in chief, as we will see.

The biblical accounts of Ezra and Nehemiah are conflated from several sources. There are letters written in Aramaic, pasted in at various places. There's Hebrew text written from the third-person point of view. And there are the so-called memoirs of Ezra and Nehemiah, written in the first-person. The original letters and documents contained in these books are invaluable sources of historical information, but the composite nature of the accounts has also made it difficult for historians to work out the actual sequence of events. But even so, the accomplishments of these two great figures are plain enough from the text as it stands.

Nehemiah had been the cupbearer of the Persian king Artaxerxes I—a position of considerable influence. Hearing of dire conditions in Jerusalem, he asked to be appointed as the governor of Judah in 445 B.C. No doubt he believed his influence in the Persian court could benefit his people in many ways, but his primary goal was to rebuild the walls of Jerusalem. In those days a city's wall was its main means of defense. Without a wall the citizens were easy prey for brigands or foreign invaders. And so a city without a wall was considered not just vulnerable but actually contemptible. Rebuilding the wall of Jerusalem was both a matter of defense and national pride. The Jews could expect no respect as a people so long as their capital city lay open and indefensible. Getting the wall back into place was a major step toward restoring the Jewish people to world significance.

The project had its detractors from both without and within. The governor of Samaria made a formal request to the Persian satrap that he halt the project. A powerful Arab sheik named Geshem and a Jewish aristocrat named Tobiah also made trouble. This Tobiah is called an "Ammonite slave," but his name is Jewish ("Goodness of Yahweh"), and he was clearly well connected with the Jews. Very likely he was the product of a Jewish-

---

[9]Primary sources for this section are Ezra 7—10; Neh 1—12.
[10]*B. Tal. Sanhedrin* 21b. For more information on the Talmud, see the text box at the end of chapter one.

Ammonite marriage, and his mixed parentage earned him Nehemiah's contempt.[11] But his family was extremely wealthy and would continue to figure prominently in Jewish affairs for decades to come. Because of these determined enemies, the Jews were forced to arm half their men so they could guard those who worked on the wall. It slowed down the project considerably. But even so Nehemiah and his crew completed the rebuilding job in fifty-two days. Since the population of the city wasn't nearly as great as it had been before the exile, the wall was smaller than in the old days. But the completion of the project brought the residents of Jerusalem a feeling of security and a great cause for celebration.

The other challenge Nehemiah faced was the problem of mixed marriages. Many Jewish leaders who returned to Jerusalem had intermarried with the Ammonites, Moabites and other Canaanite peoples around them. As in the days of the old Israelite monarchy, such marriages were often politically, not romantically, motivated. The Jewish social climbers were trying to enhance their clout by marrying into wealthy and influential local families. Tobiah, whom I mentioned above, was but one of the racially mixed sheiks who wielded power in Jerusalem. The Jews who married into foreign families were doing just as Solomon had done in the old days, cementing political alliances with matrimonial ties. Nehemiah didn't fail to remind them of what happened to Solomon: how the nation descended into apostasy because of his foreign brides (Neh 13:26). Cursing and beating the dissenters into submission, Nehemiah ordered the people to take an oath that they wouldn't allow their children to marry foreign brides (Neh 13:25).

Ezra's ministry overlapped that of Nehemiah, ideologically and probably chronologically (although many scholars dispute this notion). Traditionally his ministry has been dated to 458 B.C., thirteen years before the time of Nehemiah. But scholars have observed some problems with the traditional chronology, including the fact that the wall of Jerusalem seems to have been completed already when Ezra ministered, and that mixed marriages, outlawed by Ezra, were a problem for Nehemiah as well. If Ezra really preceded Nehemiah, it seems that his ministry had little lasting impact—an unlikely outcome considering the high esteem that Jewish tra-

---

[11]The fact that the Bible calls him an Ammonite slave could also mean that he worked as an Ammonite "lackey." Later documents show that his family estate was located in the Transjordan region where the Ammonites dwelt.

dition accords this figure. So many scholars have suggested that Ezra's work actually followed that of Nehemiah, with 428 B.C. or 398 B.C. the most popular suggested dates of his ministry. But whenever he ministered, the Bible is quite explicit about the nature of his work. His task was to "standardize" and unify the Jewish faith. Ezra's goal was to bring all the Jewish practices in line with the teachings of the law of Moses, and he had the official support of the Persian Empire to carry out the task.

Ezra's story begins in Ezra 7. Here we learn that Ezra was a priest and a "scribe"—in those days, a mid-level government administrator. He lived and worked among the Jews in Babylon. One day he made a request to King Artaxerxes for permission to return to Jerusalem so that he might instruct the people there in the laws of God. Artaxerxes honored his request, and the king even issued a decree that any Jews who refused to obey God's laws would be punished by the Persians and subject to penalty or even to death! (Whether or not the king would have actually come through on the promised support is questionable. In those days powerful parties frequently made grand promises to their allies that they would have been hard-pressed to keep. Their chief value seems to have been the psychological boost they provided for the underlings.) Furthermore the king presented Ezra with gifts to beautify the temple of the Lord. It seemed to Ezra that God moved the king to show favor on his enterprise. He gathered up the scrolls of God's law and proceeded to Jerusalem, taking priests, leaders and goods with him. In fact, five thousand people returned to Jerusalem with Ezra, swelling the city's population considerably with some "better quality" Jews.

The main thrust of Ezra's mission was to instruct the Jews in God's laws—indeed, one might even say he imposed the laws on them. With official backing from the Persians, Ezra could command the people to observe the dietary restrictions, festivals and sundry regulations to an extent that probably had never before been possible. There's no evidence in the Old Testament that any king or prophet ever attempted such a far-reaching reform as Ezra's was designed to be. Not even King Josiah initiated the kind of Bible-based obedience that Ezra commanded.

Ezra called a solemn assembly of the Jews in Jerusalem, and the law was read in their presence, with interpretation provided for those who were so used to speaking Aramaic (while living in Babylon) that they could no longer understand the old Hebrew (Neh 8:8). As the convicting words were proclaimed, the Jews wept and wailed in repentance. Apparently it

THE SCRIBES

The Hebrew and Greek words that we translate as "scribe" both mean "writer." Initially the terms denoted professionals who wrote contracts and kept records, but eventually the scribes came to have much broader duties. Writing was a difficult skill to master in ancient times, and those who wrote well were in high demand. Kings and nobles depended on scribes for drafting treaties and recording annals. A trustworthy scribe could become a very influential figure.

In Old Testament times, scribes were usually administrative officers rather than "writers" per se. The prophet Jeremiah was accompanied by a scribe named Baruch who had free access to the royal courts. By Ezra's day scribal skills were more easily obtained, and priests and Levites could serve as scribes while still performing their sacerdotal (priestly) duties. Due to their literary skills, scribes earned the reputation of being learned men, and they often served as teachers. They also were responsible for copying, editing and preserving the biblical texts. Through such activities *scribe* eventually became a synonym for "biblical scholar." Probably, those scribes who were trained in copying biblical texts were also instructed in their interpretation. In the Gospel traditions some of the scribes opposed the teachings of Jesus. Perhaps there was some jealousy involved. After all, they were trained professionals while Jesus was a mere amateur. And of course his teachings disagreed with those that had been handed down to them by their teachers.

wasn't the practice of the Jews to read the laws in this fashion. What's more, the book of Nehemiah tells us that they "discovered" during their reading that the law commanded the Jews to live in booths (Hebrew *sukkoth*) during the harvest feast. The proclamation was sent forth throughout the cities of Judah and in Jerusalem, commanding the people to observe the Feast of Tabernacles. It was the first time the Jews celebrated "Sukkoth" since the time of Joshua (Neh 8:13-18).

It's clear that Ezra gave the law of Moses a new prominence in Judaism.

Some scholars have even argued that he was personally responsible for bringing together sundry law scrolls and narratives and editing them into the collection that we now know as the Pentateuch.[12] That may be the case, but the most we can say with certainty is that Ezra gave biblical laws an official status unlike anything they had known before. The historical books of the Bible show us that in Old Testament times the laws were enforced in a haphazard manner at best. Idolatry, theft, adultery and other crimes were not punished in the ways that the law of Moses decreed. Festivals, sacrifices and sabbath days hadn't been observed as God commanded. With Ezra on the scene, however, all that was to be changed. Anyone who failed to conform to the law of Moses would have to answer not only to Ezra, but in theory at least, to Persian justice. The Jews, whether they liked it or not, were becoming the "people of the book."

Another task that Ezra took on himself was the elimination of mixed marriages among the Jews. We've seen that Nehemiah dealt with this issue too. But Nehemiah seems to have aimed the brunt of his consternation at the priests. Ezra, on the other hand, undertook a thorough investigation of intermarriage, composed a list of all the malefactors and made them pledge to put away the foreign wives and sacrifice sin offerings.[13] It seems to have been a more extensive effort to eradicate the mixed marriages than that which Nehemiah conducted. In any case, it seems odd that both men, working within a generation of one another, had to deal with the same vexing issue.

There's been considerable debate about how deep an impression the ministries of Ezra and Nehemiah actually made on Jewish society. After all, what did they really accomplish? The rebuilding of a wall, the public promulgation of the Torah, the discouragement of mixed marriages. Their contemporaries might not have found their records all that impressive, and some would have easily reverted back to their old ways as soon as both men were off the scene. But why then did later generations consider their impact to have been so profound? Why did the rabbis hail Ezra as a second Moses? Probably because these men set in motion the process by

---

[12]It's difficult to say when the Pentateuch took its current form. Since the Samaritans use essentially the same Pentateuch as the Jews, it must have occurred before the final split between the Samaritans and the Jews—but when that final split occurred is uncertain. Obviously there was some animosity between the Jews and the Samaritans already in the time of Nehemiah, but the final split may not have come until a couple of hundred years later, in the time when the Jewish leader John Hyrcanus invaded Samaria and destroyed the Samaritan temple on Mount Gerizim.

[13]Ezra 10; cf. Neh 13:23-29.

which the law, its interpretation and obedience to its commands would be firmly ensconced as the core of the Jewish religion. Sacrifice and the temple remained prominent features of the faith, but obedience came first. Of course such ideas weren't altogether new. Similar thoughts had been proclaimed by some of the prophets and psalmists even before the Babylonian exile. But with the ministry of Ezra these principles were given a new emphasis and were on the way to becoming the rule for the Jews as a whole.

Another effect of their ministries, only a little less significant than the first, was to engender a strong xenophobic or isolationist attitude in Palestinian Judaism—an attitude that would eventually earn the Jews a reputation as "haters of humanity." Ezra and Nehemiah, both of whom had held prominent positions in the Persian government, ironically encouraged the Jews to cut off all relations with their foreign neighbors. Certainly the move must have seemed justified at the time. The Jews were doing little to become a "light to the Gentiles." On the contrary, Gentiles were making their impression on the Jews. Ezra and Nehemiah recognized the need for decisive action. The rebuilding of Jerusalem's wall wasn't just a security measure. It was also a symbol of the Jews' separation from their pagan neighbors. And it represented the first necessary step toward rebuilding a kingdom—a fact that wasn't lost on the Ammonites, Edomites and Samaritans (Neh 4:1-8). Then there were the mandatory divorces, which forced the foreign wives to leave their homes and livelihoods, and return to their parents' houses (if they could) in shame. Judah's neighbors wouldn't be quick to forget such humiliation. In later centuries when the Jews would be thrust into closer relations with those very neighbors, the friction would be severe.

From Ezra to the End of the Persian Empire

We know only a little about how the Palestinian Jews fared in the last century of the Persian Empire. The book of Esther is set in this time period, and it does give us some valuable insights into the procedures of the Persian court, but it tells us little about political relations or social life of the Jews in their homeland.[14] Josephus has little to say of historical value for

---

[14]The fact is, there are several aspects of the book of Esther that seem impossible to reconcile with what we do know of Persian history (e.g., Esther tells us that there were 127 Persian satrapies, when in fact there were only 21). It also seems a bit hard to reconcile the story of Esther's marriage to the Persian king with Ezra and Nehemiah's strong opposition to mixed marriages! Most modern scholars—even some who would consider themselves conservative—are inclined to consider the book of Esther to be a creative work of historical fiction rather than a record of actual events.

this period. But some firsthand information has come down to us from a most unlikely source: a collection of papyri (documents written on sheets made from papyrus) discovered in Egypt. These ancient texts were found on the island of Elephantine, near Aswan. They include some correspondence between the Jews living in Egypt and the Jews in Jerusalem. A Jewish military colony lived on the island, and archaeologists had the good fortune to discover their ancient archives.

ANCIENT WRITING

Writing began in Mesopotamia, where the Sumerians, Babylonians and Assyrians developed a form of writing known as "cuneiform" (wedge-shaped), inscribing word-pictures on clay. The Egyptians learned writing from Mesopotamia and developed their own system of word-pictures called "hieroglyphics." The Israelites, however, never used a word-picture system. They adopted the alphabetic writing system developed by the Phoenicians. Letters were written in ink that was usually made from ash and tree sap but occasionally derived from other materials. A quill was used to inscribe letters on a variety of materials. School lessons could be inscribed on tablets covered with wax, and "erased" by leaving the tablets in the sun. Informal communications were often written on potsherds. Parchment, made from animal hide, was for more formal communications. And the Israelites also imported papyri from Egypt. Papyri were made from papyrus reeds pounded flat and woven into sheets. It's from the word *papyrus* that we get our word *paper.*

We can't say for certain when this Jewish colony was founded. They claim to have been well settled there before the Persians conquered Egypt (525 B.C.), so a sixth-century B.C. origin seems likely. The earliest texts, however, can be dated only as far back as 495 B.C. It's interesting to note that the officials of the colony wrote their letters to Jerusalem in Aramaic rather than Hebrew. So it's possible that the colonists were transplanted to Egypt sometime after the Babylonian conquest of 586 B.C., when the Jews began to use Aramaic widely. (On the other hand, they may have begun using Aramaic after the Persians conquered Egypt.) The Elephantine Jews had their own temple—a strange state of affairs considering that King Josiah of Judah banned sacrifice at any shrine but the temple in Jerusalem around 622 B.C. Apparently Josiah's reforms were quickly forgotten in that far-off land, or the colonists simply concluded that the prohibition against sacrifice outside of Jerusalem couldn't possibly apply to Jews living so far from home. (In any case, we know that the Elephantine temple wasn't the only Jewish temple located outside Jerusalem. There was also a Jewish temple at a site called Leontopolis in the Transjordan during this period.)

The Elephantine papyri give us a small glimpse of the culture and intrigues of those transplanted Jews as well as their Judean cousins. There are many legal texts and deeds, including conveyances, marriage contracts (yes, prenuptial agreements were known long ago!), sworn depositions, loans and so forth. There's one literary text, the *Words of Ahiqar*, a tale of court intrigue set in Assyria. It includes a collection of proverbs attributed to the wise hero Ahiqar. There's a historical document, a copy of the Behistun (or "Bisitun") Inscription, which records Darius I's conquests over his enemies. And there are the letters sent to and from the colony to Judah (called Yehud in Aramaic) and other locations. These letters are filled with surprises. A letter dated 419 B.C., written to Jedaniah bar Gemariah (apparently the leader of the community), was delivered on the authority of the Persian king Darius II. This letter instructed the colonists about the proper observance of the Feast of Unleavened Bread—otherwise known as the Passover. Some of these instructions come straight from the Bible; others seem to reflect an emerging set of orally transmitted instructions regarding this most important feast. We can't determine from the instructions given whether the Elephantine Jews hadn't been celebrating Passover or just that they hadn't been celebrating it properly. In either case it demonstrates the zeal with which Darius II—a Persian—sought to standardize the practices of the ethnic groups throughout his realm. Like Darius I, Darius II urged each group to live according to its "ancestral laws." Where those laws were ambiguous, he wanted them clarified. No doubt Darius II's policies encouraged the standardization of the Old Testament text and its wide dissemination among the Jews.

Another letter, written to Governor Bagohi of Judah, speaks of a situation that's almost comical. In 410 B.C. when the satrap of Egypt was away on business, the acting satrap conspired with the local Egyptian priests to destroy the Jewish temple on Elephantine Isle. And what was the motive behind this attack? Apparently it was a problem of religious sensibilities. The priests were devotees of the god Khnum, whom they worshiped in the form of a goat. When the Jews sacrificed goats in their temple, the Egyptian priests considered it an affront to their god! The colonists requested the assistance of Governor Bagohi in getting their temple rebuilt. The letter must have put the Judean Jews in a delicate spot. On the one hand they wanted to help their brethren in Egypt, but on the other their own laws forbid sacrifices outside of Jerusalem. Eventually it was decided that the Elephantine Jews could rebuild their temple, but they weren't allowed to conduct any animal sacrifices at the site—only grain and incense could be offered there. Probably the compromise was motivated as much by the desire to spare Egyptian sensibilities as Judean religious scruples.

The Elephantine papyri contain no "smoking guns." They disprove nothing we've received as truth from the biblical tradition—but then they don't prove the Bible to be true either. They do show us the tendency toward assimilation faced by Jews living in an environment of extreme religious diversity. The Jews of Elephantine honored the Lord, who they called Yaho, above all other gods. But they seem to have honored other deities as well. These Jews offered blessings in the name of the Lord *and* in the names of Egyptian and Syrian deities. Their children married Egyptians and Arameans, and they all paid respects to one another's deities. The Jews named their children after gods of Egypt and Syria as well as Yaho, "the God of heaven." At least some of the Jews of Elephantine thought of the Lord as the chief God, but not the only god.

Nonetheless, the texts of Elephantine demonstrate that the "solidification" of Judaism that was occurring in Judah was being extended to Egypt as well. Just as in Judah, the Jews here were grappling with the biblical texts and the traditions that they had received from the law of Moses. Through their correspondence with the homeland the Egyptian Jews were bringing their practices in line with those of the Judeans. For the first time in their history the Jews were trying to forge a unified identity based on the written word of the Lord.

For Further Reading

Akroyd, Peter. *Exile and Restoration*. Philadelphia: Westminster Press, 1968.
A text-based study that considers the images of exile and restoration in several biblical books.

Bright, John. *A History of Israel*. 4th ed. Philadelphia: Westminster Press, 1999. See especially chapters 9-10. Argues that Nehemiah preceded Ezra.

Clines, David. *Ezra, Nehemiah, and Esther*. New Century Bible Commentary. Grand Rapids: Eerdmans, 1984. Accessible commentary by a leading scholar.

Horbury, William; W. D. Davies; Louis Finkelstein; and John Sturdy. *The Cambridge History of Judaism*. Vol. 1. Cambridge: Cambridge University Press, 1984. A scholarly treatment, well documented.

Porten, Bezalel. *Archives of Elephantine: The Life of an Ancient Jewish Military Colony*. Berkeley: University of California Press, 1968.

Williamson, H. G. M. *Ezra, Nehemiah*. Word Biblical Commentary 16. Waco, Tex.: Word, 1985. Introduction argues that Ezra preceded Nehemiah.

3

The Persian Impact
on Judaism

One dramatic effect of the Babylonian exile was a redrawing of the Jewish map. The Jewish people, once deeply ensconced in their hard-won territory, were scattered far and wide. Some of the "cream" of Jewish society had been transported to Babylon, while other leaders had sought refuge in Egypt. Even after Cyrus issued his decree allowing them to return home, many of the Babylonian Jews chose to remain in their new homeland. A vibrant Jewish community was developing there, which would only grow in importance as the centuries passed. And with Persia's conquest of Babylon, many able and ambitious Jews now made their way east, establishing colonies in the new seat of imperial power, as the book of Esther recalls. The Jewish presence in Egypt increased as well, as merchants and mercenaries found it easy to travel from one part of the Persian Empire to another. Judaism was leaving its Palestinian cradle and going out into the world.

Meanwhile, the Jewish homeland was in dire straits. The population and boundaries of "Yehud," as Judah was now called, were reduced to a fraction of their former size, even with the returning exiles. And the influx of pilgrims created tension in Jerusalem and other Judean cities. The Jews who came from Babylon were very different from the "people of the land" who had been left behind. The returning Jews represented the Judean elite, and their experience in Babylon helped them to define and strengthen the essentials of their faith. The Jews who had remained behind, on the other hand, came to depend on the foreigners around them and adopted some of their ways. Through the prophet Jeremiah, the Lord described the returning Jews as "good figs, very good figs," while those who had remained in the land were "bad figs, very bad figs" (Jer 24:2). The repatriates came to look with disdain on their homebound brethren. A deep dichotomy had been created in Jewish society that would continue until well into the first centuries after Jesus: the rabbis of the Christian era used the term "people of the land" as an insulting epithet for any Jews who couldn't be trusted to observe the law properly.

A New Individualism

The Babylonian exile profoundly affected Jewish demographics. But it also had a deep impact on the social psychology of Judah. In preexilic Judah there always had been a strong emphasis on national hopes and collective destiny. Yahwistic faith placed more emphasis on the relationship between the nation and its God than that of the individual Israelite and God. In texts like Deuteronomy 28, Judges 2:11-23 and 2 Samuel 24, we get a clear picture of the importance of corporate guilt and national favor in biblical thought. When the Israelite nation was righteous, the people as a whole would prosper; when the nation was wicked, all would suffer together.

Another important aspect of that preexilic mindset was the role of the king. In theory the king was the spiritual barometer for all Israel. When the kings were pious, Israel was blessed. An evil king, on the other hand, meant trouble for the whole nation. God repeatedly brought judgment on the entire country because of wickedness attributed to the kings. Solomon's apostasy caused the nation to be divided in two (1 Kings 11), while Manasseh's wickedness led to the Babylonian exile itself (2 Kings 21:10-15). No doubt part of the issue was that the kings' bad examples caused some Israelites to follow suit (see 2 Kings 21:9). Prophets longed for the time when a truly righteous king would reign, leading the people in the ways of the Lord. Then God would exalt Israel over its neighbors (e.g., Is 9:1-7; 11:1-10; Amos 9:11; Mic 5:1-5). The temple of the Lord would become the envy of all the lands, and strangers would make their pilgrimages there to learn of Israel's God.

But that was before the destruction of Jerusalem. Now there was no king at all. The temple that was going to draw foreigners from the four corners of the globe had been demolished. What happened to the Jews' glorious destiny? Some Jews were probably expecting the monarchy to be restored quickly and the glorious promises of the new kingdom to be fulfilled in the near future. Already they had taken steps in that direction with the construction of their new temple. But somehow the restoration project seemed to have misfired. The second temple was nothing special to look at—nothing to draw pilgrims from foreign lands. And the monarchy wasn't restored. There was no king to serve as the center of national pride; no temple that could be the focus of religious "elitism." The Jews had to reorient themselves to a collective life without a king and a cult with few trappings of grandeur. And thus were sown the seeds of a new individualism: nationalistic hopes and collective piety were giving way to personal piety and expectation of an intimate, personal relationship with God.

It's difficult to assess the way this new psychology affected Jewish society. The problem is that we don't know very much about the popular culture and social structures of preexilic times. Consequently we're forced to draw insights from analogies to other lands. Ancient Egypt seems to provide a good comparison. In Old Kingdom Egypt (the time of the great pyramid builders), the pharaohs were the focal points of national pride and piety. They were gods on earth, and an Egyptian's greatest hope was to have the opportunity to serve them. When the Old Kingdom collapsed it initiated a great period of doubt, introspection and confusion. But it also brought into being a new age of the "common people": an efflorescence of the creative arts and a greater appreciation for individual dignity. There's little reason to doubt that the fall of Jerusalem had similar effects on the Jews. A new sense of *personal* pride at least partially replaced the old sense of *national* pride. Entrepreneurism flourished as Jewish businessmen found new opportunities for commerce, and new technologies were producing a wide array of goods. Democracy of a sort was extended as the Jewish "council of elders" began to take on tasks of government previously handled by the king and his officers. And new forms of literary and artistic expression came into being as Jewish thought was cross-pollinated with ideas and styles from the many lands that lived under the umbrella of Persian rule.

Linguistic Changes

These far-reaching social changes were accompanied by a more prosaic development: the transformation of the Jews' language. The Jews' ancestral tongue was, of course, Hebrew. But the official language of the Babylonian Empire was Aramaic, a language closely related to Hebrew. For diplomatic and trade purposes some Jews learned Aramaic even before the Babylonian conquest, since the Syrians and other neighbors used a form of that tongue. The Jews who were deported to Babylon became fluent in the language of their new homeland. Most of them continued to use Hebrew in their homes and religious services, at least for a while. But after a generation of Jews had grown up in Babylon, the use of the mother tongue was becoming more of a formality than a necessity. Even after Cyrus conquered the Babylonians, the situation remained pretty much the same for Jews living in Abar-Nahara (west of the Euphrates). Even though Aramaic wasn't the Persians' native language, they recognized the practicality of allowing Aramaic to remain the lingua franca of the western empire.

But what of the "people of the land"—the Jews who hadn't gone to Babylon? Many of them undoubtedly continued to use Hebrew. The exiles' return to their homeland created an interesting socio-linguistic situation in Judah: many members of the lower classes would have spoken a vulgar form of their ancestral Hebrew. The skilled trades people, merchants and politicians generally spoke Aramaic, although some of them retained familiarity with classical (biblical) Hebrew. It's difficult to sort out how the languages developed through the next several centuries. But it's clear that biblical Hebrew was eventually displaced by a colloquial form of the language, incorporating elements from the Aramaic tongue. Both Hebrew and Aramaic continued in use through the first century A.D.[1] But eventually Hebrew became a literary language only—it was used only in writing or official communications, just as Latin was used in Europe in the Middle Ages. We can't say exactly when this occurred. Usually it's been held that by the time the Mishnah was written down (mid-third century A.D.), Hebrew was no longer a spoken language. But some linguists now argue that Mishnaic Hebrew has all the qualities of a *spoken* language. So the jury is once again in deliberation.

Another phenomenon of note was the way that the Persian language influenced the Jews' Hebrew and Aramaic. Very quickly some Persian words

---

[1]Artifacts found at Masada and other Judean towns bear witness to the linguistic situation in Palestine in New Testament times. Potsherds and inscriptions have been unearthed written in both Hebrew and Aramaic, with Aramaic predominating. A jar in the Israel Museum bears the word *balsam* in both Hebrew and Aramaic. Obviously the original pot contained balsam that was sold at the market, and the bilingual inscription identified its contents to either Hebrew- or Aramaic-speaking customers.

were adopted into the Hebrew and Aramaic vocabulary. The Persian word *pardes*, "garden," became a regular part of Jewish usage (it entered into English as the word *paradise*). The word *raz*, "mystery"—an important word in the book of Daniel and the Dead Sea Scrolls—also comes from Persia. Certain sentence structures and turns of phrase made their way into Aramaic from Persian grammar as well.

Changes in the Jewish Religion

More interesting for our purposes than the social or linguistic changes of Judaism were the new religious concepts that came into Judaism during this period—concepts that laid the foundations for both rabbinic Judaism and Christianity. One basic change has already been mentioned: there was a new focus in Judaism on the received Scriptures. Initially we see this change manifested in a deep concern for understanding and obeying the precepts of the Mosaic law, as in the ministries of Ezra and Nehemiah, and in the Elephantine Papyri. But later in the Persian period we can observe a fast-growing reverence for the writings of the prophets. Already in the book of Zechariah we find references to the words of the "former prophets" (Zech 1:4) and allusions the prophecies of Isaiah (e.g., Zech 3:8). Haggai draws from the book of Amos (compare Hag 2:17 and Amos 4:9), and Malachi makes several allusions to the book of Isaiah.[2] This kind of inter-biblical allusion isn't totally a postexilic phenomenon, since the former prophets occasionally referred to each other's oracles as well. But the practice becomes more pronounced in the postexilic period and becomes especially prominent in intertestamental literature. The writing of prophetic oracles didn't cease during the intertestamental age. There were many people producing texts that were presented as prophetic (often under assumed names) as well as teachers who brought forth their messages as inspired revelations. But these new prophets were careful to present their messages either as commentaries on accepted biblical texts or to mix frequent allusions to biblical books into their presentations. They wanted their ideas recognized as a continuation of the biblical faith, not as innovations.

Much Jewish thought in this period *was* innovative, to a lesser or greater degree. During the Persian period a number of ideas appear in Jewish literature that are absent or obscure in the earlier Old Testament books. Some

---

[2]Compare Mal 3:1 with Is 40:3-5; 42:1; and Mal 3:2-5 with Is 1:11-28.

of these ideas were probably part of popular Israelite thought from ancient times but weren't well developed in the Old Testament for various reasons. Others arose in response to the new circumstances of the exile and the Persian domination. They developed from the divinely guided reflections of Jewish sages and were sometimes encouraged by dialogue with Persian teachers as well. That's not to say that the Jews of Judah and Babylon were following in the footsteps of their Elephantine cousins, adopting the Persian deities into a new Jewish pantheon. But there's a good deal of evidence that many Jews were familiar with some of the religious teachings of Persia and were seeking to reconcile those beliefs with their own.

The main religion of Persia in this era was called Zoroastrianism, after its prophet Zoroaster (also called Zarathustra).[3] Its basic teachings were remarkably similar to the Jews' own faith, holding to the existence of a supreme, good god, invisible and eternal. It had a highly developed sense of morals and ethics. Like Judaism, Zoroastrianism permitted no images of its great god, Ahura-Mazdah. The religion even forbade the practice of animal sacrifice, preferring to burn perpetual fires of incense as a symbol of Ahura's true light. Since it wasn't only the religion of the conquerors but also an attractive faith in many ways, Zoroastrianism presented a strong challenge to the Jews. Through interaction with priests and scholars of different faiths, the Jews undoubtedly learned a thing or two about their own God. Perhaps as the theologians of the church would later use Greek philosophy to help clarify the tenets of the Christian faith, some of the Jews found certain aspects of Persian religion instructive, while they rejected the core of Persian teachings. From our vantage point we could say that God used the Persians to reveal new aspects of his nature to his chosen people.

As we consider some examples of new developments, we'll find that the touchstone for Jewish beliefs was the teachings of the Hebrew Bible. In their progress toward becoming the "people of the book," the Jews looked to the biblical text to vindicate their beliefs and practices. Each new idea was tested against the revelations of the Scriptures and anchored firmly on the revealed word of the Lord. Ideas that stepped too far outside the circle of light cast by the accepted Scriptures found little audience among the pious Jews.

---

[3]We know little about the prophet Zoroaster himself. He may have lived around 1000 B.C., although some scholars would place him even earlier. His teachings spread slowly for centuries before becoming the official religion of Persia. The faith remains alive to this very day, although its adherents are now few.

PROGRESS OR APOSTASY?

For some people the thought of the Jews adopting ideas from their foreign neighbors is troubling. The Lord had ordered the extermination of the Canaanites in Palestine for the very purpose of avoiding such religious contamination. Wouldn't it be apostasy for the Jews to incorporate Persian religious beliefs into their own religion?

If the Jews were abandoning their own faith in favor of Persian beliefs, we might call it apostasy. But that isn't the case here. First of all, the Jews never adopted any notions from the Persians that were contrary to the revelation already given in their Scriptures. Many of the new developments in Judaism during the Persian period are firmly grounded in the faith of the Old Testament. There are no fundamental changes in the basic affirmations of the Jewish faith here. But there are some significant new concepts that relieve some tensions and fill in some gaps in Old Testament revelations.

Another important fact to keep in mind is that God could use any tool he desired, including foreign sages, to bring new revelations to his people. If he could speak to Balaam through the mouth of a donkey, he could surely speak through the lips of Persian magi! (We might also note that Balaam himself, author of several important biblical prophecies, wasn't an Israelite. According to the book of Numbers, he was from the town of Pethor near the Euphrates River.) The author of the epistle to the Hebrews wrote that God had spoken in many different ways to his people before speaking to them through Jesus Christ. God didn't simply write out a creed and give it to Israel. The Jewish religion was revealed slowly, over many centuries, as the Israelites' experiences with their God revealed new aspects of God's character. It was experiences, more than decrees, that shaped the substance of the Jewish faith. And one of those experiences was the dialogue and debate between Jewish sages and their foreign counterparts.

Angelic hosts. One area where Persia exerted some influence on Judaism was angelology. Angels appear frequently in the Old Testament, but outside of their interactions with humanity we know little about them. The Hebrew Bible says nothing about how or when they were created, and it says little about their various roles in the heavenly hierarchy. In the Bible angels usually serve as messengers—a function reflected in both their Hebrew designation *mal'ak* and Greek term *angelos*. Both terms can designate either human or divine emissaries—a fact that occasionally makes it difficult to determine whether the biblical narrative is referring to a supernatural being or a human prophet (e.g., Judg 2:1). Angels are seen bringing words of instruction, warning or judgment to human beings.[4] In their capacity as messengers they sometimes seem almost like "extensions" of God's presence, speaking God's words with both the third person "he" and the first person "I" (see, e.g., Gen 16:10; 21:17-18; 22:11-12). The earlier Old Testament books seldom describe angels or discuss their attributes. The authors were far more concerned with the messages they brought than the messengers themselves.

But angelic beings weren't limited to serving as messengers. Angels acted as God's "spies" at Sodom and Gomorrah (Gen 18—19); they guided and protected the Israelites during the exodus (Ex 23:20); and they brought plagues on them when they sinned (2 Sam 24:16-17). They could serve as God's eyes, ears and mouth in the world of humanity. Angelic figures also served as warriors, battling alongside the armies of Israel against their human foes. These forces were apparently organized like human armies, with officers and ranks, since an angel introduces himself to Joshua as "the commander of the army of the LORD" (Josh 5:14). But the Old Testament shows little interest in describing angelic ranks in any detail—at least, not before the Persian period.

After Persia came on the scene the Jewish interest in angels seems to have risen considerably. It's not until the book of Daniel—possibly the latest book of the Old Testament and certainly a book written after the Jews encountered the Persians—that we meet Gabriel and Michael, the only angels in the Old Testament to be given personal names. The Jewish rabbis noticed this fact and commented that the Jews learned the names of the angels while they were in Babylon.[5] That might well be true, but they

---

[4]See, for example, Gen 16:7-12; Judg 2:1-4; 13:1-20; 2 Kings 1:3-4.
[5]*Bereshith Rabbah* 48 (a *midrash* on the book of Genesis); *Y. Tal. Rosh Hashanah* 1.2.

CELESTIAL DENIZENS

The Bible speaks of a variety of creatures who inhabit the heavenly realms and sometimes interact with humanity. They include:

Angels—Hebrew *malak*. The term means simply "messenger." Most often angels appear in roughly human form, but they could look very impressive. Their main role in the Bible is to act as intermediaries between God and humanity.

"Sons of God"—Apparently, angelic beings who could appear human. In this case the word *sons* doesn't indicate parentage but only association (a typical Hebrew construction). See Gen 6:2, 4; Ps 82:1.

Cherubim ("powerful ones")—Often appear in ancient Near Eastern art as winged hybrid creature (like sphinxes). In the Old Testament these beings seldom interact with humanity. They frequently function as guardians of a sort (Gen 3:24; Ezek 28:14).

Seraphim ("flaming ones")—In Isaiah 6:2 these six-winged creatures serve in God's heavenly courts, proclaiming his glories.

Hosts—Angelic warriors. They could battle beside the armies of Israel, usually invisible to human eyes (2 Kings 6:15-17).

wouldn't have learned angel names from the Babylonians, who had no such beliefs. Nor did they learn the names *Michael* and *Gabriel* from foreigners: both names are Hebrew.[6] What they might have learned was the notion that angels could even *have* names of their own. The main religion of the Persian Empire, Zoroastrianism, was deeply interested in angelology and had names for legions of ministering spirits. Perhaps contact with the Persians led the Jews to explore this aspect of their faith in more depth and attach names to important angels in their own religion.

There is another possibility: perhaps angels in pre-exilic times *did* have names, but none of the names were recorded in our Old Testament. The Bible mentions lost works like "The Book of the Wars of the LORD" and "The Book of Jashar" that might have included this kind of esoteric informa-

---

[6]*Michael* means "Who Is Like God?"; *Gabriel* means "God's Hero."

tion.[7] But when the Old Testament was assembled, such information might have been edited out, since the names of spirit beings were commonly used in magical incantations throughout the ancient world. (Indeed, the names of angels and demons became one of the most prominent features of Jewish magical texts in the Christian era.) And it wasn't simply the names that were a potential problem: the ancient Near Eastern peoples commonly accorded worship to a great variety of spirit beings. Not only were the chief gods of the pantheon revered, there were also minor spirits, servants of the gods, who were worshiped in local shrines and private homes. In the era when Yahwism was still battling against beliefs in multiple gods, the prophets and sages who wrote and edited the Old Testament might have decided it was better to avoid perpetuating the idea that angels were spirit beings with individual personalities. There was a very real danger that superstitious Israelites might have constructed altars to Michael or Gabriel, offered them sacrifices and appealed for their aid (not unlike some people do today). Once the Babylonian exile had passed and the worship of multiple gods lost its appeal, the danger of angels becoming objects of worship was no longer an issue. The Jews could use the names of the angels that were remembered from antiquity, perhaps resurrect some of the lore associated with them and have little cause to fear that the practice would lead to apostasy.

And indeed the Jews did make extensive use of angel lore during this period. Even from a few references in Daniel we learn a great deal more about Gabriel and Michael than their names. We also learn that Michael is a great warrior and a prince among the angels. He is the angel in charge of Jewish affairs (Dan 10:13). We also learn that other nations have their own angelic princes—evil angels who somehow oversee the destinies of their charges. These angelic princes and their armies do battle against each other, just as human armies do battle. The outcomes of these battles determine the fate of people on earth. When the "prince of Persia" comes, it signals the ascendancy of the Persian Empire. The arrival of the "prince of Greece" means that the Greeks are coming now into power (Dan 10:20). None of these ideas are found in the Old Testament prior to the book of Daniel—they constitute a new revelation to the people of God.

And it's not only in Daniel where we find such notions. Many intertestamental texts also feature angels. The book of Tobit, written during the

---

[7]"Wars of the LORD," Num 21:14; "Book of Jashar," Josh 10:13; 2 Sam 1:18.

Persian period, features the angel Raphael ("God Heals") as one of its main characters. Raphael disguises himself as a young man and accompanies Tobias on his journey to Media, acting as a friend and adviser as the story unfolds. When he finally reveals himself to the hero, he describes himself as "one of the seven angels" (Tobit 12:15). This same number crops up again in sections of *1 Enoch*. In the section known as the "Book of the Watchers," Enoch learns that there are seven chief angels, each with his own area of specialization (*1 Enoch* 20). The Jews typically considered seven to be the number of completion or perfection, and that notion probably inspired the idea of seven archangels. But it's also possible that the authors of *1 Enoch* and Tobit were both inspired by Ezekiel 9, where seven angels carry out the judgment of Jerusalem.

ENOCH'S ANGELIC PRINCES

In the book of *Enoch*, as in Daniel 4:13, some of the angels are called "watchers." Apparently, these are beings who "watch over" human affairs. The Enochic "Book of the Watchers" identifies six chief angels:

Uriel—in charge of eternity and trembling
Raphael—over the human spirits
Raguel—taker of vengeance
Michael—over people and nations
Sariel—over those who sin
Gabriel—over the angels of Eden, serpents and cherubim

In some other texts only Uriel, Gabriel, Michael and Raphael are identified as "archangels." This tradition eventually became the standard.

Zoroastrianism, with its angelic hierarchy, also believed that there was a small cadre of angelic leaders. But unlike Enoch or Tobit the Persians held that there are but six chief spirits, not seven. The Jewish system may have been encouraged by Zoroastrian angelology, but it didn't simply copy the Persian beliefs.

Demonic minions. First Enoch also shows us another side of the angels: it tells us about angels who fell into sin. The section known as the "Book of the Watchers" elaborates on the biblical story of the fallen angels in Genesis 6. According to the Bible the "sons of God" (angels) became enamored with human women and took some of them as wives. Their union brought about a race of giants known as the *nephilim*. The whole incident takes up only four verses in the Bible (Gen 6:1-4), but it encouraged a great deal of speculation. In *1 Enoch* 6—8; 69, we're told that the angels were led by a spirit named Semyaz. These "watchers" not only took human wives, they also taught human beings various forbidden arts. Like the Greek Prometheus, a mythical Titan who gave humans the secret of fire and suffered eternal punishment, the angels were imprisoned and eternally tormented because of their wickedness (*1 Enoch* 13; 67).

Fallen angels were one class of wicked spirits. But there was another, larger class: the demons. The study of biblical demonology is a somewhat complicated affair. Unlike the New Testament, the Old Testament has no word corresponding to our word *demon,* so it's not always easy to determine if certain terms refer to evil spirits or simply to invidious natural creatures or phenomenon. But scholars generally agree that the *shedim* and *se'irim,* who appear in several Bible passages, are demonic spirits.[8] Lilith, mentioned in Isaiah 34:14, and Azazel, in Leviticus 16, were probably also demonic spirits known and feared by the Israelites.[9] There may be a few other demons mentioned in the Old Testament as well. But the authors and editors of the Bible generally steered clear of discussing demons in any depth. Not a single Old Testament passage speaks of demons opposing the work of the Lord, as they clearly do in the New Testament. Perhaps, as some have suggested, demons simply weren't considered an important aspect of ancient Israel's religion. Maybe most Israelites thought so little about demons that the biblical writers could pass over the whole subject in silence. But there's another explanation that seems even more likely: the authors and editors of the Old Testament deliberately deemphasized the subject of demons in order to avoid the confusion and superstition that such malevolent figures could engender.

Throughout the ancient Near East the line between gods and evil spirits was rather blurry. Indeed, demons could be thought of simply as evil or

---

[8]Lev 17:7; Deut 32:17; 2 Chron 11:15; Ps 106:37; Is 13:21; 34:14.
[9]The name *Azazel* can also be interpreted to mean "scapegoat." Most scholars, however, believe that Azazel was the name of a demon that the Israelites believed inhabited the wastelands.

mischievous gods. People who felt they were under demonic attack might well offer the spirit a sacrifice, just as they would offer to a major deity. No doubt some similar notions muddled the minds of many Israelites. In fact, the Bible tells us that the Israelites had a terrible tendency toward worshiping demons: Leviticus 17:7 and Deuteronomy 32:17 state that the Israelites sacrificed to demons as if they were gods, and Psalm 106:37 tells us that they actually offered their children to demons. So there was a danger in giving too much credit to evil spirits in Old Testament times—the danger that belief in such spirits could adulterate faith in the one true God. Most Israelites lacked the understanding to comprehend the darker side of the spirit world. So rather than risk giving mistaken impressions that there were gods other than the Lord, the biblical authors and editors downplayed the whole subject of demons.

But during the Second Temple Period the subject of demons became a topic of some speculation. Probably part of the reason behind this change was that the Jewish sages now had little fear of their brothers and sisters descending into demon worship. As stated above, the Babylonian exile seems to have settled the issue of who would be the God of Israel. The Jews in exile carefully guarded their cultural and religious identity. Their reflection on the apostasy that caused the national catastrophe made them all the more vigilant to avoid any tendencies toward what the rabbis called *avodah zarah,* the worship of foreign gods. It was this deep concern for preserving single-minded devotion to the Lord that led Ezra and Nehemiah to condemn "mixed marriages" so vehemently. So as the Jewish community became more solidly devoted to the Lord, demons could be brought out into the light, so to speak, and discussed openly, without the fear that some Jews would build them an altar and sacrifice a goat to them.

Another factor that might have encouraged the Jewish sages to give attention to demonology was the place of demon lore in the Zoroastrian religion. Zoroastrianism possessed a highly detailed demonology, with ranks upon ranks of well-organized devils working to tempt and torment the righteous. Apparently most Jews of the Second Temple Period didn't adopt the Zoroastrian ideas—no Jewish text from this period provides us with a catalogue of demons or descriptions of their various responsibilities. On the other hand, some Jewish authors demonstrate a definite familiarity with Persian ideas. In the book of Tobit an evil demon named Asmodeus torments a woman by killing any man she weds, but an angel instructs Tobit of a magical means to defeat the demon. The name of the fiend Asmodeus could be explicit evidence of Persian influence on the story: it's very likely the Jewish equivalent of the name of a prominent Persian demon, *Aeshma deava* ("demon of wrath"). Sometime later, Jews came to associate his name with the Hebrew verb *shamad*, "to destroy." In the apocryphal Wisdom of Solomon 18:25, a text undoubtedly written some time after Tobit, "the destroyer" is an epithet for the devil. So it would seem that Asmodeus had already come to be identified as the king of demons. His name continues to figure prominently in Jewish mystical literature up through the Middle Ages.

In the years after the fall of Persia the Jews continued to explore the subject of demonology. *First Enoch* gives us a little more insight into the origins and work of the demons. In one section of this book (possibly written before 200 B.C.), the demons are said to be the disembodied spirits of giants (the Nephilim) who were slain before the time of Noah. Like their fathers, the fallen angels, these demons are responsible for much suffering and mischief in the world. The author of the book of *Jubilees* may have been familiar with this part of 1 *Enoch,* because he tells a similar story in his own work (*Jubilees* 10:3-9). The demons are children of the fallen angels, and they tempt Noah's grandchildren into all manners of evil. When Noah prays for his descendants, God imprisons nine tenths of the demons. But at the request of the evil Mastema, God allows the rest to remain free, under Mastema's command, so that they can aid him in the work of tempting and tormenting humanity. These stories about the demons' origins have no parallel in Persian thought. They were the creations of certain Jews who were trying to account for the existence of spirit beings that opposed the work of God.

The fall of Satan. Demons received new emphasis in Persian-era Jewish thought, but this idea has deep roots in the Old Testament. However, the notion of an archfiend, an "opponent" of God, constitutes an unprecedented revelation.[10] Is there any evidence that the Israelites knew of the existence of the devil before the Persian period? A thorough search of the Old Testament throws the question very much in doubt. To begin with, the term *devil* never appears anywhere in the Old Testament. The preexilic Hebrews had no phrase denoting a chief demon or king of evil spirits. Nor do

---

[10]In this section I will use the English term *devil* to denote the chief fiend or evil opponent to the Lord. In the Second Temple Period, the Jews used several different names for this chief fiend, and it is not clear that they always had the same figure in mind.

we ever read in the Old Testament of a figure who rules over the evil spirits, as Beelzebul (Satan) is clearly said to do in the New Testament (see, e.g., Mk 3:22).

BEELZEBUL

The meaning of this epithet for the devil, which first appears in the New Testament, is uncertain. According to 2 Kings 1, Baal-zebub, "Lord of Flies," was the name of the god worshiped at Ekron by the Philistines. Ancient commentators understood Beelzebul to be a corruption of this name. Some more recent discoveries have revealed that a god named Baal-zebul, "Lord of Heaven," was worshiped in Syria. Probably Baal-zebub in 2 Kings was a pun on this title. The name may have been adopted as a title for the devil, who was the "prince of the powers of the air" (Eph 2:2).

Furthermore, the English translations of several Old Testament verses that refer to "Satan" are quite misleading. In fact there is only one verse in the Old Testament in which the word *satan* should be translated as a proper name (1 Chron 21:1). In the books of Zechariah and Job the Hebrew phrase that's usually translated "Satan" is actually *hassatan*, or "the *satan*." *Satan* is a Hebrew word that basically means an "adversary." The word is used several times to describe human beings (e.g., 1 Sam 29:4; 1 Kings 5:4 [Hebrew Bible, 5:18]). In one case the angel of the Lord is actually called a *satan* (Num 22:22, 32). The term is also used in a more technical sense to designate an accuser who brings charges against another in a court of law. When Psalm 109:6-7 says, "Appoint a wicked man against him; / let an accuser stand on his right. / When he is tried, let him be found guilty," it probably uses the term *satan* in this manner. In ancient courts such accusers were permitted to act in a very "adversarial" manner. The *satan* could badger, taunt and generally abuse the defendants in order to "trip them up" and make them demonstrate their guilt.

In a couple of biblical passages this human justice system is projected into heaven. Just as the Bible sometimes pictures God's heavenly dwelling with imagery drawn from earthly throne rooms, divine councils may be

portrayed on analogy with earthly councils.[11] In Zechariah 3:1-2 the
prophet sees a vision where the heavenly court is in session, complete with
the *satan* casting accusations at a defendant, while an angel of the Lord acts
as the defendant's advocate. Likewise the book of Job describes a heavenly
council meeting, where a *satan* comes forward to report on his activities:
"One day the sons of God came to present themselves before Yahweh, and
the *accuser* came with them" (Job 1:6, author's translation). There's no indication in the story that the *satan's* presence is unexpected or unusual.
He's only singled out because he's the central figure of the episode. According to the story the accuser reported that he'd been traversing the
earth, looking over its inhabitants. God suggests to him that he might consider the stalwart saint Job. The accuser begins his work: Job only serves
God because God has blessed him so well. If he were to lose his wealth, Job
would turn on the Lord. God allows the accuser to test his theory. With the
Lord's permission the accuser goes forth and torments Job in an effort to
demonstrate that Job's piety is false—much like an ancient accuser would
have badgered a suspect to wring a confession from them.

There are some obvious differences between the work of the *satan* in this
story and the way the devil operates in later intertestamental literature
and the New Testament. In Job's story the accuser doesn't appear to be
working against God's will. Indeed, he does precisely what God tells him
to do, testing Job's integrity. If we consider what the *satan* does to Job to be
devilish, we accuse God of devilry as well. It may be misleading to think
of the *satan* in this story as the devil. He isn't portrayed as an outcast from
heaven or the leader of legions of demons. Instead, this *satan* is simply an
angel who's been given the task of testing the righteous. Job isn't the victim of a demonic attack. Rather, he is afflicted because God is allowing the
satan to do his job in the cosmic justice system.

The system envisioned in the book of Job is truly monotheistic in its outlook, and it preserves the notion of God's sovereignty. No devilish spirit is
at work here, opposing the work of God. On the other hand, the story does
leave the door open for cynics to challenge God's love and justice. An innocent man suffered precisely *because* he was good. Job's children were
slain not because the accuser was evil and hated him but simply because

---

[11]See Is 6, where Isaiah sees God sitting on a throne, dressed in royal robes. These symbolic
visions shouldn't be understood as literal descriptions of heaven—they're presented in
human imagery for our benefit.

the accuser—and God—sought to test Job's mettle. One might wonder if a truly good God could deliberately put his people through such misery. But then that's precisely the point. The righteous often *do* suffer without any earthly reason. God of course knows why they suffer, but human beings aren't privy to that information. Our proper response to pain is to bear it patiently and hope for vindication in the end.

The book of Job wrestles with a problem rarely considered in the Old Testament. In the preexilic Old Testament books, with their collective conception of sin, righteousness and destiny, the issue of a single individual suffering unjustly was largely passed over. The *nation* was promised prosperity if the people were good and trouble if the people were evil. The book of Deuteronomy, for example, doesn't even consider the question of what would happen to the good people in Israel if God sent a plague on the country when most of the people were wicked. The stories of Noah (Gen 6) and Lot's escape from Sodom (Gen 19) demonstrated that God was able to spare good individuals from the fate of the wicked. But then there was the example of Jeremiah. In spite of his devotion and obedience to the Lord, he suffered abuse at the hands of his fellow Jews and was carried away against his will to Egypt when the Babylonians besieged Jerusalem. If this were all the reward one could hope for from faithfully serving the Lord, some Jews might well have wondered if it was really worth the effort.

With the growing sense of individualism that characterized Jewish thought in the postexilic period, the question of just recompense was becoming more pressing. Individuals would no longer be satisfied with the thought that their goodness brought blessing to their nation but might do nothing for them personally. What benefit was there in righteousness if the good could suffer just as much as, or even more than, the wicked? In pre-Persian times there were pieces of the picture that hadn't yet been revealed—pieces that would allow for the preservation of God's ultimate sovereignty *and* love. One of those pieces is the notion of the resurrection and final judgment, when the scales of justice will finally be balanced. But the other missing piece is the concept of a real cosmic struggle between good and evil—a struggle where good people might suffer not because of God's testing but because of the devil's consternation.

In contrast to preexilic Yahwism, the Zoroastrian faith of Persia seemed to account well for the problem of human suffering and temptation. The most prominent feature of this religion was a belief in cosmic dualism. In fact, Zoroastrianism is the only living world religion that can be called truly dualistic.[12] Dualism technically denotes a religion that holds to the belief in two creative spirits. They need not be equal in power, but they both must be involved in the process of creation—and one must not be the creator of the other. Zoroastrianism taught the existence of two creative gods: Ahura Mazda, the good god, and Angra Mainyu, the evil god.[13] Ahura Mazda was aided in his work by angelic officers, each of which had special duties to perform. The god and angels were the source of all the blessings that the righteous enjoy in this world. Angra Mainyu, on the other hand, was aided by demonic minions. These spirits were responsible for all the sufferings of the righteous and the spread of wickedness in the world. These two forces were locked in perpetual battle with each other for the souls of humanity.

On the surface at least, Zoroastrianism seems to deal very well with the problem of evil. Trouble occurs because there's an evil god who causes temptation and misfortune. The good god, Ahura Mazda, has nothing to do with bad things that occur. On the other hand, Zoroastrianism's belief in multiple gods was unconscionable to the Jews. No polytheistic system— even one with only two gods—could accommodate the concept of God that the Jews embraced. A god cannot be all-powerful if he shares his authority with another being. This basic incompatibility probably caused most Jews to reject the core belief of Zoroastrianism.

But even so, some Jews seem to have found value in the idea that there was a spirit being who worked to thwart the will of God. Why do the righteous suffer? Why do those who want to do good often find themselves doing evil instead? The concept of an archfiend seemed to provide a satisfying answer. The devil couldn't be granted the status of co-deity with the Lord, as was Angra Mainyu in Zoroastrianism. But some of the Jews, at least, were beginning to understand that an evil spirit striving to subvert the works of God was responsible for many of their trials and temptations. And an obvious biblical candidate for that office was the prime tempter and persecutor, the *satan*.

Satan's rising prominence is evident when we compare the story of

---

[12]Christianity is sometimes called dualistic because of its belief in the devil, but technically it's not dualistic, because the devil is a created being and is not a creator himself.

[13]According to some scholars, in the earliest Zoroastrian teachings Angra Mainyu was not considered Ahura Mazda's equal in any sense. Rather, he was the rival of Ahura's chief angel, like Michael is the rival of Satan in Christian teachings. He became elevated to the position of Ahura's chief rival just as some popular religious thought views Satan as God's evil twin.

David's census in 2 Samuel, written before the Babylonian exile, with the later version in 1 Chronicles. According to 2 Samuel 24, God was angry at Israel, and so he tempted King David to conduct a national census—considered a grave sin in those days. When David conducted the census, God punished the nation by sending a plague, killing thousands of Israelites. From a human perspective, it might seem like an unjust test. Would any decent human parents deliberately put temptation before their children and then punish them severely when they sinned? But according to 1 Chronicles 21:1, written during the Persian period, it wasn't God but Satan (here used as a proper name) who tempted David to commit the sin. Theologically, we can reconcile the accounts by recognizing that while Satan tempted David to evil, God was ultimately responsible since he allowed the test to occur. But in any case, the later version exonerates God from any *direct* responsibility for David's sin.

Is it possible that contact with the Persians encouraged some Jewish sages to separate the work of the devil from the work of the Lord? It's quite possible indeed. But the Jews didn't simply adopt a Zoroastrian notion. Rather, it seems more accurate to say that some Jewish thinkers were inspired by the exile experience *and* by their contact with Zoroastrianism to reconsider the nature of evil. Why did Israel continue to do evil when God had given them the Law and the Prophets to guide them? Why did good people like the prophet Jeremiah seem to suffer such undeserved hardship? The old answers to these questions seemed increasingly unsatisfactory, especially when the Persians seemed to provide a better answer. But the Jews weren't willing to accept any new concepts that couldn't be reconciled with the revelations received from the Lord in the Law and Prophets. The devil's new role had to be linked to ideas found in the accepted Scriptures.

Later in the intertestamental period, the image of the devil developed in a number of different directions, far beyond the simple identification of Satan as God's archenemy. In the book of *Jubilees* (c. 200 B.C.) the chief fiend is called Mastema. The name is derived from a Hebrew word that appears in only one passage in the entire Bible, Hosea 9:8: "There is only *mastema* in the house of Ephraim's God" (i.e., the temple at Bethel, ritual center for the northern kingdom Israel during the divided monarchy). The word apparently means "hatred" or "hostility," but the author of *Jubilees* interpreted it as a proper name. And he understood the "person" who lodged in Ephraim's temple to be an evil spirit—the devil. The book of *Jubilees* considers Mastema to be the chief of all evil spirits. Its author, in retelling the Old Testament stories, makes Mastema responsible for some of the more disturbing actions that the Bible attributes to God, including Abraham's temptation to kill Isaac and the incident in Exodus 4:24 where God tried to kill Moses. It's quite reminiscent of the way that 1 Chronicles absolves God of direct responsibility for David's census.

Other intertestamental texts identify the chief fiend with a variety of biblical figures. In a section of *1 Enoch* known as the "Animal Apocalypse" (c. 160 B.C.), the devil is identified with Azazel, the spirit who received the scapegoat on the Day of Atonement.[14] In Enoch's vision Azazel appears as a star that falls from heaven to the earth, an image lifted from Isaiah 14:12. In Isaiah's text the fall of the morning star represents the descent of Babylon's king from his position of power. But Enoch reinterprets the symbol: the star's fall from heaven now symbolizes Azazel's descent from God's royal courts, to lead the fallen angels into sexual relations with human women (Gen 6:1-2). Some portions of the pseudepigraphic *Testament of the Twelve Patriarchs,* possibly composed as early as the second century B.C., identify the chief fiend as Beliar. This name is the Aramaic equivalent of the Hebrew "Belial." Like the name Mastema, the name Belial was originally an obscure Hebrew word, later taken as a reference to a spirit being. In the Old Testament, it only occurs in the phrase *bene beli-ya'al,* an idiomatic expression that can literally be translated "sons of worthlessness." The scoundrels identified with this phrase were clearly children of the devil (spiritually speaking, of course), so the phrase *beli-ya'al* was taken as another name for the chief fiend.

An even more elaborate development appears in the Dead Sea Scrolls. In some of the Scrolls the dichotomy of the spirit world is projected on to the physical world as well. The *Community Rule* divides human beings into two camps. The righteous are called the "sons of light," and their patron is the archangel Michael, the "Prince of Light." The wicked "sons of darkness" are ruled by a spirit called Belial, the "angel of Darkness." Belial and his minions try to tempt the righteous to sin. They cause all the suffering that the righteous endure in this world. The *War Scroll* dramatically depicts the struggle culminating in an armed conflict between human armies on earth and angelic armies in the heavenly realms. Since the two sides are evenly matched, the struggle teeter-totters between one side and the other

---

[14]See Lev 16:8, 10, 26.

until God himself intervenes and brings the war to an end. In this world-view there's a real conflict between "good" and "evil," but God stands aloof from that struggle. The devil is no match for God, so when God enters the fray the battle is over.

FROM THE COMMUNITY RULE (1QS) 3.17-25

"He created humanity to rule the world, and set over them two spirits in which to walk until the appointed time of [God's] visitation. These are the spirits of truth and falsehood. Truth originates from the spring of Light; wickedness comes from the fountain of Darkness. The authority of the Prince of Light rules all the righteous, so they walk in the ways of Light. The Angel of Darkness has power over all the wicked, so that they walk in the ways of darkness. All the errors of the righteous come from the Angel of Darkness. All their sins, their iniquities, their guilt, and their rebellious ways are under his dominion, according to the mysteries of God, until the (appointed time of the) end. All their afflictions and their seasons of distress are under his baleful authority. And all the spirits of his lot cause the children of Light to stumble. But the God of Israel and the angel of his Truth give aid to all the children of Light."

These are just a few of the depictions of the devil in intertestamental literature. It isn't possible to trace the development of diabolical imagery in this period. Each text may represent a stream of tradition or a single author's opinions. Nor can we tell when certain ideas arose simply by noting when they first appear in the existing literature. Many texts were produced in those days that haven't survived to our time. And not even the surviving texts can tell us how long certain ideas may have been around before they made their way into a text. But it seems safe to conclude that when the Jews "discovered" God's evil adversary, they didn't automatically identify him with Satan. One writer might have identified the devil with Satan, another with Mastema, another with Azazel and so on. Consequently there was some splintering of the concept of the devil during the intertestamental period.

But by the time of Jesus it seems that many of these concepts had been brought together into a cohesive whole. There's no difference in the New Testament between the devil, Belial and Satan; the three are one. (The name Satan is the preferred designation in the New Testament, with the devil running a close second.) Because of their broader perspective, the New Testament authors were able to see the hand of the devil in many Old Testament events. In Luke 10:18 the disciples' successful ministry prompts Jesus to remark, "I watched Satan fall from heaven like a flash of lightning." The image of Satan plummeting to earth was certainly inspired by Isaiah's "fall of the morning star." Likewise, Revelation 12:9 tells of a war in heaven where Satan was cast down to the earth in the form of a dragon. This image might also have been inspired by Isaiah 14. Unlike the pseudepigrapha, which identified the devil's fall with the sin of the "sons of God" in Genesis 6, the New Testament seems to remove the event from a historical timeframe: Satan's fall *has* happened, and in some sense it *is* happening.

The book of Revelation also identifies Satan as "that ancient serpent" (Rev 12:9; 20:2). Very likely this designation refers to the serpent of Eden. Since the serpent clearly opposes God's work, who else could he have been but God's evil adversary? And even though the New Testament never identifies Job's *satan* the devil, it certainly recognized his activity to be diabolical. In Revelation 12:10, the devil is called the "accuser," the Greek equivalent of the *satan*. When Jesus tells Peter that Satan has asked to be allowed to test him (Lk 22:31), it's very reminiscent of the story of Job's test.

Another diabolic image with Old Testament roots is the identification of Satan as a "prince." The book of Daniel speaks of good and evil angelic princes who struggle with one another for supremacy (Dan 10:13, 20; 12:1). And the New Testament devil behaves in a similar fashion. He's called the "prince of demons" (Mt 9:34; 12:24 NIV, KJV), the "prince of this world" (Jn 12:31; 14:30; 16:11 NIV, KJV), and "the prince of the power of the air" (Eph 2:2 KJV). The New Testament depicts the devil as a powerful adversary to the people of God, just as the Dead Sea Scrolls depict Belial. This present world order is largely under his dominion. But his power is not absolute, and his defeat is certain (Rev 20:10). Indeed, his fall has already been set into motion by the crucifixion of Jesus Christ (Jn 12:31-32).

Not all Jewish writers immediately accepted the understanding of the devil as God's evil adversary. Several books of the Apocrypha, such as the

Wisdom of Ben Sirach (200 B.C.), 1 Maccabees (late second century B.C.) and Baruch (late second century B.C.), seem to know nothing of a devil. The Sadducees of Jesus' day didn't believe in angels or "spirits," but the Pharisees did—including, one can assume, the devil, since they accused Jesus of using the devil's power (Mt 12:24). Later rabbinic Judaism seems to have adopted beliefs very similar to those of Christianity, with a supreme devil, known by various names, accompanied by hosts of evil spirits. By the Middle Ages any Jewish sects that rejected belief in the devil had become extinct.

Life after death. The final new development we'll consider here is the concept of the resurrection of the dead. In the later part of the Persian period the Jews began to grapple systematically with what we often call the ultimate question: what happens after we die? In most of the Old Testament little is said about the fate of the dead. Rather, the Old Testament is primarily concerned with the fate of Israel as a nation. As we observed earlier, it was corporate rather than personal destiny that captured the interest of the biblical authors. No one sinned to him- or herself alone; no one was righteous for him- or herself alone. When the Israelites obeyed the Lord, according to many Old Testament passages, they would enjoy long lives, good harvests and conquest over their enemies.[15] Wicked behavior, on the other hand, threatened the health of the entire nation. If Israel fell into sin, God would punish his people with very earthly plagues, famines and defeat at the hands of their enemies.[16] And if these punishments weren't enough to cause the Israelites to repent, God would play his trump card and destroy the nation.

Of course the Bible also recognized the possibility that an individual could act wickedly, while the nation as a whole wasn't charged with sin. The Proverbs (regarded by most scholars as a late composition) are especially individualistic in their perspective, observing that habitual sinners were in danger of having their lives cut off by the Lord.[17] The prophets Jeremiah and Ezekiel explicitly state that the Babylonian exile wrought a change in the way God would deal with his people: whereas in the past the nation would suffer together because of a man or woman's sinful behav-

---

[15]For long life see, for example, Deut 6:2; 30:20; Ps 91:16; Prov 3:2; 4:10; 9:11. Bountiful harvests are promised in Deut 7:12-14; 11:13-15; 28:4-6, 8, 11-12. Destruction of enemies is found in Deut 7:23-24; 11:23-25; 28:7.

[16]See esp. Deut 28:15-68; 29:14-29; Judg 2:11-23.

[17]Prov 1:19; 5:22-23; 7:23; 10:27.

ior, in the postexilic time God would hold every person responsible for his or her own sin.[18] But even so, these prophecies say nothing about the wicked suffering damnation or eternal punishment. The sinners threaten not their eternal destiny but their lives—the person who sins will die for his or her own sin. Generally the Old Testament gives little attention to the question of whether the sinner's soul was in danger of damnation.

When the Old Testament does speak about the fate of the dead, the words are seldom encouraging. Neither sinner nor saint seems to have welcomed the prospect of dying. Apparently both the righteous and the wicked expected to end up in Sheol, the Hebrew realm of the dead.[19] No Old Testament passages speak about the righteous dead going to heaven or experiencing eternal bliss. The good king Hezekiah, when he was informed of his impending death, prayed fervently that God would spare him. When he received word that God would give him fifteen more years to live, Hezekiah rejoiced, because "Sheol cannot thank you, / death cannot praise you; those who go down to the Pit cannot hope / for your faithfulness" (Is 38:18). The patient Job, while longing for death on the one hand, also declares that those who go down into Sheol are like a mist that vanishes, never to be heard from again (Job 7:8-9). In a similar vein Psalm 6:5 declares, "For in death, there is no remembrance of you; / in Sheol who can give you praise?" The author of Ecclesiastes (considered by most scholars to be a very late, postexilic composition) is aware that some people in his time believe the spirit lives on after death, but he himself is agnostic about the issue. As far as he can see, there's no difference between the beasts and human beings when it comes to death (Eccles 3:16-22). A

---

[18]Jer 31:29-30; Ezek 18:1-4, 19-20.

[19]Some scholars have argued that only the wicked go to Sheol and that this place corresponds to hell in the New Testament. They cite the fact that the Bible never specifically says a righteous person actually descended there. But in several passages righteous individuals *do* expect that they will one day go to Sheol. In addition to Hezekiah and Job, discussed in the text, there was also Jacob in Gen 37:35. Even allowing that these passages are only hypothetical, would saints speak casually about going to hell after their death? This problem has led the translators of the New International Version to translate *Sheol* always as "grave" rather than "underworld," as in some other translations. Theologically this translation may be justifiable since the Old Testament's descriptions of those in Sheol can be interpreted as referring to dead bodies. But if Sheol is only the grave, where do the souls reside after death? Why do the Old Testament saints say nothing of going to heaven or paradise? Most likely they didn't know about heaven as a human destiny yet. Only people like Enoch or Elijah, taken directly to heaven, were thought to escape Sheol.

A "PRECIOUS" DEATH?

According to Psalm 116:15, "Precious in the sight of the LORD / is the death of his faithful ones." Many interpreters see here a testimony to belief in life after death in the Old Testament. After all, why should the faithful ones' death be precious unless God will be taking their souls to heaven?

But a look at the entire psalm renders this interpretation difficult. The psalm is a song of joy for *deliverance* from death. The psalmist clearly didn't consider death a good thing in any way. He considers the prospect of death a terror, not a blessing (116:3)!

A closer look at the word *yaqar*, "precious," also suggests a different understanding for the psalm. This Hebrew word is generally used to describe something that is prized because of its rarity or uniqueness, not because of any implicit virtue (see, e.g., Ps 37:20, where the flowers of the field are cited for their preciousness [NRSV "glory"; NIV "beauty"] because they are short-lived). In some contexts the word would be better translated "special" rather than "precious." A better translation of Ps 116:15 might be, "The LORD takes special notice of the death of his faithful ones." In other words God takes special consideration of them, not allowing their lives to come to a premature end. The psalm isn't about life after death but about God's special provision for the righteous in the present world.

person should take pleasure during life on earth because Sheol is a joyless place of inactivity (Eccles 9:10). These verses are completely true from a human point of view: dead bodies don't praise the Lord or enjoy pleasures or have any knowledge of earthly affairs. Nor can we know, humanly speaking, whether the spirit survives death. But what a far cry these verses are from Jesus' image of Lazarus resting peacefully on the bosom of Abraham (Lk 16:19-22) or Paul's confident assertion that to be absent from the body is to be present with the Lord (2 Cor 5:8). Living in the days before God revealed the blessedness of those who die in the Lord, the Old Testament authors could only report their own experiences and observations.

Their observations are true, so far as they go—but they're incomplete.

It would be inaccurate to say, however, that the ancient Israelites didn't believe in some form of life after death. There was almost certainly a popular notion of life after death among the Israelites. Belief in some form of the afterlife was common to all the peoples of the ancient Near East, and Israel was no exception. The "cult of the dead"—the worship of dead ancestors—was practiced in various forms by the Canaanites, the Syrians, the Babylonians and the Egyptians, as well as the far-flung nations across the Mediterranean. It was the "poor man's religion" par excellence. In some Canaanite cities the dead were actually buried inside the houses so their spirits (which hung around the bodies) could be fed and consulted. Babylonian graves were equipped with feeding tubes so wine or blood could be poured into the tombs to nourish the spirits of the deceased. The "feasts of the dead" were orgiastic parties, celebrated in all those ancient lands, meant to strengthen the departed spirits and ensure their good will. And the Israelites too participated in such rituals—much to the chagrin of the biblical prophets and sages. The Psalmist relates with horror that the Israelites ate the feasts of the dead at Baal-Peor (Ps 106:28), which would have been nonsense if the Israelites had no concept of an afterlife. The law of Moses and the prophet Isaiah both condemn the practice of necromancy—consulting spirits of the dead (Deut 18:11; Is 8:19). In neither case do they question whether or not the practice is effective; rather they view it as apostasy. Spirits of the dead, the *rephaim*, were often considered gods in the ancient Near East. In the story of Saul and the Witch of Endor, Saul asks the witch to call up the spirit of the late prophet Samuel so he can consult with him about the future. When the spirit appears, the witch cries out that she sees a "god" rising from the earth (1 Sam 28:13). In the popular religion of ancient Israel the dead might have been consulted regularly as if they were minor deities. Some scholars have suggested that the word *Sheol* derives from the Hebrew verb *sha'al*, "to inquire," and refers to a place where inquiries were made of departed ancestors.

So how do we reconcile the comments by the biblical authors that the dead cease all activity with the belief that the spirit lived on after death? Part of the discrepancy lies in the distinction between popular practices and biblical ideals. Beliefs in the cult of the dead belonged to the realm of the unsophisticated or even apostate Israelites. The sophisticated biblical authors had no interest in perpetuating superstitious and pagan notions about the afterlife. In preexilic times God hadn't yet given his people much insight into the fate of our spirits after death. So the biblical authors were reluctant to encourage speculation on topics where God had been silent. Theologically, we can understand their comments on the darkness and desolation of death to refer not to the spirit but to the body, which does indeed lie silent and powerless in the grave.

During the intertestamental period, however, the situation changed dramatically. I've repeatedly emphasized that the problem of foreign gods seems to have been largely settled sometime shortly after the Babylonian exile. Once the Jews decided as a people that there was but one God, the danger that spirits of the dead would become objects of adoration was minimal. The ghosts could come out of the closet, and the fate of the dead could be given the serious consideration it deserved.

Some of the Jews concluded that belief in life after death had no place in Judaism. The book of Tobit, written during the Persian period, seems to know nothing of life after death. Around 200 B.C. Ben Sirach echoes the old view that Sheol is a place of silence, where no activity occurs and no praises are sung to God. Like Ecclesiastes he argues that one should enjoy life while it lasts, but not in wickedness: God will cut short the life of the wicked.[20] First Maccabees, written later still, holds out little reward for the righteous but glory and a good name (1 Macc 2:51). This strain of thought continued into the time of Jesus in the Jewish sect known as the Sadducees, who denied that the dead could be raised to life again (Mt 22:23-32; Acts 23:8).

Other Jews seem to have retained the notion that the soul survives death, but added the idea that the righteous and wicked experience different fates. Righteous souls, they believed, would go directly to a place of bliss after death, while the wicked would go into a place of punishment. The earliest text to express this opinion (*Jubilees* 23.21) comes from about 200 B.C. and may have been influenced by Greek popular religion. Indeed, several texts that express this view come from the Hellenistic Diaspora, those Jews who lived in lands heavily influenced by the Greeks. Josephus also seems to attribute this view to the Essenes, one of the three principal Jewish sects that existed in his day (their views will be discussed further in chapter six). This view probably developed fairly late in the Second Temple Period and remained a minority opinion.

Most Jews seem to have adopted a perspective that differed consider-

---

[20]Sir 14:16; 17:22-23; cf. Eccles 7:17.

ably from either of these ideas. In this new understanding it wasn't belief in disembodied spirits that was the focus of interest but belief in a real, *embodied* existence. Proponents of resurrection taught that at the end of the age the dead would be revived and given new, immortal bodies. The concept seems to be such a departure from earlier Jewish thought that many scholars have been tempted to explain it wholly as an import from Zoroastrianism, where belief in the resurrection of the dead was prominent. But while Persian influence might have encouraged belief in the resurrection, it probably wasn't the source of the idea. Several historical and biblical streams fed into the concept of the resurrection, as it eventually came to be understood among the Jews.

Historically, the Jews experienced a national tragedy unlike any they had experienced before—their defeat and exile at the hands of Babylon. Their nation had been destroyed. Their royal house was taken away. Their temple had been reduced to rubble. All the symbols that formerly were the foci of Israelite piety had failed them. As stated earlier, the central concern of Jewish religion began to shift from national destiny to individual destiny. We can see analogous patterns in other ancient nations that experienced similar collapses. We've already talked a little about ancient Egypt. In Old Kingdom Egypt (before 2160 B.C.) the average Egyptian probably was afforded little hope for an afterlife, unless he could "hitch a ride" on the coattails of the pharaoh. The royal cult was directed at preserving the pharaoh's spirit for eternity. Great pyramids were built as monuments to the pharaohs, and the common person hoped that participation in the project would bring personal blessings. The pharaoh's most faithful servants yearned to be buried in the shadow of the pyramids, achieving immortality by serving the pharaoh in the world to come. (Common people might aspire to an afterlife by serving one of the royal officials who'd be serving the pharaoh.) But when the Old Kingdom crumbled into the nearanarchy known as the First Intermediate Period (c. 2160-2040 B.C.), Egyptian religion was transformed as well. The cult of Osiris, a god who supposedly was killed and raised to life again, grew in popularity with the masses. Private citizens began to build elaborate tombs for themselves, and even poor people would pay to have their bodies mummified (as well as they could afford), to assure themselves a decent afterlife. A similar transformation took place in Greek religion, when Greece was conquered by the Romans. Popular Greek religion became obsessed with the notion of immortality. The so-called mystery cults multiplied, promising to secure a place in the Elysian Fields (the Greek equivalent of Paradise) for those who would participate in their secret rites. It's not particularly surprising then that Judaism also underwent a change of focus during and after the Babylonian exile.

Nor should it be surprising that most of the content of this new hope came from the Jews' own Scriptures. Neither Egypt nor Greece looked far beyond their borders for hope of an afterlife. The Egyptians already possessed the myth of Osiris, dying and rising from the dead, and the Greeks had similar myths about Orpheus and Olympian heroes who cheated death. The Jews had a rich legacy of biblical imagery that provided much of the substance for their own budding conception of the afterlife.

One basic biblical belief was the essential inseparability of body and soul. In Old Testament times Israel and the other Near Eastern nations didn't have a concept of the spirit as an entity with independent existence. That's why the Egyptians were so careful to preserve the bodies of the dead. It also underlies some practices of the cult of the dead, where the "shades" were generally "fed" and consulted at their own tombs—the soul was believed to reside with the body after death.[21] In biblical teaching, unlike some popular Christian clichés, we are *not* immortal souls temporarily encased in human bodies. Rather, we are integrated beings, body and spirit together comprising "a living soul."[22] An afterlife like that envisioned in some Greek-influenced texts, which anticipated a disembodied soul floating around in heaven for eternity, would have been quite foreign to Old Testament thought (and probably New Testament thought too, for that matter—though some have argued that Paul held a more dualistic understanding of the soul and body). The concept of the resurrection wasn't based on some notion of the immortality of the human spirit, but rather on the gracious intervention of God for the sake of his holy ones. We see that idea expressed in Psalm 49:15, generally regarded as a late composition. Here, the poet writes that God will redeem him from the power of Sheol, while the unrighteous are left there to languish. Resurrection is a *gift*, not a natural human faculty.

---

[21]The story of the Witch of Endor manifesting Samuel in her home town (1 Sam 28) is an exception, but not a unique one. Witches, by means of their magical arts, were believed to be able to make spirits manifest themselves far from their bodies.

[22]See Gen 2:7, where God breathes spirit into the lifeless body, and the body becomes a "living being." This concept also fits well with what we now know about mind-body interaction. Changes to our physical body can deeply affect our personalities.

Another Old Testament motif that shaped the idea of the resurrection was the conviction that God couldn't permit injustice to continue indefinitely. Eventually, the prophets and sages knew that God would have to intervene in human affairs so the scales of right and wrong could be balanced. One recurring theme in the prophets is the expectation of "the day of the Lord," when God would give the inhabitants of the earth their due. They wrote with mixed longing and fear of God's coming intervention in human history, when terrible judgment would descend on Israel's enemies and vindication would be delivered to the righteous.[23] Cosmic upheavals—both symbolic and real—would accompany the day of God's vengeance. God's people would begin to obey the Word of the Lord as never before, and the land itself would respond with miraculous productivity. Even the animals would learn to live in peace.[24] But none of the pre-exilic prophets actually speak of the dead being raised on the day of the Lord. Rather, this time would see the restoration of Israel's *national* glory. The message wasn't of individual salvation but corporate restoration and retribution.[25] But even so, these hopeful images encouraged the notion of a final judgment, where all the wrongs would be righted and justice would be served. After Judah was destroyed and the Jews began to think more in terms of individual piety and destiny, they began to regard the "day of the Lord" as a time of personal vindication rather than simply a time of national vindication.

Yet another stream that fed the hope of resurrection was the Old Testament's use of resurrection imagery in symbolic or poetic senses. One of the earliest writers to invoke this picture was Hosea (eighth century B.C.). The Israelites, who had been punished for their sins, would return to the Lord, who "after two days . . . will revive us; / on the third day he will raise us up, / that we may live before him" (Hos 6:2). This reference makes no mention of dead bodies or graves, but its intent is clear enough. Like bodies brought back from the dead, the beaten-down nation Israel would be restored to life and vigor by God's hand. The prophet Ezekiel, writing after the destruction of Judah, takes the image much farther. In Ezekiel 37 this

[23]Some of the clearest expositions on the day of the Lord are found in Is 13, Ezek 7, Amos 5:18-27, Joel 2, Obad and Zeph.
[24]Is 11—12; 65:17-25; Joel 3:18-21; Amos 9:11-15.
[25]Some scholars have seen in Is 26:19 a promise of individual resurrection, but since the context speaks of Judah's national restoration, the verse might best be understood as symbolic of the repopulation of Judah.

prophet sees a vision of a valley filled with bones, representing broken and scattered Judah. But at the prophet's command the bones reassemble, flesh grows on them, and they come to life again. God explains to Ezekiel that he will do the same with the house of Israel—though they seem dead and hopeless, he will restore the nation to life again. The book of Isaiah also uses resurrection imagery several times to proclaim hope to God's oppressed people.[26] Nor was resurrection exclusively a symbol of national renewal: some biblical writers describe their deliverance from peril as being "raised from the dead" or "delivered from the grave."[27] None of these passages spoke of a literal resurrection, but later Jewish writers often made reference to them to demonstrate that God promised to bring life to the dead.

One writer who employed these passages was the author of the book of Daniel. This book is the only one in the Old Testament that speaks explicitly about personal resurrection. In Daniel 12:1-4 we're told that at the time that God delivers his people, there'll be a resurrection of both the righteous and the evil—some to receive their rewards and others to receive their punishments. In these few verses Daniel makes several allusions to the book of Isaiah. He writes that the dead who "sleep in the dust" will "awake," just as we read in Isaiah 26:19 (apparently a symbol of the restoration of the nation). He tells us that those who are "wise" will lead "many" to righteousness—an allusion to the work of the servant of the Lord described in Isaiah 53:11. He uses the same rare Hebrew word for the "contempt" that the wicked will experience that we find in Isaiah 66:24, a passage that tells how the corpses of the wicked would burn eternally, to be objects of contempt. Clearly, Daniel's concept of the resurrection is firmly rooted in biblical imagery.

The same can be said of Psalm 49, which was mentioned earlier.[28] In this late biblical poem the psalmist uses an image frequently found in the Old Testament, the image of God rescuing the righteous from Sheol. But unlike earlier authors who used this phrase to mean deliverance from imminent death, this writer apparently meant that he would be delivered *after* his death. The psalm lampoons the rich, who trust in their wealth but leave all

---

[26]Is 25:7-8; 26:19; 53:9-11.

[27]Ps 16:10; 71:20; 86:13; Jon 2:6.

[28]There's been much debate over the significance of this psalm. I side with those who see here a true, physical resurrection, rather than simply a deliverance from the prospect of death.

their money behind when they perish. Their money won't be able to save them from death. All other people die too, of course (Ps 49:10), but the psalm implies that some of the dead will experience different fates than others. Those who have "insight" won't be like the haughty, who will perish "like the beasts" (Ps 49:20 [Heb. verse 21]). Instead, the psalmist expects to be redeemed from the power of death because God will "take" him (Ps 49:14)—just as Enoch (Gen 5:24) and Elijah (2 Kings 2:3, 5) were "taken" to heaven. Biblical phrases and images form the substance of this author's hope for life after death.

Outside the confines of the biblical canon, several intertestamental authors used biblical imagery to describe the resurrection. The various sections of *1 Enoch*, written at times ranging from 200 B.C. to just before the time of Jesus, show a great interest in the resurrection theme. One of the earliest sections of the book, chapters 22-27, draws strongly from Isaiah 65—66 in describing the fate of those who have been resurrected. The righteous will live in the New Jerusalem, where they will be rewarded for their good deeds. The wicked will be punished in a valley burning with fire. Chapters 92-105, written in the second century B.C., emphasize that resurrection is designed to bring justice to those who were denied justice in their lives. Neither passage seems to expect a *universal* resurrection—in other words, *1 Enoch* didn't seem to expect all the dead to live again. Rather, only those who hadn't received their just reward (or punishment) during their mortal life would be raised to life again. In 2 Maccabees 7, written in the late-second century B.C., we read of seven brothers and their mother who were tortured to death, each confidently asserting that God would raise their bodies to life again and reward their obedience to his law. The wicked oppressors, on the other hand, would have no resurrection at all. This chapter draws heavily on imagery from Isaiah 53 and other biblical passages about the "servant of the Lord."

It seems clear that the primary influence on Jewish thought about the afterlife was the Old Testament itself. But was the Jewish idea of resurrection truly *inspired* by biblical teachings? Many scholars have observed some interesting parallels between Jewish expectations about the resurrection and Zoroastrian ideas. In the Zoroastrian scheme, when a person dies, the soul remains with the body for three days. On the third day the soul ascends to a mountaintop, where its works are judged. If the good outweighs the evil, the soul goes to heaven; if evil predominates, the soul descends to hell. But the soul doesn't remain permanently in heaven or hell.

At the day of judgment the body will be reconstituted and reunited with its soul. There will be a trial by fire, when all the righteous and unrighteous will have to pass through a river of flame. The flame will purify the righteous, but the wicked will be destroyed eternally.

We can see some obvious similarities between some Jewish concepts and the Zoroastrian view. Both tell us that (1) the spirit somehow rests after death, (2) there will be a bodily resurrection on the judgment day, and (3) the resurrection involves both the righteous and the wicked. Some Jewish texts even demonstrate a more intimate knowledge of the Zoroastrian scheme: the *Testament of Abraham* 20:9-12, for instance, speaks of the soul residing with the body for three days and nights after death—an idea too close to the Zoroastrian scheme for mere coincidence. But while some Jewish authors may have adopted details about the afterlife from the Persians, the Jewish concept of the resurrection itself was probably homegrown. The experience of exile, the belief in ultimate justice, the notion of the unity of body and soul, and the biblical resurrection imagery all fed the belief that God would raise the righteous to receive their reward, while the wicked would be punished for their sins.

Some scholars have put forth a more nuanced suggestion: that the Jews developed a notion of the resurrection of only certain individuals, and the idea of a universal resurrection came from Zoroastrian influence. But I believe that the development from the idea of selective resurrection to general resurrection was rather natural. Once the Jews allowed that some people could rise from the dead to have their deeds reviewed and weighed in the balance, it seems logical that they would have recognized that *all* people experience injustices in this world of one sort or another, and that a truly just system demanded the resurrection of all people. The Zoroastrians might have had the idea first, and contact with the Persians probably encouraged Jewish speculation along these lines. But the Jews seem to have received the idea of the resurrection as an independent revelation, informed by the rich biblical tradition that was wholly their own. The Jews were creative enough to develop their own understanding of life after death, and self-assured enough that they wouldn't simply soak up the ideas of the nations that happened to be their overlords.

Conclusions

Judaism in the Persian period possessed a wonderful combination of stability and flexibility. Its stability came from its dependence on the revealed

Scriptures. The Hebrew Bible provided the Jews with a touchstone for their faith. The flexibility came from its dynamic relationship with God, and its openness to his continuing revelation. The Jewish faith was capable of changing as new circumstances arose, new revelations were given or new challenges posed. The Persians proved to be a source of all three. Sometimes, contact with the Persians inspired the Jewish sages to consider aspects of their faith that simply hadn't received the attention they deserved. Some Jewish authors actually adopted ideas from Zoroastrianism to clarify their understanding of God. But in every case, any new ideas that came into Judaism during this period had to prove themselves in the light of the Scriptures, the accepted Word of the Lord.

For Further Reading

Bergquist, Jon L. *Judaism in Persia's Shadow.* Minneapolis: Fortress, 1995.

Horbury, William, W. D. Davies, Louis Finkelstein, and John Sturdy. *The Cambridge History of Judaism.* Vol. 1., chap. 11. Cambridge: Cambridge University Press, 1984.

Johnston, Philip S. *Shades of Sheol: Death and Afterlife in the Old Testament.* Downers Grove: InterVarsity Press, 2002. Argues that Sheol was not the abode of the righteous dead.

Nickelsburg, G. W. E. *Resurrection, Immortality, and Eternal Life in Intertestamental Judaism.* Harvard Theological Studies 26. Cambridge, Mass.: Harvard University Press, 1972. A classic study with extensive documentation.

Russell, D. S. *The Method and Message of Jewish Apocalyptic.* Philadelphia: Westminster Press, 1976. See chapter 9, "Angels and Demons," and chapter 14, "Life After Death."

Segal, Alan. *Two Powers in Heaven.* Leiden: Brill, 1977. An influential work on dualistic ideas in Judaism.

4

The Greeks in the East

From the Jewish perspective the visage of authority was becoming increasingly foreign. When the Egyptians conquered Judah after the death of King Josiah, there were no surprises: Judah had experienced close relations with Egypt for years and knew the Egyptians and their ways quite well. King Nebuchadnezzar's Babylonian Empire was a newcomer to the Palestinian political scene and represented a "distant land" in the opinion of the Jews (2 Kings 20:14 = Is 39:3). But they were still fellow Semites, with much culture in common with their Jewish subjects. The Persians, however, were different. Their land was still more distant than Babylon; the people were of Indo-Aryan descent rather than Near Eastern extraction. Culturally and geographically, the seat of power was becoming more remote from Jerusalem. And with the coming of the Greeks the situation took a dramatic turn. The overlords were now a people from across the sea, with whom most of the Jews had little prior contact. Their language was strange; their customs abhorrent. A new thing was happening among God's people, unlike anything they could have imagined. The center of the world had shifted from the East to the West. And Judaism would never be the same again.

The Greeks and the Persians

The Greeks had no ancient ambition to conquer the Persians. In fact, it was originally the opposite: it was the Persians who were bent on conquering the Greeks. The conflict began in 499 B.C., when some Greek colonies in Asia Minor revolted against King Darius I. Darius might have put the revolt down quickly but for some Athenian ships that came to the aid of their

brethren in the East. Before the revolt was quelled, the Greeks had burned
the city of Sardis in Lydia, a loyal subject of the Persian Empire. So Darius
vowed revenge against the Athenians. From a distance it probably seemed
that adding Greece to the Persian Empire would be no great challenge.
Greece wasn't a united kingdom; its chief city-states struggled with each
other constantly for supremacy. Athens, Corinth, Megara, Sparta and
Thebes perpetually bickered, formed temporary alliances, betrayed one
another and pursued their own best interests. When Darius I looked to the
West, he saw a plum ripe for the picking. After subduing mighty Egypt,
what kind of a challenge could the Greeks offer?

Greece proved a surprising challenge, indeed. In 490 B.C. Darius assembled a huge army and a fleet of six hundred ships. The Persian troops
landed on the east side of Attica, on the plain of Marathon. A small Athenian army stood against them. Through a brilliant stratagem the Greeks
hemmed in the Persian forces, making it impossible for them to deploy
their troops as they had planned. In utter disarray and taking heavy losses,
the Persians were forced to retreat back to their ships. Legend has it that a
Greek messenger ran over twenty-five miles from Marathon to Athens to
deliver news of the victory—thus giving us the word *marathon* for a
twenty-six-mile race.

With his military forces decimated and rebellions brewing at home,
Darius was forced to postpone his dream of adding Greece to his empire.
But the Persians weren't ready to give up their ambition just yet. In 481 B.C.
Darius's son Xerxes attempted another invasion with an even larger army.
His troops marched inland rapidly, advancing on Athens with devilish intent. But the Spartans, the most disciplined warriors of the ancient world,
came to the aid of their long-time rival. A small band of three hundred
Spartan soldiers held the Persians at Thermopylae Pass, sacrificing their
lives in a successful effort to delay the invaders long enough for the Athenians to evacuate their city. When the Persians arrived, Athens looked like
a ghost town. The invaders took out their frustrations by destroying many
of the city's glorious structures, but they didn't hold their prize for long.
The exiled Athenians appealed to the other city-states, and in 479 B.C. the
combined Greek forces drove the Persians from the Achaian (Greek) peninsula.

Persia seemed to have had its fill of Greece, at least for the time being.
Besides, the bloated empire was having enough problems keeping control
of its Asian provinces. With some weak and incompetent emperors des-

GREEK MILITARY SUPREMACY

How was it that the Greeks managed to hold off and even over-whelm much larger Persian forces? There were several factors at work. One was technology. The Greek armor was far superior to that of the Persians, giving their foot soldiers the clear advantage in hand-to-hand combat. The Greeks also had an advantage at sea. Their small, fleet fighting ships proved more than a match for the cumbersome Persian vessels in the kind of battles that the Greek and Persian navies fought. Another factor was tactical leadership. The Greek soldiers were well disciplined and fought as units. The Persian soldiers tended to fight as individuals, each more concerned about dispatching his own opponent than the overall battle plan. Finally and probably most important of all, the armies were very different in composition. The Persian army in-cluded many soldiers conscripted from the diverse lands over which the Persian Empire held sway. Some of these ethnic groups were none too happy with the Persians to begin with, and proba-bly not overly thrilled to be bringing other nations under Persian domination. Many more of the soldiers were mercenaries—hired hands. The Greeks, on the other hand, were fighting to protect their homes and their families. In spite of their squabbling they were convinced to a man that the Greeks—any Greeks—were su-perior to any other people in the world. The idea of foreign dom-ination was unconscionable to them.

perately trying to hold on to increasingly uncooperative satrapies, Persia had no stomach for further conquest. So Greece was free to explore democracy, develop its arts and philosophy, and resume its civil warfare. Athens and Sparta vied for dominance in a struggle that has become known as the Peloponnesian War. By 400 B.C. Sparta had emerged as the victor in this fray, but in 371 B.C. Thebes, utilizing new battle tactics developed by their brilliant general Epaminondas, conquered Sparta and brought all Greece under The-ban control. But that unification, too, was brief, and it dissolved when Epam-inondas was killed in battle in 362 B.C. Greece was once again a land divided.

The Rise of Macedonia

Meanwhile, to the north of Greece the small kingdom of Macedon was quietly preparing to forge its place in history.[1] In 359 B.C. Philip became king of the somewhat unsophisticated land. Philip had fought against—and lost to—Epaminondas of Thebes. He admired Epaminondas's techniques and improved on them with some ideas of his own. Philip developed an organizational plan for his army known as the *phalanx*. The phalanx consisted of nine thousand men, arrayed in squares with sixteen soldiers on each side. The soldiers stood about three feet apart, and ringed themselves in with their unique shields. The front-line soldiers were armed with thirteen-foot-long spears that extended between the shields. Moving together in formation, each group of soldiers formed a human tank, deadly and veritably impregnable. Philip also assembled an impressive cavalry and developed new siege machines and other devices that made his army most formidable indeed. Following the example of Epaminondas, Philip set out to bring the factious city-states under the rule of a single monarch—himself. By 338 B.C. Macedon conquered and united the land of Greece.

The Greeks weren't all that impressed with their new liege. They considered Macedon a barbarous realm, not actually Greek at all. But Philip embraced Greek culture and adopted Greek as the official language of his newly forged empire. The great philosopher Aristotle became the tutor of Philip's son, Alexander. Alexander also became a disciple of the orator Isocrates, whose constant theme was the utter superiority of Greek culture and the utter depravity of the Persians. Isocrates believed the time had come for the Greeks to go on the offensive against their Eastern foe. And Philip, having united Greece into a most formidable power, was inclined to agree.

But Philip couldn't carry out his plans for invading the East. In 336 B.C. he was assassinated by one of his nobles. Quickly, however, Philip's son Alexander took the reins of the kingdom. Alexander was only twenty years old when he became the king of Macedon and the Greek Empire, but he proved a more-than-worthy successor to his father. Endowed with a passionate love of Greek culture and a missionary zeal, he dreamed of spreading Hellenistic (Greek) ideals throughout the world. His immediate goal was relatively minor. On the coast of Asia Minor (modern Turkey) were several Greek colonies that had been conquered and incorporated

---

[1]These events are summarized in *Ant.* 11.8.

into the Persian Empire—the same colonies that tried to revolt against Darius I 165 years earlier. Alexander felt the time had come to liberate those cities from their barbarian overlords. In 334 B.C. Alexander led an army of forty thousand soldiers across the Dardanelles into Asia Minor. His first encounter with a small Persian army at the Granicus River (near ancient Troy) proved an easy victory for Alexander. Typical of the inept administration of the Persian Empire at this time, there were no other Persian forces stationed in Asia Minor. The current emperor, Darius III, seemed to be oblivious to the obvious threat that Alexander posed. So after only a single battle Asia Minor lay before the Macedonian general like a sheep waiting to be sheared. Facing so little resistance, Alexander was encouraged to reconsider his objectives. No longer would he be content with the liberation of some Greek colonies. Now he set his heart on the conquest of the entire Persian Empire.

Under different circumstances it would have seemed a mad undertaking. An army of forty thousand, equipped only for a short mission of liberation, now bent on a long journey of conquest in the heart of the enemy's territory? If it weren't for the widespread discontent in the Persian Empire at the time and the incompetence of Darius III, it would have never succeeded. That's not to detract from Alexander's remarkable achievement. Not only was Alexander a brilliant general, he was also a master of propaganda. Like Cyrus the Great, founder of the Persian Empire, Alexander won the favor of the locals by portraying himself as a liberator rather than a conqueror. He promised relief from oppressive taxes and misgovernment by uncaring Persian officials. Only rarely did he receive any opposition at all from the locals. He also engaged in some psychological warfare, leaving enormous horse bits lying around at the sites of his victories—giving the impression that his cavalry was supersized!

Alexander and Darius III first came face to face in 333 B.C., when Alexander was en route from Asia Minor to Syria. The encounter clearly demonstrated the Darius's lack of tactical ability. The Greeks encamped in an open field near the village of Sollioi. If Darius had chosen to engage Alexander in the open plain, as his generals advised, his massive army might have surrounded and crushed the smaller Greek force. But instead Darius met Alexander's army in a narrow pass between the sea and the Taurus Mountains, where the Persian troops couldn't be easily deployed. Their numerical advantage was thus neutralized by their leader's incompetence. Alexander's phalanxes, on the other hand, proved very effective in the close quarters. Darius's army was quickly routed and forced to retreat, forfeiting all Asia Minor to the Macedonian king.

Alexander's conquest of the East was barely begun. In 332 B.C. he proceeded through Syria and Palestine with little resistance. The Phoenician city of Tyre, long known for its arrogance, was one of the few sites to offer any trouble. Alexander captured the city after seven months' siege. In a rare show of excess he vented his rage on Tyre, selling thirty thousand women and children into slavery, crucifying two thousand men and leveling the city to its foundations. He also had some trouble with Gaza, but this city was taken after only two months. Josephus relates one version of a Jewish legend that Alexander visited Jerusalem and worshiped at the temple of the Lord there, but there's probably little truth in these stories—his crowded itinerary wouldn't have allowed such a trifling detour.

After finishing with Gaza, Alexander proceeded to Egypt, where he was received in the manner he truly desired: as a liberator from Persian tyranny. Alexander demonstrated his piety before the Egyptians by sacrificing at their temples and doing homage to the sacred Apis bull in Memphis, whom the Egyptians believed was the incarnation of the god Osiris. He also began building there the city of Alexandria, destined to become the shining jewel of the Eastern world. For a year he enjoyed Egyptian hospitality—and worship. Since they considered Alexander to be their legitimate pharaoh, the Egyptians accorded him the same kind of worship that they offered the pharaohs of old. He was, to them, a god upon the earth. But while Alexander lingered in Egypt, the Samaritans rebelled against their new Macedonian satrap and burned him alive. The king quickly proceeded to Samaria and put down the revolt ferociously, apparently with some aid from the Jews.[2] The city of Samaria was destroyed and rebuilt as a Greek settlement. It seems that Alexander rewarded Judea—as the Greeks called Judah—for its part in putting down the revolt, adding some Samaritan towns to its territory. The incident further soured the already rocky relations between the Jews and their northern neighbors. Alexander later tried to placate the Samaritans by helping them expand Shechem, the city to which most the Samaritan refugees fled. It's also possible that the Samaritan temple on Mount Gerizim was built by Alexander's order.

---

[2]Somewhat distorted references to the massacre are found in the writings of Josephus and Eusebius. Papyri and artifacts attesting to the destruction, including human remains, were found at the Wadi ed Daliyeh in 1960.

Alexander obviously relished the adulation of the Egyptians, and he returned there for a short while after putting down the Samaritan uprising. But soon the time came to complete his mission: he'd have to pursue King Darius. Up through Palestine and Syria and into Mesopotamia he traveled, until finally he crossed the Tigris River at a place called Gaugamela (near Arbela). Darius III and his huge host confronted Alexander's small but sturdy army, and once again the Persian king was soundly defeated and forced to flee for his life. Now, Alexander was the undisputed conqueror of the East. He took his time surveying his new realm, spending a year admiring the magnificent ancient cities of Babylon and Persia, which joyfully opened their gates to the conquering hero. But then word came that Darius had been taken prisoner by his own noblemen. Alexander hastened now to liberate the Persian king from his captors, hoping to take Darius alive. But in this campaign, at least, Alexander failed. On hearing of Alexander's approach, the noblemen killed the king and left his body lying in the dust for Alexander to discover. With Darius dead, and since he left no royal son to lay claim to his throne, Alexander the Great was declared the rightful king of the Persian Empire.

The Transformation of Hellenism

Alexander came to the East convinced of the barbarism of its people. His intention was to bring the light of Greek culture to a land submerged in the blackest night. But once he tasted its fruits, the mysterious East cast its spell over Alexander. The pomp and circumstance of the Persian court was so very different—and so heady!—compared to the austerity of Macedonian kingship. Soon Alexander laid aside his soldier's armor and took up the fine robes and golden jewelry of a Persian lord. He surrounded himself with servants, slaves and eunuchs, just like an Eastern potentate. As the Persians lavished their adoration on their new monarch, Alexander demanded that his Greeks treat the Persians with respect as well, and make no attempts to punish them for losing the war. He even installed Persians and other natives in positions of governmental authority. The king who came to Persia as a Greek missionary was developing a new vision. No longer interested in replacing Eastern culture with Greek culture, he now imagined a melding of the two into a glorious new system of thought and action. No more would Hellenism simply mean the importation of Greece to Asia. Now it would mean a hybrid culture combining the best that Greece and the East had to offer.

JEWS AND SAMARITANS

From the earliest times, Jews and Samaritans had rocky relations. According to 2 Kings 17 the Samaritans are a mixed race. Samaria (the old capital of Israel) was depopulated by the king of Assyria, and people of various nations were brought in to resettle the land. These people brought their idols with them to Israel. But God sent lions among the Samaritans to punish their idolatry. So the king of Assyria sent an Israelite priest to teach the Samaritans about the God of Israel. The Lord thus became the chief God of Samaria, though the inhabitants continued to worship other gods as well.

The Samaritans tell a different story. They claim to be the descendants of the true Israelites, those who were left behind in the deportation. (Since King Sargon of Syria reports exiling only 27,290 Israelites, there were obviously a great many who were left behind.) Samaritans claim that it's not they but the Jews who are apostate. The Samaritans claim that the Ark of the Covenant was originally located in their holy city of Shechem. But the high priest Eli—in their account, a renegade—created a second ark and located it at Shiloh. It was this reportedly fake ark that was eventually moved to Jerusalem.

It's interesting that this account contradicts a letter preserved by Josephus in *Antiquities* 12.5.5 (258-264). This letter, believed to be authentic by most scholars, records a petition made by the Samaritans to Antiochus Epiphanes to be exempted from the persecution of the Jews. Their argument is that even though some of their practices are similar to Jewish observances, they're actually unrelated to the Jews, being descended instead from the Sidonians (Phoenicians).

Jews and Samaritans share many characteristics. Both worship the Lord and use the Pentateuch (books of Moses) as their primary Scriptures. The rabbis observed that the Samaritans were often more scrupulous about keeping the law than they were themselves. But the Samaritans' Pentateuch differed in some substantial ways from that of the Jews. They also denied the authority of the Prophets and Writings. But most important of all, they denied the legitimacy of the Jerusalem temple, preferring to offer their sacrifices on Mt. Gerizim, near Shechem. Antagonism between the two nations was strong in the Persian period, when the Samaritans certainly outnumbered the Jews. The rift became irreparable when the Jewish priest and leader John Hyrcanus destroyed the Samaritans' temple near the end of the second century B.C.

When reading Jewish history it's important to maintain a distinction between the residents of Samaria, the city, and the Samaritans. The city of Samaria was rebuilt by Alexander the Great as a Greek city and populated with pagans. Most of the Samaritans had fled the city and settled in Shechem. When the New Testament refers to Samaritans, it means the Shechemites, not the pagan residents of Samaria.

To some of his officers it seemed that Alexander had gone too far. To see their general dressed in the delicate garb of a Persian monarch was repellent to them. To be forced into sharing power with the people they had vanquished was unthinkable! The Greeks conquered Persia, and these officers felt they should be allowed to act like conquerors. But while Alexander lived, they wouldn't openly challenge their commander in chief. At least, not in this matter.

When Alexander sallied forth to secure the eastern half of the Persian Empire under his rule, he found his troops somewhat reluctant to follow. He pressed his armies onward through Afghanistan, all the way to India. But farther than that, the troops would not go. No matter how Alexander begged, pouted or threatened, the Greek army had enough of conquest. It was time to go home and enjoy the fruit of their victories. So Alexander returned to Persia and set about the work of consolidating his new empire and implementing his dream of the merging of East and West.

As an ultimate symbolic gesture of unity, Alexander held a mass wedding in the Persian capital of Susa, where eighty noble Macedonians took Persian women as their wives. The wedding was conducted according to Persian rather than Greek ritual. In addition he bestowed gifts on ten thousand Greek soldiers who married Persian wives. The union of Greek and Persian culture was becoming a reality. Over the protests of his Macedonian officers, Alexander appointed Persians as generals in his armies and as his personal bodyguards. He held a great banquet in which Greek and Persian priests offered sacrifices and prayers for the welfare of their respective lands.

Alexander died suddenly in 323 B.C., at the age of thirty-two. His death severely set back the dream of fusing East and West, since his successors didn't share his enthusiasm for the idea. But the forces that Alexander had set in motion were irresistible. The East would seesaw back and forth between Greek customs and eastern traditions for the next several hundred years. Influential philosophies, such as Stoicism and Neo-Platonism, would arise or flourish in the East, combining systematic Greek thought with eastern understandings of divinity. Oriental ways would seep into Greece itself and then into Rome, infecting their Western austerity with the opulence of Persia and Babylon. In the end, the best of the East and the West would come together when the Christian church brought Greek thought and methods together with Eastern theological concepts, producing a faith that satisfied both the hearts and minds of people throughout the world.

ALEXANDER THE GOD

Before his death Alexander was widely worshiped throughout the East. We might expect such emperor worship to have arisen from eastern traditions. The pharaohs of Egypt were considered incarnations of the sun god, and Babylonian rulers were regarded as the gods' adopted sons. (Persian emperors, on the other hand, weren't considered divine nor accorded worship.) But interestingly enough, the impetus for Alexander's deification didn't come from the easterners but from the Greeks. The first people to worship him were probably the Greek colonists of Asia Minor. They may have been continuing a tradition begun by Alexander's father Philip, who also thought himself to be a god, a descendant of Heracles. There were legends in Greece about divine or semidivine kings, but there was little historical precedence for worshiping a living monarch. Philip somehow believed that his reign had brought the mythological to life. After his death the cult of Philip continued, and no doubt Alexander encouraged its practice. Before Alexander's death, his own divinity was being debated in Greece, where a cult was worshiping him as a living god. This exaltation of Alexander established the precedent that his successors would follow.

Alexander's Successors

Alexander's death brought chaos to his empire.[3] He was survived by a son, but the child was too young to take over the reigns of government. Alexander had made no other provisions for a successor. So it fell on Alexander's generals to determine who would rule the vast Hellenistic empire. One of them, Perdiccas, was elected as the high regent, in an effort to preserve the unity of the state. Presumably he would have ruled until Alexander's son was old enough to assume the throne. Other generals received control of various regions of the empire: Lysimachus was given Thrace;

---

[3]These events are summarized in *Ant.* 12.1.

Ptolemy was placed over Egypt; Seleucus received Babylon. Each of these ambitious men had his own agenda and treated his charge as the victor's spoils. None of them seemed wholly content with the territory allotted him. Conflicts began almost immediately, and the high regent Perdiccas found it increasingly difficult to keep the proud, unruly officers in line. In 321 the very officers who elected Perdiccas as their leader murdered him. Alexander's son was later murdered as well, leaving no one with a good claim to the throne. The generals were free to battle among themselves for control of the empire.

One of the central figures in this struggle was a certain Antigonus. Alexander appointed Antigonus the satrap of the important region known as Phrygia (in Asia Minor). Soon after Alexander's death, Antigonus set out to conquer Babylon, forcing Seleucus to flee to Egypt for refuge. Intoxicated with power, Antigonus demanded that the other generals acknowledge him as Alexander's rightful successor. But they would have none of it. Instead, they joined forces against him, and handed him some decisive defeats. Recognizing the resolve of his rivals, Antigonus signed a treaty in 311 B.C. establishing each general's territory. Seleucus returned to Babylon, and Antigonus was given control of Syria and Palestine. But Antigonus's ambition wasn't spent yet. In 306 his forces invaded Greece and Cyprus. Antigonus now declared himself king—the first of the generals to take that title. The others, however, not to be outdone, responded by declaring themselves kings as well. They formed an alliance against Antigonus, and in 302 the tough old general fell in battle. Antigonus's territories were divided between the other kings: Lysimachus added western Asia Minor to his domain; Ptolemy now held Egypt and Palestine; and Seleucus got Syria and Mesopotamia.

The struggle for Palestine, however, was only begun. Ptolemy claimed the land of Palestine should be his for strategic reasons, since it could serve as a base for the invasion of his country. In actuality his desire went beyond concern for security: the most important trade routes of the Near East passed through Palestine, and Ptolemy wanted to insure the uninterrupted flow of merchandise from Egypt to wealthy markets throughout the Mediterranean. Seleucus also coveted the bitumen, trade routes and other resources to be found in Palestine. But in deference to the king who had aided him in the struggle with Antigonus, Seleucus ceded his claim on Palestine—for the time being.

In the end Ptolemy and Seleucus proved to be the only generals capable of establishing their kingdoms. Neither could be called a great man, but both were reasonably competent. And for the time being the key to survival was to be capable, but not too ambitious. Ptolemy and Seleucus each contented themselves with the territories allotted to them, which weren't inconsiderable. World empires would wait for another age.

The Rule of the Ptolemies

There's much to be said about the way Ptolemy ran Egypt—almost all of it bad, from the Egyptians' point of view. Ptolemy had no interest whatsoever in Alexander's dream of merging East and West. Soon after Alexander was dead, Ptolemy divorced his Persian wife and dismissed the Persian officers whom Alexander had installed. To Ptolemy the native Egyptians were little more than the spoils of war, a resource to be exploited. He was their conqueror, and he intended to act like it. Egypt was rich in goods that could be exported at great profit, and Ptolemy wanted it all. He set up government officials who supervised the production of all foodstuffs and many other commodities as well. Privately owned farms became the property of the state. Native Egyptians and other Easterners were taxed as heavily as they could bear; Macedonians and Greeks in Egypt were taxed much more lightly. Under the first four rulers of the Ptolemaic dynasty, almost all government officials were Macedonians or Greeks—native Egyptians were largely disenfranchised. Even the army consisted of Macedonians and Greeks. Native Egyptians were employed by the military only as porters or manual laborers.

There was one area where the Macedonian conquerors weren't so quick to give up Eastern ways: their understanding of kingship. Macedonian kings were a rather humble lot, and there was little pomp and circumstance associated with royalty. The Greek city-states were generally democracies of a sort that nearly did away with kingship altogether. But the Macedonian generals had grown accustomed to the regal robes, fawning servants and general pageantry that went with an oriental monarchy. In fact, the adoration of the king went beyond mere respect: in some oriental kingdoms the monarch was regarded as an incarnate god. Already during Alexander's lifetime an empire-wide cult was worshiping the "divine" Alexander. In Babylon, Seleucus I wasted no time in appropriating the title of divinity for himself. He actually identified himself with Zeus, the chief god of the Greeks, and had temples constructed throughout the realm in his honor. Ptolemy I, in keeping with his practiced disdain of

Eastern customs, rejected the title of deity. But his son, Ptolemy II Philadelphus, gave his official recognition to the cult of divine kingship, and
statues of the Ptolemies were erected in every temple in Egypt.

Eventually, there came a softening in the attitude of the Ptolemies toward the people whom they ruled. Perhaps it was the adoration paid to
them by subjects who regarded them as gods on earth. Perhaps it was the
eventual triumph of good sense that made them realize there was little to
gain by provoking hatred from their subjects. Perhaps it was the fact that
the native priests formed an alliance of sorts with the king, and the priests
used their influence to secure the loyalty of the natives. Or maybe the East
finally cast its spell over them just as it had over Alexander the Great.
Whatever it was, from Ptolemy V (204 B.C.) onward the Macedonian rulers
came to identify more and more closely with their Egyptian subjects, en-
acting laws favorable to native concerns. Indeed, the time came when the
Ptolemaic "Pharaohs" seemed actually to *favor* the interest of the natives
to those of Greeks living in Egypt. Like the Pharaohs of old, the Ptolemaic
monarchs adopted the custom—quite foreign to the Greeks—of marrying
their sisters to preserve the purity of the bloodline. After several generations the distinction between native-born Egyptians and Greeks became
blurred somewhat, especially outside the major cities, so that it actually
didn't seem to matter so much anymore.

The Ptolemies and the Jews

How were the Jews affected by the Ptolemaic policies?[4] In the struggle between the generals, Judea was a hapless pawn—but a pawn of considerable strategic importance. Some ancient Jewish sources tell us that when
Ptolemy took control of Judea, a great many Jews were deported and sold
as slaves. Such an outrage would only have occurred if the Jews had actually resisted Ptolemy's conquest. According to Josephus, Ptolemy invaded
Jerusalem on the Jews' sabbath, and thus encountered little resistance. But
once the sabbath passed, the Jews would have been free to respond to his
presence with force of arms. Given the insensitive, abusive ways in which
Ptolemy administered Egypt, it isn't surprising that the Jews wouldn't
have welcomed his rule. The next Ptolemaic king, Ptolemy II, ordered that
the Jewish slaves be granted freedom, but the deportation left its mark on
Judaism. Jews were scattered throughout the Mediterranean region, and

---

[4]The primary source for this section is *Ant.* 12.1.1-12.3.4 (12.1-153).

many chose to remain in their new homelands rather than return to Palestine. Jewish outposts thus sprang up throughout the Mediterranean world. Many Jews did quite well for themselves in this era, taking advantage of freedom of movement and trade throughout the empire. Jerusalem, too, seemed to be experiencing economic prosperity, due no doubt to its proximity to some important trade routes.

JUDAISM AND SLAVERY

Slavery was a common feature of ancient life. The Old Testament allowed Israelites to keep both Gentiles and Jews as slaves, but Jews were generally discouraged from enslaving their countrymen. But if someone acquired deep debts or committed certain crimes, he or she could be sold into slavery to fellow Jews—but not to Gentiles. The law required that male Israelite slaves be released after six years of service, unless they refused to go forth (Ex 21:2-6).

Jewish prisoners of war were frequently sold as slaves to foreigners and taken away to distant lands. But if any Jewish communities existed in those lands, tradition required them to ransom their kinsman and set them free. Without funds for a return trip home, these people frequently settled in the lands to which they'd been taken. The slave trade thus became a channel for expanding the Jewish presence throughout the Mediterranean region.

Compared to other ethnic groups in the empire, Jewish population seems to have grown rather quickly. One of the reasons behind this trend was the fact that the Greeks, and eastern peoples who aped them, participated in the barbaric practice of infanticide. Some scholars have suggested that the reason the Greeks adopted the practice was the poor soil of the homeland. Because it was so difficult to grow crops in Greece, the Greeks frequently found themselves unable to feed their families. There was an obsession among them to keep family sizes small, and birth control methods were at best unreliable in those days. So the Greeks would leave many of their newborns on hillsides to be devoured by animals or collected by depraved creatures for unspeakable sacrifices. Daughters suffered this fate more often than sons; but few Greek families ever allowed more than two or three babies to live. The Greeks exported this barbarous custom to the East, and infanticide became the fashion among those who were coming to associate all things Greek with the freshest fruits of civilization. Because their religious sentiments strictly forbid the practice, the Jews tended to multiply more quickly than their neighbors. Already by 300 B.C. Jerusalem was a populous city, and it continued to grow throughout the Greek period. The Hellenists—people who held firmly to Greek ideals—looked on this rampant breeding with scorn, but the Jews were on their way to becoming a presence in the Mediterranean world.

THE ZENON PAPYRI

Zenon was a Ptolemaic financial officer during reign of Ptolemy II. His archives were discovered in Egypt in 1915. According to these records Zenon visited Palestine in 259 B.C. and remained there a year. He brought back with him several documents concerning the region. While these documents compose only a small fraction of the archives, they tell us a good deal about Judea's financial and administrative situation in early Ptolemaic times. They also reveal that the Tobiad family (descendants of "Tobiah the Ammonite slave" who opposed Nehemiah) was still very active in Judean politics in this time.

After the initial conflict with Ptolemy I, things seem to have been relatively quiet for the Jews in Palestine. Even though the region was carefully administered and heavily taxed, Judea seems to have been spared the brunt of Ptolemy's avarice. His greatest concern was with governing the coastal regions (Phoenicia) and the Transjordan, where important trade routes passed. As long as Judea was secure, providing a safe buffer between his kingdom and potential enemies to the north, he was content to offer minor interference in local affairs. A financial officer traversed the entire region of Palestine and Phoenicia, overseeing local trade and taxation. There might also have been an administrative/military official over the area. But local administration was left in the hands of native officials, who prospered quite well under the system.

Of course, that doesn't mean that the Jews had it easy. The Ptolemies did tax them heavily, and the small farmers and merchants felt the burden most keenly. The Jews couldn't even console themselves with the idea that their taxes provided much-needed public services. When taxes were collected, all the money was sent back to Alexandria to fatten the Macedonian coffers. Ptolemy initiated a system where tax collection was farmed out to local officials who used the position to their political and economic advantage. The tax farmers were responsible for raising a certain quota from their district. Anything they sent in above the quota was considered a feather in their cap—the ticket to a cushy government job or other special perks. They could also use their position to generate income for themselves by extorting extra taxes from the locals. The system was hierarchical, with village tax collectors accountable to regional collectors, who were accountable to the people above them. Among the Jews in Palestine the ultimate responsibility for seeing that taxes were paid fell on the shoulders of the high priest. In fact, it appears that the high priest also served as the Jews' governor during this period. We don't know exactly how this situation came about, but it's reasonable to assume that the high priest had already become a significant figure during the Persian period. We've seen how much importance the Bible assigned to the high priest Joshua right at the beginning of Persian rule. Later, when Nehemiah was appointed governor of Judah, he doesn't seem to have pushed anyone else out of the position. Probably the high priest served as the chief local official unless someone else was specifically appointed to the post.

The Struggle for Palestine

To Judea's north stretched a vast, covetous kingdom.[5] Like the Ptolemies, the Seleucids recognized the strategic importance of Palestine's trade and travel routes. Seleucus never formally renounced his claim on Palestine; in his mind the country was "on loan" to Ptolemy as a reward for services rendered in the struggle against Antigonus. Since Seleucus was not nearly so ambitious—nor quite as competent—as Alexander the Great, he was willing to surrender the eastern parts of the empire that he inherited, concentrating on the western lands. India was lost almost at once, and Af-

---

[5]The primary source for this section is *Ant.* 12.3-4.

ghanistan went not much later.[6] Powerless against such defections, the
Seleucid monarchs decided to concentrate their efforts on maintaining
control of the area around the Mediterranean, especially Asia Minor and
Syria. Antiochus II (261-246 B.C.) moved his capital city from Babylon to
Syria, allowing him easy access to the sea—and putting the Seleucids right
on the border of Palestine. The new capital city, called Antioch, became a
center for Greek culture in the East. (It was here, many years later, that the
disciples of Jesus were first given the name "Christians.")

Between 274 B.C. and 253 B.C. two wars broke out between the Syrians
(Seleucids) and Egyptians (Ptolemies) for the control of Phoenicia and Palestine; but each time the Ptolemies came out the victors. To seal the peace
pact ending the second war, Ptolemy II offered his daughter Berenice to
Antiochus II as wife. There was only one problem: Antiochus was already
married, and the Greeks hadn't become so "Easternized" as to countenance multiple wives. In exchange for a peace treaty and a large dowry,
Antiochus apparently deemed his marriage a small price to pay. So he divorced his wife Laodice and banished her along with her son Seleucus II.
Berenice and Antiochus were joined in marriage, and it seemed that there
would finally be peace between Egypt and Syria.

Laodice wasn't so easily dismissed, however. When Antiochus died in
247 B.C., she quickly came forward to press the case of her son, Antiochus's
firstborn, for the throne of Syria. Berenice wasn't about to give up her own
son's claim without a fight. After all, she was Antiochus's *legal* wife, making her son his legal heir. But Laodice's ambition was matched by her
guile, and she wouldn't be deterred by legal technicalities. When it appeared certain that Berenice's son would get the crown, Laodice had both
Berenice and her son assassinated.

Of course, this heinous crime enraged Berenice's brother, Ptolemy III,
now king of Egypt. In 246 B.C. he retaliated against Laodice and her son by
sending his army into Palestine, and the Third Syrian War had begun.
Ptolemy enjoyed remarkable success on this campaign. The Seleucid
armies were still in disarray over the difficulties in succession, and they
could offer little resistance. Ptolemy easily advanced through Palestine, all
the way into Syria itself. But soon Seleucus II got firm control of his king-

---

[6]The kingdom of Parthia, in Iran, won its independence from the Seleucids around 238 B.C.
Soon after, the Parthians had wrestled Babylon away from the Greeks, and the Seleucids
had a strong rival on their eastern frontier.

dom, and rallied his forces. Ptolemy's troops had to fall back. And then, to make matters worse, a revolt erupted in Egypt. Ptolemy not only withdrew from Syria, he actually had to withdraw many of his forces from Palestine. With Ptolemy's army in full retreat, Seleucus might have pressed his advantage and taken Palestine from the hands of Egypt. But this time it wasn't to be. Seleucus was confronted with domestic problems of his own—his brother decided to take the throne for himself. Syria was plunged into a civil war (the first of many to come). Thus Seleucus was diverted from his goal of snatching Palestine from Egypt's grasp.

The Jews weren't untouched by all this intrigue. During the Third Syrian War the high priest Onias II apparently revolted against Egypt and sided with the Seleucids. He demonstrated his new allegiance by withholding his tribute to Alexandria. No doubt the Seleucids made many promises to the Jews, but the move proved a bad one: the Ptolemies were victorious and retained their control over Palestine. As punishment for his duplicity, Onias was stripped of the position of chief tax collector and all his other civil authority as well. But apparently he managed to placate his overlords sufficiently that they allowed him to retain the high priesthood. The position of chief tax collector and civil leader came into the hands of Joseph, from the Tobiad family—probably the same Tobiads who opposed Nehemiah so long ago. Josephus has a great deal to say about this Joseph, but it's mostly legendary. But we can be certain that the Ptolemies were already well acquainted with Joseph's family. His father Tobiah appears in ancient Ptolemaic records as a figure of considerable wealth and influence.[7] Money spoke as loudly in those days as it does today, and the affluent Tobiad family probably bought their office through extravagant bribes and promises.

The Palestine issue wasn't settled, but only tabled for the moment. In 221 B.C. the Fourth Syrian War broke out, a seesaw struggle between Ptolemy IV of Egypt and the young king Antiochus III of Syria (see Dan 11:10-12 for a summary of the war). When this war ended in 217, Syria looked like the loser. The borders remained pretty much where they had been at the beginning, with Egypt in control of Palestine. But appearances were deceptive: the political situation was quite changed. Egypt was weakened significantly by the struggle and wouldn't be able to bear another attack. Antiochus,

---

[7]Tobiah is mentioned several times in the Zeno papyri, discovered in Egypt in 1915. As mentioned earlier, these reports are the administrative records of Zeno, a Ptolemaic financial officer who made a tour through Phoenicia and Palestine in 260-258 B.C.

however, took his setbacks as an opportunity for learning. He turned his attention for a while to the East, reconquering many of the territories that his predecessors had lost. When Ptolemy IV died in 204 B.C., he was succeeded by his five-year-old son, Ptolemy V. The already-weakened nation was thrown into turmoil. Antiochus seized the opportunity, and in 201 he invaded Palestine. The Egyptians retaliated, and bloody struggles ensued in many Palestinian cities—including Jerusalem. But in 200 B.C. Antiochus delivered a crippling blow to the Ptolemaic army at Panium (the city that would one day be known as Caesarea Philippi). Finally, the Syrians added Palestine to their own kingdom.

Seleucid Rule in Palestine

The Seleucid monarch had a very different philosophy of government than did the Ptolemies. While the Ptolemies were disdainful of their subjects during this period, the Seleucids took a deep interest in native affairs and culture. They were more deeply infected than the Ptolemies with Alexander's vision of a fusion of East and West. In fact, while the other Greek generals divorced their native wives after Alexander's death, Seleucus I kept his Persian wife and employed natives along with Greeks in positions of leadership.

When the Seleucid capital moved from Babylon to the city of Antioch on the Syrian coast, the Seleucid officials were immersed in a much more pervasive atmosphere of Hellenism (Greek culture) than that which had existed further inland. For many years before Alexander the Great, Greeks had been doing business with Phoenicia and Syria, and Greek colonies existed all along the coast. (We should remember that Alexander the Great originally came to the East to liberate Greek colonies in Asia Minor.) With support from the Greeks who now surrounded them, the Seleucids were encouraged to spread Hellenistic ideas among the people of the East. It's ironic that the Ptolemies, who initially despised the people of Egypt, did little to encourage the spread of Greek culture among them. The Seleucids, on the other hand, who seemed more favorably disposed to their subjects, zealously pursued the dissemination of Greek culture in the East, establishing throughout their realm cities modeled after the Greek city-state—the so-called *poleis* (singular *polis;* compare the word *metropolis*).

A polis was more than just a convenient place to live. Each new polis was designed to be a center for spreading Hellenism in the East. Greeks and Asians mingled freely with one another, but not as equals: under this system it was the Greeks who were to be delivering the benefits of their culture to the East, not vice versa. Non-Greek residents of these cities were not only second-class citizens—they usually weren't citizens at all. When the polis was established, the king would enroll certain select residents as its citizens, most of them Greek. Only children of citizens or those admitted by special vote could be added to the citizenship of a Greek-style city. The citizens had special rights to vote, hold public office and participate in cultural activities. The title "citizen" was a coveted one.

THE DECAPOLIS

The Decapolis was a group of Hellenized cities situated east of the Jordan River, near Judea and Galilee. The term Decapolis ("ten cities") first appears in any literature in Mark 5:20. The man whom Jesus freed from a legion of demons was from Gerasa, one of the cities of the Decapolis. The former demoniac spread abroad the news of his liberation throughout the Decapolis. "Decapolis" occurs several more times in the New Testament, along with the writings of Josephus and in other ancient texts. But there's some confusion in the sources about which cities were included, and even if it was actually limited to ten.

The cities of the Decapolis were settled on or near ancient habitations. Scythopolis, for instance, was located on the site of Beth Shean. The residents, however, looked to Greek monarchs as their founders. Gerasa claimed to have been founded by Alexander the Great; Philadelphia by Ptolemy II Philadelphus. They had no group charter or formal organization: they were bound together only by their identity as islands of Hellenistic culture amidst a sea of Easterners. Some were conquered and held by the Jewish Hasmoneans, and some were conquered by the Arabian Nabateans. But when the Romans arrived in the East in 63 B.C., they liberated the towns of the Decapolis, thinking it unconscionable that Greeks should be ruled by Eastern monarchs. The liberation initiated a golden age for the Decapolis, in which their Greek culture could flourish.

Figure 3. Hellenistic cities in the land of Israel

Religion was an important aspect of the culture that the Seleucids wanted to bequeath on the East. Each polis had its patron god—a Greek deity, often with a bit of Eastern flair. In some cities the god was the deified king. Temples and statues were erected throughout the city in the god's honor. Many institutions of the polis were established in the name of the patron god, designed to promote his or her cult. The schools, theaters and public buildings—all were designed to encourage the adoration of Greek culture and religion. But the most conspicuous institution for the dissemination of Hellenism was the *gymnasium*. These centers of culture, learning and sports were prominent features of each city. In the gymnasia, naked male contestants competed in games honoring Greek gods.[8] The traditionally modest people of the East must have been scandalized by the displays of public nudity, but for those who wanted the benefits of Greek culture and the favor of their overlords, modesty must have seemed a small price to pay. There were public funds and tax benefits available to citizens enrolled in a polis, and many city leaders eagerly sought to have their own cities converted to the Greek model. The trans-Jordanian cities known as the Decapolis, mentioned in the Gospels as an area where Jesus made a great impression, included ancient towns that had been transformed into Greek poleis.

Thus the Seleucid Empire was fully engaged in what can be accurately called "cultural imperialism" in the East. But it wasn't just a love for Greek culture that drove their proselytizing. The Seleucid Empire contained people from many different ethnic groups, all with proud traditions of their own. Any of these countries might decide to reassert its independence, forcing the Seleucids to fight a war in a hostile land. But the poleis could serve as friendly outposts in the diverse regions of the empire. Greek settlers and eastern "converts" would presumably resist attempts at native insurrection. So the poleis weren't just wellsprings of Greek culture but also of potential soldiers dependent on the empire for the high standard of living they enjoyed. The poleis also served as three-dimensional billboards advertising the glories of Greece. Theoretically, the natives would see in these cities the great benefits that the Seleucid Empire could bestow on its loyal subjects; thus they would be reluctant to bite the hand that fed them the rich dainties of Hellenism. But if not, there were still the Greek citizens,

---

[8]The Seleucids identified *Baal Shemayin*, the Aramaic storm god, with the Greek god Zeus. Other Syrian idols were also refashioned in the form of Greek deities.

concentrated in strategic pockets throughout the empire, who would rise up in troubled times to defend their king and their Hellenistic lifestyle.

Judea Under the Seleucids

When Judea was transferred from Egyptian to Syrian rule, the change of management had a dramatic effect on Judean affairs.[9] One of the most significant was the restoration of the high priest as chief civil authority among the Jews. The Seleucids remembered that Onias II supported the Syrians against the Ptolemies in the Fourth Syrian War. The move cost Onias dearly when Ptolemy came out the victor; but now his Seleucid preferences benefited his son, Simon II—remembered by later tradition as "Simon the Just." Antiochus III also used public funds to help restore the Jerusalem temple, which apparently suffered some damage during the war. Even the tax burden that weighed so heavily on Judea was alleviated. At first, at least, the Seleucid conquest must have seemed like a change for the better.

The Tobiad family, however, hadn't been left out in the cold. Ever mindful of the way the wind was blowing, seven of Joseph's sons had shifted their allegiance from the Ptolemies to the Seleucids during the war. Only the youngest son, Hyrcanus, remained loyal to the Ptolemies. He was forced to flee back across the Jordan River to the land that once was the home of the Ammonites, and there he established a sheikdom of his own. But he wasn't completely cut off from Judean affairs, as we'll see a little later. His brothers, meanwhile, ingratiated themselves to the new Seleucid monarchs and were rewarded with positions of power in Jerusalem.

So the players remained much the same, with the high priest and the Tobiad family striving for control in Judea. But the rules of the game had changed significantly. The Egyptians were largely unconcerned with internal affairs in their provinces so long as the taxes were paid. The Syrians, however, had a different imperial philosophy. The desire to spread Hellenism was only part of the picture. Judea was now much closer to the imperial capital than it had been during the days of Ptolemaic rule. Its affairs were carried out practically under Antioch's nose. The king was no longer distant and impersonal. He passed through the land and met its leaders face-to-face. Seleucid officials were headquartered in strategic towns throughout the empire, fully engaged in the affairs of the peoples under their administration. Little escaped their attention.

---

[9]The primary source for this section is 2 Maccabees 3—4.

Soon a recipe for disaster was brewing: the Seleucids were badly in need of money. Antiochus III made a poor decision and a bad enemy. Rome had started its own eastward expansion, and a number of cities in Greece were conquered. Antiochus III received a call from Greece to come to the aid of his brethren. The proud and confident monarch responded by committing a good many troops and ships to the effort. But the attempt failed, and Antiochus was forced to conclude a peace treaty with the Romans. Never gracious in victory, the Romans demanded severe concessions. Antiochus was forced to cede control of his territories in Asia Minor, to send his son Antiochus IV to Rome as a hostage and to pay a huge tribute to the victors. Faced with the prospect of raising a large amount of money quickly, Antiochus III made another error in judgment: he attempted to plunder the temple of the god Bel in the Mesopotamian city of Elam. The outraged natives rose up and killed the king.

So it was that in 187 B.C. Seleucus IV succeeded his father to the throne. Burdened with the responsibility of paying tribute to Rome, he was forced to raise taxes throughout the empire—including those of the Jews. Like his father, Seleucus also recognized that there might be money to be made from the temples throughout his realm. In those ancient times temples often operated as chief financial institutions in a country. Of course, they collected lavish gifts from the faithful, which were used to glorify the houses of the gods. In addition, wealthy individuals would often deposit funds in the temples for safe keeping, certain that no one would have the nerve to rob such holy places. Such was the case with the Jews. Josephus reports that the Jews stored all their public funds in the temple (*Ant.* 14.7.2 [113]). We've also seen how the high priest was responsible for collecting taxes throughout the region. So there was a great deal of money passing through the temple precincts. It's no wonder that the strapped Seleucid monarchs looked on the temple in Jerusalem with growing avarice.

There were others whose greed was directed toward the temple as well: the Tobiads coveted the wealth and the power that resided there. When the strong and popular high priest Simon II died in 190 B.C., the Tobiads sensed their opportunity. The new high priest, Onias III, wasn't as competent as his predecessor. So the Tobiads persuaded Antiochus III to appoint a man named Simon as the "captain" of the temple—apparently a position of financial administration.[10] No doubt they promised Seleucus that their

---

[10]The story of the struggle between Simon and Onias II is found in 2 Macc 3—4.

man would be able to raise greater revenues than Onias alone could manage. And no doubt they offered Seleucus bribes as well.

But this Simon soon came into conflict with the high priest over the administration of the temple market (the place where sacrificial animals were sold). We're never told the details of the disagreement, but we can be fairly sure it had to do with the use of revenues generated in the market. Unable to get the better of Onias, Simon resorted to slander. He reported to the governor of Palestine that the priests were hording treasures in the temple. The governor relayed the news to King Seleucus, who dispatched one of his officers, a man named Heliodorus, to investigate the matter. Onias insisted that there was no hidden treasure in the temple. The only money stored there was used to help widows and orphans, along with certain funds placed there in trust by Hyrcanus, the pro-Ptolemaic Tobiad sheik. This last remark is especially suggestive: it implies that Hyrcanus, the enemy of the Seleucids, was either a friend or ally of the high priest Onias. Which also suggests that maybe Onias himself wasn't completely loyal to the Seleucid Empire. In any case 2 Maccabees 3 reports (with its usual emphasis on the supernatural) that Heliodorus wouldn't believe Onias. So he attempted to plunder the temple treasury himself. But his attempt was thwarted by angels who struck him down and beat him with whips, forcing him to retreat empty-handed. Heliodorus returned to King Seleucus with the message that the Jerusalem temple couldn't be plundered.

Be that as it may, Onias wasn't yet free from trouble. Simon raised further problems for the high priest, even plotting his assassination. Around 174 B.C. Onias traveled to Antioch to plead his case before the king, hoping to have Simon removed from his post. But before Onias could bring forward his petition, Seleucus IV was assassinated by the very Heliodorus whom he had sent to plunder the temple. Seleucus's younger brother, Antiochus IV (who had recently returned from captivity in Rome), ascended to the throne.

Antiochus IV was one of the truly flamboyant characters of history. Convinced of his own deity, he took the name Epiphanes, meaning "God manifest." His coins were minted with his own face on the surface that usually would have borne the face of Zeus. But Epiphanes was a jovial deity. He would often leave his palace and carouse with the common folk. If he heard about a party taking place in town, he might suddenly appear, with a band of musicians accompanying him—surprising and frightening the celebrants. Like the later Emperor Nero of Rome, he enjoyed the theater and fancied himself an actor and musician. Sometimes he would parade through the streets in his royal robes, tossing gold and jewels to the crowds. Other times he would toss worthless stones or dates. Capricious and contradictory, it's no wonder that some ancient Hellenistic authors called him not Epiphanes but Epimanes—"Madman"!

Antiochus, however, wasn't so out of touch with reality that he didn't feel the weight of the tribute he owed to Rome. Eager to discover new sources of revenue and egotistical enough to believe in the infallibility of his judgment, he soon made some decisions that could have brought Palestinian Judaism to the verge of extinction.

The Hellenistic "Reform"

For a number of years a dispute had been simmering in Jerusalem between the traditionalists and the Hellenizers, Jews who wished to adopt Greek customs.[11] Since Nehemiah's day the Jews had been separatists, largely keeping to themselves. In the age of Hellenism, with its emphasis on merging Eastern and Western ideals, this attitude made them somewhat odious to their neighbors. Most of the Jews felt no real compulsion to abandon the customs they'd grown to know and love; but some others wanted to wipe away the distinctions between Jew and Gentile. Politicians and merchants would have much to gain by adopting the fashions of the Seleucid overlords and the wealthy Greek neighbors. There was money to be made in public service or through military service for those who would be willing to abandon some of their Jewish sensibilities. And then there were undoubtedly Jewish individuals of every station who felt drawn to the novelty of Greek culture. The "philo-Hellenists" (Greek lovers) probably constituted a minority, but their wealth and influence would have outstripped their numbers.

Under the Seleucid government, with its policy of encouraging the spread of Greek culture, this Hellenizing party received a boost. Some wealthy and powerful individuals in Jerusalem began to see some definite advantages to adopting Greek ways. But there was an obstacle in their way: the high priest Onias III was a conservative, opposed to the Hellenizing trend. But not all the priestly family was of the same mind. Supported by a coalition of priests and aristocrats, and possibly funded by the Tobiads (who were ever eager to curry the favor of the powers that be), Onias's

---

[11]The primary sources for this section are 1 Macc 1:10-15; 2 Macc 4.

brother Jason approached Antiochus Epiphanes with a proposal: if Antiochus would remove Onias from the priesthood and replace him with Jason, Jason promised to bestow a generous gift on the Seleucid master and to raise tax revenue as well.[12] In addition (and most troubling of all, from the conservative Judean perspective) Jason requested permission to establish a gymnasium and Hellenistic school in Jerusalem—a necessary prelude to transforming Jerusalem into a Greek polis.

How could Antiochus refuse? He was being offered the two things he most desired: a chance to promote Hellenistic culture and a good deal of money. And so, in 174 B.C. Onias III was deposed, and Jason was made high priest in his place. The gymnasium was constructed and athletic contests were begun. According to 1 Maccabees the young men of Jerusalem underwent surgery to cover the marks of their circumcision, since the Greeks considered circumcision a shameful mutilation (1 Macc 1:15). In 2 Maccabees 4, we get a most dreary picture of the situation: even the priests in Jerusalem neglected their sacrificial duties, so that they could go and participate in the wrestling matches. When the regional athletic contest was held in the city of Tyre (like our Olympic Games, they occurred every four years), Jason sent a large gift to be used to purchase sacrifices for the Greek hero Hercules, in whose honor the games were held. (According to Jason of Cyrene, author of 2 Maccabees, the bearers of the money were so offended by the apostasy that they donated the funds to the Seleucid navy, instead.) Hellenism was becoming quite fashionable in Jerusalem, and more conservative Jews considered the high priest Jason to be the basest of scoundrels.

Jason was soon to learn a lesson of his own: he who lives by the sword dies by the sword. When he purchased the office of high priest, he set a bad precedent. Now the Tobiads apparently decided that Jason was too moderate for their purposes—or perhaps he simply wasn't corrupt enough to provide them with the kind of income they thought they should be receiving. In 171 B.C. Jason sent Menelaus, brother of Simon the captain of the temple, to Antiochus with the yearly tribute. But Menelaus had other plans. He came before Antiochus with a proposal to bring an even larger tribute than Jason had raised. He bribed Antiochus with gifts—no doubt provided by the Tobiads—and the promise of more to come. So, Jason was

---

[12]A short note about the incident appears in 1 Macc 1:11-15, and 2 Macc 4 contains a more detailed account.

THE SIGN OF CIRCUMCISION

According to Genesis 17:9-14, God commanded all Abraham's descendants to be circumcised as a sign of the covenant between Yahweh and his people. But circumcision wasn't just a Jewish custom. Syrians, Phoenicians, Canaanites and even Egyptians practiced forms of the ritual. Its origins are obscure, but it's clear that the practice was known in Syria-Palestine even before the days of Abraham. But no other ethnic groups attached the same religious significance to the custom as the Jews did. It was so central to their identity that "the circumcised" became a suitable epithet for the people of Israel.

The Greeks brought great pressure against the practice of circumcision. To them it represented a mutilation, and any mutilation of the body was considered shameful. Most ethnic groups were willing to adopt the Greek fashion, but the Jews would not. They considered failure to circumcise children to be tantamount to apostasy. When Antiochus Epiphanes attempted to exterminate the Jewish faith, he correctly recognized circumcision as an act of defiance and punished it severely. Mothers who circumcised their children were tortured to death, and their babies were hung about their necks as a visible sign of their transgression.

In light of the suffering the Jews bore on behalf of circumcision, we may better understand some the resentment that St. Paul engendered among the Jews. Paul's argument that "neither circumcision nor uncircumision is anything; but a new creation is everything!" (Gal 6:15) must have sounded treasonous to his kinsmen. But Paul's point was that the Jews shouldn't trust in external rituals to secure the favor of God.

In the second century A.D., circumcision again became an issue when the Roman emperor Hadrian passed a law making mutilation of the genitals a capital offense. Hadrian was primarily attempting to ban the Eastern practice of castration, but the law effectively banned circumcision as well. This prohibition was one of the factors that led to a great Jewish uprising in A.D. 132.

deposed, and Menelaus was made high priest in his place. Jason fled for his life, taking refuge in the trans-Jordanian region of Ammonaitis. It's interesting that he would have chosen such a place for his flight: it was also the place where the rogue Tobiad Hyrcanus fled earlier, a region of pro-Ptolemaic sympathies. Could it be that Jason was deposed because of treasonous involvements as well as financial considerations?

The installation of Menelaus represented an arrogant disregard for Jewish traditions and sensibilities. For centuries the high priests were drawn only from the family of Zadok, the high priest in the time of King David. Customarily, each priest was succeeded by his eldest son. Jason broke the precedent when he displaced his elder brother Onias. But Menelaus, though a priest, wasn't even from Zadok's lineage. He was in no way qualified for the office he'd purchased. Of course, Antiochus might not have been aware of that fact. Menelaus and the Tobiads, however, most certainly were. So were the Jews of Jerusalem, who were outraged by the incident. Many of them were undoubtedly beginning to reconsider their initial infatuation with Hellenism.

Menelaus gave them even more cause to regret their apostasy. He was a cruel and capricious tyrant. He had the gold plating removed from the temple and used it for bribes and to pay off debts to his friends—but he failed to pay Antiochus Epiphanes the tribute he'd promised. When the former high priest Onias III learned about the sacrilege, he set off to Antioch to denounce Menelaus. Menelaus knew that Epiphanes probably wouldn't have been concerned about the stripping of the temple. But he *would* have been angry that Menalaus wasn't using his ill-gotten gains to pay off his debt to the king. Had Epiphanes learned that Menelaus discovered a source of revenue but wasn't using it to pay his taxes, the new high priest would have been in serious trouble. So Menelaus paid one of Antiochus's officers to assassinate Onias before he could present his charges. The king was outraged, and he had the assassin executed, but somehow Menelaus escaped justice. And so, it seemed, he was free to continue his plunder of the temple, looting its treasury and fixtures. As word of the larceny spread through Jerusalem, a mob converged on the temple. A riot erupted, and many Jews were killed.

The Jewish senate was determined to make Menelaus pay for the bloodshed. They sent a delegation to Antiochus Epiphanes with a formal complaint against the rogue high priest. But Menelaus sent a delegation of his own, one well-equipped for the task at hand: they brought great sums of money for bribing witnesses and officials. In the end it was not Menelaus who was reproved, but the Jewish senate's delegates to Antioch were executed. Menelaus once again escaped without so much as a warning. Jerusalem was paying dramatically for her flirtation with apostasy. But the worst was yet to come.

The Antiochan Persecution

The disaster began when Antiochus Epiphanes decided the time had come to extend his empire with a campaign against Egypt.[13] On the pretense of some hostility from the Egyptian king Ptolemy VI, the Seleucid king campaigned against the south in 170 B.C. The campaign went very well for Antiochus, and he extracted severe concessions from Ptolemy. In fact, Egypt was declared a Seleucid protectorate.

While Antiochus was busy in Egypt, a rumor began to spread in Judea that Antiochus had been killed in battle. For the deposed high priest Jason the news could not have been better. With an army of a thousand, he invaded Jerusalem and attempted to seize control of the government. But the high priest Menelaus barricaded himself within the city's citadel, an almost impregnable fortress. Unable to claim his prize, Jason vented his anger on the citizens of Jerusalem. But some escaped to bear news to Antiochus that Jerusalem was in rebellion. The king, more sure than ever of his might, was in no mood to hear of such insolence. He brought his army to the city in fury, and a bloodbath ensued. Men, women and children were butchered. The temple was plundered, and its treasures were carried away. Antiochus placed a governor over the city, who worked with Menelaus to maintain control of the populace. Jason, however, escaped. Unwelcome in the Ammonite lands where he previously found refuge, he traveled to Sparta, where he died in exile (2 Macc 5:8-9). (According to a popular legend of the time, Jews and Spartans were related to one another. Jason was seeking refuge with his Greek "cousins.")

It wasn't long before Egypt violated the peace treaty and declared its independence from Epiphanes. In 168 B.C. the king was prompted to under-

---

[13]There is some question concerning the course of events that actually brought about the Antiochan Persecution. The accounts in 1 and 2 Maccabees disagree somewhat on the circumstances, and Josephus provides little information that could clarify matters. Most scholars would hold to the account I present here, but significant disagreements still exist. The reader might want to compare this account to those of the suggested readings. The primary sources for this section are 1 Macc 1:16-64, 2 Macc 5—7 and Dan 11:21-39.

take a second campaign against its southern neighbor. He anticipated little resistance from the Egyptians. But what Antiochus didn't know was that a third party had decided to interpose itself in the mix. The Roman senate, determined to prevent the Seleucid Empire from expanding any further, sent its general Popillius Laenas to intercept Antiochus on his way to Egypt. Popillius informed the proud king that the Roman senate ordered him to withdraw from Egypt at once or face the displeasure of Rome. Antiochus answered that he would consider Rome's request. But the general wasn't satisfied. With remarkable disdain for the prestige of a foreign monarch, he took his staff and drew a circle in the sand around King Antiochus. Then, he said to the king, "You may consider as long as you like— but Rome requires your answer before you leave that circle." Such impudence had never been seen in the civilized world. Antiochus was outraged—but he was also helpless. He'd recently been a captive in Rome, and he knew that his kingdom wasn't yet in any position to win a war with the mighty Republic. His only choice was to withdraw.

With his ambitions for Egypt thwarted, Antiochus set his mind on another goal: securing his control over Judea. Driven by the humiliation of his encounter with Rome and by his recognition that the problem in Judea was basically a religious conflict, Antiochus decided to put an end to the trouble permanently—by doing away with the Jewish religion. Under other circumstances such a decree would have been unthinkable. Greek thought tended to be tolerant of a variety of worldviews; the idea of imposing one's religious beliefs on others was contrary to the spirit of Hellenism. But Antiochus had several reasons for believing that he was making the right move. First, the Hellenizing party in Jerusalem had actually requested assistance in bringing Greek culture to the Jews. Who knows what slander Jason and Menelaus might have told about the religion of their political enemies in order to curry the favor of Antiochus? Furthermore, the traditionalist Jews were separatists, refusing to participate in the state cult that bound together the empire. Their religious beliefs were a threat to the stability of the kingdom. The revolt in Jerusalem gave further evidence of the volatility of the region. So a unified religion might be just the thing that would prevent such outbreaks in the future. Finally, Antiochus Epiphanes was angry and humiliated. The fact that the Jews wouldn't recognize his divinity added insult to injury. He couldn't challenge the Romans, but he certainly could punish the Jews.

In 167 B.C. Antiochus sent his troops to Jerusalem, ordering them to transform the temple of the Lord into a shrine to Zeus Ouranos, the god of heaven. The Greeks massacred the residents of Jerusalem and burned private homes and public structures throughout the city. The city walls that Nehemiah labored over were demolished. A grim fortress called the Akra was erected on the site where Solomon's palace had stood. The temple itself wasn't spared from the desecration. In its most holy sanctuary an idol—the "abomination of desolation"—was erected. The Lord's altar was replaced with a pagan altar, where Gentile priests offered sacrifices to the Greek gods (Dan 11:31; 12:11; 1 Macc 1:54). Pigs and other unclean animals were slaughtered in the temple precincts. Laws were enacted that forbid the Jews from observing the sabbath day or traditional festivals. Circumcision was outlawed. Scrolls of the law were burned, and anyone found possessing a copy of the law was killed. On pain of death, all the Jews were ordered to abandon their ancestral religion and worship Zeus Ouranos, the god of the heavens. Officers of the king were dispatched to all the cities of Judea, compelling the Jews to perform sacrifices to Zeus or die. In 2 Maccabees 6—7 the stories are told of heroic Jewish martyrs who refused to eat pork or sacrifice to the pagan gods. Fierce tortures were implemented to persuade the Jews to abandon their God. Through this reign of terror Epiphanes believed he would put an end to the Jewish problem once and for all.

Many of the Jews believed that the persecution was a punishment for their own sins. The Lord brought Antiochus Epiphanes against them to chastise the nation for its double-mindedness and infatuation with Hellenism. But those same Jews confidently believed the Lord was merciful. God's wrath would soon be spent. Then it would be the tyrant who would receive the punishment that he so justly deserved.

For Further Reading

Bickerman, Elias. *The Jews in the Greek Age.* Cambridge, Mass.: Harvard University Press, 1988. Wonderfully readable study by a well-respected classicist.

Hengel, Martin. *Judaism and Hellenism.* Translated by John Bowden. Philadelphia: Fortress, 1974. Amasses vast amounts of data on the Hellenism of Judea in the time of the Ptolemies and Seleucids.

Horbury, William, W. D. Davies, Louis Finkelstein, and John Sturdy. *The Cambridge History of Judaism.* Vol. 2., chap. 2. Cambridge: Cambridge University Press, 1990.

Schäfer, P. "The Hellenistic and Maccabean Periods." In *Israelite and*

Judaean History, Edited by J. H. Hayes and J. M. Miller. London: SCM Press, 1977.

Schürer, Emil. *A History of the Jewish People in the Age of Jesus Christ.* Vol. 1, §4. Edited by Geza Vermes, Fergus Millar and Matthew Black. 4 vols. Edinburgh: T & T Clark, 1973-1987.

Tcherikover, Victor. *Hellenistic Civilization and the Jews.* Translated by S. Applebaum. New York: Atheneum, 1959. Especially strong on political and administrative details.

5

The Fight for Freedom

How did the Jews react to the persecution? The two books of Maccabees are, of course, our primary sources of information on the question. But these sources have to be handled with care. Both books are designed to praise the family and faction that resisted the oppressors and won independence for the nation. Their perspectives are biased, and both accounts are fraught with difficulties. They frequently disagree even with each other. Josephus also chronicled the revolt, but his account isn't especially helpful. He used 1 Maccabees as his primary source and adds only a little to the picture that we don't find there. So as we piece together the story of Jewish resistance, we have to infer many details from the literary and historical context, and we must supply some facets of the picture by drawing analogies to similar incidents in other times and cultures.

The books of Maccabees essentially paint a picture of the Jews capitulating to the demands of their oppressors or fleeing for their lives until Mattathias Hasmoneus rises up and leads the nation in rebellion. But that certainly isn't the whole picture. There's no reason to believe that all the Jews went compliantly to sacrifice at the pagan altar or that they silently accepted their own executions. There must have been a variety of Jewish responses to the oppression, running a whole spectrum:

- *The collaborators.* Jewish collaborators consisted primarily of the Hellenizers who were eager to see Jerusalem enjoy the cultural, political and economic benefits of adopting Greek ways. It was they who invited Greek interference in Jerusalem to start with, and they might have encouraged Antiochus to force his religion on the Jews. (It bears repeating that the very spirit of Hellenism was tolerant of religious diversity, and it seems quite unlikely that any Hellenistic monarch would have forced the state cult on a subject people unless he'd been invited to do so.) The collaborators probably welcomed Antiochus's forced conversions as a much-needed reform. As they saw it, their hard-headed opponents would be silenced one way or another, opening the door to allow Jerusalem to embrace fully the advantages of a Greek-friendly lifestyle. These people probably suffered little from Antiochus's persecution, and may very well have aided in its implementation.

- *The accommodators.* Jewish accommodators had no particular love for the Greeks, but no particular dislike for them, either. They were willing to accept the new religion being imposed on them from simple necessity, not from any particular conviction. Some of the accommodators were more ethnically Jewish than religiously Jewish: the Mishnah, the great rabbinic text of the third century A.D., repeatedly warns that the "people of the land" can't be trusted to observe Jewish laws properly. Even in rabbinic times most people didn't have access to copies of the Bible, and there weren't synagogues located on every street corner to instruct the masses in proper religious observance. If this was the case in A.D. 200, imagine how much worse it must have been four hundred years earlier, before the development of new writing materials and the construction of fine roads throughout the Near East. We may assume that many rural Jews weren't well versed in the tenets of their own faith (just as many Christians are ignorant of their faith today). Worshiping God under the name "the Lord of Heaven" may have seemed like no great crime to some of them. Then there were others who knew that it would be wrong to abandon their ancestral traditions in the manner Antiochus demanded, but their fear of persecution and death compelled them to do as they were commanded. The book of 1 Maccabees gives the impression that most of the Jews fell into this camp.

- *The pacifists.* Pacifistic Jews didn't want to abandon their faith, but they wouldn't fight to preserve their way of life. They would die for their religion, but they wouldn't kill for it (at least, not at this time). Their choice not to retaliate against the oppression probably didn't arise from some principled commitment to nonviolence—there's no evidence that such a principle existed in this era. In the Old Testament, when Jewish prophets or leaders called for pacifistic reactions to their oppressors, it wasn't because they believed it was wrong to hurt or kill one's persecutors. Rather, the Old Testament prophets sometimes urged the Jews to wait for God himself to intervene on their behalf, as he had done against King Sennacherib in the days of the prophet Isaiah. Daniel's prediction (Dan 12:1) that the archangel Michael would deliver the Jews from their travail might have inspired some Jews to remain passive in the face of oppression.[1] The books of the Maccabees tell us little about the role of these Jews in the struggle for freedom, but it's possible that the martyrs whose stories are told in 2 Maccabees 6—7 represented this point of view. Believing that God would eventually judge the oppressors and hoping for the resurrection of the righteous, they were willing to sacrifice their lives, rather than violate the laws of the Lord.

- *The defenders.* The Jewish "defenders" were willing to fight to save their lives, but they had no desire to press the battle against the Greeks. Some of them fought only when they were attacked. These people may have been isolationists, staying uninvolved until the issue came to their doorstep. As long as the Greeks didn't bother them, they were content to lay low. Others, like the Hasideans ("pious ones") first mentioned in 1 Maccabees 2:42, fought to end the persecution. They left their homes and banded together in defense of their homeland and brothers and sisters. When the oppression was lifted, this group was ready to cease its hostilities against the Greeks. They fought only so long as their rights and the rights of their fellow Jews were in danger.

- *The aggressors.* To Jewish aggressors the Antiochan persecution was a call to arms—not merely to defend themselves but to take the battle to the Greeks and drive them from the land. For these people the situation called for more than a restoration of the status quo. It was a call to liberation from all foreign domination. The books of Maccabees largely portray the liberation movement as a cohesive group rallying behind the leadership of the Hasmonean clan, but that picture should probably be taken with a grain of salt. The liberation movement was led not only by religious zealots and patriots but by men with political ambitions as well. It may have been the most factious segment of the Jewish population. There's a hint to this effect in 1 Maccabees 5, where some fellows

---

[1]The rise of Michael could mean that the Jews needed to take no action in their own defense, but it could also be a symbol of the Jewish uprising. In Daniel 10:20 the patron angel of Judah struggles with the angel of Persia, reflecting Persia's dominance over the Jews. The patron angel intimates to the prophet that the angel of Greece is coming to displace the angel of Persia, obviously reflecting the ascendancy of the Greeks over the Persians. So Michael's advent in 12:1 could well represent the Jews' revolt against the Greeks.

named Joseph and Azariah (presented as officers in the Hasmonean army) attempt to wage a war of their own against the Gentiles. They were soundly defeated, according to the narrative, because, unlike the Maccabees, their effort hadn't been ordained of God (1 Macc 5:62).

History, so it's said, is written by the victors, and that's certainly the case in the story of the Antiochan persecution and the subsequent revolt. It was the Hasmoneans who came out the winners, and it was their version of the story that's been preserved. Even Josephus seems to have had little access to information beyond that found in 1-2 Maccabees. Bear in mind, then, that the story of the revolt that I relate in this chapter may be a little lopsided and incomplete. Our sources are flawed, but probably not *fatally* flawed. When read with the proper discernment, they tell us much about the events of the era. So with the appropriate caveats issued, let's proceed to the story of the Hasmonean Revolt.

Mattathias Hashmonai

The Hasmonean Revolt began inauspiciously enough. In the town of Modein (modern Ras Medieh), a small burg some twenty miles northwest of Jerusalem, there lived a priest named Mattathias and his five sons.[2] His family name, Hashmonai (Greek, Hasmonaios), is known to us only from Josephus (the title "Maccabees," often mistaken for the family name, will be explained later). Josephus relates that Hasmonaios was the name of Mattathias's great-grandfather (*Ant.* 12.6.1 [265]). But ultimately the family name was probably taken from the place of Mattathias's ancestral origin, perhaps Heshmon or another town with a similar name.

First Maccabees 2 tells us that Mattathias had moved to Modein from Jerusalem. It wasn't at all uncommon in those days for priests to live well outside the environs of the Jerusalem temple. While many lived within the capital city, many others were scattered throughout the countryside. The caste of priests had grown very large, and not all were required to be on hand to serve in the temple. Instead, the priesthood was divided into twenty-four "courses," each of which served in its own scheduled season. The priests could travel to Jerusalem and remain in the city for their two weeks of service, then return home again. Mattathias was probably a "gentleman farmer," living off his land and his priestly salary.

The old priest was understandably appalled at the news he received

---

[2]The primary source for this section is 1 Macc 2:1-30.

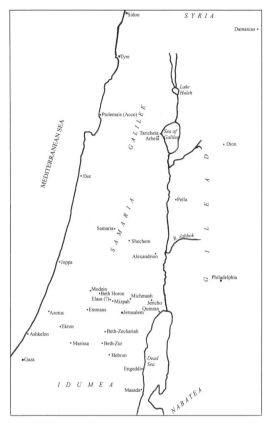

Figure 4. Palestine in Hasmonean times

from Jerusalem. Why had he lived to see such a day? He longed to take some action against the desecrators of the temple and to defend the people of the Lord, but what could he do? It seemed he was doomed to watch from afar as the great city was defiled.

But if Mattathias thought his isolation would protect him from the king's decree, he was mistaken. Soon the envoys of Antiochus Epiphanes arrived in his own small town, demanding that all the residents of Modein renounce their ancestral faith and sacrifice to the new god. An altar was built in the town square, and the residents were all assembled to hear the royal decree: "Renounce your old religion! Sacrifice to the god of heaven! Obey the command of your king!"

Mattathias and his sons stood a little way apart, watching the proceedings with a baleful eye. The king's officers observed Mattathias's priestly bearing and the apparent respect granted him by the other residents of Modein, so they decided that this man should be the focus of their persuasions. "You, sir," they said, "are clearly a leader among the people of this town. You should be the first to obey the king's decree and set an example for the others. All the nations around you honor the king's god. Why not join them? You'll be counted among the friends of the king, and you'll find that the king can be very generous to his friends."

Mattathias wasn't careful about his answer. "Even if all the nations of the world abandon their gods and worship the king's idol," he proclaimed, "I and my sons will remain true to the Lord!" No doubt his burning gaze held the people of Modein at bay for some time. But finally, an intrepid soul went forward to the altar, ready to make the king's sacrifice and accept the Greek's gifts. But Mattathias wasn't about to permit such a sacrilege in his town. He killed the Jew sacrificing at the pagan altar, and the king's officers as well. (One might wonder—what did he use for a weapon? How ironic it would be if he used the very knife that would have been used to slaughter the sacrifice!) Then Mattathias issued a challenge: "All you who are zealous for the law of the Lord, and who are true to his covenant, come and stand with me!" Mattathias, his sons and many other faithful Jews left their possessions behind and fled the town of Modein to encamp in the rugged Judean hill country. The Hasmonean Revolt had begun.

The resistance coalesces. The Hasmoneans and their comrades weren't the only Jews who took to the wilderness.[3] Already many had fled Jerusalem and other towns, and were living in bands scattered throughout the Judean countryside. Unorganized and unsure of their course of action, they didn't immediately begin any efforts to win back their homeland. Most likely they hoped only to "lay low" until the crisis passed. But the Greeks learned about a band of refugees who were hiding in the caves outside Jerusalem. A detachment of soldiers was sent to persuade the group to obey the king's orders—or to kill them if they persisted in their disobedience.

The soldiers found the group on the sabbath day, when the Jews were forbidden to do any sort of work. But to the Greeks the sabbath was nothing but an excuse for Jewish laziness. They had no sense of how deeply the religious sensibilities of the Hebrews were bound to the observance of the day of rest. And so they issued their ultimatum: "Come out now, and sacrifice to the god of heaven, and your lives will be spared!" The Jews were

---

[3]The primary source for this subsection is 1 Macc 2:31-48.

caught on the horns of a dilemma. If they refused to obey, they'd undoubtedly be attacked. As they understood the law, if they took up arms to defend themselves, they would be in violation of the sabbath rest. Would it be acceptable to break the sabbath in order to save their lives and the lives of their wives and children? They decided it wouldn't—indeed, to fight on the sabbath day would defile the very covenant they were supposedly defending. So they sent their bold reply to the soldiers, "We will not obey the king's decree, nor will we violate the law of our God!"

The Jews took up no swords or rocks. They refused even to move some stones to block up the entrances to their caves. Perhaps they were expecting divine intervention, a miraculous deliverance like the one experienced by Shadrach, Meshach and Abednego in the fiery furnace. Perhaps they hoped the Greeks would have the decency to see they were unarmed and not aggressive. Perhaps they merely accepted the inevitability of their death and placed their hopes in the rewards they would receive at the resurrection of the dead.[4] Whatever their thoughts, they wouldn't be goaded into violating the sanctity of the sabbath day. The pagan soldiers advanced on the Jews' position and slaughtered a thousand men, women and children in their sabbath observances.

When the Hasmoneans and their comrades heard of the disaster, they took council together. Apparently, they could expect no miraculous deliverances. And what use would there be for martyrs if the whole Jewish race were exterminated? The practical route, it seemed, was to suspend the usual sabbath observances until the crisis was passed. They wouldn't go forth as aggressors on the sabbath, but if the Hasmoneans and their band should be attacked on the sabbath or any other day, they would defend themselves with the every ounce of their strength and resolve.

Judas Maccabeus's fight for tolerance. Early in the revolt, old Mattathias died.[5] Probably he passed away from natural causes, since 1 Maccabees

---

[4]Beliefs in the resurrection of the dead were still very much in flux at this time. Daniel 12:2-3, 13 clearly expected a resurrection for the righteous. In 2 Maccabees 7, written some fifty years after the revolt, the martyrs endure their torture because of their hope of the resurrection. But the book of 1 Maccabees, written perhaps a generation or two after the revolt, seems to anticipate no resurrection at all. Mattathias, in his deathbed speech to encourage the rebels, can promise them only "great honor and an everlasting name" (1 Macc 2:51). For those with no hope in an afterlife, the temptation to apostatize must have been very strong indeed.
[5]The primary sources for this subsection are 1 Macc 3:1—4:61; 2 Macc 5:27—10:8; *Ant.* 12.7.1-12.7.7 (287-326).

THE JEWISH SABBATH

Observation of a sabbath day (from sunset Friday to sunset Saturday) was unique to ancient Israel—no other people had such a custom. The word *sabbath* comes from a Hebrew word meaning "to end" and probably has a dual significance: the sabbath day was the end of the week, and on that day the Israelites were to end their work. The Old Testament rationale for observing a weekly day of rest was that God had created the world in six days and rested on the seventh (Ex 20:8-11). So keeping the sabbath wasn't just a matter of Jewish custom but part of the "natural law."

There are few references to sabbath observance in the Old Testament historical books. The Israelites may have been pretty lax on the issue during the days of the monarchy. Prophets decried the profanation of the sabbath with work and trade (Is 58:13-14; Jer. 17:19-27). Nehemiah faced the task of bringing the sabbath back into its proper place as a day of rest and worship (Neh 10:31; 13:15-22). He seems to have been successful, considering how scrupulous the Jews of the Hellenistic era were about sabbath observance. Even the Roman army had to release Jewish soldiers from service on the sabbath because they refused to bear arms that day.

By the time of Jesus the Jewish sages had developed numerous regulations regarding the observance of the sabbath. There was some debate on what constituted work, and some scribes would have prohibited their fellow Jews from gathering food or tending the sick on the sabbath (Mk 2:23—3:6). Jesus chided the Pharisees of his day for making sabbath observance a burden rather than a delight, as God had intended.

The tradition of strictly defining work continued into rabbinic times. The Mishnah contains numerous regulations about sabbath observance, prescribing how far one could walk, how much one could carry and even how many letters someone was allowed to write at a time. Jews were permitted to administer first aid to save the dying, but not to relieve pain. They could pull a man out of a ditch, but not an animal. They could tie a knot, but only if it could be tied with one hand. The sages' purpose was to build a "hedge" around the law—a barrier of regulations that would assure that the Jews wouldn't even come close to violating the sanctity of their sabbath rest.

tells us no different. But with his passing, command of the revolt fell into the hands of his eldest son, Judas (the Greek form of the name Judah). Judas was given the nickname "Maccabeus," an epithet with uncertain significance. After long debate, scholars generally now agree that it probably derives from the Hebrew word for "hammer." It may have been applied to Judas because of his military exploits—he crushed his enemies like a hammer against the rocks. Or it's equally possible that he bore the moniker from his youth, perhaps because of his temperament or even some physical feature (his head?) that resembled a hammer. In any case the name seemed so apropos to his exploits and mission that it was eventually extended to his whole family. The family name, Hashmonai, has largely passed into obscurity, while the nickname Maccabees has stuck.

Judas determined that it was time to stop hiding in the shadows and go on the offensive against the Greeks. Traversing the land of Judah he recruited an army of about six thousand men. They began their counterassault with raids under the cover of darkness. Towns populated with Gentiles, and probably even those populated with turncoat Jews, became their targets. Supplies were captured, inhabitants killed and buildings were put to the torch. Soon, Judas's forces seized control of a number of strategic locations, and his fame began to spread. More Jews began to join the rebels—perhaps motivated by fear of what might happen to them if they didn't.

Judas couldn't keep his activities secret. Indeed, he wouldn't have wanted to. He depended on his reputation to draw new recruits into the movement. But the same fame that enhanced his reputation among the Jews also captured the interest of the Syrian officers. They assembled an army of Greeks and Samaritans under the command of Apollonius to crush the rebel leader and his forces. Outnumbered and poorly equipped, Judas engaged the Syrian forces head-on, trusting in the resolve of his soldiers, the righteousness of his cause and the might of his God. And sure enough, Judas won the day, killing Apollonius and taking the Greek officer's sword as his own. But the Seleucids weren't about to back down. They now entrusted the subjugation of the Jews to Seron, commander of all the Seleucid forces in Coele-Syria (the Seleucid administrative district that included Judea, Samaria, Phoenicia and Syria).[6] Judas's men were

---

[6]There has been some dispute over the meaning of the word *Coele*. The term was used from Hellenistic times and was assumed to have been of Greek origin. More recently, however, several scholars have plausibly argued that the word is a corruption of the Semitic word *kol*, meaning "all." So Coele-Syria probably meant "all Syria."

vastly outnumbered, and they were weak from fasting. But even so the Maccabees were again victorious. Eight hundred enemy soldiers were killed, and the rest were put to flight.

By this time it was probably dawning on Epiphanes that the Jewish uprising was a serious problem. But he had his hands full with other difficulties: in the East, the Parthians (an Iranian people related to the Persians) formed an empire of their own and began to press hard against the Seleucids' eastern border. Presently, the eastern threat seemed to require the most urgent attention, so Antiochus set out with half of his army to face the Parthians. He appointed his young son Antiochus V as coregent in Syria, but Antiochus's minister of state Lysias was actually in charge of affairs at home. Lysias appointed three generals to lead a large army into Judea. They were so confident of total victory that they assembled slave traders in Syria to take the Jewish captives and sell them on the international markets. The revolt would soon be over, and the Jewish rebels would be scattered throughout the known world.

Judas, too, was preparing for the inevitable confrontation. With Jerusalem occupied by Gentile forces, he assembled his army at Mizpah. New recruits were swelling the ranks, and the Hasmoneans organized them into units. Officers were chosen and placed in command of the various divisions. The troops were armed and trained—but more important, they prepared for the battle with prayer and fasting. The impending conflict was as much a spiritual struggle as a military struggle, and the Jews intended to be ready on both fronts.

The Syrian forces advanced into Judea and encamped in the region of Emmaus (modern Amwas, probably not the same place as the Emmaus of the New Testament). But how were they to proceed from there? Dispatching the entire Syrian army to search for a small guerilla band was hardly practical: it would be impossible for so large a band to travel stealthily, so Judas and his army could easily elude them almost indefinitely. On the other hand, once Judas had been located and pinned down, the Syrians would want to be certain they had sufficient numbers to crush the rebels. The Seleucid generals decided to dispatch only a portion of their forces, under the command of a general named Gorgias, to find Judas and his army and engage them in battle. The larger part of the army would remain encamped at Emmaus, ready to come into service when the Maccabees were found.

Learning that the Syrian army had been divided, Judas made a bold and

PARTHIA

The Parthians were an Iranian people who forged an eastern empire as massive as Rome's was in the West. They first rose to power in the mid 3rd century B.C., when they revolted against the Seleucids. The empire expanded greatly, reaching as far west as the Euphrates River before being stopped by the Romans. Jews in Babylon and Media were incorporated into the Parthian Empire. Even though the Parthians were polytheists, they allowed subject peoples to direct their own religious affairs, and the Jewish communities flourished. Some Parthian Jews were present in Jerusalem on the day of Pentecost when the Holy Spirit was given (Acts 2:9).

The Parthians handed many defeats to both the Greeks and the Romans before the Romans finally won a decisive victory in A.D. 116, establishing the boundary between the empires. The Parthian Empire finally dissolved in A.D. 226.

brilliant move: skirting Gorgias's contingent, he fell on the unsuspecting forces encamped at Emmaus. The huge Syrian army was caught completely off guard, and they could offer little resistance. When Gorgias and his men returned, they found their camp in flames. The Jews advanced on the remaining Gentile forces, but the Syrians were so unnerved that they fled in panic. The Jews won a decisive victory over their oppressors.

There's some confusion about the sequence of events that followed. According to 1 Maccabees 4:26-35, Lysias himself now undertook a campaign against the Jews; but 2 Maccabees 11:1-12 puts this campaign somewhat later. Both versions agree that Lysias was determined not to repeat the failures of his predecessors and chose to invade not from the west, as previous armies had done, but through the east. This area was sparsely populated, and Lysias could possibly enter the Judean territory unobserved, catching the Hasmoneans off guard. And indeed, the Greeks did make deep progress into the land before they met any resistance. The Greeks clashed with the Hasmonean forces at Beth-Zur, about twenty miles from Jerusalem. The battle went hard for both sides. Undoubtedly the Maccabees were hurt in the battle, but so were the Syrians. Lysias dealt the Jews a painful blow, but he had to withdraw without crushing the rebellion as he had hoped.

Politically, Lysias's withdrawal was as good as a victory for the Jews. The king's regent was forced to recognize that suppressing the Jews would be a long and costly undertaking, one for which he had little stomach. With Antiochus Epiphanes away in the East and political intrigue at home, Lysias must surely have been questioning the wisdom of pursuing so difficult a campaign—and perhaps the morality of it as well. If Epiphanes sought to impose Hellenism on the Jews because he believed they welcomed the conversion, subsequent events had proven him wrong. So, when delegates from Judea arrived in Syria requesting to negotiate peace, Lysias willingly listened. Without consulting the king, he agreed to end the persecution and to allow the Jews to worship as they saw fit. Second Maccabees 11:16-21 preserves a letter written by the regent to the Jews in 164 B.C. granting them their rights if only they would pledge their loyalty to the Seleucid government.

Judas wasn't among those who had negotiated for peace. But when he learned of Lysias's decree, he heard the knock of opportunity. He seized the moment and invaded Jerusalem itself. His goal wasn't to take control of the throne, and rule the entire nation. Nor would he challenge the Akra, the mighty citadel where many Greek soldiers were garrisoned. He had but one aim: to liberate the temple of the Lord and put the worship of Israel's God back in its proper order. Indeed, at the time it must have looked as if he were simply taking it on himself to carry out Lysias's decree—although the course of events would soon show otherwise.

For now, however, the task at hand was the restoration of the temple. Judas hand-picked the priests who would be charged with this duty. Pagan altars in the temple precincts were demolished. Even the old altar of the Lord, which had been desecrated with the blood of pigs and other unclean animals, was demolished. Its stones were set aside until a prophet could come and tell them what should be done with them. A new altar built of uncut rocks was set up in its place. On December 14, 164 B.C., the preparations were complete. The daily burnt offering, neglected now for two years, could once again be kindled on the altar. For eight days the Jews celebrated the dedication of the new altar and the purification of the temple. Jewish tradition says that Judas and his companions found only enough holy oil for one day, but it miraculously burned for the entire eight days of rededication. An edict was passed that the days of "dedication"—in Hebrew, *Hanukkah*—would be celebrated as a perpetual ordinance among the Jews. And thus was born the "Festival of Lights," still observed by the Jews to this very day.

From restoration to liberation. A major victory had been won—but the war wasn't over yet, at least not in Judas's mind.[7] In anticipation of further conflicts he began fortifying the precincts around the temple as well as the city of Beth-Zur, a strategic outpost on the western front. Judas and his brother Simon led campaigns to evacuate Jewish residents from cities in Galilee and Gilead (today, southern Syria), where they were being harassed by hostile Gentiles. Then came the news that changed the nature of the conflict: Antiochus Epiphanes fell ill and died on his way home from Persia. To the Jews his downfall was a divine judgment for his war against the Lord. Indeed, 2 Maccabees 9 declares that Antiochus repented of his great wickedness and would have proceeded to Jerusalem and become a Jew himself, had he not died on the way. (The historical value of the story is probably small.) Epiphanes had appointed one of his generals, Philip, to conduct the affairs of state until the young prince Antiochus V came of age. But Lysias refused to step down. He had been running the empire, and he intended to continue, at least until Antiochus V was older. Philip was forced to flee to Egypt and seek refuge with the Ptolemies. But he wasn't about to give up without a fight the position that Epiphanes had bequeathed on him.

Faced with rivalry and unrest within Syria itself, Lysias had little energy to give to the war against the Jews. Indeed, he probably believed they'd make good allies, should he need to defend his claim to the empire's leadership. So sometime early in 163 B.C. Lysias again extended the olive branch to the Jews. Antiochus V would restore to the Jews their rights and allow them to live in peace. They could worship their God as they pleased. The temple would be inviolable. And the law of God would be binding once again on all Israel. The Antiochan persecution was officially over.

How would the Jews respond to such an offer? To Judas it seemed to promise him little that he didn't already possess. The fact was, the Syrians weren't able impose their will on the Jews. Judas and his people

---

[7]Primary sources for this subsection are 1 Macc 5:1—9:22; 2 Macc 10:9—15:37; *Ant.* 12.8.1-12.11.2 (327-434).

could already live as they pleased, conducting temple worship in their own fashion. But the Hellenizing Jews who had caused the problem still remained a powerful force in Judea. And worst of all, the Akra—the great citadel that housed Syrian troops—still stood in the center of Jerusalem. So late in 163 B.C. Judas decided it was time to lay siege to the citadel and rid Jerusalem of the contaminating presence of the Gentiles for good. He tried to trap all the inhabitants in the structure to prevent them from summoning reinforcements. But some of the Syrians escaped, along with some of the Hellenizing Jews. They went to Antioch (the Seleucid capital) and complained to Lysias that they were under attack. The Jewish envoys were especially pathetic: "How long will you delay giving us justice? We are loyal citizens of the kingdom. We obeyed your father and did as he commanded. And for this, our own brethren hate us. This Judas, he attacks our towns, kills our men and boys and seizes our homes! He lays siege to your citadel and fortifies towns against your soldiers! If you don't act swiftly, who knows what will come of it all?" (1 Macc 6:22-27, paraphrased).

Lysias realized that he had to respond. With enemies in Egypt and Parthia, and intrigues in his own kingdom, Judea was a territory he could hardly afford to lose. So he raised a mighty army to invade Judea. He gathered a hundred thousand foot soldiers, twenty thousand cavalry and thirty-two battle elephants. Coming in from the east, they attacked Beth-Zur, and after a long siege they forced it to surrender. Judas had to lift his assault on the Akra and mustered his troops at the town of Beth-Zechariah. But soon the Jewish forces were overwhelmed, and Judas's own brother Eleazar was killed in the fighting. The Hasmonean forces retreated, taking refuge in Jerusalem itself. Lysias and his army advanced and brought the siege to the capital city, sure of their victory. But then there was a rather abrupt turn of fate: Philip, the general who fled to Egypt, had returned to Syria to take the throne by force. Lysias was forced to hasten back to Antioch, so he concluded a peace treaty with the Jews that essentially allowed them to settle their affairs on their own. Judas's fortifications on Mount Zion were demolished, and the Syrian troops remained stationed in the Akra. But once again the Jews were assured of their right to order their religious affairs without Syrian interference. The conflict in Judea became what it had been before Antiochus Epiphanes had imposed his "reforms": a struggle between the Hellenizing party and the traditionalists for the control of Judea.

Lysias and the young Antiochus V put down Philip and his attempted coup, but their security was short-lived. In 162 B.C. Demetrius I, Antiochus Epiphanes' nephew, escaped from Rome, where he'd been held hostage. He raised an army and invaded Syria. Demetrius quickly gained much popular support, and after a short struggle the throne was his. Lysias and Antiochus V were executed, assuring Demetrius of at least a short season without rival claimants dividing his hard-won empire.

It wasn't long before the new king was facing a delegation from Jerusalem, led by a certain Alcimus. The ambassadors explained the state of Judean affairs, with factions fighting for control of the nation. Alcimus and his delegates represented the loyal faction; Judas and his troops were rebels against the empire. Unless Demetrius made a strong show of force now, he'd lose control of the country. That wasn't a loss that Demetrius was willing to bear, with the Ptolemies ever threatening to the south. So Demetrius agreed to install Alcimus as the high priest over the Jews. He sent him back to Jerusalem escorted by an army under the direction Bacchides, the new governor of the region, just to be sure there'd be no trouble.

Most of the Jews, weary of war, accepted the new high priest. Apparently Alcimus had a reputation of piety, since even the scribes (Jewish scholars) and the Hasidean sect, who had fought with the Hasmoneans, accepted his leadership. Together, they implored Judas to lay down his arms and discuss peace. But Judas would have none of it. He had ambitions of his own and little trust for Alcimus and his cohort. And as it turned out, there was good reason for mistrust: Alcimus soon had seventy Hasidean leaders executed. Bacchides, pleased that affairs in Jerusalem were under control, returned home to Syria. He left a small army at the high priest's disposal.

Judas and his troops continued to harass Alcimus and the Hellenizers. And once again, finding his forces insufficient to crush the rebels, Alcimus had to appeal to Demetrius for assistance. Early in 160 B.C. a large Syrian army under the leadership of a general named Nicanor invaded Judea. But the rebels utterly routed the Syrian forces, and Nicanor himself was slain. The freedom fighters entered Jerusalem exultant, bringing the head and right arm of the Syrian general as trophies. Astutely enough, Alcimus realized he was in serious danger. He fled to Syria and appealed to Demetrius to commit further troops to the task of putting down Judas and his cohorts. But Alcimus didn't have to beg. The Syrians were of no mind to

THE SELEUCID MONARCHS

The later years of the Seleucid Empire were fraught with intrigues and rivalries. The chronology of rulers from Antiochus Epiphanes forward seems to be as follows:

- Antiochus Epiphanes: 175-164 B.C.
- Antiochus V Eupator (son of Epiphanes): 164-162 B.C.
- Demetrius I Soter (nephew of Epiphanes): 162-150 B.C.
- Alexander Balas (claimed to be son of Epiphanes): 150-145 B.C.
- Demetrius II Nicator (son of Demetrius I) 145-140 B.C.; Antiochus VI (son of Alexander Balas): 145-142 B.C.; Tryphon (Alexander's general): 142-138 B.C. These rival claimants each ruled a portion of the kingdom.
- Antiochus VII Sidetes (brother of Demetrius II): 138-129 B.C.
- Demetrius II Nicator (again): 129-126 B.C.; Alexander Zebinas (alleged son of Alexander Balas): 128-122 B.C. (rival claimants; Zebinas defeated Demetrius in 126 B.C. and became sole ruler, until the rise of Seleucus V)
- Seleucus V (son of Demetrius; soon assassinated): 125 B.C.
- Antiochus VIII Grypus (brother of Seleucus V): 125-113 B.C.
- Antiochus IX Cyzicenus (cousin of Grypus): 113-95 B.C.; Antiochus VIII Grypus (again): 111-96 B.C.

From 96 B.C. to 89 B.C., the Seleucid Empire was divided among several rival claimants. It was conquered by Tigranes, king of Armenia, in 89 B.C.

excuse such humiliation, and Bacchides mustered another army—twenty thousand choice Syrian foot soldiers and two thousand cavalry—to march against the rebels.

Judas was ill-prepared for the assault. Since the Jews were no longer fighting for the right to worship God as they pleased, the Hasmoneans had lost much of their popular support. Judas went searching for foreign allies and entered into a treaty with Rome. But even though the Romans were happy to sign any agreement that would nettle the Seleucids, they weren't about to commit troops to such a minor cause. So Judas had few soldiers at his disposal. He encamped near Elasa with three thousand men, and it was there that the two armies met.[8] When the Jewish troops saw the great Syrian host drawing near, they appealed to Judas to flee—but he would have none of it. Confident in his God, expecting a miracle, he refused to be intimidated by the Syrian numerical superiority. But his soldiers weren't quite so faithful. Many of them deserted, until his army dwindled to only eight hundred. Still, Judas refused to back down from the fight. He encouraged the irresolute, "If this is where we're to meet our end, then let us meet it bravely." There at Elasa the armies met, but the short conflict can hardly be called a battle. Judas was killed early in the skirmish, and the rest of his army scattered. His brothers Jonathan and Simon gathered up his body and carried it away for burial in the family tomb at Modein.

So ended the career of the great national hero Judas Maccabees. But the battle for Jewish independence had only just begun.

Jonathan Hashmonai. Judas's death was a major blow to the rebellion.[9] Alcimus was now the undisputed leader of the Jews. Many of the rebels were rounded up and brought before Bacchides for punishment. But somehow the Hasmoneans eluded capture. With Judas gone, their leadership fell on the shoulders of the next eldest sibling, Jonathan. But they had little to do now but keep out of sight, at least for the time being.

Alcimus seemed to enjoy unopposed power for the short time he ruled over the Jews. But his career was brought to a rapid close by his untimely death. According to our historians, the forward-thinking high priest attempted to remove a partition in the inner court of the temple, which would have "destroyed the work of the prophets" (1 Macc 9:54). The purpose of the offending wall is uncertain. The temple was divided into several courts, and the layout varied from time to time. Some scholars have tried to identify the wall as one that separated the Court of the Gentiles from the Jewish courts, or the Court of the Women from the areas frequented by men. But neither identification is certain. The important point here was that changes in temple architecture were never arbitrary affairs—they were matters of divine revelation. God revealed the tabernacle plans to Moses on Mt. Sinai. Ezekiel had seen a vision of the ideal temple, and its layout was quite different from that of Solomon's temple. One of the

---

[8]The precise identification of Elasa is a matter of some dispute, but it was located northwest of Jerusalem, probably in the vicinity of Gezer.
[9]Primary sources for this subsection are 1 Macc 9:23—12:53; *Ant.* 13.1.1-13.6.6 (1-212).

Dead Sea Scrolls, the Temple Scroll, also presents a prophetic description of a new temple. Temple architecture was a holy affair, not a matter of personal taste. Probably, the wall Alcimus demolished had been constructed under the direction of one or more prophets. So it wasn't so much the function of the wall that was at issue, but the fact that Alcimus was putting his personal opinions ahead of God's word. The Lord struck the high priest down in the midst of his remodeling, and he died in agony in 159 B.C.

None of our accounts give us a clear picture of what happened next. Josephus claims the high priestly office was unoccupied for the next seven years, and most scholars accept this statement as fact. But I believe such a lengthy vacancy of the high priesthood is highly unlikely. After having fought so hard to restore the daily sacrifice and temple rituals, the Jews wouldn't have allowed such high and holy days as Yom Kippur (the Day of Atonement) to have gone unobserved. Our sources also tell us nothing of any politician or officer assuming administrative leadership in Jerusalem. Who was collecting the taxes and enforcing loyalty to the king, if not the high priest? Surely someone must have been filling this most important sacerdotal and administrative office in Judea, but who? Apparently the person gave so little offence or accomplished so little that the chroniclers felt they could pass him over without mention. Josephus, with no information about who filled the office for these seven years, concluded the office was vacant.

Meanwhile, Jonathan took advantage of the weakness in Jerusalem to begin securing his own position. Within two years the Maccabean resurgence was such that the Hellenizers again sent messengers to Bacchides, asking him to put down the rebels. When Bacchides arrived, however, he found no small band of ragtag revolutionaries, but a large, well-organized political faction. Finding himself unable to put down the Maccabean forces, he decided instead to make peace with Jonathan, and chided the Hellenizers for misrepresenting the conflict. These Maccabees were no longer a troubling band of marauding desperadoes—they'd become a political party of considerable influence.

Jonathan was now free from the threat of Syrian intervention. With the help of his brothers and compatriots, he established an alternative government in the city of Michmash. Many Jews regarded the official Sanhedrin—the Jewish senate—in Jerusalem to be corrupt, being controlled by members of the Hellenizing party. So Jonathan and his officers began to "judge the people" from their newly established home. Thus he started building a large base of popular support and could press toward his ultimate goal: the utter extermination of the Hellenizing party.

Soon circumstances arose that seemed to make Jonathan's position even more favorable. The Seleucid government was now constantly struggling against political intrigues at home, and each aspirant to the throne was in search of potential allies. In 153 B.C. Alexander Balas, claiming to be Antiochus Epiphanes' son, made a bid for the empire. Demetrius could hardly afford to devote his attention to Judea while dealing with a civil war at home. The support of a vigorous young fighter like Jonathan might come in handy. Demetrius was willing to negotiate with the Hasmoneans. He gave Jonathan the right to raise troops and produce weapons, and ordered the release of political prisoners held in the Akra. Jonathan accepted all these concessions graciously and took his liberty a step further: he actually entered Jerusalem with his troops and began to "judge" the people in the capital city itself.

Alexander Balas proved to be an even shrewder bargainer. Recognizing that the traditionalists represented the more vital element of Palestinian Judaism, he curried their favor by offering a most tempting package: the high priesthood itself. Balas offered to appoint Jonathan Hashmonai, the former outlaw, as the chief religious and political figure in Judea. Jonathan made no effort to demur or play humble. He accepted the offer immediately. His first public act as high priest was presiding over the Feast of Tabernacles in 153 or 152 B.C.

Jonathan's installation as high priest must have presented a dilemma for the true traditionalists. On the one hand, he and his family had worked hard to end the Antiochan persecution and restore proper worship in Judea. Jonathan was well recognized as a leader and a figure of pious influence over the people. On the other hand, he wasn't a descendant of Zadok, from whose lineage all high priests had been drawn for centuries. In fact, the office of high priest was passed from eldest son to eldest son since time immemorial. True, the tradition had been disrupted when Jason bribed his way into office, displacing his brother Onias III. But Jason and Menelaus were regarded as usurpers and criminals. Now Jonathan's appointment to the high priestly office represented an even *greater* departure from received tradition. Had the revolutionary's thirst for power made him forget the very principles that his family had been fighting for?

If any of the traditionalists protested about Jonathan's high priesthood, our sources haven't recorded it. It wouldn't have served their purposes to point out a troubling lapse in Jonathan's commitment to Jewish tradition. Instead, Jonathan is presented as the unambiguous hero in the struggle against oppression and apostasy. Our sources almost imply that he accepted the high priesthood not from any personal ambition but only for the good of the nation.

Back in Antioch, Demetrius tried to trump Balas's offer. He made extravagant promises to Jonathan, including the release of all Jewish captives, removal of foreign troops stationed in Jerusalem, exemption from taxation and other equally improbable offers. But Jonathan wasn't taken in. Maybe he realized that Demetrius was the weaker party in the struggle, since he was very unpopular in Antioch. Maybe Jonathan simply decided the promises were too good to be true. But as it turned out, Jonathan and the Hasmonean partisans gave no aid to Demetrius or Alexander Balas. Having accepted the favors of both parties, they now simply stood on the sidelines and waited to see who would come out ahead. Alexander Balas proved the victor, and Jonathan retained his position as high priest and the leader of the Jews. In fact, when a delegation from Jerusalem presented Balas with a petition against Jonathan, the Seleucid monarch responded by clothing Jonathan in the royal purple and parading him through the streets. A herald went before him, proclaiming that the king would hear no more complaints against Jonathan. Jonathan was also designated a "chief friend of the king," and named the *strategos* (chief military official) and *meridarches* (chief civil official) of Judea.

Jonathan seemed to have the situation well in control in Judea, but the situation in Syria was still volatile. In 147 B.C. Demetrius II, son of Demetrius I, began to press his claim for the throne. The Jews remained aloof from the conflict until 145, when Apollonius, the governor of Coele-Syria, defected to the usurper. Apollonius challenged Jonathan to a battle in the plains, where he presumed the God of Israel had no power.[10] But the Jewish forces routed Apollonius's army, prompting the grateful Alexander Balas to name Jonathan a "Kinsman of the King," and grant him the Philistine city of Ekron as a Judean possession.

Alexander Balas found that his other "kinfolk" had little family loyalty. His officers and governors were defecting to Demetrius. His own father-in-law, Ptolemy VI of Egypt, brought his army to Syria on the pretense of aiding Balas—but instead, he attacked the loyal Syrian forces. Obviously, Ptolemy thought he could use the Seleucid rivalry to conquer the Syrian

---

[10]Among pagan nations it was commonly assumed that the gods were limited to certain geographical locales. Since the God of Israel often manifested himself on mountains, foreigners assumed he was powerless in the lowlands. See, for example, 1 Kings 20:23.

empire for himself. But in this effort he was only partly successful. Alexander Balas was indeed driven from the throne. He had to flee to Arabia, where he was finally assassinated. But Ptolemy was mortally wounded in the conflict and never took control of Syria. Demetrius II, the last man standing, became ruler of the Seleucid Empire.

Realizing that Demetrius would have his hands full consolidating his new position, Jonathan sprang into action. In the center of Jerusalem stood the last symbol of foreign power: the Akra. The foreign troops housed inside this citadel were like the sword of Damocles hanging over the Jews' heads. Jonathan immediately laid siege to the structure—a clear assertion of his independence from the Syrians. But once again a party of Jews who were still loyal to the Hellenistic monarchs informed Demetrius II of Jonathan's treachery. Demetrius summoned Jonathan at once to answer for his actions. And Jonathan went, accompanied by a large company of Jewish nobles—an obvious attempt to demonstrate his popular support. He also brought rich gifts for the new monarch. The two parties were well aware of their positions. The Jews weren't ready for a war against the full might of the Seleucid Empire. But Demetrius had no desire to become involved in what promised to be a long and difficult struggle against the tenacious Hasmoneans. So a compromise was struck: Jonathan lifted his siege of the Akra and agreed to remain a loyal vassal of Syria. But in return he was confirmed in his position as leader of the Jews and as "king's kinsman." Jonathan was given three Samaritan provinces to add to his own domain, and he was exempted from taxation. It's obvious that Jonathan's prestige had grown considerably in the last few years. Called on the carpet for treason, he actually came out ahead in the deal.

The political instability in Syria that had benefited Jonathan soon turned against him. One of Alexander Balas's generals, a man called Tryphon, brought forward the late king's son Antiochus VI as a new contender for the throne. Faced with an uprising in Antioch, Demetrius promised Jonathan that he would give him control of the Akra and several other Judean fortresses in exchange for his aid. Jonathan sent three thousand troops, and the revolt was put down, for the time being. But Demetrius, recognizing the Hasmonean's ambition, reneged on his promises. Enraged by this duplicity, Jonathan threw his support to the young aspirant and his sponsor, Tryphon. The Jewish armies went forth to secure the territories lying round about Judea for Antiochus VI. Some went over willing to the new king; others required some military persuasion, which

Jonathan obligingly provided. He also subdued Beth-Zur and other Syrian fortresses in Judea that remained loyal to Demetrius. In this fashion he was accomplishing two goals: he was ostensibly serving the interests of the usurping monarch, but he was also expelling the foreign presence from Judea and increasing his hold over his own territories.

At the same time, Jonathan sent emissaries to Rome and Sparta. The purpose of these visits was to reaffirm the old treaties that Judas made with these foreign powers. Jonathan could hardly have believed that the Romans would actually come to the Jews' aid. It hadn't happened in all the years since the treaties were first signed, and there was no reason to believe the situation had changed much. On the other hand, the mere possibility of Roman assistance must have been reassuring to the Hasmoneans and troubling to their enemies. To the Syrians it would also have smacked of insubordination. Why should a loyal subject of the Seleucids need to make treaties with their sworn enemies, the Romans?

Tryphon wasn't oblivious to Jonathan's ulterior motives. He recognized the potential threat that this ambitious ally presented. So as soon as he had the situation in Syria well in hand, Tryphon entered Judea with a large army. Jonathan marched out to meet him with forty thousand men of his own. But Tryphon immediately turned on the charm, presenting Jonathan with gifts and introducing him to his soldiers as an officer who was to be obeyed without question. Tryphon assured Jonathan that the Seleucids wished to honor the Hasmoneans' efforts by presenting them with the city of Ptolemais (ancient Acco, on the Phoenician coast) to add to the Judean realm. Would Jonathan accompany Tryphon to Ptolemais and survey his new port?

Jonathan was completely taken in. He had little reason to be suspicious. After all, he'd made a good show of faithfully serving the king, even though he'd actually been advancing his own cause. And the promise of Ptolemais was a temptation that could cloud the judgment of any ambitious leader. Such a fine port was exactly what the Hasmoneans needed to conduct trade across the Mediterranean Sea or to receive foreign military assistance. So Jonathan dismissed his army, and set off for Ptolemais, accompanied by only one thousand of his own men. But as soon as they entered the city, Tryphon sprung his trap. The city gates were closed, Jonathan's soldiers were massacred, and the high priest himself was taken captive. With Jonathan as a hostage, Tryphon set out to subjugate Judea.

The remaining Hasmonean brother, Simon, was ready for him. He immediately secured the port city of Jaffa (Joppa), from which he could summon Roman aid if necessary. He also fortified Jerusalem against a possible siege. As Tryphon's army entered Judean territory, Simon met him with a formidable Jewish host. Tryphon sent envoys with words of reassurance. Jonathan was only being held, they claimed, because he had failed to pay tribute money in exchange for the honors conferred on him. If Simon would send the tribute along with Jonathan's sons as a show of good faith, Tryphon promised to release the high priest.

Simon now faced a difficult choice. Could he trust Tryphon to keep his word? Probably not. But if he refused the demand, he could be accused of abandoning his brother in order to take the high priesthood for himself. So Simon sent the tribute and Jonathan's sons to the Syrian camp. As expected Tryphon didn't release Jonathan. Instead, he took his money and captives and set off to cross the Jordan River. His plan was to circumvent Simon's army entirely and invade Jerusalem from the east. But a freak (miraculous?) snowstorm stopped his troops short, and Tryphon had to withdraw to Gilead. He'd been prevented from conquering Jerusalem, but he would not be denied at least one prize. There in Gilead, in 142 B.C., Jonathan was executed. Tryphon then returned to Syria, where he'd cause even more mischief. Simon recovered his brother's body so that he could be properly mourned by his people. They buried Jonathan in the family tomb in Modein, with his father and brothers Judas and Eleazar.

For Further Reading

Bar-Kochva, B. *Judas Maccabaeus: The Jewish Struggle Against the Seleucids.* Cambridge: Cambridge University Press, 1989.

Bickerman, Elias. *The God of the Maccabees.* Leiden: Brill, 1979. Interesting reading from a distinguished scholar. Emphasizes the religious struggle.

Goldstein, Jonathan. *I Maccabees.* Anchor Bible Commentary. New York: Doubleday, 1976. Often brilliant and occasionally quirky treatments, but highly influential.

———. *II Maccabees.* Anchor Bible Commentary. New York: Doubleday, 1983.

Horbury, William; W. D. Davies; Louis Finkelstein; and John Sturdy. *The Cambridge History of Judaism.* Vol. 2, chap. 9. Cambridge: Cambridge University Press, 1990.

Schürer, Emil. *A History of the Jewish People in the Age of Jesus Christ.* Edited by Geza Vermes, Fergus Millar and Matthew Black. Vol. 1, §§4-7. Edinburgh: T & T Clark, 1973-1987.

6

Jewish Diversity
in the Hasmonean Era

Near the end of his narrative on Jonathan's career, Josephus makes a
rather unexpected digression onto the topic of Jewish religious sects:

> At this time there were three sects among the Jews, who had different opin-
> ions concerning human actions; the one was called the sect of the Pharisees,
> another the sect of the Sadducees, and the other the sect of the Essenes. Now
> for the Pharisees, they say that some actions, but not all, are the work of fate,
> and some of them are in our own power, and that they are liable to fate, but
> are not caused by fate. But the sect of the Essenes affirm that fate governs all
> things, and that nothing befalls men but what is according to its determina-
> tion. And for the Sadducees, they take away fate, and say there is no such
> thing, and that the events of human affairs are not at its disposal; but they
> suppose that all our actions are in our own power, so that we are ourselves
> the causes of what is good, and receive what is evil from our own folly. How-
> ever, I have given a more exact account of these opinions in the second book
> of the Jewish War.[1]

This is the first time Josephus mentions these sects in his account of Jewish history.[2] The paragraph seems wholly an intrusion into the narrative,
with no connection to the material before or after. There's no visible reason
for its inclusion here, leading scholars to conclude that in Josephus's

---

[1]*Ant.* 13.5.9 (171-73).

[2]The word *sects* is traditionally used to describe these various Jewish groups, but it is not
meant to imply that there was a certain normative Judaism from which these groups
diverged. Rather, these groups represented different varieties of Judaism that coexisted and
competed with one another for power.

sources the sects played some part in the narrative that Josephus chose to omit in his account. We can hardly reconstruct the circumstances now. The importance of this reference, then, is that it gives us an idea of when the three major Jewish sects of New Testament times began to have a public presence in Judea. And since two of these groups—the Pharisees and Sadducees—will play significant roles in events to come, it seems a good time for us to pause and consider their origins and beliefs.

Jewish "Sectarianism"

The division of Judaism into various sects was no new development. Long before the coming of the Greeks, the Israelites had been divided into various parties and perspectives, usually coexisting but often competing for the control of the nation. There were strict monotheists, syncretists and apostates. There were those who believed that only Jerusalem should be the center of Yahwistic worship and those who held that one could worship the Lord anywhere that there were stones to build an altar. There were some with a very high view of kingship and its religious implications and others who held a more secular understanding of royal power and authority.

Both during and after the exile, vigorous efforts were made to bring some kind of normalcy to Judaism. Syncretistic and apostate groups were largely subdued in Judea during the Babylonian exile, but Judaism was still far from unified. There were differences of opinion on theological questions like the resurrection of the dead. There were disagreements about marriage between Jews and foreigners, with Ezra and Nehemiah taking a hard line against the practice, while the author of Esther seemed to have no moral difficulties with it. The book of Malachi actually chronicles the formation of a sect: a group of those who "feared the LORD" got together and entered into an agreement that they would be faithful to God's laws (Mal 3:16). Some scholars argue that there was a "wisdom" sect, with a universalistic outlook; an "apocalyptic" sect, anticipating an imminent end to the world; and numerous other groups besides.

In the decades before and during the Maccabean Revolt, there existed a group known as the Hasidim, or "pious ones." There are but three references to this group in the literature (1 Macc 2:42; 7:13; 2 Macc 14:6), but they were obviously influential in their day. They initially aided the Hasmoneans, but once their religious rights were restored they broke with the revolutionaries and sought peace with the Seleucids. The scant references are tantalizing, spawning hundreds of articles written on reams of paper.

It's long been argued that the Hasidim were the forerunners of the Pharisees, and more recently, of the Essenes. But evidence for either identification is scant. We know nothing of what the Hasidim believed or how they
worshiped, and little of why they fought against the Greeks.

We shouldn't feel compelled to somehow associate the Hasidim with
the three sects in Josephus's scheme. Scholars have come to recognize that
early Judaism was far more diverse than once believed. There has been a
stubborn tendency to take Josephus's description of Judaism existing in
three sects as literal. But Josephus tells us there were only about six thousand Pharisees and about four thousand Essenes—and the Sadducees constituted only a small group of aristocrats. Obviously, these three sects
together account for only a fraction of the millions of Jews living in those
times. So apparently many Jews weren't aligned with any particular sect,
while others were members of sects that Josephus failed to include in his
tripartite scheme. Josephus himself tells us about a "fourth philosophy,"
similar to the Pharisees in their beliefs but characterized by their unwill-
ingness to submit to foreign domination. He also wrote about the Jewish
Christians, who already constituted a substantial group in Josephus's
day—but they were excluded from his tripartite scheme.[3] So we need not
try to make every religious movement of the day fit into the Pharisee-Sad-
ducee-Essene scheme; other factions were present and active throughout
the era. They simply weren't as prominent, or at least not as interesting to
Josephus, as these three were.

We should also beware of the old understanding, coming from rabbinic
tradition, that there was a single unbroken stream of pure Judaism deriving
from Moses, going through the prophets to the Pharisees and to the rabbis.
Scholars now understand that it's really impossible to speak of "normative" Judaism until well into the rabbinic era (fourth century A.D. and beyond). Throughout the biblical and intertestamental period, Judaism was
actually a cord of interwoven strands, bound together by belief in the Lord,
the holy Scriptures (even though they disagreed on what constituted those
Scriptures) and their reverence for Jerusalem. Occasionally one group or
another would step forward and redefine orthodoxy for a time, as when

---

[3]*Ant.* 18.3.3 (63-64). The text has obviously been reworked by the Christian copyists who
preserved Josephus in order to make it more theologically orthodox, but there's little
reason to doubt that the core of the report—that there was a man named Jesus who
performed wonders, that he was crucified under Pontius Pilate and that his followers
persisted until Josephus's day—is genuine.

Ezra and Nehemiah imposed their understanding of Judaism on the people of Jerusalem. Of course, in a theocratic society, a sect could claim to be the normative expression of Judaism because its members controlled the Sanhedrin or the priesthood. But there was always room for differences of opinion. The Pharisees might have been for a time the largest and most popular sect, but they were no more "true" Judaism than the others.

The Problem of Sources

Before we can consider the nature of the Jewish sects, we have to take into account the nature of our sources. Josephus talks about the Pharisees, Sadducees and Essenes, plus the fourth sect, which we'll discuss in a later chapter. The New Testament and early rabbinic literature (the so-called Tannaitic literature, produced before the mid-third century A.D.) speak of the Pharisees and Sadducees. Philo of Alexandria, the Hellenized Jewish philosopher who lived around the time of Jesus, gives us some extensive descriptions of the Essenes. (Many scholars would also include the Dead Sea Scrolls among our sources for the Essenes, but we'll consider the Dead Sea Scroll sect separately.) The Babylonian and Palestinian Talmuds, as well as the midrashic literature, record many traditions about the Pharisees and Sadducees. But these texts were produced centuries after the time when the sects existed and must be used with caution.

Our sources largely agree in their descriptions of the sects, but each has its own interests and emphases. Josephus, writing for his Hellenized and Roman audience, often projects concepts and categories from Greek philosophy onto his subjects. In the text quoted above he describes the various sects' positions on the role of "fate." Fate was an important and highly debated concept among the various schools of Greek philosophy, but it was an idea utterly foreign to Palestinian Judaism. The Jewish sects might have argued about the role of divine providence, but providence is a very different notion than the Hellenistic conception of fate. (Providence refers to God's ordering of the world according to his will; fate speaks of an impersonal force that orders the universe—even the gods being subject to its decrees.) Josephus was trying to explain Judaism in terms his audience would have understood and appreciated. But in doing so, he certainly distorted the picture significantly. "Fate" would hardly have been a major issue of division among the Jews.

Furthermore, both Josephus and Philo devote far more attention to the Essenes than their influence would seem to warrant. But both authors knew that ascetic bands like the Essenes fascinated the Greeks and Romans. Similar associations existed in other Mediterranean societies, and their members were often held up as paragons of virtue. Philo in particular cited the Essenes as examples of the high standards of righteousness and discipline that could be found among the Jews.

The New Testament also presents its facts from a particular point of view. Modern writers frequently accuse the Gospels of being anti-Semitic, painting a hate-filled distortion of Judaism in the time of Jesus. Someone might get that impression as they read some of the strong rhetoric in the Gospel accounts. But such charges fail to consider the context in which Christianity arose. The New Testament authors were themselves Jewish, and they directed their criticisms not against Judaism in general but against the leaders and the groups with whom they clashed most fiercely. Even when the Gospel of John, for example, speaks disparagingly of "the Jews," it usually means only the Jewish political establishment. (Some newer translations have recognized this fact and translate "the Jews" in John as "the Jewish leaders.")

The New Testament's depiction of the Pharisees and Sadducees has been shaped by both theological and sociological considerations. On the sociological side, when the Gospels were written, Christianity was still largely a Jewish sect. The Gospels were designed in part to help Christians distinguish themselves from the other prominent Jewish groups. Ideas central to Christianity's identity—the resurrection of the dead, the importance of the Jewish laws, the significance of sacrifice—were the issues that the Gospels emphasized in their presentations of the sects. It was especially important for Christianity to distinguish itself from the Pharisees, the Jewish sect that was most vigorously recruiting the very people to whom the Christians appealed and the group with whom they had the most in common. The polemical language that Jesus levels against the Pharisees might well be compared to the vehemence with which Martin Luther attacked the Catholics of his day. Not all Pharisees were evil hypocrites, and not all Sadducees were aristocratic schemers.[4] The rhetoric must be put in its context or it will be misinterpreted.

---

[4]From time to time even the Gospels intimate that the portraits painted of rival Jewish groups were broad generalizations: for example, in Jn 3:1; 19:39 Nicodemus is depicted as good, sincere man and a Pharisee.

THE PHARISEES AS HYPOCRITES

The Gospels reserve their most scathing rhetoric not for murderers, thieves or adulterers but for the Christians' closest kin—the Pharisees. Jesus accuses the Pharisees of hypocrisy—acting pious on the outside, while actually being full of wickedness (see esp. Mt 23). For Jesus this wickedness isn't so much a matter of the typical moral failings—greed or lust or the like. Rather, their failings were a lack of love and compassion (Mt 23:23; Lk 13:15-16), or the desire to have human approval (Lk 11:43; 18:9-14). For some of the Pharisees the law had become an end in itself rather than a means to communion with God. It seems that some believed people were created to benefit the law, not vice versa (see Mk 2:27).

Not all Pharisees were hypocrites. Yet there's little reason to doubt that hypocrisy was a troublesome problem in Pharisaism. Even the Babylonian Talmud, the compendium of rabbinic teachings from the fifth to sixth century A.D., denounces six types of hypocritical Pharisees (*Sotah* 22b). Some of the sins named here are the very faults condemned by Jesus. If Jesus' criticisms seem strong, it's because many Pharisees were sincerely trying to please God, but some were being entrapped in a web of legalism. Christians and Pharisees shared much the same faith, and Jesus struggled to save those he considered to be redeemable.

The rabbinic literature too must be read in context. The rabbis regarded themselves as the scion of the Pharisees. In rabbinic Judaism, in contrast to Christianity, the Pharisees were not the enemy but the heroes. The Sadducees were the Pharisees' archenemies, so they could serve as a convenient straw man when the rabbis wanted to make a point of law. It didn't hurt, too, that the Sadducees were probably nearly extinct by the time when the Mishnah and Tosephta, our primary Tannaitic sources, were put into writing. So the rabbis didn't have to be too concerned about misrepresenting what the Sadducees actually believed or taught. In some cases the rabbinic literature attributes teachings to the Sadducees that seem highly suspect (e.g., that the Sadducean women followed the teachings of the Pharisees in matters of ritual washings, M. Niddah 4.2; T. Niddah 5.3). But from the Tannaitic sources we could conclude that the major points of contention between the Sadducees and other groups didn't concern providence or the resurrection of the dead but matters of proper washing and food preparation.

The problem of sources has made some scholars reluctant to attempt any synthetic description of the various Jewish sects. Instead, many treatments today simply summarize the descriptions found in the various literary works, noting their points of agreement and discrepancy. While this reluctance to systematize the data is understandable, it seems to me unwarranted. There's enough agreement between our sources to allow us to develop a fairly reliable picture of the different groups. We simply need to stick to the general picture and not attempt to bring too much detail into our descriptions.

The Pharisees

Of the groups named by Josephus, the largest and most influential was surely the Pharisees. The origins of the group are shrouded in veils of mystery. Their name apparently derives from the Hebrew verb meaning "to separate." In the rabbinic texts they are called the *perushim*—a passive form, suggesting the translation "the separated ones." That fact could mean that the Pharisees separated themselves from the masses. In the rabbinic sources the Pharisees are frequently contrasted with the "people of the land." So perhaps they took their name because they had self-consciously set themselves apart from those they deemed less scrupulous about observing the law. If that was the case, it's somewhat ironic that Josephus considered the Pharisees to be the "people's party" in Jewish society. On the other hand, they might have taken the name "Pharisee" because they were scrupulous about making "separations" (distinctions) between people and things that were clean and unclean. In that case they weren't so much separated as *separators*.

The Pharisees are never mentioned in the Old Testament. They play no role in the Hasmonean Revolt. They step on to the stage of history for the first time during the reign of Simon Hashmonai (Jonathan's successor). Theories that place their origins back in Old Testament times, then, would seem to have very little foundation. The Pharisees probably coalesced early in Hasmonean times as a number of Jews with similar opinions came

together and established a formal fellowship. Perhaps they emerged in response to the Antiochan persecution. Often, times of hardship build cama-
raderie among like-minded souls. It's possible that groups of faithful Jews
huddled together to comfort one another with the hope of the resurrection
of the dead, and to encourage each other in the careful observance of the
law. Once the persecution was lifted they might have remained bound to
one another by the fellowship of suffering and their emerging *halakhah* (legal interpretations). But that's pure speculation. We have no real information on the beginnings of the Pharisees and must be content with
descriptions of their beliefs and practices.

One of the most distinctive features of the Pharisees was their adherence to what is often called "oral law." Josephus and the Gospels agree that
the Pharisees, in addition to the biblical laws, ordered their lives by means
of a great many traditional teachings (*Ant.* 13.10.6 [297]; Mk 7:2-4). These
halakhot (plural of *halakhah*) were surely the foundation for the great rabbinic legal work of the third century A.D., the Mishnah. But while the Mishnah was a written, edited collection of debates and decisions, the Pharisees
hadn't yet committed their rules to writing. Most likely their rules weren't
considered "law" in the same sense as biblical laws. Rather, these *halakhot*
were traditional interpretations of the laws of Moses, deemed somehow
authoritative but without any official status. (It's difficult to discern how
the Pharisees' oral laws would have differed from those of the Sadducees
and Essenes; but Josephus insists that the authority granted to traditional
interpretations was a major distinction between the Pharisees and the
other sects.) The oral law developed gradually as the Jewish sages
throughout the ages debated fine points of various biblical statutes. How
much could a Jew physically exert himself on the sabbath day? How could
Jews be sure that their food hadn't been contaminated by contact with
nonkosher items? Under what conditions could a man divorce his wife?
The Bible is seldom explicit on such questions. So the Pharisees' teachers
and the later rabbis discussed these matters in detail so they could provide
clear guidelines for pious Jews.

It was the issue of oral law that would become the main point of contention between Jesus and the Pharisees. Jesus' approach to the ambigu-
ities of Old Testament, according to the Gospels, was to emphasize the
spirit or intention of the laws over the letter of the laws. For example, Jesus
emphasized that the sabbath was designed to be a day of rest and refresh-
ment, and therefore relieving pain or hunger on the sabbath was perfectly

acceptable. The Pharisees, on the other hand, emphasized that the sabbath was a day for ceasing from work. They developed strict definitions of what constituted work and rigidly imposed these rules on their followers. In matters like the keeping of kosher (dietary rules), washing before meals, marriage laws and so on, the Pharisees of Jesus' day had developed a large number of traditional regulations. But undoubtedly these rules had come into being over a long period of time, and they probably were far less burdensome in the Hasmonean era.

The Pharisees initiated some new emphases in Judaism. But we must bear in mind that the Pharisees weren't self-consciously seeking to become religious innovators. They based their ideas firmly on the Scriptures as they understood them. Their ideas about God, human destiny and obedience to the law were either derived from biblical passages or attached to biblical passages through any of a variety of interpretive devices (methods that sometimes look to us like "proof-texting"). They had no desire to be known as innovators—but that's what they most certainly were. And their flexibility in adapting to new situations and ideas gave their brand of Judaism the necessary resiliency to survive and thrive even after the destruction of the second temple in A.D. 70.

The religious views of the Pharisees are well attested. The New Testament and Josephus agree on the major points. As we read earlier, Josephus tells us explicitly that the Pharisees believed that some things in this world are caused by fate, while others are left to human will. Translating the statement into something more compatible with Jewish thought, we might say that they believed in limited providence: God willed certain things to happen but allowed for a certain amount of human freedom as well. (The rabbis argued a similar view, holding that God ordered most world events, while allowing human beings the freedom to choose good or evil. See *M. Aboth* 3.16.) Individuals are free to choose whether they will do good or evil. And on the basis of that choice, the Pharisees argued, God would determine the eternal destiny of each individual. Those who had done good would live forever in heaven, while those who had done evil would suffer torment in hell (*Ant.* 18.1.33 [14]).

Josephus, in one of his descriptions of the Pharisaic view on the afterlife, presents their beliefs in his characteristic Greek guise. He states that the Pharisees believed the soul to be immortal (*Ant.* 18.2.3 [14]). In this passage Josephus tells us that the Pharisees believed that both good and evil souls descended to the underworld after death, where the good were rewarded and the evil punished. Here again Josephus has projected a notion from Hellenistic philosophy on to the Jews. Some of the Greeks—like Plato—believed that human beings were animated by an immortal soul, which was released when the body died. The Jews, on the other hand, believed that the soul didn't exist separate from a body of some kind. As we observed earlier, Jews didn't consider immortality to be a natural human faculty but a gift of God. Josephus came a little closer to this position in his earlier discussion of the Pharisees in the *Jewish War* 2.8.14 (162). There he wrote that the Pharisees believed all souls were immortal, but only the souls of the righteous received a new body after death. Probably the New Testament is more accurate in stating simply that the Pharisees believed in the resurrection of the dead (Acts 23:8). While it's possible that a Jewish sect might have believed in an intermediate state for the soul between death and the final resurrection, it seems unlikely that a large number of Judean Jews would have conceived of a soul remaining immortal and eternally disembodied.

The New Testament tells us of another Pharisaic distinctive: the Pharisees believed in angels and spirits; the Sadducees did not (Acts 23:8). In this case it appears that the issue isn't the simple existence of such beings. Surely if the Sadducees believed in the Bible at all, they must have believed in angels! Rather, the question must have been whether or not such beings communicated to people in the Pharisees' day. The Pharisees in the Sanhedrin actually defended Paul against his detractors by arguing that an angel or spirit might have spoken to him—a notion that the Sadducees seem to have rejected (Acts 23:9). And the rabbis, the heirs of the Pharisees, frequently give witness to the Pharisees' belief that God could speak to his people through angels or even heavenly voices in their own day.

As for their social relations, Josephus praises the Pharisees for their civility and respect for their elders. They lived simply, choosing to eschew worldly luxuries. In Josephus's day the Pharisees were largely excluded from the circles of wealth and influence—but that wasn't always the case. Their fortunes varied based on who held power in Jerusalem. Even so, when the Pharisees were denied official positions of power, they could often get their way. The masses generally followed the Pharisaic positions and resisted efforts to impose laws or customs that were contrary to the Pharisees' teachings (*Ant.* 18.1.3-4 [15-17]). There were a number of reasons behind their popular appeal. First, the Pharisaic positions on the afterlife coincided most closely with popular beliefs. No doubt Jewish folk religion of the day maintained a belief in an afterlife, and the Pharisees represented a more sophisticated set of adherents to that belief. Furthermore, the Pharisees' simple lifestyles helped them to connect better with the common person. The aristocratic Sadducees were far removed from the circumstances endured by the masses. Finally, the Pharisees, according to Josephus, were simply nicer than the Sadducees. When the two sects were at odds, the common folk would be far more likely to side with the one they found pleasant and agreeable.

The Sadducees

Josephus, in fact, describes the Sadducees as rude and boorish. A small, aristocratic sect of a few thousand members, the Sadducees represented the highest economic stratum of Judean society. But in spite of their wealth, Josephus claims that in his day the group could accomplish little, being forced pretty much to bend to the will of the Pharisees. Such was not always the case—there were times that the Sadducees managed to wield a great deal of influence over the Jews. When they could forge alliances with the ruling powers, the Sadducees could almost have their way in spite of popular disapproval. For the most part, the extent of their influence depended on who was in control of Judea at the time, just as it did for the Pharisees.

Unlike the Pharisees, the Sadducees were religious conservatives. According to Josephus, they rejected oral tradition and accepted as binding only that which could be explicitly demonstrated from the Scriptures. Indeed, Josephus says they observe nothing apart from the law of Moses (*Ant.* 13.10.6 [297], 18.1.4 [16]). Primarily, Josephus is trying to say that the Sadducees rejected the oral traditions of the Pharisees. But some scholars have argued that these passages imply the Sadducees accepted only the five books of Moses—Genesis, Exodus, Leviticus, Numbers and Deuteronomy—as Scripture. Such a position wouldn't be unprecedented, since the Samaritans accepted only these books as Scripture. It might also explain why Jesus, when debating with the Sadducees over the issue of the resurrection of the dead, made no reference to the explicit statement about the resurrection in Daniel 12 nor to the less explicit references in Isaiah and the Psalms. Instead, he referred them to Exodus 3:6: "I am the God of your father, the God of Abraham, the God of Isaac, and the God of Jacob" (see Mt 22:23-32). If the Sadducees didn't recognize the authority of the Prophets or Writings, they would hardly have been convinced by arguments based on these passages of Scripture.

Both the New Testament and Josephus agree that the Sadducees didn't believe in the resurrection of the dead. The rabbinic literature hints to this fact as well, observing that the Sadducees used to mock the Pharisees for afflicting themselves in this world, hoping to receive rewards instead in the next life.[5] Their lack of faith in the afterlife might partially explain their apparent addiction to luxury. Without hope of a "world to come," the Sadducees assessed their spiritual performance according to the blessings they enjoyed in this life. If they were wealthy, it meant God was pleased with them. If they were poor, it meant they must be doing something wrong. The Sadducees had no qualms about enjoying the benefits of wealth and power in life because these gifts were the rewards for righteous living. We shouldn't assume that because they didn't believe in an afterlife they felt they could live immorally. None of our sources ever accuse the Sadducees as a group of impiety or immorality, only of arrogance and ignorance.

Josephus also tells us that the Sadducees rejected the notion of fate altogether. In other words, they didn't believe that God directed human affairs. No doubt Josephus exaggerates their position somewhat. No one could accept the Pentateuch as Scripture without believing that God intervenes in human affairs. Nor would there be any reward for righteousness if God didn't respond to good or evil actions. Perhaps Josephus meant only that the Sadducees believed in some kind of radical freedom of the will: God neither directs nor foreknows human decisions, making us wholly responsible for our actions. Or maybe the Sadducees believed that the days of divine intervention had passed. Such a belief would be consistent with their rejection of angelic messengers (Acts 23:8). Miracles, angel visitations and the like might have happened in the old days, but the time for such showy manifestations of divine power was long gone.

For a long time, common wisdom has held that the Sadducees' power base lay in their close affiliation with the temple and priesthood. Recently, some scholars have asked if there's really enough evidence to posit such a connection. Josephus says little about the priests being drawn from the ranks of the Sadducees. He explicitly identifies only one high priest, Ananus, as a Sadducee (*Ant.* 20.9.1 [199]), and his account

---

[5]*The Fathers According to Rabbi Nathan* A 5, trans. Judah Goldin (New Haven, Conn.: Yale University Press, 1955).

implies that some priests were allied with the Pharisees.[6] The rabbinic literature tells us that some high priests were Sadducees, but it also identifies some as Pharisees. In the New Testament the high-priestly establishment at the time of Jesus and Peter seems to be allied with the Sadducean party (Acts 4:1-4; 5:17-18); but at least one priest mentioned in the New Testament—Zechariah (Lk 1:5-7), father of John the Baptist—can't be in any way associated with the Sadducees. So clearly not all priests, and not even all high priests, were Sadducees. And yet I believe there *is* sufficient evidence to suggest a connection between the Sadducean party and the priesthood. Most of the Hasmonean high priests were allied with the Sadducees, as we will see in events to come. The temple represented the single largest concentration of wealth in all Judea. Remember that in those days the temple wasn't merely a place to worship and sacrifice; it was a major financial institution where the rich could deposit their funds for (more or less) safekeeping. If the Sadducees truly represented the wealthy class in Judea, then they'd naturally have wanted a good deal of influence in the operations of the temple complex.

If the Sadducees were indeed associated with the priesthood, it could shed some light on the sect's name. *Saddouk* is the Greek form of the Hebrew name "Zadok," meaning "righteous." The name "Sadducee" simply means "of Zadok," and so the Sadducees were probably partisans of someone who bore that name. It was a fairly common name in intertestamental times, so "Zadok" could simply have been the name of the group's forgotten founder. On the other hand, the name Zadok had certain *special* significance in the early Hasmonean era when the Sadducees came into existence. Before the Antiochan persecution the high priests traditionally had been drawn from the family of Zadok, the high priest in the days of King David. The descendants of Zadok would have been known as Sadducees (using the Greek spelling). So the sect of Sadducees might have represented adherents of the displaced Zadokite high priests. If such were the case it might help explain why we'll see the Hasmoneans currying the favor of the Sadducees over that of the Pharisees. If the Sadducees were associated with the traditional high-priestly regime, it would have been politically expedient for the Hasmoneans to gain their support in order to

---

[6]The Hasmonean high priest-king Hyrcanus II was probably allied with the Pharisees; see chap. 9 for evidence. Certainly Matthias, high priest in the days of Herod the Great, was (see *Ant.* 17.6.2-4 [149-167]).

lend some legitimacy to their usurpation of the high priesthood.

A final point on relations between the Pharisees and Sadducees: as noted above, rabbinic literature speaks frequently about conflicts between the two major sects. But with only a couple exceptions those conflicts have almost nothing to do with theological beliefs. Rather, the major disagreements between Pharisees and Sadducees in rabbinic texts appear as matters of interpreting ritual law or *halakhah*. If this picture is accurate, then the Pharisees probably would have found it easier to have forgiven the Sadducees for not believing in the resurrection of the dead than to forgive them for, say, improperly washing their hands before dinner. We have a bit of corroborating evidence for this picture in Dead Sea Scrolls. In one text (*Miqsat Ma'aseh Hattorah*, designated 4QMMT), the Scrolls sect states explicitly why it separated from the rest of the Jews. The text never mentions theological differences between the Scrolls Community and other groups. Rather, it was matters of *halakhah* that made them so unwilling to fellowship with others. Washings, festival observances, sacrificial practices—these were the issues that splintered Judaism of the time. Again we're reminded that for early Palestinian Jews, orthodoxy—proper beliefs—wasn't nearly so important as orthopraxis—proper actions. This quality would come to distinguish Christianity from the dominant Jewish groups of its day.

The Essenes

Josephus has more to say about the Essenes than any other Jewish sect of his day (*Ant.* 18.2.5 [18-22]; *War* 2.8.2-13 [119-161]; and various scattered references). Philo of Alexandria also devotes a good deal of attention to this sect, while virtually ignoring the Pharisees and Sadducees (*Every Good Man Is Free* 12.75-87; *Hypothetica* 11.1-8). These sources sometimes contradict one another and even contradict themselves as they try to make sense of this somewhat quirky faction. Many scholars would add the Dead Sea Scrolls to our list of sources about the Essenes. But due to the difficulties in interpreting and reconciling the Scrolls with Josephus and Philo, we'll give the Scrolls sect separate treatment.

The Essenes never appear in the New Testament. Old theories that identified Jesus and John the Baptist as Essenes are largely discounted these days. (Although some scholars do observe points of contact between these principal figures of the Gospels and the Scrolls sect.) Their roles in the significant events following the time of Jesus are minor. They never appear in rabbinic literature, having become extinct well before the rabbis' heyday. The Essenes are little more than a historical curiosity, one of those radical splinter groups that capture human imagination but do little of lasting significance. So we'll not devote quite so much attention to the Essenes as Josephus and Philo have done.

The name "Essene" has been the subject of much debate. Philo connected it with the Greek word *hosioi*, "pious ones," but this derivation is both improbable on cultural grounds and impossible on linguistic grounds. The name is almost certainly of Hebrew or Aramaic origins. Some scholars have tried to connect it with the Syrian Aramaic word for "pious," or the Hebrew verb meaning "to do" (i.e., the law), but each proposed etymology has its weaknesses. So we have to admit that we're pretty much in the dark.

Josephus tells us that the Essenes believed earthly events were under the control of fate. Like hyper-Calvinists, they believed that God ordered all things in the world, including acts of the human will. They were unwilling to leave a matter so important as one's eternal destiny to human reason and order. They believed in the immortality of the soul, giving this doctrine special emphasis. Josephus attributes to the Essenes the Platonic belief that the soul is preexistent and becomes imprisoned in a mortal body at birth. At death the soul receives joyful release from the body. Righteous souls enter eternal life in a blissful realm beyond the seas, while the wicked experience eternal imprisonment beneath the earth (*War* 2.8.11 [154-55]). Josephus compares their idea of the afterlife to the Greek ideas about the Elysian fields and Hades, but he says nothing of whether the Essenes held to the very non-Greek notion of the bodily resurrection.

Josephus also seems to imply that the Essenes in some manner identified the sun with God. He writes that the Essenes would rise up before the dawn and pray to the sun, as if entreating him to rise (*War* 2.8.5 [128]), and that they would cover themselves when going to the toilet, so as not to offend "the rays of the Deity" (*War* 2.8.9 [148]). These passages have given scholars of early Judaism fits—sun worship is impossible to reconcile with any form of orthodox Jewish faith. But Josephus never speaks of these practices as if they were unusual or offensive to fellow Jews. This leads us to believe that either he has once again projected onto this sect a practice more at home in the Hellenistic world, or he meant his words to be understood more figuratively than we have usually taken them.

The Essenes had peculiar beliefs regarding the temple and sacrifices.

Philo writes that they did not sacrifice at all, devoting themselves instead to purification of their minds (*Every Good Man Is Free* 12.75). But Josephus more reasonably states that the Essenes practiced a sacrificial cult of their own, attended to by their own priests (*Ant.* 18.2.5 [19]). They sent sacrifices to the temple, but they wouldn't enter the temple precincts because they believed that the purification rites practiced there were incorrect. So the Essenes regarded the temple as defiled—a position that would clearly set them against the majority of their kin.

Josephus and Philo agree that the Essenes had some unusual customs. Both report that the Essenes lived together in communities, although their communities were spread throughout various cities. They held no private property but gave their wealth to the leaders of the community for distribution to all in need. They dressed in white and abstained from earthly pleasures. The Essenes were ever respectful of those in authority, believing that all authority was given by God. Both Josephus and Philo tell us that the Essenes would gather for communal meals, governed by a prescribed order of prayers and rituals. The Essenes didn't own slaves, and they were celibate, for the most part—although Josephus does tell us that there was a subgroup of Essenes who took wives (*War* 2.8.13 [160-61]). Both of our sources agree that the Essenes were masters of herbs and esoteric arts. They vowed to share their secrets with none outside of their sect. Philo also tells us that the Essenes devoted themselves to the "arts of peace," and no one would be found among them who would make or trade weapons (*Every Good Man Is Free* 12.76). Josephus, however, tells us of an Essene who was a general in the Great Revolt against Rome (*War* 3.2.1 [9-12]), and he informs us that the Essenes suffered torture and other afflictions during that war (*War* 2.8.10 [152-53])—clearly indicating that the Essenes were not as pacifistic as Philo seems to imply.

The picture that these sources have drawn of the Essenes is reminiscent in some ways of early Christianity: communal meals, sharing of the wealth, eschewing of earthly pleasures and respect for authority are all characteristic of the first generation of the church (Acts 2:44-47; 4:32—5:11). The Essenes are also similar to the Community that produced the core of the Dead Sea Scrolls (and may, in fact, be one and the same). The members of that Community also pooled their property, engaged in ritualized meals and followed a strict code of conduct. But recent studies have demonstrated that similar ascetic groups existed throughout the Hellenistic world. These so-called friendship groups lived communally, adhered to high moral standards and bound themselves by secret rules and rites. Members of these groups were highly esteemed among the Greeks and Romans for their discipline, even if they were regarded as something of a curiosity. Undoubtedly this is the reason that both Josephus and Philo devote so much attention to the Essenes: they wanted to let the world know that there were Jews who lived in the same laudable fashion as those who were regarded as paragons of virtue by the Hellenistic world.

The Dead Sea Scrolls Community

In the case of the Dead Sea Scroll Community (Hebrew *yahad*) we have a situation that occurs all too rarely in the study of ancient history: instead of us hearing their story second-hand, a group tells us its own story. Of course, the situation is complicated by the fact that the Dead Sea Scrolls aren't all products of the Community. Among the eight or nine hundred scrolls, about a third are biblical, a third are nonbiblical but previously known (such as the book of *Jubilees* and sections of the book of *1 Enoch*) and a third are previously unknown nonbiblical compositions. But even of these texts only a fraction are original compositions created by the sect itself. Others were collected and preserved by the sect but may not represent its actual point of view. So reconstructing the history, beliefs and practices of the Community is a challenge.

The Dead Sea Scrolls very likely represent the Community's library. Based on these texts, most scholars identify the Community as Essene. This identification has much to commend it. First, there's the circumstances around the Scrolls' discovery. Hidden in caves near the Dead Sea, the Scrolls were far removed from any major human habitation. Only a small ruin, Khirbet Qumran, existed in the vicinity of the Scrolls' repositories. But a Roman author, Pliny the Elder, writing in about A.D. 75, observed that there was a group of Essenes living on the western bank of the Dead Sea in his day (*Natural History* 5, 15.73). Many scholars concluded that this group of Essenes must have dwelled at Qumran, since it was the only known habitation in the area.[7] They believe that many of the Dead Sea scrolls were composed at this very site. (Recent archaeological studies have confirmed that the pots in which some of the scrolls were

---

[7]One problem with this identification is that Khirbet Qumran was apparently destroyed by the Romans during the Great Revolt (A.D. 67-74). In that case, Pliny couldn't have seen a group of Essenes living there in A.D. 75.

stored are identical to those found at Khirbet Qumran.)

Another basis for identifying the Scrolls Community with the Essenes is the communal lifestyle shared by the groups. The points of contact are numerous. Both the Community and the Essenes required new recruits to endure a lengthy trial period before they were fully admitted to the group. Only after this trial were members allowed to pool their resources with those of their brethren (1QS 1.11-12; 6.17-22). The Community members eschewed wealth, as did the Essenes (and the Pharisees too, for that matter). Both groups ate communal meals that were presided over by the ranking priest. No one was allowed to be loud or disorderly during the Community meals, and anyone who desired to speak had first to ask permission and be recognized (1QS 6.4-13). Likewise, Josephus observed that the Essenes' meals were orderly affairs, accompanied by a mysterious silence (*War* 2.8.5 [129-33]). Scholars have also observed that both the Essenes and the Dead Sea Community were conspicuously attentive to ritual bathing, but the same observation could be made about most Jewish groups of the day.

More significant, it seems, are the theological similarities between the Essenes and the Dead Sea Community. The Essenes were the only major Jewish sect to teach a form of predestination, arguing that human affairs were entirely in the hands of God. The Dead Sea Scroll Community held a similar view. Each person on earth is born into a "lot," either good or evil. It's the lot that determines a person's conduct in this world, not vice versa. Several texts speak about God's foreordaining of earthly events, including human nature (e.g., 1QS 3.15-16; 9.23-24; 1QH 9.7-8 [= 1.7-8, 31-32]; 7.12-22 [= 15.12-22]). Such ideas would have been very foreign to the teachings of the Pharisees, rabbis or (if Josephus can be trusted on this point) the Sadducees.

Does that mean the group must be Essene? Based on some annoying difficulties with the case, a few scholars have argued against the identification. First, not a single Dead Sea Scroll ever uses the term *Essene,* or anything that could be a Hebrew or Aramaic equivalent. Since both Philo and Josephus know the sect by this title alone, shouldn't the term appear *somewhere* in the group's library? Also, several of the Community's practices can't be reconciled with the descriptions of the Essenes found in our ancient sources. Both Josephus and Philo state emphatically that the Essenes do not marry—although Josephus did allow that there was a subgroup of Essenes who would marry for procreation only. More to the point, Pliny states explicitly that the Essenes who dwelt by the Dead Sea in his day were celibate and no women lived among them. But none of the Dead Sea Scrolls forbid marriage, and one important text—the *Damascus Document*—clearly assumes that the Community members did marry (CD 7.6-8; 4Q266 frag. 9, col. 2). This same text instructs Community members on the sale of slaves (CD 12.10-11) and includes several regulations regarding oaths (e.g., CD 15.1-6; 16.6-12). Josephus and Philo both tell us explicitly that the Essenes did not own slaves and that they refused to take any oaths. Philo tells us that the Essenes didn't perform sacrifices—a position that Josephus probably didn't share. In any case, sacrifice was an extremely important part of the Community's life, as both the *Damascus Document* and the *Songs of the Sabbath Sacrifice* make clear.

Certainly, the Qumran Community was more akin to the Essenes than to the Pharisees or Sadducees. Perhaps they represent a different Essene faction, or perhaps both Josephus and Philo were inaccurate in their descriptions of the Essenes. At any rate there are sufficient differences between the Essenes as described by Josephus and Philo and the Qumran Community to warrant a separate treatment of the groups. Given the diverse landscape of Second Temple-period Judaism, we needn't insist on identifying every Jewish movement as either Pharisee, Sadducee or Essene (after all, no one insists on identifying early Christianity as a sect of the Pharisees!).

It's hard to determine exactly when this group came into existence. There are a number of hints in the scrolls, but no conclusive data. The earliest of the scrolls—a copy of the book of Lamentations—has been dated to around 200 B.C., but the sect may have added that text to its collection when the manuscript was already very old. Most of the texts, according to radiocarbon and other dating methods, were produced in the first century B.C., with some produced earlier and some later. One text, the *Damascus Document*, gives us a good deal of detail regarding the sect's formation—but little, unfortunately, that can be fit into the historical picture provided to us by Josephus and other sources. Other details about the group's history can be gleaned from the *Nahum Pesher* (commentary) and the *Habakkuk Pesher*. The *Nahum Pesher* contains one of the few identifiable historical references in the Scrolls: it refers to an event that occurred during the reign of the Hasmonean priest-king Alexander Janneus (103-76 B.C.), when some Pharisaic leaders attempted to return Judea to Seleucid rule (we'll discuss this affair in chapter seven). Unfortunately, we have no way of knowing if this event happened near the time when the Community was founded or only near the time when the *Nahum Commentary* was written. So as intriguing as the reference may be, it doesn't help us to fix the time when the Community came into existence.

According to the *Damascus Document*, the Community was founded when a group of Jews was disturbed by what they perceived as unrighteousness in the nation's leadership. Specifically, it mentions the sins of polygamy, uncles marrying nieces, leaders amassing wealth and priests defiling the temple (CD 4.13-5.15). This group was leaderless for forty years, until God raised up for them the Teacher of Righteousness. The Teacher was persecuted by a wicked priest and forced to flee with his followers "to Damascus" (perhaps a cryptic term for another location). The *Damascus Document* was written before, or not long after, the Teacher's death, for it predicts that forty years after his demise the righteous would rise up and expel the wicked from the land (CD 20.13-15). In a later text, the *Habakkuk Commentary*, the interpreter tells us that God in his inscrutable wisdom decided to lengthen the "last days"—obviously the time of the end hadn't arrived on schedule (1QpHab 7.5-8). The *Habakkuk Commentary* also witnesses to a new emphasis in the group's eschatological expectations: not only would the wicked Jews be punished, but God would take his war against the Romans as well. The *War Scroll* (1QM; 4QM) describes in detail the seven-year war that would give the "sons of Light" triumph over the "sons of Darkness" (apostate Jews) and the forces of the Kittim (Romans).

From these texts alone we can safely say that the Community came into existence during the Hasmonean era and continued until well into the Roman era. The wicked priest who persecuted the Teacher might have been one of the Hasmonean rulers, since probably only a high priest would have been able to exercise the influence that the "wicked priest" demonstrates. But the long-standing notion that the Community and the Hasmoneans were bitter enemies has been thrown into question by the recent publication of a fragmentary manuscript designated "4Q448." This text has been said to "praise" King Jonathan, but at best it can be said to pronounce a blessing on him. Even that, however, is significant, since the only King Jonathan ever to rule over the Jews was Alexander Janneus, a Hasmonean ruler. Does this text represent the actual views of the Community, or was it a nonsectarian text that somehow ended up in their library? If it represents the Community's views, it might signify a realignment of the Community with its former enemies. Another text, 4QMMT, is a letter in which the Community members explain their reasons for separating from the majority of the Jews. The letter is addressed to someone in authority in Jerusalem, whom the Community members believe will be sympathetic with their position. The letter compares this leader to the ancient kings Solomon and Jeroboam and tells him to remember King David—which suggests that he too was a king. Perhaps here, then, is further evidence of an alliance between the Community and Alexander Janneus. When Janneus died, his successor developed an alliance with the Pharisees—a group the Community largely despised. Once again they would have found themselves to be persona non grata in Jerusalem.

The Community's beliefs are well documented. I've described their semidualistic worldview, similar to that of the Zoroastrians, in chapter three. In the Community's theology God seems somewhat distant from human affairs. Instead, intermediary spirits are in charge of earthly events. The Prince of Light, who apparently is the archangel Michael, governs the "children of light." He's aided in his work by angelic beings. The children of darkness are governed by Belial, the sect's preferred name for the devil. Any evil that befalls the children of light, or any evil they commit, is due to the work of Belial and his minions. The forces of light and darkness are locked in combat from which God remains aloof until the final battle.

The Community shared a belief in a form of predestination with the Essenes. Every human being is born into the children of light or the children of darkness. Astrological factors, such as the positions of the planets at one's birth or the appearance of a comet or other celestial phenomena, may reveal the lot of someone's birth. Unattractive physical features were also considered indications that a person belonged to the children of darkness. But primarily the lot of one's birth was revealed by a person's conduct. Those who adhered to the teachings of the Community, of course, were part of the children of light. The *War Scroll* declares that at the end of the age, the spirits of light and darkness will do battle in heaven while the children of light and darkness battle on earth. Finally, God himself will intervene, and the battle will be decided in favor of the light.

There are only a few vague references in the Dead Sea Scrolls to a resurrection of the dead at the end of time. Clearly, this notion wasn't a prominent feature of the Community's thought. More significant to them, at least in the later period, was the group's actual participation in the final conflict. They expected to be led by two "anointed ones" (messiahs): a messianic high priest and a messianic prince. The high priest seemed to

JEWISH FAMILY STRUCTURE

Most scholars agree that the Old Testament prefers monogamy over polygamy. The creation of Adam and Eve established the pattern for the ideal marriage. The fact that the first polygamist is a descendant of Cain and is a murderer is also significant (Gen 4:19-24). The stories of polygamous marriages are always characterized by strife, as in the case of Abraham and Jacob, or even apostasy, as with Solomon. But in the Near East multiple wives were a sign of wealth and power, and assured many sons to carry on the family name. The Israelites adopted the custom, and God allowed it to persist for a season. Polygamy went out of style in the Hellenistic era for reasons I'll discuss in a later chapter.

The Old Testament encouraged endogamy—marriage with other Israelites only—and promoting endogamy was an important aspect of Ezra and Nehemiah's ministries. Leviticus 18, however, prohibits Israelite men from marrying their close kin, including their sisters, mothers or stepmothers, daughters or stepdaughters, in-laws, granddaughters, or aunts. The prohibition against marrying one's aunt was understood narrowly by most Jews, and the rabbis considered it fine for a girl to marry her uncle. But the Dead Sea Scroll Community argued that a law addressed to men covered women as well, and prohibited uncles from marrying their nieces.

"Levirate marriage" (*levir*, Latin, "brother-in-law") is the name given to the custom of a man marrying his brother's childless widow in order to produce a son in his brother's name. The Old Testament considers it a brother's duty to "raise up seed" for his sibling (Deut 25:5-10). But John the Baptist criticized Herod Antipas for marrying his brother's widow (Mk 6:18). John regarded Herod's marriage as a violation of Leviticus 18's prohibition against in-law marriage because the widow already had children—so the levirate clause didn't apply.

enjoy preeminence in most ritual and legislative matters. The primary role of the "prince of the congregation," as the messianic prince is called, is to lead the children of light in the final battle.

The Community's beliefs certainly distinguished them from the major Jewish sects of the day. But in their texts and letters they place little emphasis on their unique doctrines. Rather, it's their unique *practices* that they emphasize as the cause of their separation from the Jews at large. One of the most divisive issues was the proper understanding of the calendar. In the intertestamental period (and on into our own day), the ritual calendar used by the majority of the Jews was based on observations of the moon. When the last vestiges of the moon disappeared—when the "new moon" occurred—it was declared a new month. And after twelve such months, it was a new year. The Jewish fasts, festivals and sacrifices were celebrated on certain fixed days of the *month* rather than fixed days of the *year*. This system worked well for ancient societies where printed calendars would have been a luxury that not everyone could afford. The peasants could simply count the days from the new moon to know when they should fast or sacrifice or bring their crops to market.

The problem with the lunar calendar is that it's about ten days shorter than the solar year—the time the earth actually takes to revolve around the sun. So with each passing lunar year, the holy days would arrive ten days earlier in the solar year. If the situation weren't corrected, the Jews could have ended up celebrating their autumn harvest festivals in the early summer! The Jews developed a system in which they would periodically add an additional month to the year—the "second Adar"—to bring the calendar back into line with the seasons (a system we call "intercalation"). So twice every seven years, the Jews would celebrate a "leap year," with a full extra month. By this method they kept the position of the special days relatively stable.

Some of the Jews, however, believed that this system was a corruption of God's original plan. The earliest evidence of this discontent comes from the "Astronomical Book" of 1 *Enoch* (chaps. 72-82), written probably in the third century B.C. This book advocates a 364-day "luni-solar" calendar, divided into twelve lunar months and fifty-two weeks. The book of *Jubilees*, written in the mid-second century B.C., also argues for a solar year rather than a lunar year. (Neither text makes provision for a "leap year," so this calendar too would have eventually been out of sync with the actual $365\frac{1}{4}$-day solar year.) The Community preserved these documents and may have read them as

THE JEWISH CALENDAR

The Old Testament records the names of several months used in ancient Israel. They are Abib (the first month, see Ex 13:4), Ziv (1 Kings 6:1, 37), Ethnaim (1 Kings 8:2) and Bul (1 Kings 6:38). But during the Babylonian exile, the Jews abandoned the old names and adopted those given to the months by the Babylonians. In their Hebrew forms the names of the months are:

1. Nisan (March-April)
2. Iyyar (April-May)
3. Sivan (May-June)
4. Tammuz (June-July)
5. Ab (July-August)
6. Elul (August-September)
7. Tishri (September-October)
8. Marcheshvan (October-November)
9. Chislev (November-December)
10. Tebeth (December-January)
11. Shebat (January-February)
12. Adar (February-March)

In the leap years they added another month, Adar Sheni (Second Adar). These same months are still used by Jews today in their calendar of religious holidays.

Scripture. They adopted the luni-solar calendar as their own and castigated the majority of the Jews for failing to observe feasts and sacrifices on their proper days. The letter mentioned above, 4QMMT, includes a detailed exposition on how the luni-solar calendar would work, which days would be observed as sabbaths and when the major Jewish festivals would be celebrated.

Other issues addressed in 4QMMT included marriage customs, with the Community arguing against not only polygamy and the marriage of uncles to their nieces but also of priests marrying women from nonpriestly families. They also had much to say about proper methods of sacrifice and maintaining the holiness of the temple by barring anyone with physical defects. In contrast to our day when churches, synagogues and public buildings are striving to become barrier-free, the Community was outraged that the handicapped were permitted access to the temple precincts. They were also concerned with proper methods of purification. For instance, it was the Jewish custom when performing a ritual washing to simply pour water from a single container over the hands of several people. But the Community argued that the impurity on the first person's hands traveled up the stream of water and rendered the water in the container unclean. Anyone else who washed with water from the same container was simply adding to his impurity!

With all the theological matters that could have set them at odds with each other, it might seem strange to modern Christians that the Jews "quibbled" so much about matters of *halakhah*. But the Jews believed that these rituals and rules had to be properly observed or the nation's relationship with God was in jeopardy. If the Day of Atonement, when the priests made atonement for the sins of the nation, were not observed properly, would the Jews still be forgiven? If the sacrifice was performed on the wrong day or the priest was sacrificing with unclean hands, would God still accept the offering? The Community believed that the nation was continuing to bear its sins because the priests who served in the temple were not following the proper calendar and were performing the rituals in a state of impurity. So while it might sound to us like quibbling, to these Jews it would be *we* who are quibbling, when we divide into sects over matters so "unimportant" as whether or not God predestines us for salvation! An important distinction between Christianity and Judaism is that Christians teach that we establish and maintain a relationship with God through *believing* the right things; Jews emphasize that the relationship is established and maintained by *doing* the right things. In their opinion, correctly performing the sacrifices, sabbath observances, purification rites and so on would make the difference between national prosperity and destruction.

So to the various sects the power to dictate how the Jewish people would observe their feasts and sacrifices was very significant. Each group was convinced that theirs was the right way and coveted the authority to impose their practices on the nation as a whole. In the decades to come, power struggles between the various sects would come to play a most significant role in Judean politics.

For Further Reading

The official publications of the Dead Sea Scrolls are found in the *Discoveries in the Judaean Desert* series, published in Oxford by Clarendon. They contain facsimiles, translations and commentaries. Some popular translation editions are listed at the end of chapter one.

Brooke, George J. *Exegesis at Qumran.* Sheffield, England: Sheffield Academic Press, 1985.

Cook, Edward. *Solving the Mystery of the Dead Sea Scrolls.* Grand Rapids: Zondervan, 1994. Written especially for Christian laypeople.

Neusner, Jacob. *Rabbinic Traditions About the Pharisees before 70.* Leiden: Brill, 1971. Multivolume set deals critically with a wide variety of literature.

Nickelsburg, George W. E., and Michael E. Stone, *Faith and Piety in Early Judaism.* Philadelphia: Fortress, 1983. Chapter 1, "Sects and Parties," collects source data from ancient authors. It uses the Dead Sea Scrolls as primary sources for the Essenes.

Porton, Gary G. "Diversity in Postbiblical Judaism," in *Early Judaism and its Modern Interpreters.* Atlanta: Scholars Press, 1986.

Rivkin, Ellis. *A Hidden Revolution: The Pharisees' Search for the Kingdom Within.* Nashville: Abingdon, 1978. An influential but controversial work that tends to take rabbinic traditions very literally.

Saldarini, Anthony J. *Pharisees, Scribes and Sadducees in Palestinian Society.* Wilmington, Del.: Michael Glazier, 1988. As the name implies, this work makes extensive use of sociological theory and categories.

Sanders, E. P. *Jewish Law from Jesus to the Mishnah.* Philadelphia: Trinity, and London: SCM Press, 1990. Chapter 2, "Did the Pharisees Have Oral Law?" argues that the Pharisees didn't have an oral law in the way it's usually conceived.

Schürer, Emil. *A History of the Jewish People in the Age of Jesus Christ.* Edited by Geza Vermes, Fergus Millar and Matthew Black. Vol. 2, §§26, 30. Edinburgh: T & T Clark, 1979.

Talmon, Shemaryahu. "The Internal Diversification of Judaism," in *Jewish Civilization in the Hellenistic-Roman Period.* Edited by Shamaryahu Talmon. Philadelphia: Trinity Press, 1991. Addresses the question of Jewish "sectarianism" and unity.

VanderKam, James. *The Dead Sea Scrolls Today.* Grand Rapids: Eerdmans, 1994. Argues that the Scrolls were written by Essenes, but presents other views fairly.

7

The Second Jewish Commonwealth

It's amazing how much the Jewish rebels managed to accomplish, given their circumstances. They had brought an end to the persecution; they had secured their rights to live and worship as they pleased; they had won for themselves a measure of respectability. They'd even managed to commandeer the high priesthood—a position that allowed them to impose their own understandings of Judaism on the entire nation. But there remained one prize that had eluded the Hasmoneans: national independence. As long as the Jews remained under the "yoke of the Gentiles," as they called it, their fate was insecure. And only when they were truly independent would they be completely free from the reproach that had hung over them since the days of the Babylonian exile. It would be the ultimate evidence that God had forgiven his people and restored them to his favor. So it was to this end—the complete liberation of Judea—that the Hasmonean attentions were directed.

Simon Hashmonai

After Jonathan's execution the Hasmonean partisans installed Simon as high priest and ruler of the Jews.[1] Undoubtedly, there was some controversy regarding this move; the high priests had been appointed by the foreign monarchs for as long as anyone could remember. And in spite of the circumstances, the Jews were still very much the subjects of the Seleucid

---

[1]Primary sources for this section are 1 Macc 13:1—16:22; *Ant.* 12.4.9 (213-29).

Empire. Jews who were loyal to Syria would have insisted on waiting until the king himself—Demetrius, of course (not the usurper Antiochus VI)—made the appointment. Some of the pious, too, might have been reluctant to make such a move, preferring to wait for prophetic guidance (see 1 Macc 14:41). But by now Simon and his supporters were acting almost independently of the Syrians. Having won an end to the persecution and having pried control of Jerusalem from the Hellenists, it seemed to them that the Hasmoneans had a right to rule, regardless of what the Syrians might have supposed.

Meanwhile, the Syrian general Tryphon had decided that he too had the right to rule. Abandoning his pretense of working as regent for Antiochus VI, the tyrant now had the young monarch murdered and proclaimed himself king. Of course, it was out of the question for Simon to acknowledge the sovereignty of this pretender. Instead, he pledged Jewish support to the former ruler Demetrius II—the very king whose reneging on early promises had led the Hasmoneans to their fatal alliance with Tryphon. But Simon knew that Demetrius wouldn't betray him again. He was in desperate need of allies, and the Jews had proven their usefulness. So Simon presented his bold demand: the Jews were to be exempted from paying any tribute to the Seleucids henceforth. Essentially, it was a demand for autonomy. If the Jews paid no tribute, the Syrians gained no benefit from having them as subjects. The tribute was not only a source of revenue for the empire, it was a sign of submission. Simon was declaring his independence, and Demetrius was in no position to refuse. He accepted the conditions and confirmed Simon as high priest and ruler of the Jews. Officially, at least, the Jews were now free from "yoke of the Gentiles" (1 Macc 13:41). Indeed, the event was considered so significant that the Jews began to date their treaties from, say, "the year one of Simon, the high priest," instead of dating them by the Seleucid chronology.

Simon then began to make his nation secure. His first campaign took him against Gazara, an important fortress on the border of Philistia. He took control of the city, expelled its Gentile inhabitants and replaced them with pious Jews. Then he turned his attention to the prize that had eluded both of his brothers: the Akra in Jerusalem. The Syrian troops stationed there had pledged their support to Tryphon, so Simon could wage war on them under the guise of loyal service to the king. Soon the men inside the Akra were starved into surrender and expelled from Jerusalem in 141 B.C. Simon incorporated the sturdy fortress into the temple complex and began to reside there himself.

Things seemed to be going very well for Simon in this period. Indeed, the book of 1 Maccabees portrays this portion of his reign as something of a golden era, drawing on the imagery used by the prophets for the messianic age. With the nation at relative rest and his popularity high, it seemed a good time for a public acknowledgement of Maccabean rule. Interestingly enough, to this point the Hasmonean brothers had led the Jews without having official recognition from their own people. The foreign monarchs had recognized their rights to serve as the leaders of the Jews, but the Jews themselves—as a people—had not. So in 140 B.C. a great assembly was held in Jerusalem, bringing together priests, scribes, politicians and military leaders. Simon was officially proclaimed high priest, governor and supreme military commander of the Jews. What's more, the position was made hereditary. This meant Simon's sons would fill the office after him. It was a landmark day—the Jews themselves now acknowledged that the old order had passed away. Earlier, Menelaus had stolen the high priesthood away from the Zadokite family through bribery, much to the consternation of the Jews. Now, the Jews were giving the high priesthood willingly to the Hasmoneans.

It was about that same year, 140 or 139 B.C., that Demetrius was captured by the Parthians. Quickly his brother, Antiochus VII Sidetes, rose to claim the throne. It took him several months to secure his command over the empire, and he had to enlist Jewish aid to dislodge the troublesome tyrant Tryphon. Free (for the moment) from rival claimants on the throne, Sidetes could begin consolidating his realm. And one of the first issues that needed attention was the uppity attitude of the Jews. Simon had expanded his realm at the expense of some Gentile towns, and Sidetes felt some compensation was in order. His demand was simple and direct: the Jews were to release their claims on Jaffa, Gazara and the Akra. But Sidetes was willing to negotiate with his allies. If the Jews refused to release these towns, they could instead pay one thousand talents for them.

Considering that the Jews had taken the cities by force without order from their sovereign overlords, it must have seemed like a reasonable request. But to Simon and his party it was out of the question. If they surrendered Jaffa, their communication route to the sea would be cut off. With Syrians garrisoned in the Akra the Gentiles would once again brood over Jerusalem. Apparently Simon's party believed that Sidetes lacked the will to take the towns from them. So Simon refused to release the Akra and offered to pay not one thousand but only one hundred talents for the contested towns—an offer that he must have known would be refused.

Sidetes was still engaged in his pursuit of Tryphon, so he sent his general Cendebeus to deal with the Jews. Setting up his base in Jamnia, Cendebeus began to launch assaults into Judean territory. Simon was now too old to take to the battlefield, so he put his sons John and Judas in charge of the counterattack. The armies met on the plain near the Hasmoneans' hometown, Modein. And once again the Jews were victorious, and Cendebus was forced to flee for his life. Sidetes made no more attempts to invade Judea while Simon reigned as governor and high priest.

We might have hoped that Simon, unlike his brothers, could have gone to his grave in peace. But such was not to be the case. His son-in-law, Ptolemy, governor of the plain of Jericho, had ambitions of his own. In 135 or 134 B.C. he invited Simon and his sons Judas and Mattathias to a feast at a little stronghold called Dok. When the old priest and the young men were quite drunk, Ptolemy and his accomplices killed them. He then sent messengers to King Sidetes, offering to deliver the country into his hands. Assassins were dispatched to Gazara to kill Simon's other son, John Hyrcanus. But John got word of the plot, and the assassins were arrested and executed. He then rushed to Jerusalem to secure the city against the assault that inevitably would follow.

John Hyrcanus

The book of 1 Maccabees ends with the ascent of John Hyrcanus to the high priesthood, but it tells us almost nothing about his reign.[2] From this point forward we depend on Josephus for information about the Hasmoneans. Where Josephus got his information is anyone's guess. To date there's been no definitive answer for that question. So we're forced to take him largely at his word, occasionally supplementing our account with information from Greek and Roman sources.

Simon's surviving son bore the sobriquet "John Hyrcanus." The name Jonathan, meaning "gift of the Lord," was well attested in Jewish circles, its most famous bearer being the son of King Saul. The name Hyrcanus, on the other hand, requires some explanation. Hyrcania was a territory in Persia that ran around the southern edge of the Caspian Sea, north of modern Tehran. The church historian Eusebius and others claimed that

---

[2]Primary sources for this section are *Ant.* 13.8.1-10.7 (230-300); *War* 1.2.3-2.8 (55-69).

John Hyrcanus had earned his title by conquering the Hyrcanians with the Seleucid army. And that could well be the case. John did fight with Antiochus VII Sidetes against the Parthians in the east, perhaps actually serving in Hyrcania. On the other hand, the name Hyrcanus is attested in Jewish sources well before the time of Simon and John. Any Jew who had lived in Hyrcania (as many had) and migrated back to Israel could have been identified as "the Hyrcanian," just as Uriah in 2 Samuel 11 was called "the Hittite," even though he appears to have been thoroughly Israelite. Such a geographical epithet might continue to serve as a family name for generations after its significance was lost. So there may have been a Hyrcanian Jew somewhere in the Hasmonean family tree, and the name might have been passed down to Simon's son as a family tradition. In any case, John Hyrcanus is often identified in the literature simply by his cognomen, Hyrcanus.

When the treasonous Ptolemy arrived at Jerusalem, he found the city already securely in the hands of Hyrcanus. Unable to take control of Judea, the murderer fled back to the fortress city where he had committed the crime, Dok. Hyrcanus pursued him there and began to lay siege to Dok's small but formidable ramparts. He would have taken the city rather quickly if not for one tragic complication: Ptolemy held Hyrcanus's mother as a hostage inside the city. Each time it looked as if the city would fall, Ptolemy would have her brought to the city wall and threaten to throw her to her death. Hyrcanus stayed his hand in hopes of finding some way to rescue his mother. But soon the sabbatical year arrived, and according to Jewish law Hyrcanus had to lift his siege and return to Jerusalem. Ptolemy, in a crowning act of craven spite, killed Hyrcanus's mother and escaped from Judea.[3]

It wasn't a good way for the reign of John Hyrcanus to begin, but things would get worse before they got better. Antiochus VII Sidetes hadn't forgotten the debt owed to him by Simon, nor the way his army had been humiliated. In about 135 B.C. he invaded Judea, vented his wrath on the land and laid siege to Jerusalem itself. After the city had been besieged for over a year and reduced to near starvation, Hyrcanus requested Sidetes's terms for surrender. After some negotiation it was settled that the Jews would relinquish their arms, pay tribute for the cities they had conquered and send

---

[3]Josephus's account of these events is somewhat muddled, and some scholars suggest that the siege of Dok might have occurred later in John's reign, perhaps around 129 B.C.

hostages to Syria. Perhaps most humiliating of all, the walls of Jerusalem were demolished as well.

It was certainly an inauspicious beginning for Hyrcanus's career. But the tide was soon to turn. In a remarkable stroke of luck an ancient tomb was found in Judea—identified by Josephus as none other than the tomb of King David. Considering the dire circumstances that gripped his nation, Hyrcanus felt justified in raiding the tomb. He used part of the treasure to pay his tribute to Syria and still had funds to begin rebuilding his army. In what must have been a very controversial move, he hired foreign mercenaries to fill out the ranks of the army. (After all, Jewish soldiers fighting for their homes and their rights had proven themselves capable of some extraordinary victories.) But in spite of shoring up his defenses, Hyrcanus's troubles weren't over. In 131 B.C. Sidetes decided to undertake a campaign against Parthia. The king didn't trust Hyrcanus to remain loyal while Sidetes was in the East, so he forced Hyrcanus and a band of Jewish soldiers to accompany him on the campaign. After some initial success Sidetes decided to push into the very heartland of the Parthian Empire. There, he fell in battle, but Hyrcanus was able to return safely home to Jerusalem.

When a strong and competent sovereign led the Seleucid Empire, the Jewish state couldn't resist its will. Antiochus VII Sidetes, however, was the last Seleucid monarch who could be described in those terms. When he was killed in 129 B.C. the incompetent Demetrius II, having been released from Parthian captivity, once again laid claim to the throne. Almost at once a rival appeared, presenting himself as the son of Alexander Balas. So once again the Seleucid Empire was at war with itself, and so it would remain, with only brief respites, for the next sixty years. It was this fact alone that made it possible for the Hasmoneans to forge something of an empire of their own.

In the midst of the Syrian confusion Hyrcanus followed in the footsteps of his predecessors by seeking to expand Judean holdings in Palestine. A number of considerations shaped this aggressive policy. National security was surely one factor. With the Syrians to the north and the power of the Arabic Nabateans waxing in the southeast, Judea needed as much of a buffer zone around its homeland as it could get. By securing territories on its borders Judea gained a measure of protection from invaders coming in through the "back door." Religious considerations also were a factor. Judea was a small nation with a fierce sense of national destiny. Its God wasn't one of the many gods worshiped by the nations; he was the true Lord of heaven and earth. The Jews were probably engaged in proselytizing in this era, and they weren't above spreading their faith through conquest. Some scholars have even argued that Hyrcanus was driven by a desire to fulfill biblical prophecies about God's conquest of the nations. He may have believed that his victories over the Gentiles would usher in the reign of God and his people, the Jews. But it seems difficult to believe that Hyrcanus saw himself as a crusader in a holy war, considering how many Gentile mercenaries he employed in his army. A holy war can hardly be waged by unholy troops!

Whether motivated by piety or politics, Hyrcanus wasted little time setting his war machine in motion. He first turned his attention to the east, where he conquered the fortress of Medaba on the other side of the Jordan River. By securing this Moabite city for the Jews, Hyrcanus provided his country with an important outpost on its eastern border. It would be very difficult to invade Judea from the east as long as the Jews held Medaba.

The strategic importance of this move is obvious. But his next conquest was more remarkable both for its religious dimension and its far-reaching impact. Hyrcanus turned his attention to the north, the land of the Samaritans. In this period the Samaritans were a substantial people, perhaps as numerous as the Jews themselves. Hyrcanus captured the city of Shechem and Mount Gerizim, destroying the Samaritan temple located there. The move was both indicative of the troubled relations that already existed between the two groups and further fuel for the flames. Jews and Samaritans continued in bitter enmity for centuries to come.

Hyrcanus then turned his attention to the south, to the land of Idumea. Here, he conquered the towns of Marissa and Adora. The inhabitants of these towns were offered a choice: they could go into exile from their land into the harsh countryside, or they could convert to Judaism. By offering them this option Hyrcanus may have thought he was fulfilling the requirements of Deuteronomy 23:7, "You shall not abhor the Edomite, for he is your brother." But he may have had political motives as well as religious motives. Conversion to Judaism would do much to insure the Idumeans' loyalty to their conquerors. They would be bound to the Jews by religion and estranged from their own people by apostasy. But the forced conversions are bitterly ironic. The Hasmonean Revolt had begun because Antiochus Epiphanes had tried to impose his religion on the people of Judea. The Jews had fought for the right to decide for themselves how they would worship the Lord. But now the Judeans were imposing their faith on their own subjects on pain of death. The lesson of religious tolerance had been lost on them.

WHO WERE THE IDUMEANS?

The Idumeans were significant figures in New Testament times. Herod the Great and his son, Herod Antipas, were both of Idumean descent. But who were these people?

Idumea was located to the southeast of Judea. It was a strategic location, crisscrossed by important trade routes. The name Idumea implies that the region was populated by descendants of the biblical Edomites, but the historical relationship between the former and latter is unclear. Idumea was located further west than Edom had been, and the Arabian Nabateans now inhabited the territory once known as Edom. Most likely Arab invasions had forced the Edomites to migrate west. At any rate the Jews believed that the Idumeans were descended from the Edomites, and it sometimes worked to their advantage, since the Old Testament orders, "You shall not abhor any of the Edomites, for they are your kin" (Deut 23:7). The Edomites were the descendants of Esau, Isaac's elder son.

Before their conversion to Judaism, the Idumeans had been polytheists. Their chief god was called Qaus. They might also have worshiped the Lord as part of their pantheon, since some important Yahwistic sites were located in Edom.

If the forced conversions alone weren't cruel enough, the Idumeans also had to contend with the Jews' haughty condescension. Many of the converts made a sincere attempt to adopt the religion of their conquerors, albeit with some inevitable elements from their former faith brought into the mix. After a generation or two the Idumean proselytes thought of themselves as good Jews. But to the native-born Jews the converts were (in Greek) *hemiioudaioi,* or "half-Jews," even several generations after the conquest. They were considered suspect in observance of Jewish laws, unfit for marriage to a priest's daughter or even to enter the temple. In spite of their good faith, they were held in contempt.

Hyrcanus continued to expand his territory throughout the Promised Land at the expense of Syrian holdings. The procedure he devised for dealing with the Idumeans became the rule for all his conquests: those who would not convert would face exile or death. Around 114 B.C. the Seleucids managed to push back the Hasmonean forces and reclaim some lost territory, but another civil war cost them these gains. Hyrcanus was establishing a sizable realm for himself, as large as the kingdom that had been ruled by Solomon. He was acting in utter independence of the Seleucid Empire. He apparently minted coins for use in the land and reaffirmed the long-standing alliance between the Jews and the Romans. Yet he never took for himself the title "king." Such a step would have scandalized the pious, since the prophetic promises stated that only a descendant of King David was to reign in Judah (2 Sam 7:11-16). The prophets had predicted that a monarch from the line of David would rule the nation and restore its glory (Is 11:1-10; Jer 23:5-8; Ezek 34:23-24). It was one matter to set aside the tradition of Zadokite high priesthood; it was quite another matter to disregard the words of holy Scripture. Hyrcanus satisfied himself with the high priesthood and "presidency" of Judea.

One of the last conquests of Hyrcanus's long reign was that of the city of Samaria. By 111 B.C. Hyrcanus was too old to take part in the battle himself. Instead, he entrusted the task to his two eldest sons. The names by which they are known to us are Antigonus and Aristobulus—Greek names rather than Hebrew. It was quite common in those days for upper-class Jews to be given a Hebrew name that they used in their homeland and to adopt a Greek name for use in international situations. But it's somewhat striking to see the sons of Hyrcanus identified primarily by their Greek names before the Hasmonean dynasty was barely established. Perhaps this identification is due to the changing nature of our sources. Previously, Josephus had relied primarily on the nationalistic Jewish document 1 Maccabees for information about the Hasmoneans—a text that would have naturally preferred using the Hasmoneans' Hebrew names, since it depicted them as defenders of traditional Jewish culture. Now, Josephus may have been relying on Roman or Greek sources, or accounts by Hellenistic Jews, or diplomatic records from the Hasmonean dynasty. These sources would very likely have employed the sons' official Greek names rather than their given Hebrew names.

The two young men received ample opportunity to test their mettle at Samaria. For many decades the capital city of Samaria had been populated not by native Samaritans but by Greek soldiers, foreign mercenaries and other colonists. So when the brothers began their siege, the residents appealed to Antiochus IX Cyzenicus for help. Cyzenicus came quickly to their aid, bringing a sizable army with him. But the Hasmonean brothers proved equal to the challenge. Cyzenicus blunted his sword against them for a while, then he returned to Syria, leaving the defense of Samaria in the hand of his underlings. With Cyzenicus and the bulk of his forces out of the picture, the Jews achieved easy victories over the Syrian army, forcing them to withdraw. Samaria was abandoned to its fate. After a year's siege the city was taken and razed completely to the ground.

Little else is known about the political events of Hyrcanus's long reign. When he died, around 104 B.C., he left a Jewish nation as strong as any in its history. But just as the kingdom of David and Solomon had enjoyed its success because of the relative weakness of Egypt and Assyria, John's commonwealth could thrive only so long as the mighty empires around him were distracted by internal affairs. A strong Jewish nation was still no match for the huge Seleucid and Ptolemaic empires. The Hasmonean's best hope for success was the continued bickering within and between the two empires.

One more development of Hyrcanus's reign deserves notice here. During this period the Pharisees and Sadducees begin to figure prominently in Josephus's narrative. Josephus first mentioned the Pharisees in connection with the high priesthood of Jonathan, Hyrcanus's uncle. But it's not until the reign of Hyrcanus that these Jewish sects appear as political forces. According to our historian, Hyrcanus first favored the Pharisees in his administration. But Eleazar, one of the Pharisaic leaders, told Hyrcanus that he should step down from the high priesthood since he understood (incorrectly) that Hyrcanus's mother had once been taken captive by the Greeks. (In Jewish tradition the son of a former captive was not qualified for the priesthood because he might be the product of rape and not a "pure" Jew.) Hyrcanus demanded that the Pharisees punish the offender severely, but they would only agree to imprison Eleazar for a time. John Hyrcanus became so enraged that he broke with the Pharisees and allied with the Sadducees instead (*Ant.* 13.10.5-6 [288-96]).

How much historical fact lies behind the account? It's difficult to say. The *halakhah* (Jewish legal regulation) concerning the parentage of the high priest might not have been in existence in the time of Hyrcanus. But the

Pharisees might well have taken issue with Hyrcanus's high priesthood on other grounds: this sect placed a strong emphasis on the authority of tradition, and the Hasmoneans had certainly violated tradition by assuming for themselves the role of high priest. Whatever the reason, Josephus is probably correct in assuming that the Hasmoneans weren't ideologically opposed to the Pharisees, but rather it was the Pharisees who had difficulties with the Hasmoneans.

The alliance between the Hasmoneans and Sadducees had some profound political implications. According to Josephus, the Sadducees were an elitist party, closely affiliated with the wealthy and powerful families in Judea. He also tells us that they were considered boorish and contentious. The Pharisees, on the other hand, were the populist party, more in touch with the average Jew. None of the sects could lay claim to many members—most Jews were simply Jews, never thinking of themselves as belonging to one group or another. But if Josephus's picture is accurate, the Pharisees had much popular sympathy. So the alignment of the Hasmoneans with the Sadducees had the effect of deepening the rift between Judea's leadership and the majority of its people. The heroes of the revolution were beginning to accumulate offences against traditions, morals and public sensibilities.

A final note on John Hyrcanus: according to Josephus this accomplished high priest was honored not only with military success but with the gift of prophecy as well (*War* 1.2.8 [68-69]). We're told that he correctly predicted the turmoil that would fall on the kingdom after his death. Whether or not Hyrcanus was actually a prophet is hard for us to say. But the statement does give us some interesting insights about the understanding of prophecy in Josephus's time. It indicates that the Jews didn't believe that prophecy had completely ceased during the intertestamental period, as scholars often claim. Rather, Josephus tells us that there had been no precise succession of prophets since the days of the Persian king Artaxerxes.[4] Josephus believed there had been a change in the prophetic office since the time of Artaxerxes, but the precise significance of his statement is unclear.

Aristobulus I

The reign of John Hyrcanus certainly had elements of moral ambiguity,

---

[4]Josephus *Against Apion* 1.8 (41).

CLERICAL ("PRIESTLY") PROPHECY

In the Second Temple Period, some Jews came to believe that prophecy adhered to certain offices, irrespective of one's piety or wisdom. One of the most important prophetic offices was the priesthood. Ezra 2:63 (= Neh 7:65) gives the responsibility of using the *urim* and *thummim*, or divinatory apparatus, to the priests. Divination isn't exactly prophecy, but it does require certain special gifts. John Hyrcanus is said to have possessed the gift of prophecy, and his power probably derived from his role as high priest (*War* 1.2.8 [68-69]). Josephus also claimed to possess some prophetic abilities and ascribes his gifts to his priestly heritage (*War* 3.8.3 [350-54]). In the New Testament the high priest Caiaphas prophesied about Jesus, saying, "it is better for you to have one man die for the people than to have the whole nation destroyed." His ability to prophesy is attributed to his role as high priest (John 11:47-52).

but we can't lay the same charge against the administration of his eldest son Aristobulus: if Josephus can be trusted at all, Aristobulus's reign was unambiguously wicked.[5] Hyrcanus had never intended for Aristobulus to become ruler of the Jews, perhaps recognizing the young man's ruthlessness. Instead, he'd instructed that Aristobulus would take over as high priest (apparently one's moral character was scant consideration in holding that high office in those days), while his widow would reign over the country. It would have been quite an innovation for Judea to have a female sovereign. The only queen who had ever ruled over the Jews, Athaliah (842-837 B.C.), had been notoriously evil. But thanks to the vigorous leadership of the Cleopatras in Egypt, attitudes about women leaders had un-

---

[5]Since Greek sources report on his reign quite favorably, some scholars have suggested that Josephus's sources exaggerated or fabricated Aristobulus's evil deeds. It is, in fact, impossible to say with certainty, since no one but Josephus bothers to give us any details about Aristobulus's rise to power. Primary sources for this section are *Ant.* 13.11.1-3 (301-19); *War* 1.3.1-6 (70-84).

dergone some change. These Ptolemaic femmes fatales had already proven just as vigorous and competent as their male counterparts. So even though Hebrew women had traditionally been relegated to the private sphere of life, John Hyrcanus felt confident that his widow's leadership would be accepted.

What he hadn't taken into account was Aristobulus's colossal ambition. Unsatisfied with the high priesthood alone, he immediately conspired to have his mother thrown into prison. But knowing that her existence would always pose a threat to his rule, he also ordered that she be given no food, and she starved to death. His brothers, who might try to avenge their mother, were also imprisoned. Only Antigonus was deemed above suspicion. This favored brother was even allowed to share the seat of government for a short while. But the favors bestowed on Antigonus inspired other ambitious men in the Judean court to jealousy. They began to exploit Aristobulus's paranoia, warning him that Antigonus planned to murder him and take the high priesthood himself. Aristobulus ordered his bodyguard to watch for Antigonus. If he should attempt to come into Aristobulus's presence bearing weapons, the guard was to kill him. Thus the trap was set. The enemies then sent word to Antigonus that Aristobulus had heard he'd gotten new weapons and wanted to see them. So Antigonus set out for the citadel decked out in his full amour and carrying his weapons, never suspecting his danger. He was never asked why he had come to the citadel; he was simply executed at once. Aristobulus, to his credit, was overwhelmed with grief and guilt. He sank into a dark state of mind that broke his health and brought about his rapid death in 103 B.C., after a reign of only a year.

In that short period of time Aristobulus managed to dramatically alter the shape of the Hasmonean legacy. Not only did he set standards for morality that would have made King Ahab blush; he also abandoned entirely the emphasis on tradition that had been so much a driving force behind the revolution. Both Simon and John Hyrcanus had exercised sovereign authority in Judea, but neither of them had dared to take the title "king." The offense that such an arrogation would have given the conservative Jews restrained the brothers. Aristobulus, however, didn't deny himself the royal title. He combined in his person both the royal and sacerdotal offices, destroying the separation of powers that had existed for as long as Israel had been ruled by kings. He also laid aside any pretense of resistance to the spread of Greek culture in Judea. Indeed, he apparently assumed the title *philellen*, "Greek lover." A rather ironic cognomen for the first Hasmonean to claim the royal throne of Judea!

In spite of his rejection of tradition Aristobulus continued one of his father's policies: he expanded the kingdom even further and compelled the inhabitants of conquered lands to convert to Judaism. Aristobulus added part of the land of Iturea, in Lebanon, to the Judean kingdom. Even more important, it was during his reign that much of the land of Galilee, home of Jesus, was conquered and converted to Judaism. Like the Idumeans the inhabitants of this realm would long be regarded with suspicion by the Judean Jews. For many years to come it was called "Galilee of the Gentiles" because the population of the area was largely non-Jewish. But many Galileans now became Jewish converts, and many Judean Jews would move north to the lush, cosmopolitan region and make it their home.

Alexander Janneus

Aristobulus was survived by his rather remarkable widow, Alexandra Salome. Alexandra ordered the surviving sons of Hyrcanus released from prison and married the eldest, Jonathan (Greek, Janneus).[6] Jonathan took the grandiose title "Alexander" as his cognomen, and followed in his brother's footsteps by claiming the title "king" as well as high priest. He began his reign in 103 B.C. and continued in office for about twenty-seven years—a long reign that allowed him to accomplish far more mischief than his brother ever managed.

Like his ancestors before him, Janneus had his mind set on expanding the Judean kingdom. He began with an expedition to the Mediterranean coast, to the city of Ptolemais (Acco). It would have been a good acquisition, giving the Jews easy access to the sea and the wealthy markets beyond. But the residents of the city had other ideas. They resisted successfully at first on their own. But then Ptolemy IX Lathyrus, who had been banished by his mother Cleopatra III to Cyprus, arrived on the scene with a large army, forcing Janneus to lift the siege of Ptolemais. Janneus lost his intended acquisition, but in consolation he formed an alliance with Ptolemy, promising to help him conquer Egypt if he would help Janneus conquer Phoenicia. But Janneus was a treacherous ally. He had sent messengers to Cleopatra, informing the queen of Ptolemy's invasion plans. When Ptolemy learned of the duplicity, he was justifiably furious. His

---

[6]Primary sources for this section are *Ant.* 13.12.1-15.5 (320-404); *War* 1.4.1-8 (85-106).

army invaded Judea, reducing towns to rubble, slaughtering women and children, and decimating Janneus's army.

Cleopatra wouldn't allow her son to conquer Judea—she hated and feared him too deeply to allow him to grow so strong. Nor would the Jews of Egypt remain quiet while their country was threatened with destruction. Two high commanders in Cleopatra's army were Jewish, and they persuaded her to mobilize against her son before he could gain a foothold in Judea. Cleopatra's army drove Lathyrus back to Cyprus. Janneus presented himself before his deliverer, and threw himself on her mercy. The queen of Egypt had the fate of Judea in her hands. Should she allow Janneus to continue to rule over Judea as king? Or should she annex his kingdom to her own realm? Judea's forces were clearly no match for Egypt's—indeed, it's not entirely certain that the Jewish army would have supported Janneus against Cleopatra, so distressed were they at the disaster his treachery had brought on the land. But one of Cleopatra's Jewish generals persuaded the queen to leave Janneus in command of Judea. It would be better to have grateful friends on the northern border, he argued, than recalcitrant subjects. So Cleopatra returned to Egypt, leaving the Jews to rebuild their land and their self-esteem.

Janneus wasted no time in setting forth again. Having been stymied in the west, he decided to try his luck in the east. His armies invaded the region across the Jordan River, where they conquered Gadara and other cities. He then turned back to the west, conquering Gaza and other important coastal sites. So in spite of his mistakes he managed to expand Judean holdings further. On the foreign-affairs front Janneus seemed to live a charmed life. The nation was strong and as large as it had ever been in its entire history.

On the domestic front Janneus wasn't faring quite so well. We've already seen how John Hyrcanus had put himself at odds with the Pharisees, who commanded the general sympathies of the masses. Janneus made the breach much worse. He had broken Mosaic law and offended the religious scruples of many Jews when he married Alexandra Salome, since biblical law forbids the high priest from marrying a widow (Lev 21:10-14). Rumors also persisted from the days of Hyrcanus that Janneus's grandmother had been taken captive by Antiochus Epiphanes—and so his parentage was dubious. And on top of it all he was simply regarded as a scoundrel. Stories of his immorality circulated freely in Judea, enraging the pious. We're told that at a celebration of the Feast of Tabernacles, probably fairly early in his reign, a riot broke out. The celebrants at the feast customarily carried tree branches and lemons. As they watched the unworthy cleric leading worship, they found the fruit handy missiles to throw at him. Enraged, Janneus ordered his guards to attack the unruly crowd, killing six thousand Jews. After so great a slaughter in the holy city, Janneus could scarcely hope to regain the favor of his people.

Later in his reign Janneus gave his enemies both cause and opportunity to depose him. Around 88 B.C. he had gone to campaign against the Arabic Nabateans in the southeast. But Janneus managed to lead his army into an ambush, and the troops were slaughtered. The king himself barely escaped with his life. He returned to Jerusalem humiliated and unprotected, and some of the leading Pharisees decided it was time to have this source of embarrassment removed from office. They conspired to invite Demetrius Eucerus, one of several contenders for the throne of Syria, to invade Judea and do away with Janneus. Demetrius came with a large army, and after a hard-fought battle that bloodied both sides, Janneus was driven into the hill country. It looked as if the Greek forces would be victorious. But to many of the Jews, even the reign of a wicked Jew was preferable to foreign domination. Six thousand Judean men turned out and threw their support to Janneus. Demetrius, whose own forces had been seriously depleted, decided this was a battle he couldn't win, so he returned to Syria.

Now it was time for Janneus to take his vengeance on his betrayers. The Pharisaic leaders were captured and brought to Jerusalem, where Janneus pronounced a sentence on them that had never been inflicted by a Jewish monarch before, nor would be again: he ordered eight hundred of them crucified in the center of the city. While the men hung there in agony, the wrathful monarch had their wives, sons and daughters brought to the feet of their crosses. The king's soldiers slit the throats of the helpless women and children before the dying eyes of the men on the crosses. Janneus secured a ringside seat for the spectacle. He watched the whole affair from his balcony, celebrating his revenge with wine and the pleasures of his concubines.

This mass slaughter was only the beginning of a reign of terror. Eight thousand Judeans were forced to flee and live in hiding until Janneus was dead. The whole affair made such a deep impression on the Jews that decades later, the author of one of the Dead Sea Scrolls interpreted some verses from the book of Nahum as a prophecy about the incident. It's one of the few times that the Scrolls speak clearly about historical events. According to the interpreter Alexander was the "lion of wrath" who hung alive the "seekers of smooth things" (the usual Scrolls epithet for the Phar-

isees) who sought to bring Demetrius (mentioned by name) into Jerusalem. But the interpreter tells his readers that God had ordained that
Jerusalem wouldn't be trampled under the Gentiles' feet until the coming
of the Kittim—the Romans (4QpNah 1.2-4). He makes little comment
about the cruelty of the punishment. Maybe he considered it a just penalty
for a group that would have betrayed Judea's independence.

Janneus had put down the revolt at home, but new problems appeared
on the international scene. The Seleucid Empire was divided into warring
factions, and Janneus wasn't able to stay completely out of the crossfire.
But when King Aretas of Nabatea defeated one of the Seleucid armies and
killed one of the Seleucid kings, Nabatea took Syria's place as Judea's most
dangerous enemy. Janneus clashed with Aretas at Adida, deep in Judean
territory, and he could only persuade Aretas to withdraw by offering him
concessions. With so powerful a rival to the south, Alexander turned his
attention to the northeast. Between 83 and 80 B.C. he added further conquests in the Transjordan to the already considerable Judean kingdom.
Following the policy of his father before him, all the residents of the conquered lands were forced to become Jewish. Evidently, Janneus was immoral, but not impious. At the same time, his Hellenizing tendency is also
evident, and not merely in his disregard for Jewish law and sentiments.
The evidence has been preserved in the coins minted during his reign,
which bear both Hebrew and Greek inscriptions. Instead of a royal crown,
they bear the image of a diadem—a Greek, not Jewish, symbol of kingship.

Janneus died in 76 B.C., after suffering for three years from an alcohol-
induced illness. By the end of his reign much of the animosity against him
seems to have been replaced by national pride in his military conquests.
Yet, in Alexander Janneus's reign we have a clear illustration of how far the
Hasmoneans had strayed from their original goal. They had fought to restore religious freedom and reduce foreign influence. But now they imposed their religion on those about them; they viciously suppressed their
critics; they brought foreign customs into Jerusalem. It's all quite reminiscent of George Orwell's *Animal Farm*, where the animals expelled the ruling humans from the farm, and then their leaders began to act like the
tyrants they had deposed: "The creatures outside looked from pig to man,
and from man to pig, and from pig to man again; but already it was impossible to say which was which."[7]

---

[7]George Orwell, *Animal Farm* (New York: Signet Classics, 1974), p. 128.

Alexandra Salome

When Alexander died at the age forty-nine, he designated an older and wiser head as his successor: his widow, Alexandra Salome.[8] She couldn't serve as high priest, of course—that role was strictly reserved for men, no matter how progressive the times might have been. So, while Alexandra assumed the title "queen," she appointed her eldest son Hyrcanus II as high priest. A rather phlegmatic fellow, Hyrcanus II could serve competently in his office, causing little trouble to the queen. Her younger son Aristobulus II was given command of the armies. He was more ambitious than his brother, but he didn't challenge the wily matriarch—at least not for the time being.

Alexandra's reign proved to have been as different from Alexander's as night is from day. Whereas he was despised by the people, she was generally loved. (The Jews believed that she had been as victimized by her husband's excesses as they had been, and they sympathized with her.) While Alexander was constantly involved in warfare, her reign was relatively peaceful. While he allied himself primarily with the Sadducees, she cast in her lot with the Pharisees. According to Josephus's account in the *Antiquities* Alexander himself advised her to make this shift in policy. Alexander told his wife that she should attempt to win the favors of the Pharisees so they would treat his body with respect after his death—and so she could have peace within her kingdom. But instead of simply winning their favor, she became something of a pawn in their hands, according to the *Antiquities*. It's a rather different picture than the one Josephus had presented earlier in the *Jewish War*. That work told of no deathbed advice from Alexander. Instead, Josephus had written that the Pharisees had insinuated themselves into power little by little, and that Alexandra favored them primarily because they were more pious than the Sadducees. There may be an element of truth in both accounts. It seems likely that Alexandra realized her reign would represent such an offence to the traditionalists and to her ambitious son Aristobulus that she would desperately need the support of the masses. The Pharisees, with their ever-growing popularity, were more useful to her than the snobbish Sadducees. It seems unlikely to me that Janneus had actually given her instructions regarding the Pharisees, but it's hard to say where Josephus would have come up with such a story. Male chauvinism, perhaps?

---

[8]Primary sources for this section are *Ant.* 13.16.1-6 (405-32); *War* 1.5.1-4 (107-19).

Whatever the reason for the policy change, it's clear enough that during the reign of Alexandra the Sadducees were out and the Pharisees were in. Josephus and rabbinic tradition agree that the Pharisees began exercising unprecedented power in Judea. They were able to reinstitute their own interpretations of Judaism as the law of the land, and they even began to take vengeance on those who were responsible for the death of their eight hundred kinsmen in Alexander's day. The only way the Pharisees could have exercised such power is if they had taken control of the Jewish high council, the Sanhedrin (or as it's sometimes called, the *gerousia*). Apparently, Alexandra used her influence to install a Pharisaic majority in the Sanhedrin.[9] Since the reign of John Hyrcanus, if not earlier, the council had been filled with aristocratic Sadducees. Now, with the tables turned, the Sadducees found that their money and family ties couldn't buy their safety.

The high priest Hyrcanus might have been sympathetic, but he lacked the will to oppose his mother and the masses. So the Sadducees appealed to Aristobulus to see if he could persuade his mother to call off the Pharisaic dogs. A delegation of Sadducean leaders came before the queen requesting to be restored to favor, or at the very least granted the protection of living in some of the fortress cities, where they'd be beyond the reach of their enemies. Aristobulus proved to be less of a supporter than they expected. Pressed for his opinion on the matter, he simply commented that the Sadducees had brought their troubles on themselves by allowing a woman to reign over them when Alexander had left behind sons who were capable of filling the office. Alexandra wasn't without sympathy for her former allies, but she could concede little without alienating her new friends. She gave the Sadducees permission to live in the fortresses.

After the Pharisees' wrath was spent, the rest of Alexandra's reign was fairly uneventful. The rabbis of later centuries, who regarded the Pharisees as their forefathers, characterized the time as a golden age of prosperity. The crops grew bigger, the grass was greener, and the people were happier because the Pharisees had been empowered to make the people behave according to God's will (as they understood it, of course). Josephus is less ef-

---

[9]We have little information on how members of the Sanhedrin were chosen during this period. Certainly the queen must have had considerable influence in the process. Jonathan had probably installed his own ruling council when he was appointed the high priest and governor of the Jews, and the power of appointment may have become hereditary.

THE SANHEDRIN

The Jewish council of elders was an important legislative body throughout the Greek and Roman periods. It was led by the high priest and included members of the priestly aristocracy. Mainly, these individuals were Sadducean in sympathy. Other elders filled out a quota of seventy (or seventy-one) members. Alexandra Salome had appointed many Pharisees to the Sanhedrin, switching for a while the balance of power.

Unlike our modern senates, the principal duty of the Sanhedrin appears not to have been legislative but judicial. We most frequently read of the Sanhedrin trying criminals (or perceived criminals) for serious infractions of Jewish law. Its power varied greatly, depending on the whim and ability of the king or governor. At times the Sanhedrin actually wielded the power to impose capital punishment, and at other times it was essentially impotent.

In the second century A.D. the Romans abolished the official Sanhedrin. An unofficial rabbinic council filled its place, but its power to punish lawbreakers was very limited.

fusive in his praise, but he agrees that the days of Alexandra were generally peaceful. An expedition against the Syrians in Damascus led by Aristobulus met little resistance. And a threatened invasion from Tigranes, an Armenian king who conquered the fractured Seleucid Empire, was averted by some diplomacy and generous gifts. Alexandra didn't attempt to expand the kingdom as her predecessors had done, but she lost nothing either.

When Alexandra grew ill near the end of her life, Aristobulus II decided that the time had come for him to seize control of the kingdom. He gathered an army and invaded Jerusalem. The coup alarmed Alexandra, who had appointed Hyrcanus to succeed her to the throne, but there was little she could do to stop it. When she died in 67 B.C. the kingdom was destined to fall into the hands of Aristobulus.

Aristobulus II

Before Hyrcanus II had the opportunity to secure his place on the throne, Aristobulus's army had overwhelmed the high priest and his soldiers.[10] Hyrcanus was forced to flee to the Akra. With his enemy ensconced in the impregnable fortress, it seemed like Aristobulus would have a lengthy siege on his hands. But trapped and with little support among the Jews, Hyrcanus was willing to make large concessions in exchange for his life. He'd never been a particularly ambitious man. So the high priest offered to give up both the throne and the priesthood, and to retire from public life, as long as he was guaranteed security and a tidy income. Aristobulus agreed to the arrangement, and the brothers shook hands and embraced before the eyes of Jerusalem. Aristobulus II probably had no desire to begin his reign by killing his brother, as his ill-fated uncle Aristobulus I had done. So Hyrcanus was allowed to retire in peace.

There were others who weren't so eager to see Hyrcanus abdicate the throne. Chief among these instigators was the native governor of Idumea, a man named Antipater. Wealthy, influential and corrupt, Antipater had little desire to see the strong and ambitious Aristobulus II ruling Judea. And there were Jews who shared Antipater's opinion. Undoubtedly the Pharisees had little love for Aristobulus, who was perceived as an ally of the Sadducees. And there were other powerful Jews who could expect their influence to be curtailed significantly under the reign of Aristobulus. These various forces managed to persuade the gullible Hyrcanus that his life would never be safe while Aristobulus was on the throne. (Of course, they might have been right.) Antipater made an arrangement with Aretas III, the king of Nabatea, to give Hyrcanus refuge and support. The Nabateans, as Judea's chief rivals in the area, had no more desire to see a strong king on the Jewish throne than did Antipater or the Judean aristocrats. This consideration, along with Hyrcanus's promise to return to Nabatea twelve cities that had been conquered by Alexander Janneus, persuaded Aretas to help the deposed priest reclaim his throne.

The first encounter between the army of Aretas III and that of Aristobulus II resulted in a rout for the latter. The high priest fled back to Jerusalem and barricaded himself within the temple complex—a veritable fortress itself. The fickle Judeans, seeing how Aristobulus had been humbled, now gave their support to Hyrcanus and the Nabateans. They joined with

---

[10]Primary sources for this section are *Ant.* 14.1.1-4.5 (1-79); *War* 1.6.1-7.7 (120-58).

Hyrcanus in laying siege to the temple. The crowds even brought forth a saint named Onias, renowned for his powerful prayers, and asked him to curse Aristobulus. But instead of offering a curse, Onias prayed that God would honor neither side but bring peace to Judea. The mob became indignant with the holy man, rose up in anger and stoned him to death. As the days dragged on, Aristobulus requested that the Jews provide sacrificial animals so the daily offerings could continue. At first, they required him to pay exorbitant prices for the animals. Later, they took his money but refused to send the animals. On one occasion they even sent a pig to the temple—a mocking violation of the Mosaic law and disturbingly reminiscent of the crimes of Antiochus Epiphanes. With the people so clearly against him and little hope in sight, it must have appeared that Aristobulus was doomed.

Aristobulus's fate wasn't sealed yet. In Syria another power had come on the scene. The Romans, concerned that the political turmoil in Syria would disrupt their own Mediterranean interests, had sent the general Pompey to bring the faltering kingdom under Roman control. While Pompey went to Armenia to deal with the vigorous King Tigranes (Tigranes had conquered Syria several years earlier), Pompey's lieutenant, Aemilius Scaurus, went on ahead to Syria. Aristobulus and Hyrcanus wasted no time sending their envoys to Syria to appeal for Roman aid. Both men offered a bribe of four hundred talents for a decision in their favor. Scaurus considered the circumstances and determined that Aristobulus was the more capable leader and more likely to pay. He ordered Hyrcanus and the Nabateans to withdraw. The Nabateans were a scrappy people, but they weren't stupid. They wouldn't risk an encounter with Rome. They withdrew from Jerusalem, but not with impunity: a vengeful Aristobulus followed behind, inflicting heavy casualties on his erstwhile captors.

Aristobulus II was once again in control of Judea—but for how long? Soon Pompey himself arrived in Antioch, where he was met by three delegations from Judea. One wanted Hyrcanus replaced as the legitimate high priest; the other represented the interests of Aristobulus. But a third embassy came as well, claiming to represent the greater will of the Judean people. They requested that both men be removed, and the Jews be allowed to choose a new high priest. Pompey said he would make a decision in the matter after he had paid a visit to the Nabateans. In the meantime he ordered the brothers to keep the peace until he returned. But something about the meeting worried Aristobulus. Believing his position was in peril, he raced back to Jerusalem and began fortifying the city against a siege.

Pompey received word of Aristobulus's activities and rightly interpreted them as insubordination. The Roman general decided that Nabatea would have to wait. He needed to deal with Aristobulus before the renegade king could complete his preparations. As the Roman troops approached Jerusalem, the city gates swung open to welcome him. But Aristobulus had taken refuge within the temple complex. Pompey, determined to extricate Aristobulus, ordered his men to lay siege to the temple. The mighty structure withstood the Roman assault for three months, while the priests inside dutifully continued their appointed sacrifices. But on the Day of Atonement in 63 B.C., the holiest day on the Jewish calendar, the gates of the temple finally gave way. The Romans charged in and slaughtered the priests, who refused to defend themselves or even to flee while they were in the midst of their prayers and sacrifices. Pompey himself marched into the holy of holies, the central sanctuary that only the high priest was allowed to enter. He didn't despoil the temple, however, and he did make provisions to assure that the worship of God would continue there uninterrupted. The short reign of Aristobulus, however, had been brought to an end. The former monarch was captured and taken to Rome. The other leaders of the uprising were beheaded.

Judea paid a high price for Aristobulus's insolence. Many Jews were taken to Rome as captives. Hyrcanus was reinstated as high priest—but he no longer bore the title of king. He was now a vassal of the great foreign power whom the Hasmoneans had once called allies. And as a final indignity, Judea was forced to pay tribute to Rome. After eighty years of liberty, the yoke of the Gentiles once more lay on the shoulders of the Jews.

Assessing the Hasmonean Dynasty

How should history judge the accomplishments of the Hasmoneans? Opinions have varied widely. Ancient Jewish authors expressed a spectrum of opinions. An ambivalent nod may be given to the Hasmoneans in Daniel 11:34, where it speaks of the "little help" that will come to the persecuted during the time of Antiochus Epiphanes (as opposed to the true help of God). The so-called Animal Apocalypse of 1 *Enoch*, composed early in the revolt, expected Judas to establish nothing short of a messianic kingdom on earth. He was a God-ordained hero whose victories would bring glory to the Jewish people. Once the Hasmoneans had begun to rule as monarchs, Jewish opinion of them remained divided. But the lines of division are hardly clear-cut. Both books of Maccabees, written from very different theological perspectives, hold the Maccabees in high regard. The Dead Sea Scrolls Community, once thought to have been a strongly anti-Hasmonean group, also preserved a "Hymn in Praise to King Jonathan" (4Q448)—actually a hymn to the Lord, but it does pray for peace for King Alexander Janneus. It was quite surprising to discover among the Dead Sea Scrolls a text that seems to support the most immoral of the Hasmoneans. On the other hand, the *Psalms of Solomon,* a pseudepigraphon written soon after the fall of the dynasty, regarded all the Hasmoneans as usurpers. Of course, the rabbis had little love for the Hasmonean dynasty, with the single exception of Alexandra Salome. The New Testament passes over this entire chapter of Jewish history without comment.

Christian scholars, following the presentations given by Josephus, generally have had a positive regard for the Hasmoneans' accomplishments. Jewish writers, influenced by the rabbinical traditions, tended to be more critical. In recent years, however, both Christian and Jewish scholars have tended to view the Hasmoneans' contribution to history as a good thing. One standard text states that the Hasmoneans saved monotheism from extinction—as if the Jews were the only people in the world capable of monotheism! In actuality there were several religions and philosophical schools heading toward monotheism in that era. If monotheism was all that was at stake, the world had little to fear—there were Greek philosophers ready to step in to the gap and provide a system of philosophical religion that would surely have fit the bill.

It wasn't monotheism that Antiochus Epiphanes threatened to extinguish: it was only its Judean variety that was on the chopping block. So the question isn't whether or not the Hasmoneans rescued the world from a religious dark age of polytheism. Rather, it's simply a matter of the preservation of a certain form of Judaism. If the Hasmoneans hadn't led a rebellion against Antiochus, would "orthodox" Judaism have perished? To me, it seems unlikely. There were Jews far beyond the borders of Judea who were faithfully holding to the tenets of their religion. In Babylon, Egypt and other lands, vibrant Jewish communities were keeping the faith. Even in Judea itself, persecution alone could probably not have destroyed true faith. Through the ages tyrants have attempted to extinguish Christianity; but when the veil of oppression lifted, the faith usually emerged even stronger than before, without the Christians having taken up the sword in

THE PSALMS OF SOLOMON 17.4-9

Lord, you chose David to be king over Israel,
And swore to him about his descendants forever,
That his kingdom should not fail before you.
But (because of) our sins, sinners rose up against us,
They set upon us and drove us out.
Those to whom you did not (make the) promise,
They took away (from us) by force;
And they did not glorify your honorable name.
With pomp they set up a monarchy because of their arrogance;
They despoiled the throne of David with arrogant shouting.
But you, O God, overthrew them, and uprooted their descen-
    dants from the earth,
For there rose up against them a man alien to our race.
You rewarded them, O God, according to their sins;
It happened to them according to their actions.
According to their actions, God showed no mercy to them;
He hunted down their descendants, and did not let even one of
    them go.
[James Charlesworth, ed., *The Old Testament Pseudepigrapha*
(Garden City, N.Y.: Doubleday, 1985), 2:665-66]

its defense. Judaism could have survived Antiochus Epiphanes, even without the Maccabean uprising. Indeed, given the immorality of some of the later rulers, it's a wonder that Judaism managed to survive the Hasmoneans.

So what did the Hasmoneans actually accomplish? Perhaps the most significant legacy of the Hasmoneans is the rebirth of Jewish nationalism. From 586 B.C. to 142 B.C. the Jews had been under the authority of foreign empires. For the most part they'd been model subjects. But what effect did such submission have on the collective Jewish psyche? Had the Jews, as a people, become soft—prey to the dominant cultures that surrounded and overwhelmed them? Had they lost their vision of a kingdom that would

THE HASMONEAN DYNASTY

1. Mattathias Hashmonai (167-165? B.C.): priest from Modein, started Hasmonean Revolt.
2. Judas Maccabeus (165-161): son of Mattathias.
3. Jonathan (161-142): brother of Judas.
4. Simon (142-135): brother of Judas and Jonathan.
5. John Hyrcanus I (135-104): Simon's son.
6. Aristobulus I (104-103): son of John Hyrcanus; first Hasmonean to claim the title "king."
7. Alexander Jannaeus (103-76): surviving brother of Aristobulus I.
8. Alexandra Salome (76-67): wife of Alexander Jannaeus (and Aristobulus before him).
9. Aristobulus II (67-63): younger son of Alexandra Salome.
10. Hyrcanus II (63-40): served as high priest only under Roman and Herod's rule.

subdue the nations and take its light to the Gentiles? There's some evidence that they had. The Jews were moving toward a complacent acceptance of their overlords' cultures. But the Antiochan persecution and the Hasmonean revolt surely reversed that trend. The Jews were forced to recognize the distinctiveness of their faith. Their eyes were opened to the preciousness of what they had almost given away. They were allowed to see how close they could come to fulfilling the promises made to the patriarchs and prophets of old. Even if the Hasmonean dynasty had failed to be the kingdom that the prophets had envisioned, it whetted the nation's appetite for the real thing. A renewed sense of Jewish destiny had been awakened, and it would not be quickly extinguished.

For Further Reading

Horbury, William, W. D. Davies, Louis Finkelstein, and John Sturdy. *The Cambridge History of Judaism.* Vol. 2, chap. 9. Cambridge: Cambridge University Press, 1990.

Mendels, Doron. *The Rise and Fall of Jewish Nationalism.* New York: Double-

day, 1992. Chaps. 1-6 consider the significance of kingship, land and
temple as symbols of Jewish nationalism in the Hasmonean period.
Schalit, A., ed., *The World History of the Jewish People*. Vol. 6, *The Hellenistic
Age*. New York: Rutgers University Press, 1972. A highly readable account of the Hasmonean dynasty.
Schürer, Emil. *A History of the Jewish People in the Age of Jesus Christ*. Edited
by Geza Vermes, Fergus Millar and Matthew Black. Vol. 1, §§8-12. Edinburgh: T & T Clark, 1973.

8

The Hellenistic Inheritance

The natives of Greece and the Near East weren't utterly alien to one another, even before the time of Alexander. Trade (including slave trade) and immigration had been occurring throughout the region from time immemorial, so there was a certain amount of common culture shared by the entire Mediterranean region. Fundamentally, though, we could say that the East and the West looked at the world from different angles. It's been said that the peoples of the East considered the universe and asked Who? but the Greeks considered the universe and asked How? That characterization is certainly a bit extreme. There were many superstitious Greeks as well as some scientifically inclined Easterners. But there was, perhaps, an inclination toward analytical thought in Greece that was foreign to the more intuitive Easterners. Philosophy wasn't an Eastern discipline; among peoples of the East ultimate questions on the nature of reality fell into the realm of theology.

There was also a different understanding of social class in the West, where the Greek democracies like those of Athens and Sparta regarded all citizens as more or less equal. Women and slaves, however, were considered genetically inferior to male Greek citizens. "Barbarians"—meaning any non-Greeks—were generally considered contemptible. In the East, on the other hand, there was a more hierarchical understanding of authority, and lower social classes were expected to treat their betters with appropriate respect. Yet many eastern nations had a higher regard for women than nations in the West had. Slaves, too, were often considered unfortunate victims of fate in the East rather than natural-born servants. And while all ancient peoples were given to some ethnocentrism, the Greeks seemed to excel in the area of national pride. There were other differences between East and West as well: art, literature and musical tastes were different. The famous Greek love for athletic competition was quite foreign to the peoples of the East. Such contrasts set the stage for the Hellenistic age to be a time of mutual enrichment—and a time of conflict.

The View from the West

Alexander the Great had dreamed of merging East and West into a glorious new culture combining the best of both worlds. His successors shared little of that vision. In Egypt the Ptolemies initially treated the natives with the utmost contempt, taxing them oppressively and barring them from public office. But the Greeks soon came to hold Egyptian culture in esteem. Greeks had a great deal of respect for cultures they considered ancient, and the evidence of Egypt's antiquity was visible everywhere in the great monuments of the Pharaohs. The Greeks had a difficult time maintaining their air of superiority over the venerable Egyptians. Eventually, the Ptolemaic court adopted many Egyptian practices. The Ptolemies allowed themselves to be revered as gods; they mimicked the clothing of the ancient Pharaohs; and they even began to practice extreme endogamy—the marriage of brothers to sisters. In the palaces of the Ptolemies and Cleopatras a true blending of East and West occurred. But in the Egyptian cities and countryside, that wasn't always the case. There, the Egyptians, Greeks and other ethnic groups lived in uneasy tension that occasionally erupted in outright conflict. Once the Ptolemies had abandoned their policies of oppression and recognized the rights of their native subjects, the peoples of the East and West were obliged to find ways to coexist.

At first the Seleucid monarchs seemed to have been more favorably disposed to the natives. They allowed Babylonians and Persians to serve in positions of authority, and they didn't impose the same kinds of oppressive taxes and limitations on their subjects that the Ptolemies had imposed on the Egyptians. Yet, ironically, it was the Seleucids who vigorously promoted the spread of Hellenistic culture, more so than did the Ptolemies. Undoubtedly, part of the reason for the Seleucids' missionary zeal was their low regard for the native Syrians and Jews, who they tended to view as a group. The Greeks thought the Syrians, who (as far as the Greeks could tell) had never produced a great civilization, were contemptible neophytes on the world scene. Aristotle (384-322 B.C.) had instructed Alexander the Great to treat the Egyptians in his army as an officer would treat his soldiers, but to treat the Syrians as a master would treat slaves.

The Jews initially fared somewhat better. A few early Greek writers had expressed some admiration for the Jews, being impressed by their high morals and disdain of images. About 300 B.C. the philosopher Theophrastus declared that the Jews were a race of philosophers, an opinion echoed a few decades later by the historian Megasthenes and the philosopher Clearchus. But as the novelty of the Jewish religion wore off, the Jews' prestige slipped in the Hellenistic opinion polls. Their standoffish ways and resistance to the state cult made them targets of criticism. Late in the third century B.C. rumors began to circulate that the Jews worshiped a donkey's head and performed human sacrifices. Josephus records that an Egyptian priest named Manetho, whose history of Egypt may have been composed in the third century B.C., wrote that the Israelites had been expelled from Egypt not at the command of the Lord but because of their moral debauchery and the fact that they were a race of lepers.[1] (Manetho might also have originated the story that the Jews worshiped a donkey.) Josephus also reports that Apollonius Molon, a well-known orator of the first century B.C., vilified the Jews as cowards, isolationists and generally contemptible creatures. Apollonius's most famous pupil Cicero, the Roman orator (106-43 B.C.), described all Jews and Syrians as creatures fit only for servitude.[2] Because the Greeks were so certain of their innate superiority, they probably expected the Jews to admire and emulate them. They were doing a favor to the Eastern peoples in bequeathing on them the accoutrements of true culture. If some of the natives seemed a little reluctant to accept such a precious gift, the Greeks might have been a little puzzled—or they might have written the rejection off as further proof of the natives' inherent ignorance.

We might imagine that many in the East resented the Greeks' swagger. Most of them probably saw little reason to consider themselves inferior to the invaders. The fact is, some of the oldest cities in the world were located in Syria and Palestine. Much of the Near East had already been civilized and literate when the Greeks' ancestors were still huddling in caves. It had been the peoples of the Near East who had developed both agriculture and the alphabet; and they had taught these innovations to the Greeks. These

---

[1]Josephus preserves portions from Manetho and other unflattering authors in his work *Against Apion.*
[2]Cicero *On the Consular Provinces* 5.10-12. In other writings Cicero describes Judaism as a superstition.

STOICS AND EPICUREANS

In today's common usage, the word *Stoic* describes a person who isn't emotional, while an *Epicurean* is a person devoted to pleasure. But originally these two schools of Greek philosophy weren't as opposite as they sound. Stoicism began around 300 B.C. One of its main teachings was that the universe was ordered by a principle called the *logos* (commonly translated "word," but also meaning "thought" or "reason"). There was logic and reason to the cosmos, and the highest good for humankind was to live in harmony with the natural order. Unlike Plato, who believed that people possess spirits that are liberated after death, the Stoics were materialists. They believed that the human being simply ceased to exist after death. Because unbridled passion was deemed inconsistent with logic and because human beings were naturally social creatures, the Stoics maintained very high morals and ethics.

Epicurus founded his school of thought in Athens around 307 B.C. He and his followers were also materialists, arguing that all matter consists of a combination of atoms and empty space. Because the soul does not survive death, the Epicureans held that the goal of human life should be to maximize pleasure. But maximum pleasure, they held, came from a serene mind and the elimination of pain. Any forms of immoderation—in food, drink, sex or emotionalism—cause pain and should be avoided. The Epicureans founded communes where students were led in meditation to obtain true serenity.

Stoicism and Epicureanism remained prominent philosophies well into New Testament times. Paul debated their teachers at Athens (Acts 17:18), and their teachings and methods shaped some ideas of the early church fathers.

facts were already known in classical times, and Josephus had no qualms about reminding his readers about them (*Against Apion* 1.2 [10-12]). Indeed, both Josephus and Philo of Alexandria attempted to demonstrate to the Hellenistic world that the Jews truly were an ancient and noteworthy culture. If they occasionally exaggerated their people's accomplishments—as when they made Abraham the inventor of astrology or dated Moses to an impossibly early time—they only demonstrate the great pride that the Jews took in their own culture and history. The disdain of the Hellenized world was, in the Jews' opinion, utterly unwarranted.

Worlds in Collusion

In spite of their antiquity and nobility, the Eastern peoples weren't immune to the influence of the Greeks in their midst. The conqueror's culture exerted a subtle—and sometimes not-so-subtle—pressure on the natives to adopt the ways of the West. One rather heavy-handed policy was the overlords' insistence on using Greek as the language of government and commerce. It was very different from the Persians' policy, which had allowed the Eastern satrapies to continue using Aramaic. Now anyone who wished to climb the social ladder and any merchants who desired to engage in international trade had to have at least a basic knowledge of Greek. Some Near Easterners seem to have progressed fairly far in their study of the classical tongue: in Phoenicia and Syria archaeologists have unearthed tombstones bearing Semitic names with epitaphs written in flawless Greek.

Language was only one aspect of Greek culture that found a home in the East. Throughout Syria and Palestine, coins were minted with Greek inscriptions and motifs, and public buildings were constructed after Greek fashions, with Hellenistic decorative friezes and flourishes. In Syria and in the non-Jewish cites of Palestine, temples were erected to Greek gods. Native Near Easterners offered sacrifices to Dionysus, Artemis and other Western divinities. They cheered at athletic contests held in honor of the deified hero Heracles. Local deities, like Baal Shemayin ("Lord of Heaven"), were renamed in honor of Greek gods or heroes. The Greeks even influenced Eastern speculative thought. During the Hellenistic age Near Eastern sages began to consider such questions as the composition of matter, the nature of spirit and the meaning of fate. Stoicism, one of the major schools of philosophy in the Mediterranean world, may have originated in the Near East. It combined some purely Greek concerns, like the composition of the soul and the ordering properties of the universe, with a bit of Eastern mysticism—the tendency to personalize the cosmos and to seek a relationship with its guiding powers. Some Epicurean philosophers had their roots in Syria and Phoenicia. Egypt too had some major philosophers, not the least of whom was the Jewish Philo of Alexandria. Clearly, the Greek presence was exerting a substantial influence on Near Eastern culture.

The ease with which the Phoenicians, Philistines and Syrians adopted some aspects of Greek culture may seem somewhat surprising, but it's hardly inexplicable. As we noted earlier, the peoples of the Mediterranean coast had been trading with the Greeks for centuries before Alexander the Great stepped foot on their shores. The Phoenicians and Syrians were already familiar with Greeks and their ways. The Philistines, in fact, were probably descended from the Mycenaeans (an ancient Greek civilization). Even the adoption of Greek deities is hardly unexpected. In those days nations often adopted the gods of their conquerors. Usually, they just added the new gods to their pantheons, but occasionally the victor's deities actually displaced the gods of the vanquished. Among polytheists the gods who prove most capable are often granted the greatest honor. And polytheism always has a tendency toward syncretism, combining similar gods under a single name or even combined names. Syrian texts from prebiblical times bear witness to the way that gods were adopted from various nations, added to the pantheon and occasionally fused with other gods into a single deity. So it's no surprise that the Syrians would identify their chief god Baal, a storm deity, with the Greek archdivinity Zeus Ouranos, who was also a storm god.

What of the Jews? Could they remain isolated from such developments? Some scholars have produced a good deal of data suggesting that Greek language and culture made significant inroads into Judaism. But interpreting that data has proven a challenge. Was a shallow veneer of Hellenistic culture laid over an essentially Jewish way of life and thought? Or had the Jews been substantially altered by their contact with the Greeks, so much so that their Old Testament forebears would have hardly recognized them as Jews at all? There's a widely argued theory that after the time of Alexander the Great, the Jews rapidly adopted many aspects of Greek culture and were on the way to losing their distinctiveness entirely. But when Antiochus Epiphanes attempted to force the Jews to Hellenize, they reacted strongly and the process was reversed. But how accurate—

and how probable—is this scenario? Scholars are divided on the issue, and careful studies by equally competent researchers have come to very different conclusions.

The Study of Jewish Hellenization

Research into Jewish Hellenization presents some major difficulties. First and foremost we have the problem of sources. When modern anthropologists want to study the changes in societies that come into contact with foreign influences, they draw from both written descriptions and direct observations. Universities will send in teams to take pictures, conduct interviews and observe daily life so they can produce detailed before-and-after pictures of societies in transition. Likewise, if we want to determine how contact with the Greeks changed Jewish culture, we need a good understanding Jewish culture before the coming of the Greeks. But there's the rub: our knowledge of Jewish culture in Old Testament days isn't particularly detailed. Our principal source of information about Jewish society in Old Testament times is the Old Testament itself. Most of the Jewish literature produced before the intertestamental period—literature that included noncanonical religious works, daily correspondence, official records and inscriptions—has perished. Archaeology has given us some data about daily life in ancient Palestine, but not much. The parade of conquerors who marched through the Promised Land left deep footprints, and some of the areas we'd most like to investigate have been continually inhabited for ages and remain so to this day. Reconstructing the culture of preexilic Judah is a daunting task. So when we attempt to study the effects of Hellenism on the common person's Palestinian Judaism, we're trying to document changes in a culture about which we know precious little.

Furthermore, the evidence from the Hellenistic age isn't easily interpreted. We can gather up examples of Greek inscriptions, Greek names and Greek texts, but what do these things really tell us about what the average Jew thought about the Greeks? We're hampered by the fact that our sources generally reflect the upper crust of urban Palestinian Jewish society—the very group that would have been most likely to adopt Greek traits because they had the most face-to-face contact with the Greeks and the most to gain by emulating them. We know little about the rural peasant culture, the group that comprised the majority of Palestinian Jews. Our ancient historians also must be handled with care. Josephus was from Palestine, but he wrote for a Hellenized audience and employed the forms of speech and thought that would be well received in elite Gentile society. The Talmud, frequently cited in discussions of Hellenism, was probably written down in the sixth century A.D. and represents a strongly traditional element in Jewish society. Its occasional polemics against Hellenized Jews can hardly be taken as evidence of the spread of Greek culture in Judea.

Given these difficulties, it's no wonder that scholars have disagreed strongly on the extent to which the Jews became Hellenized. On the one hand, there are some who have argued that all Jews of the era drank deep at the wells of Greek culture, while others have claimed that the average Palestinian Jew knew little of the Greeks and their ways. My own position would be midway between these extremes: there were certainly many Jews, especially in the Western Diaspora (Egypt and the Mediterranean lands), who were substantially influenced by the Greeks, but there were many others who had little contact with Greek culture and little chance or reason to adopt it as their own. Judaism was diverse in those days, and so were the Jewish responses to the Greeks.

A Diversity of Responses

Scholars have only recently come to appreciate the diversity of Jewish society in the Hellenistic era. For a long time it was commonly held that there was a pure, "orthodox" Judaism—Pharisaism—and that groups like the Sadducees or Essenes were heretical offshoots. But religious diversity is only part of the complex picture. Faith is but one aspect of that collection of traits we call "culture." In America today a Christian, Unitarian, Buddhist and atheist might all share the same language, clothing styles, diet and popular icons. Their religions may be different, but their culture is otherwise essentially the same. On the other hand, there will be vast cultural differences between a Methodist born and raised in Michigan and a Methodist born in Beijing. Our shared religious beliefs don't obliterate all the other aspects of our culture.

Likewise, all Jews of the Hellenistic era shared a common ethnic background (proselytes excepted) and religious traditions. Basically, all believed in the same God, revealed through the Law and the Prophets. They looked to Abraham as their father, Moses as their lawgiver and Jerusalem as their holy city. But the Jewish communities in various lands or social settings might have shared little else in common. So when we consider the Hellenization of the Jews, we must bear in mind the fact that not all the Jews would have reacted the same way to the Greek presence.

One very basic distinction we can make is that between Palestinian Jews and Diaspora Jews (in this chapter, *Diaspora* will refer only to the Jews of Mediterranean regions, not to the Jews of Babylon and Persia). Jews in ancient Palestine would have shared many cultural traits with their neighbors. All around, there were fellow Jews with similar religious ideals, clothing styles and dietary restrictions. They would support each other's customs and beliefs, reinforcing conformity to the accepted norms and discouraging radical innovations. In other words, Palestinian peer pressure would have hindered the spread of Hellenism. Even the landscape would have discouraged culture change. Palestinian Jews were surrounded by monuments, shrines, sacred places and institutions that reminded them of their rich heritage. The structure of Judean society encouraged the transmission of cultural traditions from one generation to the next, preserving Jewish disctinctiveness to an extent far greater than that which we see happening in ethnic ghettos in modern America.

None of these things were true for the Jews of the Diaspora. Most of them settled in urban areas where their neighbors represented a variety of ethnic groups and cultures. In order to live and work in such places, the Diaspora Jews had to learn the common language of the land. They had to adjust their diets to the foods readily available. The clothes they wore, the games they played and even the cut of their hair were influenced by contact with their neighbors. These Jews had to change some major aspects of their culture simply for the sake of survival. Such changes initiated a process that social scientists call "unfreezing"—destabilizing the culture in such a way that it becomes open to new ideas and fashions. Most Jews of the Diaspora, then, would have been more open to Hellenism than were most Palestinian Jews.[3]

In addition to this basic difference between Palestinian and Diaspora Judaism, there were other social distinctions that shaped Jewish responses to the Greeks. There was the urban-rural divide: cities tend to be centers of innovation, where new ideas are initiated and adopted. In the days before mass communication, fads and fashions originating in the cities spread slowly to outlying areas, if they spread at all. Rural Jews, then, were far less likely to have encountered Hellenistic ways than urban Jews would

---

[3]We must not forget, however, that not all Jewish communities in the Diaspora were identical. There were some small, isolated Jewish communities in North Africa that seem to have resisted Hellenization quite strongly.

have been. No doubt this is why the Hellenizing movement led by the high priest Jason and his cronies began in Jerusalem, the largest urban center of Palestinian Judaism, while the revolt began in the countryside.

Social class, too, was a factor in Hellenization. Upper class Jews, politicians and merchants had more to gain by identifying with the ruling Greeks than would lower-class Jews. The social climbers and business people might have tried to curry the favor of their overlords and customers through imitation—the "sincerest form of flattery." Lower-class Jews, on the other hand, would gain little by adopting the trappings of Greek culture. These folks would tend to identify with their peasant peer group, not with the Greek rulers in Antioch. Probably a Palestinian Jewish peasant who tried to dress and act like a Greek would have been considered an oddity among his fellows, if not an outright buffoon.

So then, we can't speak of the Hellenization of the Jews as if it were a uniform phenomenon. Different Jewish cultures responded differently to the Greeks. But rest assured: they *did* respond to Hellenistic culture. Greek influence was stronger in some settings than others, but it was probably impossible to avoid it altogether. If the residents in an isolated village knew no Greeks personally, they probably knew someone who knew someone who knew Greeks. Friends and relatives who ventured into the "world" would have brought back news of the latest trends. The question isn't whether or not the Jews were influenced by the Greeks. Rather, the question is, How did diverse groups of Jews respond to the intentional and unintentional dissemination of Greek culture throughout the Mediterranean world?

Greek Language Among the Jews

One of the most obvious manifestations of Hellenization was the spread of Greek as the common tongue. Just as Aramaic had been the official language of the Persian Empire, Greek was the official language of the Ptolemaic and Seleucid regimes. In the markets, on the streets and in the public squares, Greek was commonly spoken. Contracts and deeds of sale were composed in Greek. For most Diaspora Jews a basic grasp of the imperial tongue would have been essential. In many Diaspora communities Greek actually displaced Hebrew and Aramaic as the Jewish tongue.

The best evidence for this process is the Septuagint itself. The legend preserved in the *Letter of Aristeas* tells us that the translation of the Old Testament into Greek was undertaken at the initiation of King Ptolemy

THE GEOGRAPHY OF JUDAISM

During the Second Temple Period, the Jewish population expanded dramatically. In the days of Zerubbabel the Jews in Judea numbered perhaps a quarter million; but by the mid-first century A.D. one ancient historian reported that there were nearly seven million Jews in the Roman Empire alone (not counting those in Babylon and Persia). There were several factors behind this expansion. One was the Jews' disdain for the Hellenistic-style small family, preferring their own tradition that "children are a gift from the Lord." Another source of growth was the Hasmonean conquests, which added not only land but converts to Judea. And then there was proselytizing, which must have been conducted with vigor in the latter portions of this period (cf. Mt 23:15).

Most of the Jews lived in Palestine. In the Second Temple Period, Jerusalem had the greatest concentration of Jews, with about 100,000 inhabitants. But there were large Jewish populations in Galilee, Idumea, Syria, Phoenicia, the Transjordan and even in Samaria. Near the end of the Second Temple Period, the Jewish population in Palestine was probably over two million.

Other ancient sources tell us that there were about a million Jews living in Egypt in the first century A.D. Many of these dwelled in Alexandria, where one fifth of the city was designated a Jewish "quarter." There were Jews in North Africa as well. Simon of Cyrene, on the north African coast, was likely a Jewish immigrant (or a child of immigrants), not a native African. There was a substantial Jewish community on the island of Cyprus.

Many Jews settled in the cities of Macedonia and Greece, and Paul found vibrant Jewish communities in these regions during his travels. In the first century B.C. Rome became the site of a large Jewish community. The imperial capital may have been the home of about 50,000 Jews in New Testament times.

Babylon and Persia were also home to many Jews, but we have little data on their numbers in this era. After the destruction of Jerusalem in A.D. 70 and in the aftermath of further insurrection in Judea in A.D. 135, Babylon emerged as the center of Jewish culture and learning.

Philadelphus, who wanted a copy of the Pentateuch for his library in Alexandria. Seventy-two (or seventy, in some versions) Palestinian rabbis were recruited for the project. Working independently of each other, all seventy-two produced identical translations. But there's probably little history behind this legend. Literary analysis of the Septuagint has revealed that it wasn't the product of a single individual or team. Rather, it's a composite work completed in at least three stages, with different portions displaying a variety of styles, theological perspectives and skill with the Greek language. It was undoubtedly undertaken not for the sake of the Greek king but for the Jews themselves, who were finding it increasingly difficult to understand their own Scriptures in the original languages. It was this translation that was read in the synagogues of the Western Diaspora and quoted by Paul and other New Testament authors.

Were these translations of the Scriptures truly read by the masses of the Jews, or were they produced only for a Hellenized handful? Could it be possible that most Diaspora Jews had forgotten how to speak Hebrew and even Aramaic? The evidence suggests that such was indeed the case. In the New Testament we read of several instances where Paul spoke in the synagogues of Greece and Asia Minor, preaching to the Jews while Gentiles listened as well.[4] Such a scene could only have occurred if the language of the synagogues was Greek. And there's other pertinent evidence as well. As far as we can tell, all the literary texts produced by Diaspora Jews in the Hellenistic era were composed in Greek.[5] The vast majority of Jewish inscriptions from the Diaspora (mostly epitaphs) were composed in Greek as well—some in flawless classical style. No doubt there were always some Jews in the Diaspora who could read Hebrew and Aramaic. But once the Scriptures had been translated into Greek, the occasions for using the mother tongue were few. From the evidence that remains, it appears that by the second century B.C., the primary language of Diaspora Jews was a simplified form of Greek that we call *koine* ("common"). And there were some Jews—most notably, Philo of Alexandria—who even managed to master the idioms of classical Greek.

---

[4]Acts 13:14-50 (Pisidian Antioch); 14:1 (Iconium); 17:1-4 (Thessalonica), 10-12 (Beroea); 18:1-4 (Corinth).
[5]For example, 2 Maccabees, the Wisdom of Solomon, the Jewish *Sybilline Oracles* and the letters of St. Paul in the New Testament. Unfortunately, it's not always possible to determine where a text was written. When the author does not tell us where he's writing from, we must depend on internal clues, like references to historical events and personages.

In Judea the situation was more complex. Certainly there were Palestinian Jews who could speak Greek. There were plenty of cities in Palestine where Greeks and Jews lived in close contact—especially along the coasts, in Galilee and in the Decapolis. In those towns the Jews would very likely have picked up at least some Greek. Of course, anyone who was involved in government or international trade could hardly have functioned without some skill in the lingua franca of the Mediterranean world. In fact, there's a good deal of archaeological evidence of the importance of Greek for Palestinian Jewry. Coins minted by the Hasmonean king Alexander Janneus actually bear Greek inscriptions. There are also a great many Jewish tombs in Palestine with Greek inscriptions. Quite a few Greek contracts, lists and even some letters were found among the Dead Sea Scrolls and in caches of first and second century Jewish manuscripts discovered at Masada and the Wadi Murabba'at. So there's abundant evidence that many Jews in Palestine were skilled in the Greek language.

But unlike the Diaspora communities, the Greek speakers in Judea were almost certainly not the majority. On the one hand, it simply makes sense that most Judean Jews would have been unmotivated to learn Greek. The majority of them lived in small towns and villages where contact with Greeks was rare, and occasions to use the Greek language were infrequent. No doubt in Jerusalem and the other urban centers the situation was different from that of the small towns. There were some Greeks living in Jerusalem, and in cities like Beth Shean (renamed Scythopolis by the Greeks) Jews and Gentiles lived side-by-side, in amiable company. Also, the urban centers played host to many Greek-speaking soldiers and merchants who passed through in the course of their business. The Jewish residents of these cities would have heard a lot of Greek, and some would have been skilled in its use.

Even so, the situation for urban Palestinian Jews was nothing like that of the Diaspora Jews. Judean Jews were never far from a great many people who shared their ancestral culture. Opportunities to use the traditional languages abounded. And in Jerusalem, the major population center, the situation was even more conducive to preserving the ancestral tongue. Jerusalem was the home of Judaism. If there were anywhere that the atmosphere itself would have encouraged the Jews to maintain their cultural identity, it would have been Jerusalem! No doubt, after the Antiochan persecution the Judeans had a sour taste in their mouths for Greek culture in general. After almost having their heritage forcibly stolen from them, the Jews of Palestine surely came to appreciate it more than ever before.

DID JESUS SPEAK GREEK?

The New Testament depicts Jesus speaking to a wide variety of people. Direct quotations from Jesus are recorded in Aramaic (e.g., Mk 7:34). But Jesus is also recorded to have spoken to Gentiles who would have probably known only Greek (e.g., Mk 7:24-30; Jn 18:28—19:13). Of course, Jesus might have had translators, but many scholars suggest that Jesus must have known some Greek.

Jesus was raised in Nazareth, a small town of about five hundred residents in his day. It was a peasant town devoted almost wholly to subsistence agriculture. Joseph, Jesus' father, was probably the only carpenter in town. Jesus grew up in an insular little village, and probably no Greeks ever spent much time there.

Nazareth was situated in the region of Galilee. Galilee was located far north of Judea, north even of Samaria. It was the site of several Greek cities, which earned it the epithet "Galilee of the Gentiles." Sepphoris, a short distance from Galilee, was a large Hellenistic city. If Jesus did much business there, he must have known some Greek. But the life of a Galilean peasant would not have been conducive to deep study and mastery of a difficult foreign tongue. Nor would such study have been encouraged, as Josephus makes clear (*Ant.* 20.11.2 [264]). If Jesus knew any Greek, his knowledge was probably basic.

Those arguments are based on social theory and common sense. But there's also a good deal of physical evidence that Aramaic and Hebrew remained the primary languages of Jewish Palestine. One source of data is the New Testament. Several Aramaic words and phrases appear embedded in the Greek text (e.g., Mt 27:46; Mk 5:41; 1 Cor 16:22), a good indication that the Jews of Palestine spoke Aramaic. That notion has been corroborated by intertestamental Jewish literature, the Dead Sea Scrolls and other manuscripts discovered in Palestine. Religious texts composed in Palestine from the second century B.C. to the first century A.D. were written either in Hebrew (e.g., *Ben Sira; Jubilees;* the Dead Sea biblical commentaries and rules) or Aramaic (e.g., Daniel 7—12, sections of *1 Enoch* and many non-Community Dead Sea Scroll texts).[6] At Masada, where a band of Jewish rebels made their last stand against the Roman army in A.D. 74, a cache of manuscripts and ostraca—inscribed pottery—was found that reveal a great deal about the common languages used in Judea at the end of the first century. Hebrew, Aramaic, Greek and Latin appear in various contexts, but the majority of the materials were written in Aramaic, with Hebrew coming in second. Yes, some Judean Jews used Greek, especially in drawing up deeds and other legal papers. But when they wished to compose religious texts or write letters to other Jews, they generally used Aramaic or, to a lesser extent, Hebrew.[7]

These manuscripts pretty much confirm the statements that Josephus made about the use of Greek by Judean Jews. He was himself a highborn Judean from a priestly family. He was well educated and well traveled, and undoubtedly knew the fundamentals of Greek language. But he apparently still wrote in Hebrew or Aramaic and depended on translators to prepare the Greek versions of his histories (*Against Apion* 1.9 [50]). In his usual less-than-humble fashion, Josephus tells us (*Ant.* 20.11.2 [263]) that he exceeds all his kindred in his knowledge of Greek wisdom, and yet he still feels compelled to apologize for his lack of skill with the language. He writes:

> For our nation does not encourage those that learn the languages of many nations, and so adorn their discourses with the smoothness of their periods; because they look upon this sort of accomplishment as common, not only to all sorts of freemen, but to as many servants as please to learn them. But they give him the testimony of being a wise man who is fully acquainted with our laws, and is able to interpret their meaning.[8]

So essentially Josephus agrees that his people put no value on the mastery of Greek. It's not knowledge of the new and different but of the an-

---

[6]That is, Dead Sea Scrolls that contain no language or imagery that must be identified with the Dead Sea Scroll Community. They include a retelling of some stories from Genesis (the *Genesis Apocryphon*), an addition to the book of Daniel *(Prayer of Nabonidus)*, an Aramaic translation of the book of Job and numerous apocalyptic fragments. The Community apparently preferred Hebrew for its own compositions.

[7]The preference for Aramaic is also evident in the fact that Palestinian Jews produced their own translation of the Pentateuch in Aramaic. It is called the Targum Yerushalmi (or Palestinian Targum).

[8]*Ant.* 20.11.2 (264).

cient and traditional that was esteemed by the Jews of Judea. Again we see that Palestinian Jewish society encouraged the preservation of traditional culture rather than the adoption of Greek ways.

Physical Culture and Customs

Physical culture—things that can be seen, touched and used—are often the first traits to be exchanged when cultures come into contact. Human beings delight in novelty, and if the innovations prove useful they might become part of the lifestyle. The Jews were quick to adopt many aspects of Greek physical culture. Architectural styles in both Palestine and the Diaspora quickly began to reflect the Greeks' taste for pillars and elaborate ornamentation. The Greek-style *agora*—a courtyard in the center of town—displaced the city gates as the place where Jews would gather to discuss current events. But the changes weren't all kept out-of-doors. Inside the Jewish homes there were also some new styles. No longer content to sit on the floor, families adopted the Greek custom of reclining on benches when they dined. In wealthier homes utensils decorated with Greek motifs replaced the unadorned devices of pre-Hellenistic times. However, the designs were limited in this era to geometric patterns—no gods or heroes cavorted on the Jewish dinner table.

But it wasn't merely the household furnishings that were affected by the Greeks. Family life itself was influenced in substantial ways. Polygamy (marrying multiple wives), once a common feature of Jewish society, was increasingly frowned on in Hellenistic times. Among the Greeks, strict monogamy was the rule. The soil of Greece made poor farmland, and the people of the Achaean peninsula developed a national phobia about famine—a phobia that was partly manifested in small families. No Greek man would have prided himself on having more than one wife or many children. Rather, an indiscriminate breeder would have been treated as a pariah. The Jews, like other Near Eastern people, began to follow the Greek custom, partly because it seemed consonant with their Scriptures. Some sages further argued that women were a distraction from godliness (*Ant.* 18.2.5 [21]; M. *Aboth* 1.5), that they promoted witchcraft (*M. Aboth* 2.7) or that they were such untrustworthy creatures that it would be foolish to have any more around than absolutely necessary (*War* 2.8.2 [121])! Such misogynistic attitudes contributed to changes in the traditional Jewish marriage contract. In Old Testament times the groom was required to pay a "bride price" to his future father-in-law for the privilege of acquiring a wife. In Hellenistic times the Jews adopted the Greek custom of the dowry, where the bride's family paid money to the groom to take the girl off their hands.

The Jews didn't indiscriminately absorb Greek tastes, though. For instance, the Greek adoration for the human figure is famous. Greek statuary, mosaics and paintings usually featured realistic depictions of gods, goddesses and heroes. But the Jews were reluctant to mimic the Greeks in this fashion. From the second century B.C. to the second century A.D., Palestinian Jews were scrupulous about avoiding any human representations in their art—indeed, they avoided any representational art at all. In this period the second commandment, "You shall make for yourselves no graven images," was broadly interpreted not only as a prohibition against idols but against any representations of humans or beasts. Around 6 B.C. there was actually a riot in Jerusalem, incited by the presence of a Roman imperial eagle in front of the temple. Josephus reports that the citizens considered its presence a violation of their law (*Ant.* 17.6.2 [151]). After the second century A.D., the Jewish understanding of the second commandment became more liberal, and human and animal imagery came into wide use in Jewish Palestine. Even the synagogues were decorated with mosaics and statues, some representing heroes, astrological figures and even gods from Greek mythology!

In this matter Judaism eventually accepted the Greek customs. But in some matters the Jews could countenance no compromise. Circumcision, so central to Jewish identity, was one of these nonnegotiables. In the Greek mind any "mutilation" of the human body was abhorrent. Circumcision, practiced not only by the Jews, but by some other Near Eastern peoples as well, was strongly discouraged by the spirit of Hellenism. Some Near Easterners apparently conformed to Greek fashion on this matter. But the Jews defended their ancestral custom and adhered to it tenaciously. Except for the brief period when some Hellenizers in Jerusalem had abandoned the practice and even tried to reverse it (1 Macc 1:15), and for a few radicals who insisted that Old Testament circumcision laws should be interpreted "spiritually" rather than literally, the Jews of both Palestine and the Diaspora held fast to the ancestral custom. Wherever St. Paul traveled on his missionary journeys, he found circumcision to be a sensitive issue: there were Jewish Christians who insisted that Gentile converts to Christ should be circumcised, just as converts to Judaism would have been.

Keeping kosher also seems to have been regarded as a nonnegotiable. Even so Hellenized a Jew as Philo of Alexandria insisted that the Jewish

WOMEN IN JUDEAN SOCIETY

Ancient Jewish society, like that of most of the Mediterranean world, was patriarchal and patrilineal. That is, men held a dominant position in both public life and in the family. Family lineage was traced through the fathers. A woman was expected to leave her parents' home and reside in her husband's home, becoming a member of her husband's family. While a woman was never considered her husband's property, her legal status was in some ways dependent on her attachment to a male custodian.

The Old Testament laws made no provision for daughters to inherit property from their parents. Generally, it was expected that husbands would provide for the daughters, while the sons would need the inheritance to establish their households. Unmarried daughters were probably rare. There were few professions open to women, and many unmarried women were forced into a life of prostitution. The normal course of life for a woman was daughter to wife to mother to widow (who would be cared for by her children). A young woman was under the supervision of her father until her marriage. If it was discovered that she was not a virgin at the time of her marriage, she could be stoned to death (no such stipulations were made about the virginity of the husband). After marriage her primary occupation was to bear and raise children. A barren wife was usually considered cursed in some way and could be divorced by her husband, although that fate was by no means certain (cf. Sarah, Gen 15—21; Hannah, 1 Sam 1—2). There was no provision in the Old Testament for wives divorcing their husbands. The concept was probably unthinkable: a divorced woman would have found few suitors, and her career options would have been limited in ancient Israel.

In spite of all that, a woman's life probably wasn't as bleak as it might seem. Women seem to have enjoyed a high status in the home and exercised a great deal of authority in household management. They were responsible for the children's primary education and for the maintenance of the home. Wives secured and prepared food; they spun fibers into cloth and made clothing; and they supervised the children and household servants. In Proverbs 31, the wife is depicted engaging in real estate transactions and selling garments in the market place. The wife's many key roles in the family assured her a certain measure of security. Few Hebrew men would have imagined all women to be stupid or incompetent! Occasionally, ancient Israelite women held public positions of considerable power (e.g., Miriam, Deborah, Huldah, Athaliah).

In the Second Temple Period women's status seems to have improved in some ways. The institution of the marriage contract (Hebrew *ketubah*) assured women's rights, including a right to alimony if her husband divorced her. The recent discovery of the archives of a Jewish woman named Babatha has illuminated ancient Jewish women's legal status. The archives were deposited in a cave where Babatha took refuge during the last days of the second Jewish war against Rome (A.D. 132-135). Babatha was obviously a wealthy business woman, and her archives included deeds of sale and property conveyance. From these texts we learn that Judean women in the second century A.D. were fully engaged in commerce; some of them were literate; and they already had the right to divorce their husbands. The pax Romana created opportunities for ambitious women, just as it created opportunities for men. Conditions differed in various regions: women in Egypt had many rights, while those in Greece had few. So the status of Jewish women in Hellenistic society wasn't uniform.

dietary laws defined for human beings the most healthful and edifying way to eat. Not only the Jews but all people should avoid pork or shellfish. After all, Philo argued, anything that tasted so good had to represent a wicked self-indulgence (*Special Laws* 4.17-23 [100-123])! Philo did know of a few Jewish teachers who would have explained away the kosher laws through some tricky biblical interpretation, but they represented a very small minority. For the most part keeping kosher was held as a fundamental Jewish principle. The same was true of observing the sabbath. Criticized in the Hellenistic world as an excuse for laziness, the Jews ignored such barbs and held fast to their ancestral ways. They were so insistent on observing the sabbath that even the Roman army had to exempt Jewish soldiers from service on Saturdays.

These were some of the distinctive Israelite practices that the Jews wouldn't give up. At the same time, there were Greek customs that the Jews wouldn't tolerate. Two of the customs the Jews rejected probably arose from the Greek efforts at population control: infanticide and homosexuality. The common Hellenistic barbarism of abandoning unwanted infants was universally rejected by the Jews and frequently cited in Jewish literature as evidence that the Greeks weren't so superior as they pretended to be.[9] Homosexuality, accepted and even encouraged in some Greek circles, was also considered a contemptible violation of God's law and utterly incompatible with Judaism.[10] The Jews recognized the practice as a violation of Mosaic law (Lev 18:22; 20:13).

So neither the Jews of Palestine nor those of the Diaspora were indiscriminate in adopting Greek styles and customs. They had to weigh whether certain innovations would violate their identity as Jews. Some aspects of Greek culture could be easily assimilated into their Jewish lives and actually enrich them. Others threatened to separate them from their heritage. Always, the Jews were challenged to define what it really meant to be the children of Abraham and the followers of Moses. How much Hellenism was too much? Where should they draw the line?

Synagogue and Sanhedrin

There were two very significant institutions of Hellenistic Jewish society

---

[9]See, for example, Philo *Special Laws* 3.20 (110-19); *Sibylline Oracles* 2.282; *Pseudo Phocylides* 184-85; Josephus *Against Apion* 2.25 (202).
[10]See, for example, *Sibylline Oracles* 3.185, 595-600; *Pseudo Phocylides* 190-92; *2 Enoch* 34.2; *Jubilees* 13.18; 16.5-6; Josephus *Against Apion* 2.25 (199).

that may or may not have been shaped significantly by contact with the Greeks. One of these institutions was the synagogue. The synagogue was the primary institution through which Jewish religious instruction was passed on from one generation to the next. It was here that Jews would gather for prayer, fellowship and to hear regular readings and expositions of the Scriptures. Josephus and Philo claimed that the synagogues were established by Moses himself as a place for weekly study of the Scriptures.[11] But scholars give little credence to that claim. Rather, most historians argue that the synagogue system originated among the Jewish exiles in Babylon, in the sixth century B.C. It's widely believed that the Jews in that foreign land began meeting regularly to preserve their religious traditions in the absence of the temple and sacrificial cult. Indeed, the facts that the Jews maintained their religious identity throughout the exile and that the Babylonian Jews developed a strong orthodox community suggest that some kind of a teaching institution existed in Babylon. But it's only a probability: there aren't any clear references to synagogues in any Jewish literature composed before the Hellenistic era.

The earliest extant references to Jewish meeting places come from Ptolemaic Egypt. In the third century B.C., Egyptian Jews dedicated a "house of prayer" to King Ptolemy Euergetes (247-221 B.C.), and the inscription has survived. We have other synagogue inscriptions from elsewhere in the Diaspora, and Philo mentions Alexandrian synagogues several times. But up until New Testament times there are no references to synagogues in Palestine itself. In the accounts of Antiochus Epiphanes' persecution of the Jews in Judea, we read of him desecrating the temple, setting up altars in town squares and burning incense in front of houses, but there's no mention of attacks on synagogues—strong evidence that they didn't yet exist in Judea. But by the end of the first century B.C., synagogues had obviously spread to Palestine, since both the New Testament and Josephus attest to their existence in Judea by that time.

With such deep roots in the Diaspora, it's not surprising that the synagogue institution had a strongly Hellenized flavor. This fact is apparent, first of all, in the terms used to denote synagogues. Up through the first century A.D. the only words used to describe these institutions were Greek: *proseuche*, "(place of) prayer," and *synagoge*, "assembly." The term *proseuche* seems to have been earlier and was clearly preferred in the Diaspora

---

[11]Josephus *Against Apion* 2.18 (175); Philo *Life of Moses* 2.39 (216).

up through the first century A.D. It's frequently found in inscriptions and in the writings of Philo of Alexandria. But in the New Testament and Josephus the preferred term was *synagoge*—and this was the word that eventually stuck. Later, the rabbis translated these terms into Hebrew and Aramaic, so that the most common term for synagogues in rabbinic literature was *bet knesset*, "house of assembly."

The organization of the synagogue was very democratic. Unlike the assemblies or "holy convocations" of the Old Testament days, there was no priest who performed sacrifices and no prophet who proclaimed God's indisputable commands. Any priests or Levites who attended synagogue services were granted no more important a role than any other Jewish man. Each man had a voice in the synagogue. A democratic vote was taken on who would serve as its "captain," and he was responsible for scheduling readers. The men would engage in debates over the meanings of Scripture passages, just as the Greeks would gather in their town centers to discuss the latest philosophies (see Acts 17:16-21). All in all, the whole institution reflects the Greek exaltation of democracy and free inquiry. In such an atmosphere Jesus seemed quite an anomaly because he "taught them as one having authority, and not as their scribes" (Mt 7:29).

The case of the Sanhedrin, the Judean Jewish legislative assembly, is somewhat different. Apparently, members of the Sanhedrin were elected from among the people to serve as a kind of trial court for serious crimes, just as Greek cities had legislative councils elected from their citizens. There were "sanhedrins" in most Jewish towns, and a "Great Sanhedrin" in Jerusalem. Some scholars believe this ruling body originated in the Hellenistic era, a result of the Hellenistic spirit of democracy spreading among the Jews. These scholars note too that in Josephus's history the first mention of the Sanhedrin appears in a decree from Antiochus III (223-187 B.C.; see *Ant.* 12.3.3 [138]). And finally, the term applied to this ruling senate, *sanhedrin* (Greek for "assembly"), is the same term used by the Greeks for their ruling councils. It would seem to constitute a fairly strong case for regarding the Sanhedrin as a Hellenistic invention.

The case isn't so airtight as it might appear, though. To begin with, the term *Sanhedrin* wasn't the Jews' term of choice for the ruling council. Actually, that term was first applied to the Jewish council by the Romans: in pre-Roman times the Jews referred to their judicial council as the "council of elders" (Greek *gerousia*). There's nothing particularly Hellenistic about that title. References to assemblies of the elders appear in the Old Testament as early as the book of Exodus (Ex 3:16) and continue throughout the Bible. In Exodus 24:1, God summons Moses, Aaron and seventy elders to stand before him. Rabbinic traditions claim that the same number of elders served in the Sanhedrin in Jerusalem. It might be that various "councils of elders" had existed from ancient times among the Jews, chosen by popular assent from the graybeards. There was probably some formalization of the group in Persian times, when the high priest became its official head. The Greeks would have been quick to recognize the authority of such a group, since they had similar councils in their own city-states. They might even have encouraged extending the Sanhedrin's powers. The assembly of elders may have obtained new prominence in Hellenistic times, but the institution itself can't be regarded as a product of Greek influence.

Religious Syncretism

Nowhere was the tension to Hellenize more keenly felt than in the realm of religious beliefs. Even before the coming of Alexander the Great, there had been a growing tendency among the enlightened peoples of the East to stress the basic unity of religions. The Syrians worshiped a storm god, and the Greeks worshiped a storm god, so where was the conflict? The Egyptians revered the sun, but so did the Greeks and Babylonians. Why couldn't the gods really be one and the same? To the philosophically minded the various deities were all manifestations or aspects of the same godhead. The universal deity simply appeared in different guises in different lands or settings.

Of course, not everyone was so philosophically minded. But that doesn't mean that the less sophisticated would have had difficulty assimilating new religious beliefs. For the average polytheist there was always room in the pantheon for another god or two. They saw no problem with paying their annual tribute to Zeus while still doing their daily homage to the local deities.

Surely the Jews must have been tempted to take a similar path. We've already seen how the Jews at Elephantine paid homage to Egyptian gods, while giving their chief loyalty to the Lord. Those Jews represented an unsophisticated branch of the family tree—mercenaries and laborers far removed from the guidance of the sages. On the other hand, the people who tried to insinuate the cult of Zeus into Jerusalem were hardly from the lower classes. Those Hellenizers were influenced by the universalism of the day: the Lord of Israel and Zeus Ouranos of the Greeks were simply two manifestations of the same deity, so there'd be no harm in changing the name on the mailbox. But beyond that incident, evidence of a hybrid religion that combined Judaism with the worship of Greek gods is scant. The fourth-century synagogue art mentioned earlier can hardly be taken as evidence for Jewish worship of Greek gods, but rather as appreciation for Greek creative expression. It's similar to the way a modern Christian might display African art or Eastern religious images in their homes without giving thought to their significance. We also find that many Jews gave the names of Greek gods to their children. But this practice, too, simply represents the popular style of the day, and not any actual veneration of the pagan deities. To my knowledge no texts have ever been discovered in which a Jew addresses prayers to Apollo or Athena or Dionysus. That's not to say that there were no Jews praying to Greek gods. There undoubtedly were some who did so, just as there are Christians today in various lands who worship pagan gods alongside Jesus Christ. But such syncretism couldn't have been widespread, since there's no manuscript evidence of its existence and no Jewish teachers seem concerned about the problem. It seems, rather, that any Jews who wanted to worship the Greek gods just abandoned their ancestral faith altogether. Jewish literature has left us a good many examples of such apostates, including Philo of Alexandria's nephew, Tiberius Julius Alexander, who rose to some prominence in the Roman government.

The Jews, though, didn't reject all aspects of Greek religion. One realm in which Judaism was very open to Greek influence was astrology. The Greeks weren't the first to look to the stars for guidance—that dubious honor should probably go to the Babylonians. The ancient Mesopotamian concept of the universe assumed that all things in heaven and earth were somehow interconnected, and significant events couldn't occur in isolation from one another. So if a major battle was lost on the same day that a comet appeared in the sky, the Babylonians could conclude that the appearance of a comet was a bad omen for battle. They developed extensive catalogues of such coincidences and referred to them often when planning for the future. So heavily did the Babylonians rely on astrology that the terms *Chaldean* (the ethnic group that established the neo-Babylonian empire) and *astrologer* came to be synonymous. The Jews were aware of Babylonian astrology and lampooned it fiercely (Is 47:13; Jer 10:2). And the fact that many ancient peoples worshiped the stars only added to the Jews' disdain for astrology.

In the fourth century B.C. the Greeks—probably inspired by Babylon—began to develop some unique forms and methods of astrological inquiry. The Greeks based their form of astrology on the notion that the stars not only reflected earthly events but somehow shaped them as well. For the Greeks, astrology wasn't just a popular superstition. They tried to raise it to the level of a science. Even the Greek philosophers attempted to devise rationalizations for the practice based on Aristotle's conception of the universe. Aristotle taught that the Earth was situated at the center of a series of concentric heavenly spheres. These spheres moved about each other, and the movement of each affected the movements of the other spheres. So indirectly the movements of the stars would affect events on Earth. Such a "scientific" discipline could be very useful. Just as some do today, the Greeks would use astrology to predict a person's character based on his or her birth date. Astrologers also claimed to be able to foretell coming events based on signs in the heavens. Clients might also pay an astrologer to cast a horoscope to determine the best time to undertake a trip or plant crops or set out to battle.

Some Jews seem to have resisted the spread of Greek astrology: one author in the *Sibylline Oracles* (a composite work that includes material from pre-Christian times) praises the Jews for rejecting the practice. But the resistance apparently wasn't sustained. Astrology was already spreading among the Jews in pre-Christian times. Numerous pseudepigraphic works contain references to astrological phenomena. Many horoscopes were included among the Dead Sea Scrolls, including some that seem to predict the coming of a messianic figure and perhaps an antimessiah as well. We've already mentioned the use of astrological motifs in fourth-century synagogue art. Even the rabbis of the Talmud seem to have found little reason to complain about astrology. This particular Greek import managed to infiltrate Judaism quite thoroughly. By the Middle Ages, astrology had become such a prominent aspect of Judaism that Jewish sages were frequently employed as court astrologers. Among the great medieval rabbis astrology was considered a science quite compatible with the Jewish faith. Only the eminent Maimonides (A.D. 1135-1204) questioned the efficacy and morality of the practice.

Philosophical Thought and Method

One of the most striking aspects of Greek culture was its predilection for—indeed, its invention of—philosophical inquiry. In their speculations the

Greeks logically and systematically investigated questions that the Jews had rarely considered: What is the nature of matter? What is time? Is there such a thing as free will? Of what do the gods consist? They also considered many ethical issues, like the responsibilities of the individual to the state or to his or her fellow human beings. Some of this speculation certainly overlapped the concerns of theology and would have interested any thoughtful Jews who were aware that such questions were being asked.

That's where the question lies: how cognizant were most Jews of Greek philosophy? In the Western Diaspora, there were certainly Jewish thinkers who were conversant in Greek thought. Chief among them (but by no means unique) was Philo of Alexandria. Philo demonstrates a fine grasp of the philosophical ideas and methods employed in the world of his day. Some of the principal influences on his thinking were Plato and the Stoics. But the foundations of his philosophical-theological system were the Scriptures and his Jewish faith. In order to reconcile Greek philosophical concepts with the Scriptures, Philo employed the method of allegorical interpretation. In this method each element of a story or narrative is understood to have some symbolic significance that points to a greater truth. (George Orwell's modern allegory *Animal Farm,* for example, uses a farm and talking animals as symbols of a revolutionary state.) Allegory has been used from very ancient times as a rhetorical device, appearing even in early Old Testament passages (e.g., Judg 9:7-20; Ezek 16).

But the Greek allegorists of the Hellenistic era weren't so concerned about writing allegories as *finding* allegories. They interpreted passages from ancient myths and epics—texts that weren't originally written as allegories—as if they *were* allegories, conveying deep philosophical truth through apparently naive stories. The allegorists argued that the divine spirits that had inspired the texts had embedded profound truths in them which could be mined out by later insightful readers. When Philo and other Hellenistic Jewish interpreters applied these methods to Scripture passages, they discovered truths remarkably compatible with the teachings of the philosophers. Thus Philo, interpreting the first chapter of Genesis (*Allegorical Interpretation* 1.1.2 [2-3]), argues that the six days of creation weren't to be taken as a literal six days, since, he says, only a simpleton would believe the world was created in a literal six days. Rather, the number six is used because it represents the most perfect number, being divisible into either two or three equal parts; and because it's the product of two and three: numbers that represent the two states of matter and the three dimensions.

The allegorical method proved useful to Palestinian Jews as well. According to rabbinic tradition the sages were interpreting the Bible allegorically already in the time of Jesus. But unlike Philo, the Judean rabbis didn't use allegorical interpretation to bring the Scriptures in harmony with Greek philosophy. Rather, their interests were in making difficult or mundane Bible passages express profound truth—usually by harmonizing them with the rabbis' understanding of the greater Scriptural revelation. As an interesting example of rabbinic allegory, take this interpretation of Genesis 1:2:

> NOW THE EARTH WAS TOHU (Hebrew, 'unformed') symbolizes Babylonia: '*I beheld the earth, and, lo, it was tohu*' (Jeremiah 4:23); AND BOHU (Hebrew, 'void') symbolizes Media: '*They hastened* (the Hebrew, 'wa-yabhillu,' sounds similar to 'BOHU') *to bring Haman*' (Esther 4:14). AND DARKNESS symbolizes Greece, which darkened the eyes of Israel with its decrees . . . UPON THE FACE OF THE DEEP—this wicked state (i.e., Rome): just as the deep cannot be plumbed, so one cannot plumb (the depths of iniquity of) this wicked state.[12]

This quote, from the third century A.D. Rabbi Simeon Lakish, used the allegorical method developed by the Greeks to demonize the nations that had ruled over the Jews. And this example isn't unique: the rabbis were finding allegory everywhere in the Bible. If they were aware that their method had been inspired by the Greeks, they never acknowledged the fact.

Perhaps another area where Greek philosophy made its impact felt in Judaism was in a temporary avoidance of anthropomorphic language and imagery for God. Greek philosophical thought maintained that the God (whoever they conceived that ultimate being to be) was quite remote from the universe and generally impersonal. How could the creator of all things interact with mere humans? How could the "unmoved mover" be moved by human pain? Some speculated that God, as perfect spirit, couldn't interact with matter at all, or he would become imperfect. So they posited that if God interacted with the world, it would be through intermediaries, like the *logos* ("word" or "logical principle") of the Stoics. To the philosophers, the God of the Bible was simply too "human" to be divine.

---

[12]H. Freedman, *Midrash Rabbah: Genesis* (New York: Soncino Press, 1983), Gen 1:2. The translation has been slightly altered for clarity.

ALLEGORY VERSUS PARABLE

Allegory is one of the literary devices used by the New Testament authors to explicate the gospel. Paul uses allegorical interpretation in Galatians 4, where he compares Hagar and Sarah to the old and new covenants between God and his people. Many scholars consider the typologies in the book of Hebrews to be allegories: in Hebrews 7, Melchizedek is interpreted as a type of Jesus, and in chapters 9-10, various elements of the Old Testament sacrificial system are taken as types of Jesus' sacrifice.

But the style of teaching we associate with Jesus is the parable. Parables are short, highly visual stories that convey a moral or spiritual message. Allegories, on the other hand, might convey several messages, since each element has symbolic significance.

In Hebrew the same word was used for both parables and allegories *(mashal)*, and it's sometimes difficult to maintain a strict separation between the categories. Jesus' parables of the soils (Mk 4:1-20) and the wicked vine-growers (Mk 12:1-9) are both allegories; the various elements have symbolic significance. The "parable" of the Prodigal Son (Lk 15:11-32) is also an allegory—the father and the two sons are each symbols, and several lessons are conveyed. But the allegorical interpretation shouldn't be pushed too far. There's no reason to believe that the pods fed to the swine, for instance, have some deep symbolic meaning. The interpreter of Jesus' parables must sometimes rely on common sense to determine which elements of the stories have deeper significance and which simply add "vividness" to the narrative.

Philo, understandably enough, was deeply concerned with this problem. He dealt with the most difficult biblical stories, where God is depicted in very anthropomorphic images, by allegorizing them. He also adopted the Stoic notion of the *logos* to serve his Jewish purposes.

Philo's point of departure was the growing trend in popular Jewish literature to personify the Word of the Lord. The seeds of this trend were already present in the Old Testament. The book of Isaiah sometimes seems to "hypostatize" (attribute independent existence to) God's word, as in Isaiah 9:8: "The Lord has sent a word against Jacob, and it fell on Israel" (see also Is 55:11). Similar images appear in Psalm 33:6, which speaks of the word of the Lord creating the cosmos, and Proverbs 8, where "wisdom" is personified and made God's "partner" in creation. In Hellenistic times some Jewish authors went further still. Ben Sirach personified wisdom, who comes from the mouth of the "Most High" and sits on a heavenly throne (Sir 24:3-4). He also apparently hypostatized the Word of God, stating that the Word of the Lord goes forth to perform God's work (Sir 42:15). Similar ideas can be found in the first century A.D. apocalypse *4 Ezra,* which makes God's word the creator of heaven and earth (*4 Ezra* 6:38). But the most striking personification of God's Word in this era comes from the Wisdom of Solomon (a book of the Apocrypha probably written in the first century A.D.), which says that God's "all-powerful Word" leaped from the throne of heaven to carry God's commands to earth (Wis 8:15). It was in this tradition that Philo stood, and he took the logical step of identifying the personified Word with the *logos* of the Stoics. For Philo, the *logos* was a literal intermediary between God and creation. He was divine, but not God, and so an appropriate mediator between the immutable God and the very mutable natural world.

Philo seems to have anticipated some of the ideas we find in early Christian literature. In fact, there's been a great deal of speculation on whether or not his teachings inspired the theology of John 1, where Jesus is identified as the preexistent Word of God. But there are some significant differences between Philo's Word and John's Word. Philo carefully avoided identifying the *logos* with God, but that identification is the basis of John's Christology (doctrine of Christ): "In the beginning was the Word, and the Word was with God, and the Word was God" (Jn 1:1). Philo's Hellenistic theology wouldn't have countenanced the notion of the Word becoming flesh, which is the climax of John's hymn to the *logos* (Jn 1:14). So it seems more likely that John developed his thoughts on the Word of God independent of Philo, both men drawing on the same Old Testament traditions and their own unique insights. Nonetheless, Philo's ideas were profound, and later Christian theologians found them extremely useful.

Palestinian Jewish authors seem to have shared Philo's concerns about Old Testament anthropomorphism. Their efforts to avoid such imagery are manifest in the early rabbinic literature (first to second centuries A.D.). There's a tendency to eschew language that attributes humanlike actions (e.g., eating, expressing doubts, changing his mind) or passionate feelings to God. The Mishnah is remarkable in its "earthiness": there's little of the miraculous, divine speech or even authoritative revelations. It's a book of dialogue and argument, where God lurks in the background but seldom asserts himself. And like Philo the rabbis found the concept of the "word of the Lord" a useful one for distancing God from creation. In rabbinic texts the word of the Lord isn't called the *logos* but the *dabar elohim* (Hebrew) or *memra* (Aramaic). In some of the targumin (the Aramaic translations of the Old Testament), biblical passages that depict God interacting with creation are consistently altered or "glossed" by inserting the phrase *"the word of* the Lord" in place of "the Lord." So in Genesis 2:2, it wasn't "the Lord" who completed the heavens and the earth but "the word of the Lord." It wasn't "the Lord" who spoke to Adam and Eve or visited with Abraham or delivered Israel from Egypt; it was "the word of the Lord" who did all of those things. God himself somehow stayed aloof from the cosmos. We never find the Palestinian rabbis developing a theology of the Word like we find in Philo and John. But such circumlocution surely implies that the rabbis had been at least subtly influenced by the Hellenistic conception of the divine.

Scholars have combed rabbinic literature for more substantive examples of Greek influence. They frequently observe that the rabbis talk about the books of Homer. Yes, the rabbis certainly knew of Homer's existence, and the major role his works played in Greek literature. On the other hand, they never give any impression that they've actually *read* Homer's works. There are no quotations from the *Iliad* or the *Odyssey* in Palestinian or Babylonian Jewish literature. Nor is there any indication that the rabbis were familiar with the burning issues of Greek philosophy, except in the most general terms. No rabbinic texts ever mention Plato or the Stoics. Epicureans are held up as examples of infidels, but once again there's no evidence that the rabbis had the slightest idea of what the Epicureans believed. Indeed, the term *Epicurean* was a generic epithet for any immoral Gentile, or even for immoral Jews. The rabbis demonstrate familiarity with some of the ethical questions posed by the Greek philosophers, but they don't appear to have any command of the intricacies of the philosophers' arguments. There were issues being raised by Greek ethicists that caught the attention of the general public, and the rabbis were part of that public. It seems quite doubtful, to me at least, that the rabbis had ever actually read Plato, let alone Epicurus.

Conclusions

Hellenism was a complex phenomenon. The Jews of the urban Diaspora communities were the most deeply affected by contact with the Greeks, while the Jews of rural Palestine were the least affected. But all the Jews who were exposed to Greek culture were faced with some difficult choices. Who did they most identify with—their own ethnic group or their Greek overlords? How much of their heritage could they abandon, and yet remain truly Jewish? How much Greek culture would be too much? We're used to thinking of Hellenization as a social phenomenon. But we mustn't forget that it was a psychological phenomenon as well. Each individual had to grapple with the dissonant impulses of assimilation and resistance. There was so much personal identity at stake, but the potential for personal enrichment was great as well.

There was also great potential for apostasy. Hellenization was a spiritual phenomenon, as well as a social phenomenon. There was a struggle afoot between invisible forces—Michael, the angelic prince of Israel, struggled with the prince of Greece (Dan 10:20-21). The gods of the Greeks were as seductive in their own ways as Baal had been in old days. Their philosophers sought to remove some of the mystery from the universe; but did they rob it of some majesty as well? Would fusions of Judaism and Hellenism result in apostasy or heresy or epiphany? Could the God who used the Persians to expand the Jewish understandings of the spirit world not use the Greeks in the same manner?

Indeed, God could use any tool he desired, including the Greeks. We've already seen that rabbinic Judaism owed much to the Greeks. The allegorical methods of biblical interpretation, the notions of democratic decision making, the methods of debate—all were influenced by Greek ideas. And Christianity may owe even more to the Greeks. The apostle Paul, the evangelist Luke and the author of the book of Hebrews all employ Greek styles and methods in their presentations. The early theologians of the church commonly believed that some of the Greek philosophers had been divinely inspired and made extensive use of their writings. The church father Tertullian (c. A.D. 160-220) protested the trend, posing his famous question, "What hath Athens to do with Jerusalem?" But Tertullian's disapproval couldn't stem the tide of Hellenism. Faith and philosophy naturally complement each other; both deal with issues of ultimate significance. Some of the greatest theologians of the church consciously drew on Greek philosophers in developing their understandings of God and creation. Origen used the allegorical method extensively in his explication of the Scriptures; Augustine of Hippo depended on Platonic thought; and Thomas Aquinas, the great medieval thinker, drew on the philosophy of Aristotle. So in Christianity, East and West met and merged in a remarkable Gestalt—a whole greater than the sum of its parts. Alexander the Great's vision was fulfilled in a way much different—and greater—than he could ever have imagined.

For Further Reading

Collins, John J. *Between Athens and Jerusalem: Jewish Identity in the Hellenistic Diaspora.* New York: Crossroad, 1983.

Collins, John J., and Gregory E. Sterling, eds., *Hellenism in the Land of Israel.* Notre Dame, Ind.: University of Notre Dame Press, 2001. A recent collection of articles.

Eddy, Samuel K. *The King Is Dead: Studies in Near Eastern Resistance to Hellenism, 331-34 B.C.* Lincoln: University of Nebraska Press, 1961.

Feldman, Louis H. "Hengel's *Judaism and Hellenism* in Retrospect." *Journal of Biblical Literature* 96 (1977). A helpful review and corrective of Hengel's magisterial work.

Hengel, Martin. *Hellenism and Judaism.* Translated by John Bowden. Philadelphia: Fortress, 1974. Hengel argues here for a rather pervasive Hellenization of both Palestine and the Diaspora. He later softened his position, admitting that differences between Palestine and the Diaspora would have been significant. Nonetheless, this book remains the classic study on Hellenization for the vast amount of data it incorporates.

Momigliano, Arnaldo. *Alien Wisdom: The Limits of Hellenization.* Cambridge: Cambridge University Press, 1975. A collection of essays by a Jewish classical scholar.

Smith, Morton. *Palestinian Parties and Politics that Shaped the Old Testament.* London: SCM Press, 1971. See chapter 3, "Hellenization."

Tcherikover, Victor. *Hellenistic Civilization and the Jews.* Translated by S. Applebaum. New York: Atheneum, 1959. Note especially part 2, chapter 4, on the cultural climate in the Diaspora.

9

The Romans and the Jews

No one really knows when the city of Rome was founded. History took no notice when a band of Latins emigrated from the Italian highlands to settle on the Mediterranean coast. Archaeologists haven't been able to determine when the region was first inhabited. The Romans themselves had two main legends about their beginnings. According to one, a hero named Aeneas, a refugee from fallen Troy, founded Rome around 1100 B.C. The other claimed that Romulus, son of the god Mars and a mortal woman, established the boundaries of the city around 753 B.C. Probably little history resides in either tale. All we can say with certainty is that various Indo-European tribes from around Italy settled in the area well before the seventh century B.C. They were an unassuming, somewhat primitive people content to be left to themselves. But around 600 B.C. their village was transformed by an invasion of people called the Etruscans. We know little about them either, but they probably migrated to Italy from Asia Minor. They took over Rome and subjugated the natives. But through their technology, religious beliefs and administrative systems, they lifted the city far above the cultural level of its neighbors. Marshlands were drained, walls were built, and new territory was annexed to the city. By the time the Latin natives had ousted their Etruscan king and established a republican government (according to tradition, around 509 B.C.), Rome had become the leading state of central Italy.

The Roman Republic was governed by a senate (from the Latin word *senex*, "elder") selected from the wealthy class of Roman society, the *patricians*. The working class, called the *plebians*, was largely unrepresented in the government. Membership in these classes was hereditary, and there

THE END OF THE ROMAN REPUBLIC

Trouble in the Roman republic had been brewing for ages. Even though the lower-caste plebeians were growing in wealth and influence, the aristocratic patricians were loath to share power with them. Economic woes added to the tension. During the struggle between Rome and Carthage in the third and second centuries B.C., many farmers had been conscripted to serve in the army. While they were away and unable to work their land properly, their wives were reduced to poverty. Taking advantage of the women's dilemma, wealthy barons bought up huge tracts of land and slaves to work it. The former soldiers who returned to their farms found themselves unable to compete with the plantations. Many of these proud but impoverished people made their way to Rome, looking for opportunities to make a new life. But there was little work to be had, and the displaced veterans put tremendous strain on the city's already taxed resources. Rome needed room to grow, and it needed to put the idle to work. The answer to both problems seemed to be through military expansion. The Roman legions conquered many lands and ruled them as "provinces."

But the tensions between plebeians and patricians continued. Calls went up repeatedly for relief and democratic reforms. Political factions battled and bartered for control of the Senate and the sympathies of the masses. On several occasions Rome erupted in class riots. "Democrats"—those in favor of broader popular representation—sometimes massacred their aristocratic rivals in a manner that foreshadowed the French Revolution. In 85 B.C. a Roman general named Sulla used his wealth and soldiers to violently suppress the democrats. With the Senate paralyzed by power struggles, Sulla took it on himself to run the city as a dictator. But once peace was restored, he voluntarily laid down his office and retired from public life.

Sulla's "reforms" had temporarily secured the aristocratic rule, but the underlying problems remained. The Senate was caught on the horns of a dilemma. On the one hand, it needed a strong military presence in Rome to keep the peace. On the other hand, the Roman constitution forbade generals from acting in Rome without Senate approval, but the Senate was so divided that it couldn't agree on a course of action. In 60 B.C. three generals—Pompey, Crassus and a young democrat named Julius Caesar—formed a league called the First Triumvirate. Technically, their sphere of operation was the provinces, but in reality they exercised great influence in Roman politics. These three ambitious men weren't content to share power forever, and soon the Triumvirate collapsed. Julius Caesar emerged as dictator of Rome. The Senate feared Caesar's power and popularity. They assassinated him in 45 B.C.

After Caesar's death, chaos and violence erupted. Caesar's assassins led a campaign to restore Senate rule and curtail the influence of the military in Roman politics. Three Roman generals, Antony, Lepidus and Octavian (Julius Caesar's nephew), formed the Second Triumvirate to oppose them. They soon had defeated the Senate forces and began struggling with each other for supremacy. When Antony forged an alliance with Cleopatra, Octavian argued that the general was planning to turn over Rome to the Egyptians. Fears of Antony and Cleopatra motivated the Senate to grant great authority to Octavian. After Antony was defeated, Octavian stood as supreme power in Rome. He ushered in far-reaching reforms, but once peace was achieved, he restored to the Senate the power to oversee nonmilitary domestic affairs (27 B.C.). The grateful senators rewarded Octavian by declaring him emperor and bequeathed on him the title "Augustus." The stability he brought to the empire ushered in an era of unprecedented prosperity that continued even during the reigns of his less-capable heirs. His popularity was epitomized in the state cult established in his honor.

was little social mobility. There were, however, economic opportunities for enterprising individuals of any class. As decades passed and some plebeians began to accumulate wealth and power, they demanded more voice in government. Tension between the two classes intensified until 366 B.C., when the Senate was forced to open its membership to some of the wealthiest plebeians. With the internal strife temporarily quelled, the Romans were free to turn their attention to external conquest. Through warfare and alliances the Romans quickly conquered most of Italy, including several strong Greek colonies on the peninsula. In a wise political move, Rome offered the conquered peoples citizenship in its state. Rome would be their "mother," coming to their aid if they were attacked. They, in turn, were expected to defend Rome. The tactic worked so well that when General Hannibal of Carthage invaded Italy in 218 B.C., he wasn't able to raise the natives in rebellion against Rome. The Latin cities remained loyal to their "mother," viewing themselves as Romans rather than subjects of a foreign power.

But not all of Rome's conquests received this favored status of allies and citizens. When Rome captured western Sicily from Carthage in the mid-third century B.C., it found the people of the island too "primitive" to serve as valuable allies. Without even a well-organized government, the Romans couldn't conceive of entering into a treaty with the natives. Unwilling to place such unsophisticated folk on an even par with Roman citizens, Rome developed the idea of the "province," or "sphere of influence." Under the administration of a military governor, the people of a province weren't regarded as friends or allies but only as subjects. They retained a good deal of local rule, but they paid taxes to Rome and answered ultimately to the Roman official stationed in their land.

Once the policy of creating provinces was established, Rome began extending it to other conquests. By the first century B.C., Rome was adding no new allies to the republic. All her conquests, civilized and uncivilized alike, were then annexed as provinces.

The High Priesthood of Hyrcanus II

With Pompey's conquest of Jerusalem, Judea had the privilege of being incorporated into the Roman province of Coele-Syria.[1] There was no local military governor in Judea itself. Rather, the Jews answered to the gover-

---

[1] Primary sources for this section are *Ant.* 14.5.1-14.13.10 (80-369); *War* 1.8.1-1.13.11 (159-273).

nor of Syria—from 65 B.C. to 62 B.C., Aemilius Scaurus, the Roman general who had first met the Jews in Syria. Hyrcanus II was high priest, the chief civil and religious authority in Judea, but he was no longer king. In their usual fashion the Romans allowed the Jews to order their own internal affairs. But the governor had ultimate authority, and the Jews were once again paying taxes to a foreign power. The days of an independent Jewish state were essentially over.

The days of a Jewish "empire" were over too. One significant effect of Rome's conquest of Judea was a redrawing of the national boundary lines. Some of the territories conquered by John Hyrcanus and Alexander Janneus were now freed from Judean control. The Samaritans could once again pursue their own religious and political ideals. The Gentile cities of the coastlands and Galilee were liberated from the Jews. (The Romans, like the Macedonians, had a deep appreciation for Greek culture, and so it was particularly unconscionable to them that the Jews should rule over Hellenized cities.) In some of these cities the Jewish residents now found themselves persona non grata, and they had to return to Judea for fear of their lives. Others returned to the motherland simply for the sake of enjoying a friendlier environment. No doubt some Jewish citizens had become wealthy from their holdings in Gentile lands. But now they were forced to abandon their property and find new lodgings. The population of Jerusalem swelled with refugees and the newly impoverished. Resentment against the Romans surely seethed in many Jewish hearts.

In spite of the upheavals, the Judean situation wasn't so bad as it's sometimes portrayed. It's very likely that Hyrcanus II, given his unambitious nature, would have been a model subject to the Roman state. Since the Romans generally avoided interfering in internal politics of their conquered lands, the Jews might have enjoyed relative peace and even prosperity as part of a Roman province. After all, the Romans came building roads, public buildings and providing for the general protection of the citizenry. The Roman navy put down piracy on the sea, and the Roman armies terrorized robbers. Trade passed more freely throughout the Mediterranean region than ever before. State-sponsored building projects offered employment and trade, enhancing local economies. All in all the Jews could have done quite well as part of the Roman Republic. The Romans weren't cruel overlords, even if they appear at times to have been insensitive to local customs and beliefs. So there may have been some truth to Josephus's intimation that a delegation of Jews wanted Pompey to incorporate Judea into the Roman province. The potential peace and prosperity of life under Rome must have seemed preferable to the misery that the internecine conflict between Hyrcanus and Aristobulus had brought about.

Several problems, however, prevented the Jews from realizing peace. One was the fact that Roman prisons seemed to leak like sieves. In 57 B.C. Aristobulus's elder son, Alexander, escaped from Pompey's custody and made his way back to Judea. He gathered around himself a substantial army and seized control of several important fortresses. The high priest Hyrcanus, on the other hand, had few forces at his disposal. He had to concentrate on Jerusalem's defense by rebuilding the walls that Pompey had demolished. So it was up to the Romans to deal with Alexander. The new governor of Coele-Syria, Gabinius, pursued the fugitive to the environs of Jerusalem, where Jews and Romans engaged in battle. But unlike the glory days of the Hasmoneans, when small bands of determined Jews could overwhelm massive hosts, there would be no miraculous deliverance for Alexander. The Romans utterly defeated the rebel forces. Three thousand of Alexander's followers died, and three thousand were taken captive. Alexander himself escaped to Alexandrium, a fortress located north of Jericho, while his remaining partisans held two other fortresses. As the Romans laid siege to his citadel, Alexander sent his mother out to offer his surrender and plead for his life. Gabinius accepted the surrender, and—incredible as it seems—he apparently granted Alexander his freedom in exchange for receiving the fortresses intact.

As a result of the invasion, Gabinius decided that Hyrcanus lacked the competence to rule Judea—a charge that undoubtedly had a measure of truth to it. He ordered Judea divided into five administrative districts, each governed by its own "sanhedrin." Hyrcanus retained his position as high priest and religious authority—including his role as administrator of the temple and the financial resources it possessed. But his civil authority was now nearly nonexistent. For the first time in many generations the high priest was not the official leader of the Jewish nation.

Trouble came again in 56 B.C. The Romans had another lapse in security, and Aristobulus himself, along with his son Antigonus, escaped from prison. They quickly assembled an army and set up their headquarters in Alexandrium. But as Gabinius's forces advanced on Alexandrium, Aristobulus's soldiers escaped to the east, heading toward an old fortress called Machaerus, on the east bank of the Dead Sea. The Romans overtook them before they reached their intended refuge, killing five thousand of Aristobulus's soldiers. But the former king and his son slipped away yet again. They ensconced themselves in Machaerus, and began hasty preparations for the inevitable siege. But their work was in vain: the old walls were no match for Roman siege engines. After only two days the city had fallen. Aristobulus was sent back to Rome, but once again, at his mother's request, Antigonus was allowed to remain in Judea. Obviously, she had remarkable powers of persuasion.

In 55 B.C. Pompey ordered Gabinius to undertake a campaign into Egypt. Pompey's goal—unauthorized by the Roman senate—was to re-instate Ptolemy Auletes, who had been deposed as the Egyptian king. Hyrcanus and Antipater (the Idumean sheik who had persuaded Hyrcanus to challenge his brother for the high priesthood) provided money, arms and other supplies to Gabinius, ingratiating themselves to the governor's good favor. But no sooner had Gabinius set out for Egypt than Aristobulus's son Alexander raised the Jews in revolt against Hyrcanus. The Roman general sent Antipater to persuade the Jews away from such a dangerous course, but 30,000 men still rallied around Alexander. So as soon as he had successfully concluded his campaign in Egypt, Gabinius raced back to Judea. The Roman forces met with the rebels near Mt. Tabor. Ten thousand Jews lost their lives—but once again, Alexander escaped.

In the end, it wasn't their attempts at seizing power that led to the demise of Aristobulus and his son Alexander. Ironically, it was the great machine of Roman politics that ground them between its gears. In 49 B.C. the Roman civil wars had begun. Powerful generals struggled with one another for control of the nation and its provinces. Pompey had brought the East under Roman dominion, and he sought to maintain control of the region with the aid of his native allies. Judea was an important pawn in the game, primarily because it could serve as a platform for launching an invasion of Egypt or Syria. Hyrcanus and Antipater were called once again to Pompey's aid. But Julius Caesar also recognized the strategic importance of Judea. He needed an ally there who could rally the Jews against Hyrcanus and Pompey. For him the logical choice was Aristobulus, a man who could quickly raise an army of followers. Caesar released him from his Roman cell and put two legions of soldiers at his command. But Aristobulus never made it to Judea. The former king and high priest was poisoned to death in Rome by Pompey's men. A similar fate befell his son Alexander, who was arrested by one of Pompey's generals, taken to Antioch in Syria and beheaded. Only Antigonus escaped. He and his sisters fled to Egypt, where they won the favor of King Ptolemy.

Hyrcanus and Antipater had thrown their support to the wrong man: it was Caesar who emerged triumphant in this struggle. Pompey fled to Egypt in hope of aid, but instead he was assassinated there in 48 B.C.—an end that many in Judea would have deemed fitting for the man who had dared invade the sacred precincts of the temple. Caesar arrived in Egypt on Pompey's heels, but finding his rival already dead he became embroiled instead in the local politics. King Ptolemy XIII had become the official ruler of Egypt by marrying his older sister Cleopatra VII. Cleopatra had taken over the kingdom when their father, Ptolemy XII, had died, and she considered herself the true ruler of Egypt. But since most Egyptians refused to recognize her rule, she had fled into exile. Caesar set up his headquarters in the royal palace of Alexandria. He planned to meet with the new King Ptolemy in one of the palace's great halls, seeking an alliance that would reinforce his battered army. But before the scheduled audience, a large, rolled carpet was carried into the meeting hall. As it was spread out before Caesar, it revealed its hidden splendor: Cleopatra had smuggled herself inside. It's hard to imagine how the queen could have looked anything but comical, rolling out of the carpet unto the floor. But somehow she immediately captivated the powerful Roman general, and Julius Caesar and Cleopatra became lovers.

When Ptolemy came before Caesar, he found himself not only in the company of the general but of his estranged wife as well. He immediately perceived that Cleopatra had made Caesar an offer that he wouldn't be able to match. Recognizing his peril the king tried to flee from the palace, shouting "Treason!" to anyone who cared to listen. But Caesar's men apprehended and imprisoned him in the palace.

King Ptolemy wasn't without friends in Alexandria. One of his generals rallied the Egyptian army and assembled the Alexandrian citizens outside the palace. Now it was Caesar's turn to be the captive. He found himself besieged in the royal palace of Alexandria, cut off from support and escape. It could have been a disaster for Caesar, but it was a golden opportunity for Hyrcanus and Antipater. Here was their chance to ingratiate themselves to their new overlord. Hyrcanus persuaded the Jews of Egypt to side with Caesar, and Antipater raised an army of three thousand men to come to his aid. Antipater himself led the army to Egypt and distinguished himself by his heroism. Soon, Roman troops arrived as well, and Caesar was rescued. King Ptolemy died attempting to escape from the palace, and Cleopatra became the unopposed ruler of Egypt.

The new queen journeyed to Rome with her lover, seeking to cast her spell over the people of the great metropolis, just as she had captivated their leading general. She surrounded herself with splendor, comporting herself in a fashion befitting a queen—or a goddess. Her ostentatious displays were partly effective. The exotic lady fascinated the masses. The Senate, on the other hand, had a different reaction. They represented conservative Roman values and abhorred the notion of a woman wielding political power. They were also scandalized by the immorality of Caesar and Cleopatra's relationship, since both had been married when their affair began. But most of all, the senators had no doubt that the queen of Egypt had her sights set on ruling Rome. It didn't help matters when she and Caesar bore a son, Caesarion. Keeping a mistress was one thing, but flaunting her child was another matter altogether. Cleopatra was certain that Caesarion would one day rule the world. The Senate, however, was making different plans.

Even while Caesar was making enemies in Rome, he was cementing his friendships in the East. His Jewish benefactors were rewarded handsomely: Antipater was made a Roman citizen and exempted from taxation. He was also made the "procurator" of Judea, essentially meaning that he was Rome's emissary among the Jews. Hyrcanus was confirmed in his role as high priest and also made the "ethnarch"—chief governmental authority—of Judea. Caesar had restored to Hyrcanus the civil authority that Gabinius had stripped from him. The Jews were also permitted to rebuild the walls of Jerusalem. Perhaps most important of all, Caesar enacted legislation that protected the Jewish religion. Throughout the Roman realm, the Jews were free to practice the customs of their ancestors without interference from local authorities.

While Hyrcanus was ostensibly the ruler of Judea, it appears that the power behind the throne belonged to Antipater. He used his own considerable wealth, as well as pilfered public funds, to purchase the favor of Sextus, the new Roman governor of Coele-Syria. Through such bribery and other favors the Idumean sheik secured government positions for his two oldest sons. The eldest, Phasael, was appointed governor of Jerusalem. The second son, Herod, became the governor of Galilee. Herod was an impressive young man, intelligent and strong. At the age of twenty-five, he was already displaying the drive that would serve him so well later in his life. One of his first acts as governor was to clean out the bandits who made their homes in the Galilean countryside. Such bandits had an ambivalent status in Jewish society. On the one hand, they were certainly criminals, making their living by stealing from others. Their operations jeopardized any who traveled through Galilee. On the other hand, they generally preyed on the rich—foreign traders, Roman lackeys and others who represented the power elite. So in the eyes of many Jews, some of these bandits were nothing less than freedom fighters and almost came to be considered folk heroes.

Herod didn't see them that way. To him they weren't just a danger to trade but a threat to the very stability of his realm. On his orders a prominent brigand named Hezekiah was captured and executed, along with many of his men. The swift, effective operation was highly praised by some Galileans and the Syrians. But many of the Jews must have been displeased by Herod's actions. Even the Sanhedrin in Jerusalem was enraged. Officially, they argued that Herod had overstepped his authority: only the Sanhedrin could try and execute criminals, not the governors. Unofficially, some Sanhedrin members saw the incident as an opportunity to curtail the growing power of Antipater and his sons. So Herod was summoned to Jerusalem to stand trial.

Herod wasn't ignorant of the Sanhedrin's intentions. Nor was he feeling particularly repentant for what must have seemed to him like a perfectly reasonable course of action. He responded to the Sanhedrin's summons—but not as they would have expected. He didn't appear before the ruling council dressed in mourning clothes, as was typical for a man accused of a serious crime. Instead, he came dressed in the purple robes of a ruler. And even more distressing, he was surrounded by a retinue of armed men—ready to defend Herod, should the Sanhedrin attempt to take him into custody.

The Sanhedrin was cowed by Herod's impressive display and nearly dismissed the charges at once. But one of the elder councilors, a rabbi named Sameas, stood and gave an impassioned speech reminding the Sanhedrin of its duties. The tide was turned, and it looked as if the Sanhedrin was going to convict Herod of murder. But then the high priest Hyrcanus intervened and called for the court to recess. He took Herod aside and advised him to flee Jerusalem before the trial could resume. Chafing under such humiliation, Herod nevertheless heeded the advice. He snuck out of Jerusalem and escaped to Damascus and the company of the Roman governor Sextus. Through blandishments and bribery Herod was confirmed in his position as governor and given further authority as the *strategos*—a term of uncertain significance but probably a military commander—of native forces in Syria-Palestine. Now, the rash young man had an army at his disposal. And Herod was determined to show the Sanhedrin that he couldn't be pushed around. He set off with his forces toward Jerusalem, intent on revenge. Only Antipater's intervention prevented a bloodbath. The old sheik persuaded his hotheaded son to take his troops and return home in peace. So Herod headed back to Galilee, consoling himself with the knowledge that he'd demonstrated to the Sanhedrin that he was no one to trifle with.

Roman politics continued to wreak havoc on internal affairs in Judea. In 44 B.C. Caesar was assassinated, and there commenced a long and difficult struggle for leadership of the Republic. One of Caesar's assassins, Cassius, now began to amass an army to fight against Caesar's lieutenant, Mark Antony. The governor of Syria pledged his support to Cassius, and Hyrcanus and Antipater were obligated to follow suit. Cassius taxed the province heavily in order to supply his troops. To assure that his war chests would be full, he made harsh examples of any towns that failed to raise their tribute, selling their populations into slavery. Antipater and his son Herod proved themselves most helpful in persuading the Jewish towns to pay their taxes. Cassius was so impressed by their abilities that he decided to retain Herod in his position as strategos.

The next year Herod's career took a tragic turn. Until now Antipater had proven to be the only person capable of restraining the headstrong young man. But in 43 B.C. an assassin who had been hired by a prominent Jewish politician poisoned Antipater to death. Herod knew who was behind the assassination, but he could do little to prove a case against him. So with no legal recourse he had the murderer assassinated. It seemed a justified vengeance to both Hyrcanus and Cassius, who assured Herod of his continued support. But with Antipater now dead, Herod had lost an important steadying influence in his life. From now on he'd have to learn how to restrain his impulses on his own.

In 42 B.C. Cassius and his legions left Syria to carry his struggle to other fronts. With the Roman presence removed, insurrection erupted throughout Palestine. Antigonus, the remaining son of Aristobulus, seized the opportunity to make a play for the throne. Aided by foreign allies, he attempted to invade Judea. But Herod was ready for him and drove Antigonus and his forces back just after they'd crossed the Judean borders. On his return to Jerusalem, Herod received a hero's welcome. The crowds cheered, and Hyrcanus himself placed a garland on Herod's head. The old high priest believed it was in his own best interest to promote Herod before the Jews, since the young Idumean was engaged to take Hyrcanus's granddaughter as his second wife. It must have seemed to Hyrcanus that the Hasmonean line was destined to survive through Herod.

Meanwhile, Cassius and his ally Brutus had been defeated by Mark Antony and Octavian (who would later be called Augustus). The two conquerors, along with their partner Lepidus, divided the realm between them: Octavian and Lepidus ruled in the West, while Antony went to Asia. Antony's first priority in the East would be to milk the province for all it was worth. His army had been seriously depleted by the war, and he had many debts to pay. He needed money, and he desperately needed allies. When a delegation of Jews approached him with a list of complaints against Herod and his brother, Antony would hear none of it; Herod's generous tribute spoke louder than their complaints. Besides, Herod and Phasaelus had proven themselves competent at maintaining order in the realm, and they'd been loyal to the Roman governors. Antony had no reason to doubt that they'd be loyal to his man as well. He confirmed them in their positions, conferring on them the title "tetrarch"—a position second in eminence only to that of ethnarch. Hyrcanus retained that title and continued as the high priest and figurehead leader of Judea. Antony further demonstrated his good will by emancipating the Jews whom Cassius had sold into slavery.

Obviously, Antony had a far more important issue to attend to than some peevish Jews. He had to normalize Rome's relationship with Egypt. When Julius Caesar had been assassinated, Cleopatra had fled Rome in fear. The Senate had no love for the ambitious queen, and Cleopatra rightly suspected that her life and that of her son Caesarion were in danger. She had returned to Egypt and had spent the last three years rebuilding the kingdom that she had neglected while aspiring to become the queen of Rome. Antony recognized that Cleopatra was the second-greatest power in the East (after himself), and he knew that she might be an important ally. He invited her to meet him in Tarsus (the city of Paul's origin) in 41 B.C. Cleopatra, for her part, knew that any hopes for an empire of her own lay in forging an alliance with the Roman general. She quickly assessed Antony's character and appealed to his vanity—and his libido—by arriving in a fabulously decorated barge equipped with silver oars and purple sails. Cleopatra lounged on the deck, dressed as Aphrodite, the goddess of love, attended by scantily clad nymphs. Like Julius Caesar before him, Antony instantly became her lover. But it wasn't just lust that motivated him. An alliance seemed just as advantageous to him as it did to Cleopatra. On the one hand, the vain general relished the idea of having a highborn lady—former lover of Caesar, no less!—to share his bed. On the other hand, he desperately needed money to pay his soldiers and rebuild his army, and Cleopatra's gaudy barge seemed to confirm the rumors of Egypt's great wealth. (In reality, the nation had suffered greatly from civil war and famine, and was on the verge of economic collapse.) Antony spent the winter of 41-40 B.C. in Alexandria, enjoying the company of the queen.

With Antony's army still crippled and his attention so fully occupied, another power that had been biding its time now went on the move. The Parthians, who had already proven themselves a match for the Romans, invaded Syria and Palestine. Antigonus immediately sought an alliance with the invaders. With bribes and a promise of plunder, he secured the aid of a contingent of Parthian cavalry. As he advanced on Jerusalem, Jewish partisans joined him as well. Antigonus's forces managed to insinuate themselves into Jerusalem, and the city erupted in rebellion. But Herod and Phasaelus fought valiantly, and Antigonus's partisans were unable to get the upper hand. Antigonus was frustrated but not yet defeated. If he couldn't gain the kingdom through military mastery, he'd take it through treachery. A contingent of Parthians was admitted into Jerusalem on the pretense that they would bring an end to the bloodshed. They persuaded Phasaelus and Hyrcanus to accompany them to the Parthian camp. Herod was suspicious and kept his distance. But Phasaelus and Hyrcanus, hoping to get on the good side of the Parthian invaders, went to the meeting. The two Judeans were treated as royal guests, wined and dined and presented with lavish gifts. The Parthians were proceeding cautiously, hoping to capture Herod in Jerusalem and their "guests" simultaneously. But Phasaelus was informed that treachery was afoot. He sent messengers to Herod, warning him of a possible trap. Herod was now on the alert, but there was little he could do to help his brother. Soon, the Parthians took Hyrcanus and Phasaelus captive, and sent word to their lieutenants in Jerusalem that Herod was to be lured outside the city walls and taken prisoner there.

Herod received intelligence of his brother's capture. He knew he couldn't defeat the Parthian host with the few troops he had at his disposal. His only choice was to flee from Judea. He took his wives, children and a sizable company of men, and escaped to Idumea—fighting against Jewish rebels along the way. From there he went east toward Arabia, hoping to get some aid from Nabatea, the small but powerful Arabic kingdom. The king of Nabatea owed Herod money and a favor, and Herod felt this was as good a time as any to collect. But the king of Nabatea had no interest in repaying his debt, nor in a possible conflict with Parthia. For now, Herod was on his own.

Hyrcanus and Phasaelus were now in Antigonus's power, and the tyrant wasn't inclined to mercy. Antigonus feared that the Jews might try to reinstall Hyrcanus as high priest, so to permanently disqualify him from the office, he cut off the old man's ears. (According to Old Testament law, only men with no physical defects could serve as high priest.) Phasaelus recognized that his doom was certain. But rather than allow himself to be executed by his enemies, he threw himself to the ground and bashed his head against a stone. As he lay on his deathbed, one of his nurses informed him that his brother Herod had escaped. Phasaelus died confident that he would be avenged.

Antigonus I

It was 40 B.C. when Antigonus began his reign in Judea.[2] Like the old Hasmonean monarchs, Antigonus declared himself both high priest and king. The coins he minted identified him by his Hebrew name, Mattathias—the same name borne by the father of the Hasmoneans, who had set the entire revolt in motion. It was an ironic epithet, since Antigonus would be the last of the Hasmonean priest-kings.

Josephus tells us little of internal affairs during Antigonus's brief reign. His primary source of information for this period was Nicolaus of Damascus, King Herod's chronicler. So it's not surprising that we read more about what Herod was doing than what Antigonus was up to. What's clear from our sources is that Antigonus first had to deal with the Parthians who had installed him in his new office. They took a good deal of plunder from Jerusalem, and then set to work on the surrounding countryside, looting a number of cities. Eventually, the Parthians' greed was sated, and they

---

[2]Primary sources for this section are *Ant.* 14.14.1-14.16.4 (370-491); *War* 1.14.1-1.18.3 (274-357).

withdrew from Judea. Antigonus was left with the task of securing the kingdom they had won for him. His first order of business was dealing with Herod's supporters. A contingent led by Herod's younger brother Joseph had taken control of Masada, a veritably impregnable wilderness fortress. Antigonus's forces laid siege to Masada, but they weren't able to gain access to the stout enclave.

Meanwhile, Herod was on his way to Rome. He knew there was no way he'd be able to take Judea without Roman support. While the Jewish masses might have had sympathy for Hyrcanus, they had little love for Herod himself. To the Jews he was an Idumean "half-Jew," a convert whose thin veneer of Judaism could hardly conceal his barbaric lineage. Herod traveled first to Egypt, to rally his supporters there and raise money for the bribes he'd need in Rome. Then, he was off to Rome. Antony was there, and he granted Herod an audience. Herod, no less canny than Cleopatra, knew how to approach the general. He gave him gifts and promised him much more if Rome would take down Antigonus and restore Herod to power. Antony needed little persuading: he had found Herod useful in the past and had little love for the rebel Antigonus. Coming before the senate, Antony related the story of Antigonus's treachery and urged them to declare Herod the king of Judea. Herod himself must have been taken by surprise. Being declared king was more than he could have hoped for. His family was rich, but it wasn't of noble blood. The Romans—following their policy of noninterference in local affairs—generally conferred kingship only on those who actually stood in line for the throne. But convinced of Herod's usefulness, and perhaps fed up with the Hasmoneans, the senate agreed with Antony. In less than seven days Herod had gone from being a pitiful refugee, to being named the king of Judea.

Being declared king was one matter, but actually taking the throne was another matter altogether. Back in the East a general named Ventidius had been appointed governor of Coele-Syria. He expelled the Parthians from Syria and restored some order to the Asian province. Then he led his troops into Judea on the pretense of rescuing the besieged Herodians in Masada. But instead of engaging Antigonus's army in the wilderness, Ventidius set up camp outside Jerusalem. He demanded tribute from Antigonus, and the Hasmonean king was forced to turn over whatever public wealth the Parthians hadn't taken. Ventidius then returned to Syria, leaving his general Silo stationed in Judea. But Antigonus was left unmolested, and he began to cultivate a warm relationship with Silo—a relationship based entirely on graft. As long as Silo was profiting from Anitgonus's bribes, he felt no inclination to oust the usurper from office.

Herod entered Judea with his army in 39 B.C. His first priority was liberating his family and friends who were holed up at Masada. Now, Silo couldn't avoid lending his aid any longer, so he assigned some Roman troops to Herod's band. These combined forces overwhelmed Antigonus's besieging army at Masada, and Herod's family was free. Several cities volunteered their men and services to Herod's cause, and he went about the country subjugating rebel cities and gaining further support. When the Roman forces were drawn away from Judea by another Parthian invasion, Herod conducted a campaign in Galilee, routing out bandits and any Parthian forces in the region. His troops clashed frequently with Antigonus's supporters in a seesaw struggle for Judea. Antigonus won some substantial victories, including a battle in which Herod's brother Joseph was killed. But it was only postponing the inevitable. By 37 B.C., with the Romans back at his side, Herod was ready to begin the assault on Jerusalem itself. The Romans erected their mighty siege engines, and the walls of the city were bombarded. But Jerusalem was well fortified, and its walls didn't give easily. It took forty days to breach Jerusalem's outer perimeter, and then the Romans set to work on the inner wall that protected the temple mount. After several more weeks, Herod's forces broke through that wall. Antigonus, who had taken refuge there, was delivered to the Romans. He was taken to Antioch in Syria, where—at the request of Herod and Mark Antony—he was beheaded. It was the first time the Romans had ever carried out such a sentence on a king.

So ended the reign of the last Hasmonean priest-king and a brief gasp of Jewish self-determination. The Jews were once again vassals of Rome, subject to the whims of its generals and senate. But this time they were governed by a Roman client king, the crafty and volatile King Herod.

Herod the Great

Readers of the New Testament know Herod as the man who was responsible for the Slaughter of the Innocents.[3] In the insane paranoia that characterized his final days, Herod had deemed all the male children of

---

[3]Primary sources for this section are *Ant.* 15.1.1-17.8.4 (15.394-17.205); *War* 1.18.1-1.33.9 (347-673).

Bethlehem a small price to pay for the destruction of the Messiah.[4] So his legacy has been one of incredible villainy, the ancient equivalent of a Hitler or Stalin. But it wasn't for naught that history has conferred on Herod the title "the Great." An energetic and generally competent ruler, he elevated the Jews' status in the Roman Empire and brought an almost unprecedented splendor to Jerusalem. He was a complex, conflicted and ultimately tragic figure, an ambitious man who truly cared for the kingdom he ruled—a kingdom that generally despised him.

The early years. Historians conveniently divide Herod's reign into three sections: the period of consolidation, the period of prosperity, and the time of domestic turmoil. After taking the throne in 37 B.C. and for about a decade to come, the task that demanded all the new monarch's attention was establishing his kingdom against potential rivals. As Herod had already learned, being granted a kingdom was altogether different from actually ruling one. He had to obtain at least some measure of cooperation from his subjects. There were friends to reward and enemies to eliminate. Herod killed two birds with one stone by executing all of Antigonus's supporters. Not only did he do away with potential troublemakers, but he took their property and used it to pay off his benefactors. His ruthless efficiency probably didn't win him any friends in the Jewish populace, but it certainly instilled some fear in the potentially rebellious masses. And for an Idumean usurper and Roman lackey, perhaps fear, at least for the time being, was the best he could hope for.

Of course, Herod was well aware of the fact that most Jews would regard his kingship as illegitimate—especially while there were still Hasmoneans who could have filled the office. Following the dictum "Keep your friends close, and your enemies closer," Herod ransomed Hyrcanus from the Parthians and gave him a position of honor at all public affairs. Josephus tells us that Herod's real intention was to bring Hyrcanus close enough to eliminate him—a goal he eventually achieved. For the time being, though, Hyrcanus was treated as an honored patriarch. He couldn't serve as the high priest, which suited Herod fine. Recognizing the potential power of that position, Herod installed an old friend named Hananel (also called Ananelus) in the office. Hananel came from an undistin-

---

[4]This incident is recorded in the New Testament (Mt 2:16) only; Josephus says nothing of it. But the story is hardly out of character for the last days of Herod's reign, when he seemed to have been on the verge of madness. Capricious, wholesale murder was not beyond him in the least.

guished family, and he'd been living in Babylon, so he had no political clout in Jerusalem at all—a seemingly safe appointment from Herod's point of view. However, the Hasmoneans weren't going to take such an affront lying down. Herod's mother-in-law, Alexandra—daughter of Hyrcanus and mother of Herod's wife Mariamne—was a shrewd and strong-willed woman. She demanded that Herod install her son Aristobulus III, a sixteen-year-old, as high priest. Herod protested that the lad was too young to fill the priestly office, but Alexandra would have none of it. She enlisted the aid of another ambitious mother, Queen Cleopatra. Cleopatra interceded with Antony, and Antony ordered Herod to install the young Hasmonean as high priest. Herod made it known that he believed the whole scheme was an attempt by Alexandra to seize power for herself and her family, but he had no choice but to comply. He grew to hate Alexandra and kept her under close watch. But he didn't dare touch her, considering the friendship she had developed with the queen of Egypt.

Aristobulus III was a handsome lad, and he became immensely popular as high priest. That popularity Herod would not countenance. While Aristobulus was sporting in a pool at his mother's house in Jericho, Herod's servants "accidentally" drowned the young man. He hadn't served even a year as high priest. The innocuous Hananel took over the high priesthood once again. Alexandra complained bitterly to Cleopatra, and the Egyptian queen persuaded Antony to call Herod to account for his actions. (Cleopatra, of course, had designs of her own. She was hoping for Herod's execution, believing that once he was dead the kingdom of Judea would be hers.) So Herod appeared before Antony, well prepared for his trial with gifts and promises of unwavering support. Antony accepted the bribes and allowed Herod to return home in peace. Alexandra was frustrated, but not yet defeated. The proud matriarch bided her time, looking for opportunities to avenge her loss. She also fomented her daughter Mariamne's growing mistrust of the ruthless king.

Cleopatra, on the other hand, wasn't so patient. She was determined to add Judea to her Egyptian empire. Antony wouldn't give her Herod's kingdom because he considered the Idumean a valuable ally. But he did make her a gift of Syria and the Phoenician coast. He also gave her some land in Judea itself—the palm and balsam groves on the Jericho plain. Herod had to lease these lands from the Egyptian queen in order to sell their produce. Cleopatra further interfered in Judean affairs by embroiling Herod in a conflict with Nabatea. The king of Nabatea was withholding his tribute, and Cleopatra persuaded Antony to make Herod responsible for collecting the money. The conniving queen was confident that the two feisty kingdoms would exhaust one another, making them easy prey when the opportunity arose for her to conquer them. And her plan almost worked: Herod and the Nabateans engaged in a seesaw struggle that was crippling both sides. Cleopatra added to the trouble by sending her own army to fight *against* Herod's troops. When an earthquake decimated Judea in 31 B.C., Herod tried to negotiate a truce with the Nabateans. But Herod's peace envoys were murdered, and the request for an armistice was refused. The show of brutality enraged Herod and all Judea, and they mustered an army to confront the formidable Arabians. This time, however, the Jews were fighting for a cause, and their anger made them efficient. Herod routed the Nabateans, demonstrating again his resourcefulness—and his luck.

Herod's problems with Cleopatra soon came to a dramatic end. Antony and Octavian were struggling for control of Rome. At the Battle of Actium in 31 B.C. Mark Antony was dealt a decisive defeat. Herod recognized that change was afoot, and by this time he probably welcomed it. But even so, his position had been granted to him by Antony. Octavian wasn't beholden to Herod at all and might choose to replace him. Herod felt his position could be in jeopardy. So his first order of business before meeting his new overlord was to make certain that there could be no rival claimants to the Judean throne. So Herod had Hyrcanus accused of conspiring with the Nabateans against Judea and Rome—a charge that almost certainly had no basis in reality, since Hyrcanus had neither the ambition nor the nerve for such an undertaking. The old priest was convicted and executed, and Herod felt his claim on the throne was more secure than ever.

Before leaving to present himself to Octavian in Rhodes, Herod placed Alexandra and Mariamne in one of his fortresses, under the guard of an officer named Soaemus. Herod gave his lieutenant an order: if it goes badly for Herod and Augustus executes him, then Mariamne was to be executed as well. In his wild jealousy Herod couldn't bear the thought of another man having her.[5] The two women chafed under their imprisonment,

---

[5]According to *Ant.* 15.3.5-6 (62-70), Herod gave the same instructions to his uncle Joseph before he had gone to meet with Antony (after he had murdered Aristobulus). The many similarities between the two episodes leads one to suspect that they're both based on a single incident. Josephus simply included both accounts, uncertain which (if not both) was historical.

and Mariamne began to question Herod's love for her. But Soaemus would hear none of it. He protested, "Of course he loves you, madam! He's even given me instructions to kill you if he doesn't return home, so the two of you can be together forever!" Not surprisingly, Mariamne didn't feel especially flattered.

Herod turned on his charm with Octavian, presenting himself as the hapless victim of Antony and Cleopatra's treachery. Nor did he fail to recount all his glorious deeds, proving how useful he could be to his overlords. But all the fawning was probably unnecessary. Octavian's policy was to leave the client kings in their positions, so long as they had demonstrated their loyalty to Rome. Herod was supposed to support Antony. He couldn't be considered a traitor for doing his duty. Besides, Herod had often proven quite competent. So Octavian confirmed Herod as the king of the Jews and conferred other honors on him as well. After Antony and Cleopatra's suicide, Octavian gave back to Judea the lands that Cleopatra had taken, along with Samaria and several important coastal cities. Herod came out of the situation very well indeed.

Herod returned home exultant in victory, only to find his wife colder than ever. The king was confused and heartbroken—how could Mariamne despise him so? Hadn't he proven himself the equal of a Hasmonean? The marital tension presented an opportunity for some other ambitious characters to eliminate their rivals. Herod's mother, Cyprus, and his sister Salome envied the powerful Mariamne and resented her aristocratic airs. So they began to spread rumors, encouraging Herod's insecurity. How could Mariamne possibly reject the king, unless she had found another lover? What had she been doing with Soaemus during Herod's absence? Salome even bribed the king's cupbearer to claim that Mariamne had tried to poison Herod. To get at the truth, Herod had Mariamne's eunuch tortured. The poor man knew nothing of poison, but he did reveal that Mariamne hated Herod because she knew he had ordered Soaemus to kill her. To Herod, the fact that Soaemus had divulged such a confidence was proof enough that the two had been intimate. Soaemus was executed at once. Mariamne was tried and executed in 29 B.C.

Herod was devastated by Mariamne's "adultery," and even more so by her death. He went on a wild drinking binge. He sulked, stared into space and called out to his dead wife. He went on a hunting expedition in Samaria and returned ill and exhausted. Seeing Herod in such a state, Alexandra thought her hour had come. Soon Herod would be dead, she believed, and Alexandra needed to act at once if she were to be the next ruler of Judea. She approached the commanders of two of the Judean fortresses and attempted to win them over to her cause. But she had put her confidence in the wrong men: the officers exposed Alexandra as a traitor. In about 28 B.C. Alexandra was executed.

Herod recovered from his illness, but he never fully recovered from Mariamne's death. He had truly adored the young woman, even if he didn't actually "love" her in any mature sense. And in spite of the triumphs he would go on to obtain, the ghost of Mariamne would haunt Herod until the end of his days.

The prosperous period. Most historians would date the beginning of phase two of Herod's reign to about 27 B.C. He'd successfully eliminated any potential rivals for his throne. He was free from the interference of Cleopatra, and under the rule of Octavian—who (in 27 B.C.) was proclaimed emperor and given the title Augustus—the Roman Empire finally enjoyed unprecedented peace and prosperity. Judea shared in that prosperity, and Herod built a kingdom whose magnificence may have rivaled that of King Solomon.

Herod's greatest resource proved to be his political savvy. He was in a difficult position, trying to appear like a loyal subject of the pagan Romans on the one hand, and trying to look like a devout Jew on the other. He managed the former quite well, but his success in the latter is questionable. In Rome he was well respected. He traveled to Rome on several occasions, and his two sons by Mariamne lived in Rome "to enjoy the company of Caesar" (*Ant.* 15.10.1 [342]). Herod also met with the emperor when he came to Syria. He formed a friendship with Augustus's second-in-command, Vipsanius Agrippa, and even named one of his grandsons in Agrippa's honor. And these friendships paid dividends. Several times new lands were added to Herod's realm. At its greatest extent, his realm was at least as big as the Hasmonean kingdom. Augustus honored Herod by conferring on him the title *rex socius*—"allied king." It was a position that granted Herod a measure of autonomy far above that of most Roman "client kings." He still had to pay tribute to Rome. He couldn't wage war without Rome's approval, and he was still expected to come to Rome's aid should he be summoned. But in all internal matters of state Herod had almost complete autonomy. In this period Judea was basically free from Roman interference.

King Herod didn't come into all this good favor without some effort on his part. Recognizing the Roman infatuation with Greek culture, he sur-

ROMAN EMPEROR WORSHIP

In the ancient world, lines between the human and the divine were often blurred. We have seen already how Alexander the Great, Antiochus Epiphanes and others were worshiped as gods. The Romans, too, had myths about divine rulers like Romulus, who had founded the city. Prophecies circulated in the Roman Republic that in a time of need, a divine deliverer would appear to bring order and peace.

After many years of turmoil Augustus had brought an end to violence in Rome and its environs. It's no wonder that many people saw him as the fulfillment of the prophecies and set up shrines in his honor. Whether or not Augustus believed himself divine, we can't say. But it's clear that he found the cult a useful means of bringing unity to his empire, and he made no attempts to discourage it. Augustus became the embodiment of the Roman Empire, and worship of Augustus was a sign of loyalty to Rome.

Later emperors honored divine Augustus, but most discouraged worship of themselves, at least during their lifetimes. One exception was the mad Caligula (37-41 A.D.), who almost brought the Jews to revolt by his insistence on being worshiped throughout the empire. Generally, the first-century emperors respected the Jews' refusal to worship them because the Jewish religion had been granted protection by both Julius Caesar and Augustus. Christians, however, who were officially distinguished from the Jews during the days of the emperor Nero (57-68 A.D.), were granted no such protection. Their refusal to worship the emperor was considered not only an act of heresy but of treason.

rounded himself with Greek tutors and counselors. His children received a fine Greek education in Rome. He rebuilt several cities according to the model of the Greek *poleis*, and gave them Greek names. The ancient port city of Strato's Tower was renovated in Greek style and renamed Caesarea. Equipped with a theater, hippodrome and amphitheater, it became the foremost port of Asia, and a showplace for Greek culture and religion in the East. Samaria, too, was rebuilt, equipped with a temple for the royal cult and renamed Sebaste (Greek for "Augustus"). In the Gentile cities of Herod's realm he built or embellished many temples dedicated to Augustus Caesar and the Greek deities. At great personal expense he constructed gymnasia in Tripolis, Acco and Damascus—all cities *outside* his realm whose residents were primarily non-Jewish. He was a patron of the dramatic arts, gladiatorial games and athletic events. Herod's treasuries paid for the trophies given to the winners at the games—a fact many Jews found repulsive because the trophies resembled pagan idols. He even constructed a theater in Jerusalem itself. While there was nothing in the law against theatrical performances, many Jewish leaders were convinced that so Greek a custom had to be contrary to the commandments of God.

For the most part Herod confined his overtly non-Jewish activities to the Gentile cities. He scrupulously tried to avoid offending the Jews in Judea. The coinage he minted contained no portraits of himself or of Augustus, because some Jews would have regarded such images as a violation of the second commandment. His buildings were decorated with geometrical patterns or plant images devoid of any artwork that would have offended pious Jews. All the palaces that he built included immersion pools so he and his company could observe the ritual purity that the rabbis of the day prescribed (washing before meals, bathing after sexual relations or menstrual periods, etc.). He carefully observed the Jewish dietary laws, even when he traveled abroad, provoking one Roman author to quip that he'd rather be Herod's pig than Herod's son (the latter having a nasty tendency to die young). He forbade his daughters to marry any men who weren't circumcised. He also worked hard to secure the rights of Jews throughout the Roman Empire so that Jewish people everywhere would be free to observe their customs unmolested.

Herod's greatest demonstration of piety was to be found in his work on the Jerusalem temple. He lavished his personal and public funds on the structure, expanding and beautifying it until it was a wonder of the ancient world. Much of the architecture followed the Greek styles popular in the day, with stairs and cloisters and rows of pillars with Corinthian capitals. But again Herod avoided any human or animal imagery that might offend Jewish scruples. Even the rabbis, who had nothing good to say about Herod, remarked that no one could claim to have seen beauty unless they had seen Herod's temple.

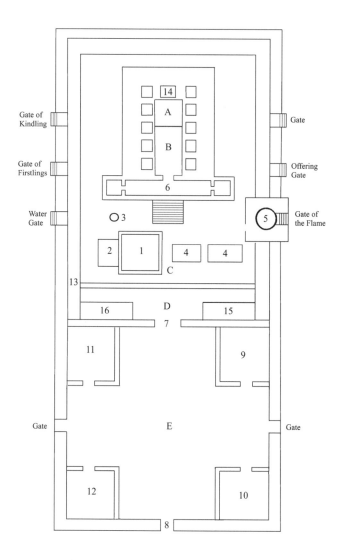

Figure 5. Plan of Herod's temple

A Holy of Holies	1 Altar	9 Chamber of Lepers
B Sanctuary	2 Ramp	10 Chamber of Wood
C Court of Priests	3 Laver	11 Chamber of Oil
D Court of Israel	4 Slaughter Area	12 Chamber of Nazirites
E Court of Women	5 Chamber of the Hearth	13 Chamber of Hewn Stone
	6 Porch	14 Chambers
	7 Nicanor Gate	15 Chamber of Vestments
	8 Beautiful Gate	16 Chamber of Baked Cakes

When people are predisposed to take offense, there's little one can do to appease them. Such was the case with the Judean Jews. Most of them probably didn't like Herod to begin with, and the favors he bestowed on "pagan" towns did nothing to improve their opinion of him. So in spite of Herod's efforts to avoid offending the Jews, they still regarded him as an apostate. The pitiful king wanted desperately to be admired, and he craved affection. But all he could inspire in his subjects was contempt. It's little wonder that he didn't always seem to have a firm grip on his sanity.

Certainly, Herod's domestic policies did nothing to enhance his standing with his subjects. He was, in a word, a despot. He would endure no challenges to his authority. The Sanhedrin was gutted of its power. Many of its members were massacred because they had supported Antigonus over Herod. Herod bestowed honor on two members of the Sanhedrin, rabbis named Pollio and Sameas, because they had encouraged the city to open its gates to him. (Many scholars believe that these rabbis are none other than the legendary Hillel and Shammai, regarded by the Talmud as the fathers of rabbinic Judaism.) But apparently, he deprived the Sanhedrin of all its civil authority, leaving it to judge religious matters alone. He also deprived the high priesthood of its power and prevented it from becoming a center for nationalistic ideals by filling the post with obscure figures and foreigners. His last appointee to the post, an Alexandrian Jew named Simon, was awarded the position by virtue of the fact that Herod had fallen in love with Simon's daughter and couldn't marry a mere "commoner." The paranoid monarch even went so far as to ban public assembly or any speech that might be deemed seditious. Spies were dispatched throughout Herod's realm, ready to report back any suspicious behavior or talk. Josephus reports that Herod himself would go out in disguise among the people to find out what they were saying about him. Suspected rebels were dealt with harshly, being tortured before they were allowed to die. Civil liberty suffered heavily during Herod's reign.

Herod's paranoia also fueled many of his building projects. In Jerusalem he fortified his palace and had the old Akra (fortress) rebuilt, naming it the Antonia, in honor of his former patron. (This project was completed before Antony's debacle.) He had a secret exit installed in the temple so he could slip out into the safety of the Antonia, should the occasion demand. He also had a number of fortresses constructed throughout Judea, including one called Herodium. Masada was rebuilt and made more impregnable than ever. These strategically placed refuges were part pleasure

THE SCHOOLS OF HILLEL AND SHAMMAI

According to Jewish tradition the oral law (nonwritten regulations about Jewish religious requirements) was passed on
through several generations by "pairs" of rabbinic sages. The last
of these pairs consisted of two looming figures called Hillel and
Shammai. If these figures were historical (which seems likely),
they would have lived at the end of the first century B.C., contemporaries of Herod the Great. It's quite possible then that they
should be identified with the Jewish leaders that Josephus calls
"Pollio" and "Sameas"—substituting similar Greek names for the
Hebrew. Other scholars prefer to identify Pollio with the legendary rabbi Abtalion, who would have lived in the same era.

Hillel and Shammai established two "schools," or groups of
disciples, whose opinions dominated Pharisaism in the first century A.D. Jewish tradition regards Shammai and his disciples as
more conservative, holding closely to the letter of the law. Hillel
and his disciples were more liberal, often understanding the law
more figuratively. According to tradition the school of Hillel dominated the Sanhedrin in the first two centuries A.D., but it seems
unlikely that the Pharisees ever dominated the Sanhedrin. It's
clear, however, that the positions attributed to the school of Hillel
eventually won out in rabbinic Judaism.

There's no mention of Hillel or Shammai in the New Testament. But the conflict between the schools seems to lie behind the
question posed to Jesus in Matthew 19:3: "Is it lawful to divorce
one's wife for any cause?" The school of Hillel argued that a man
could divorce his wife for any cause, even dislike for her cooking.
The school of Shammai argued that adultery or abandonment
were the only true bases for divorce.

palaces, part military bases. In the latter years of his reign Herod often se-
questered himself away in one or another to make himself inaccessible to
any potential assassins.

Of course, all this construction required money, and lots of it. The principal source for Herod's income was taxes, and many of these taxes were exacted from the citizens of Judea. Herod's officers collected taxes directly from the citizens, and these were used to pay tribute to Rome and fund public services. There were also taxes on the transportation of goods, and a special "temple tax" that supported the temple complex. But not all Herod's tax income came from the Jews. He also earned considerable income through his taxation of trade routes. Nabatean traders had to pay tribute to bring their goods through Judean territory. Caesarea and other port cities charged tariffs to merchant ships. Herod's considerable land holdings generated a good deal of income, which he generously put into public projects. So while the combination of tribute, taxes and tithes might have seemed like a heavy burden on the Judeans, it probably wasn't what we'd call oppressive in this period.

Herod's "prosperous period" continued until about 13 B.C. In fourteen years he had made the Jews significant figures in the Roman Empire. His building projects were renowned, and the friendship he had forged with the Romans would continue to pay dividends to the Jews for centuries to come.

The period of domestic turmoil. Herod's family life had never been anything but a mess. The years of prosperity and expansion didn't make his problems go away—if anything, they intensified them. As a powerful and prosperous king he could have almost anything he wanted, and one thing he wanted was wives. Herod married ten times and fathered many children. His first wife was a commoner named Doris, who had borne him a son named Antipater. He divorced her and sent her away after he married Mariamne the Hasmonean. He had a deep affection for Mariamne's two sons, Alexander and Aristobulus. The boys were only about seven years old when their mother was executed, and they posed no threat at the time. But in 17 B.C. they returned from Rome as young men. Herod bestowed special honors on them and arranged excellent marriages for each of them.

The grown boys carried some heavy baggage from their mother's death, and they had a hard time reciprocating the king's affection. They weren't above putting on regal airs, considering themselves, as Hasmoneans, superior to their Herodian kin. Herod's sister Salome exacerbated the situation. Perhaps she had her own designs on the throne and knew that Mariamne's sons would have to go if she or her own children were to have any chance of taking power some day. Or perhaps she was motivated simply by jealousy and hatred. In any case, she appealed to Herod's paranoia, warning him that the young men were plotting to assassinate him and claim his throne for themselves. To Herod, who seems to have been incapable of understanding any motive but ambition, Salome's accusations seemed plausible. But he responded in a way Salome couldn't have expected: he had his first wife Doris and his son Antipater recalled from their banishment. Herod believed that Mariamne's sons wouldn't dare try to assassinate him because Antipater would be the first one in line for the throne.

Herod first brought formal charges against the brothers in 12 B.C., but he later dropped them. Nonetheless, he proclaimed that his eldest son Antipater would be heir to his throne, with Alexander and Aristobulus next in line. Still, Salome persisted in causing trouble. In 7 B.C. she, Antipater and Herod's brother Pheroras fabricated evidence that the two sons of Mariamne were plotting Herod's assassination. Herod had no choice but to condemn them to death. They were executed by strangulation in the city of Sebaste (Samaria)—the very city where he and Mariamne had been married thirty years earlier.

With the two Hasmoneans out of the way, the elder son, Antipater, set to work to take the throne. If he had only waited a few years, it probably would have come to him naturally. But the impatient prince feared that his vigorous father might actually outlive him, and then he'd never have a chance to rule. Or worse yet—knowing how Herod's favor could change in an instant—the king might change his will or perhaps even do away with Antipater himself. After moving to Rome to separate himself from suspicion, Antipater conspired with his uncle Pheroras to poison King Herod. But through a strange twist of fate, the tainted cup accidentally came to Pheroras instead. When Herod learned his brother had been murdered, he was determined to bring the perpetrators to justice. After he had tortured nearly everyone involved (and probably not a few people who weren't involved), Herod discovered that the poison had been intended for him and that it had come from Antipater. Antipater was recalled from Rome and taken into custody.

By now Herod's health was failing. Fearing to name a successor—lest his appointee should decide to hasten the king's demise—he changed his will a number of times in the last days of his life. At one point he named his youngest son Antipas, whose mother was a Samaritan woman named Malthace, as his successor. Then he changed his will and named Archelaus, Antipas's older brother, as his successor to the throne. Antipas was designated to take over as tetrarch of Perea and Galilee. Another son, Philip, was named as tetrarch of Gaulanitis, Trachonitis, Batanea and Panias (territories east of the Jordan).

At the age of seventy Herod was rapidly approaching his death. But he wasn't yet so decrepit that he couldn't administer justice in his realm. Hearing of his impending doom, two Jewish leaders, Judas and Mattathias, incited a riot in Jerusalem. The cause of the uproar was a golden eagle that Herod had installed at the temple gates. The presence of the eagle seems to represent a departure from Herod's earlier policy of avoiding offence to Jewish religious sensibilities. Had he placed it there in a deliberate act of defiance? In any case, the religious conservatives believed the time had come for its removal. They incited a crowd to tear down the offending bird and cut it to pieces. The operation was a success, but the ringleaders were captured. Herod showed them no mercy: he had them burned alive.

He also had the satisfaction of living to witness the execution of his son Antipater. Since Antipater was a member of the royal house, the execution had to be approved by Caesar himself. But once the approval was granted, Herod wasted no time in seeing the sentence carried out. Antipater was slain and buried in a common grave.

Herod himself died five days later. He was buried at Herodium with all the pomp befitting a king. The people of Judea made fitting lamentations; but how many truly mourned the death of the Idumean half-Jew is uncertain. There were probably some who had loved the man and appreciated his many contributions to Jewish life and culture. There were many who despised him as a usurper and a pretender. Even today historians' assessments of Herod's career vary greatly. Some, looking at his political accomplishments, believe that the title "Herod the Great" was well earned. Others, considering his ruthlessness, promotion of paganism and self-serving ambition, regard him as a consummate scoundrel. To me, it seems impossible not to respect Herod's many significant accomplishments. We can surely appreciate his promotion of Judaism without liking him or approving of his methods. He was on the one hand a vulgar, insecure despot, and on the other a self-serving sycophant. But perhaps he was precisely what was necessary at the time to insure the survival of the Jewish state in the midst of perilous circumstances.

Herod's Successors

When Herod died, Judea erupted in violence.[6] His son Archelaus immedi-

---

[6] Primary sources in this section are *Ant.* 17.9.1-17.13.5 (206-353); *War* 2.1.1-2.7.4 (1-116).

ately had to put down a riot in Jerusalem, where crowds were demanding vengeance for Judas and Matthias. He then traveled to Rome, where he expected to be confirmed as king of Judea. But as soon as Archelaus had departed, the violence broke out anew. This time Varus, the governor of Syria, had to bring Roman soldiers into Jerusalem to stop the fighting. He left the city under control of a Roman officer named Sabinus. Sabinus believed he would be able to use his position to line his pockets and sent his soldiers about plundering Judea. But the Jews were in no mood to endure such abuse. Again a revolt broke out, this one more organized than before. The most furious fighting occurred on the Temple Mount itself and resulted in the destruction of several buildings.

In Archelaus's absence brigands began to run rampant throughout Judea. Some even aspired to take the throne for themselves. In Galilee, Judas ben Hezekiah—possibly the son of the bandit whose execution had caused Herod to be called before the Sanhedrin so many years earlier—actually plundered the royal arsenal in the city of Sepphoris and set out pillaging throughout the region. In Perea a man named Simon was declared king of the Jews. Governor Varus had to bring in more Roman troops and even called on reinforcements from the Nabateans. He began his campaign in Galilee, which was fast becoming the hotbed for Judean insurrection. He then took his army throughout Judea, purging it of insurrectionists. The operation has become known as the "War of Varus."

Meanwhile, in Rome, Archelaus found that his kingship was a matter of some dispute. His younger brother Antipas argued that Herod's final will was invalid, and that *he* should be awarded the throne. Other members of the Herodian family were also protesting Archelaus's appointment. In 4 B.C. Augustus essentially confirmed Herod's final will, but with an important exception. Archelaus would indeed become the ruler of Judea, but with the rank of ethnarch, not king. Philip was installed as the tetrarch of Batanaea, Trachonitis, Auranitis, Gaulanitis, Panias and other territories east of the Jordan. Antipas—who became known simply as Herod—became the tetrarch of Galilee.

Philip and Herod Antipas proved themselves capable rulers. Philip's was the most peaceful reign, untouched by scandal. Like his father, he was a builder. His most noteworthy project was building a city at Paneas, which he named Caesarea. It came to be known as "Caesarea Philippi," to distinguish it from the important coastal city of the same name. He died in

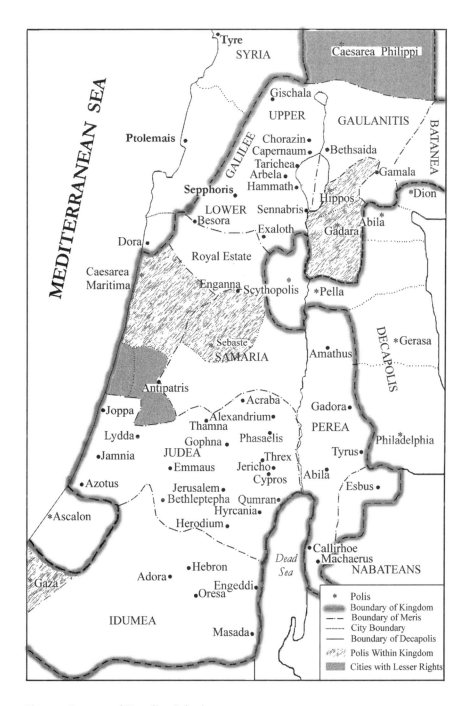

Figure 6. Roman and Herodian Palestine

THE HIGH PRIESTHOOD
IN NEW TESTAMENT TIMES

We've seen the prestige of the high priesthood rise and fall throughout the intertestamental era. It reached its zenith under the Hasmonaeans, who combined the powers of high priest and king in one person. It was at its lowest under Herod the Great. Herod usurped the power to appoint the high priest, which had been a hereditary position, and that power was retained by his successors Archelaus and the Roman praefects. Nonetheless, the appointments weren't arbitrary. Between 6 B.C. and A.D. 66 most of the high priests were drawn from about four families—families with aristocratic bloodlines and ties to the Sadducean party. (There were, however, some exceptions.)

Since the high priesthood was such a prominent position, its occupant naturally exerted a good deal of influence. After Herod's day this influence was formalized so that the high priest served also as president of the Sanhedrin, just as he had in pre-Maccabean times. Both Jesus and Paul stood before the Sanhedrin and were tried by the high priests (Mt 26:59-66; Mk 14:53-64; Jn 18:19-23; Acts 23:1-5).

A.D. 33 or 34. Herod Antipas was an ambitious and wily leader, similar in temperament to his father, though not quite as competent. He was prominent in New Testament affairs because much of Jesus' ministry occurred in his realm. John the Baptist was executed at his command (Mt 14:1-12; Mk 6:14-29; Lk 9:7-9), and Herod also played a role in the trial of Jesus (Lk 23:6-12). He died in exile after being deposed by the emperor Caligula in A.D. 40 for actions Caligula deemed seditious.

Philip was loved, and Herod Antipas was tolerated. But Archelaus managed to alienate not only his subjects but his overlords as well. The son of an Idumean and a Samaritan, he had two strikes against him, in Jewish eyes, before he ever took office. Yet prejudice alone can't account for the animosity he generated. Josephus tells us few details about his reign, but it must have been disastrous. In A.D. 6, when Augustus launched an investigation of Judean affairs, a joint Judean-Samaritan delegation traveled to Rome to present formal complaints against Archelaus. Considering how rocky the relationship between the Jews and Samaritans had been, only a thoroughly corrupt governor could have brought them together. Augustus sympathized with their complaints, and he banished Archelaus to Gaul. Judea was taken from the hands of the Herodians and placed under the direct administration of a Roman governor— a "praefect" in Jesus' day but later called a "procurator." Generally, only unruly provinces obtained such treatment, where it was deemed necessary to have a military presence on hand that could be mobilized quickly. But even so, such governors interfered little in local affairs unless it became necessary to do so. They were responsible for seeing that the tribute was paid and peace maintained in the territory. They also had the power to execute lawbreakers, but most internal issues were left in the hands of the local officials. In the case of Judea this meant that the Sanhedrin and the high priest—essentially stripped of authority under Herod the Great—were once again empowered to order civil affairs.

Such was the political situation in the days of Jesus. All things were now in place for the events of the New Testament to unfold.

For Further Reading

Richardson, Peter. *Herod: King of the Jews and Friend of the Romans*. Columbia: University of South Carolina Press, 1996.

Safrai, S. and M. Stern, eds. *The Jewish People in the First Century: Historical Geography, Political History, Social, Cultural and Religious Life and Institutions*. Vol. 1. Assen: Van Gorcum and Philadelphia: Fortress, 1974. See especially Stern's "The Reign of Herod and the Herodian Dynasty" (pp. 216-307) and "The Province of Judaea" (pp. 308-76).

Sanders, E. P. *Judaism: Practice and Belief, 63 BCE-66 CE*. London: SCM Press, 1992. Covers important religious developments of the time in light of changing social issues.

Schürer, Emil. *A History of the Jewish People in the Age of Jesus Christ*. Edited by Geza Vermes, Fergus Millar and Matthew Black. Vol. 1, §§15-17. Edinburgh: T & T Clark, 1973.

Smallwood, E. Mary. *The Jews Under Roman Rule*. 2nd ed. Leiden: Brill, 1981. Especially strong on the political consequences of Roman rule in Judea.

10

Oppression, Resistance and Messianic Hopes

Sometimes we overestimate the changes in Jewish society effected by the Roman conquest. Judea wasn't turned into an occupied territory with Roman soldiers goose-stepping through the streets of Jerusalem. The Jews weren't forced to study Latin or memorize the names of Roman gods. Culturally, things remained pretty much as they had been. The Romans continued to use the Greek language in the provinces. But otherwise they compelled no one to adopt Greek culture. The state cult was encouraged, but Roman subjects weren't required to worship the emperor during the first century A.D. Not even Herod the Great, for all his patronage of Greek culture, attempted to force the Jews into violating their traditions. Indeed, he worked hard to ensure that Jewish rights—to live and worship as they pleased—remained intact. Hellenism continued to spread through the normal channels: trade, immigration and personal contacts. It was still advantageous for aspiring social climbers to adopt the ways of the world. But Jewish religion and culture continued relatively unmolested. If anything, the Judean Jews in this period seem to have been more tenacious than ever about keeping their faith and culture "pure," as evidenced by their sensitivity to anything that even resembled a graven image.

Socially, the changes were more pronounced, but still not drastic. The Roman presence would have seemed unobtrusive to the average Judean Jew. The governor's office was located in Caesarea, a predominantly

Gentile city on the coast. He traveled to Jerusalem only when his duties demanded it. Few Roman soldiers were permanently stationed in the Jewish towns of Judea. When trouble arose, the Romans had to bring in troops from Caesarea, Samaria, or Syria. Certainly, Roman troops would move through Galilee or Judea on occasion, but their presence wasn't especially oppressive. Roman officers could conscript local residents for manual labor or force them to put soldiers up for a night. But there were strictly defined limits on how much of a burden the Roman military could impose on loyal subjects. Daily life continued much as it had under the primary jurisdiction of local Jewish authorities. The only time that situation really changed much between the late first century B.C. and the mid first century A.D. was during the reign of Herod the Great. Herod, at some point in his reign, instituted a kind of martial law in Judea, suppressing free speech and public assembly. But his successors were far more lenient, and except in times of trouble, most Jews never even saw their Roman governor. Business and government affairs were carried out with little Roman interference.

Perhaps the one area where the Jews felt the Roman presence most keenly was in their purses. The Roman conquest made a big difference in the tax burden. Judea had to pay tribute to Rome, and that tribute was raised through taxes. There were poll taxes to be paid (based on the population census), land taxes and taxes on the transport of goods. There were also the traditional taxes paid to the temple as well as tithes for the priests. The average Jew must have seen a hefty chunk of his money siphoned away before he spent any of it. Add to that burden some corruption in the administration of taxes, and we have one of the principal sources for Jewish discontent in the first century of Roman rule.

Most likely none of these factors was as crucial in shaping Jewish attitudes toward Rome as the blow given their collective pride at losing their independence. For about eighty years Judea had been a sovereign state. Few people living when the Romans arrived would have remembered a time when Judea had paid tribute to a foreign power. In the common mind, Judea had defeated the Greeks because Judea was righteous. Judea's God was the only God, and the gods of the nations were but idols. Yes, God had once used the Babylonians to punish the Jews for their apostasy. But the nation had repented, and his wrath had been spent. Judea was no longer apostate. In fact, the Jews scrupulously avoided the very appearance of idolatry. Why then were they again subject to a foreign power?

Different groups and individuals had their opinions. For the author of the *Psalms of Solomon,* a pseudepigraphon written late in the first century B.C., the answer was the Hasmoneans. This text argues that the Hasmoneans' impiety had forced God to judge the Jews (*Pss. Sol.* 17.4-9). This author probably spoke for many of his countrymen. But the members of the Dead Sea Scroll Community had a different opinion. The debacle had come about for a variety of sins, but mainly because the majority of Jews rejected the biblical interpretations of their Righteous Teacher, following the Wicked Priest instead.[1] Some other authors noted that the book of Daniel predicted the coming of four kingdoms that would rule over the Jews (Dan 2:36-43; 7:15-27). They interpreted the fourth kingdom to be none other than the Roman Empire. Rome's hegemony wasn't so much a matter of divine punishment as divine destiny.[2] But on one point all these authors agreed: the rule of Rome is but a temporary affair. Soon God would deliver the Jews from oppression. Then the impious Romans, along with all the other nations, would be judged for their wickedness and their harsh treatment of God's people.

Jewish Collaboration

Not all the Jews were eager for Rome's demise. Some were quite willing to work with the foreign overlords in view of the opportunities they represented. With peace established throughout the empire, there were new markets to be exploited. A shrewd merchant could become very wealthy in those days. There were also opportunities for political advancement. The Romans weren't so ethnocentric as the Greeks had been; an able administrator of any race could rise through the imperial ranks. Philo of Alexandria's nephew, Tiberius Julius Alexander, once served as governor of Judea and eventually held a high position in Rome itself. Then there was Herod the Great, the consummate opportunist. He realized that by playing his cards right Roman rule could work to his advantage. His grandson, Herod Agrippa (the King Herod of Acts 12), also used his political connections to secure a kingdom in Palestine. For many ambitious, well-connected Jews, Roman rule was nothing less than a gravy train. For many others, Roman rule wasn't necessarily a good thing, but it

---

[1]CD 1.1-18; 1QpHab 1.1-4.15; 4Q171 (Commentary on the Psalms) 1.12-19; 4.7-10.
[2]Such is the implication of *4 Ezra* 11—12 and *2 Baruch* 35—40, although both texts seem to imply also that Jerusalem's ruin is a punishment from God for the Jews' sins.

wasn't a particularly bad thing either.

Conditions under the Hasmonean rulers had been far from ideal. Alexander Janneus had defiled the high priesthood by his debauchery. Alexandra Salome had allowed the Pharisees to persecute the Sadducees and conduct a witch hunt throughout the Judean realm. Hyrcanus II and Aristobulus II had divided the nation and taxed its resources in their efforts to secure the throne. Foreign powers threatened to overrun the nation more than once during those last days of the Judean commonwealth. No doubt a good many Jews were more than happy to see the Hasmonean monarchy abolished. If nothing else, Rome seemed to offer stability and an end to the internecine strife that was devouring Judea. The Roman Civil Wars may have tarnished that offer somewhat, but Augustus's able and prosperous reign must have restored confidence in the promise of pax Romana. For some Jews, high taxes might have seemed a reasonable price for the security that Roman rule afforded.

Roman rule must have seemed like a godsend to the missionary-minded as well. According to the book of Matthew the Pharisees of Jesus' day were zealous to win converts: "Woe to you, scribes and Pharisees, hypocrites! For you cross the sea and land to make a single convert, and you make the new convert twice as much a child of hell as yourselves" (Mt 23:15). To some, the freedom to travel about the Mediterranean region in search of proselytes was an important benefit of the Roman Empire. The Pharisees established synagogues in a great many Gentile cities, and these centers of worship and learning attracted both converts and "God-fearers"—people who appreciated the Jewish teachings but weren't willing to endure the ordeals of circumcision and the *mikvah* (ritual baptism) required of Gentiles converting to Judaism. Christianity, too, owed much of its success to the fact that Paul and other missionaries could traverse the empire in relative security. For those who had visions of converting the world rather than conquering it, the Roman Empire—at least in the first half of the first century—wasn't a bad thing at all.

Passive Resistance

In spite of these benefits, most Judean Jews probably had little love for the empire. Some were opposed to the very notion of foreign rule; some were aggravated by the tax burden; others were grieved by real or imagined affronts to the Jewish faith. For various reasons these Jews felt that Rome's

CHRISTIAN SUBMISSION TO GOVERNMENT

The issue of whether or not Christians should engage in civil disobedience was thorny. Jesus was tested with the question, "Is it lawful to pay taxes to the emperor, or not?" (Mt 22:15-22; Mk 12:13-17; Lk 20:20-26). The problem was significant, not only because most Jews considered the taxes oppressive, but also because the taxes paid to Rome could be used to build pagan temples. Jesus responded by asking for a coin. Given a silver denarius, which bore the image of Caesar, Jesus said, "Render to Caesar that which is Caesar's, and render to God that which is God's." Since the Jews used Caesar's coinage, they placed themselves under Caesar's authority. You cannot enjoy the benefits of an empire without accepting its responsibilities.

But the flip side of Jesus' instruction is crucial: he also said, "Render unto God the things that are God's." The statement implies that when the interests of God and government are in conflict, the ultimate allegiance must go to God.

Paul (Rom 13:1-7) and Peter (1 Pet 2:13-17) likewise urged Christians to submit to the government. They argued that God had instituted the government as a means of securing justice. By submitting to the government Christians could enjoy peace in this world and have good repute among its people. And of course, it wouldn't benefit the church's missionary efforts to have Christians labeled as troublemakers.

Although the New Testament urges submission to the government, the book of Revelation addresses government's dark side. Written in a time of persecution, its author recognized that God and human governments couldn't always coexist in peace. The kingdoms of this world, epitomized in Rome (the city that sits on seven hills; Rev 17—18), are diametrically opposed to the interests of the kingdom of God. One day God himself shall destroy the earthly powers. But there is no call to arms here: the book of Revelation is a call to patient endurance for God's kingdom to come.

domination of Judea was wrong. But most of them weren't about to initiate violence against the Romans. They wouldn't go out of their way to cooperate with Rome, but they remained passive in the face of oppression.

There were different reasons for this passivity. Most people just saw little reason to work against the empire. While the average Jewish peasant gained few benefits from Roman rule, he or she realized that causing a ruckus wouldn't improve the situation. The peasantry tends to be a practical, phlegmatic segment of society. So long as there's food on the table and a roof over their heads, they usually accepted their lot in life. So Jewish peasants would grumble and mutter curses on the Roman officials. They might secretly cheer for the bandits who robbed the Romans and their collaborators. They might even cheat on their taxes. But for the most part, they weren't about to get themselves in any *real* trouble with Rome. They would merely complain and comply. So too with many of the skilled tradesman and merchants. They might not have liked the Romans, but they had little to gain through resistance. For a significant segment of Jewish society, passive acceptance would have seemed the most prudent course of action.

Other Jews had different reasons for accepting the Roman yoke. Jesus and his disciples could hardly have been called collaborators. Their message about the kingdom of God was subversive in its way, if not actually seditious. But Jesus taught his followers a form of "principled pacifism"—a moral commitment to nonviolence (see especially Mt 5:5, 9, 38-43). The Gospels don't record Jesus ever explicitly stating his reasons for this position. There are few Old Testament passages that prescribe nonviolence in the face of oppression. Jesus recognized this fact, and he states in Matthew 5 that the Old Testament ethics were an insufficient guide for his disciples' conduct. Instead, his ethics seem to be based on the concept of the sacred worth of all persons, including the Gentiles. God allowed his blessings to fall on both the evil and the good, and God's children should do the same (Mt 5:45). So while the Law allowed a person to take vengeance in proportion to the injury they had suffered, Jesus commanded his followers to repay evil with good. They weren't to fight against those who oppressed them, but to bless them and pray for them (Mt 5:38-48). The Gospels also record that Jesus had extended his ministry to non-Jews, and the church followed suit by including the Gentiles as full heirs of God's promises. The growing numbers of Gentiles in the church made it difficult for Jesus' Jewish followers to maintain any nationalistic prejudices.

Another important feature of Jesus' pacifism can be found in his teachings about eschatology: the end of the world. In Jesus' discourses on the
"end of the age" (Mt 24; Mk 13; Lk 21), he makes no provision for human
involvement in the overthrow of the nations. The destruction of the
wicked would be God's work, not the work of his people. Any conquering
to be done wouldn't come about through the sword but through the proclamation of the gospel (Mt 26:52; 28:19-20; Lk 24:46-48).

Jesus and his followers seem to have been an oddity in ancient Judean
society.[3] Some of those who complied with Roman rule had no moral opposition to violence per se, but they simply believed that the time for violence hadn't arrived yet. There were Jews who were waiting for the right
opportunity to present itself before they arose in rebellion. The Pharisees
who destroyed the eagle in front of the temple waited until Herod was on
his deathbed, and then they seized the moment to start a riot. It must have
seemed that their limited rebellion had a better chance of success under
the circumstances. But to others, there would only be one proper time for
violence—the time when God would give his people a sign that they
should rise up and throw off the yoke of Roman oppression. The Dead Sea
Scroll *Manual of Discipline* (1QS) says:

> I will not repay a man evil for evil; rather, I will pursue each person with
> good. For the judgment of every living thing is in the hands of God, and he
> will repay each one according to his deeds. . . . I will not insist on disputing
> with men destined for destruction until the Day of Vengeance; yet I will not
> suppress my anger against the wicked, nor be satisfied until justice has been
> established.[4]

This "Day of Vengeance" was the time of the final battle between the
forces of light and darkness. The Community members were instructed to
be passive in the face of oppression, until the hour of God's justice had arrived. But at God's signal they would rise up as an army and slay the
wicked. Like the author of the *Psalms of Solomon*, the members of the Community would bide their time until God had raised up his anointed deliverer—the Messiah, son of David. Then there would be no question of

---

[3]It's sometimes argued that the Essenes were pacifists based on Philo's statement that they
made no weapons (*Every Good Man Is Free*, 12.78). Actually, Philo argues only that the
Essenes stayed out of the arms trade because the sale of weapons was so lucrative, and the
Essenes were committed to a simple lifestyle. Josephus makes it quite clear in a number of
passages that the Essenes were not morally opposed to war—an Essene even served as a
general during the Great Revolt of A.D. 66-74.
[4]1QS 10.17-20, author's translation.

whether the Jews would have the resources to win a war with Rome. Their victory would be guaranteed under the supernatural leadership of God and his anointed king.

Active Resistance

There were yet other Jews who had no intention of waiting for the right time to resist the Romans. To these freedom fighters the time for action was now. Even if the Romans couldn't be overthrown, they figured, at least they could be harassed. These patriots joined together with like-minded folk and formed resistance cells within Judea and Galilee. Josephus mentions several different groups or factions of the resistance, each distinguished by different leadership or a preferred mode of operation. In his biased opinion they're all scurrilous rogues, and yet even he cannot help but express some appreciation for their determination and grit.

The Lestai. Some of the *lestai* (Greek for "bandits") that Herod harassed in Galilee probably represented this kind of resistance. Of course, there were always bandits who stole from the rich simply to fill their own pockets. But there were other bandits who had a true political agenda. These *lestai,* as they're called in Josephus and the New Testament, demonstrated their refusal to comply with foreign rule by stealing, sacking and occasionally killing their oppressors. They wanted to strike a blow for the oppressed people of Palestine by making life miserable for the Romans and their allies. Some of these bandits became very popular with the masses. While Jesus seemed to promise little concrete relief to the poor, Barabbas the *lestes* had actually struck a blow against their foreign oppressors. When the people were offered a choice, Barabbas was their man (Mt 27:15-23; Mk 15:6-15; Lk 23:18-25; Jn 18:39-40).

Sociologists call this kind of antigovernment activity "social banditry." Social banditry is a common feature of peasant societies. In the bandits, the frustrations of the commoners often find an outlet. Their exploits can become legendary, and some bandits even take on the proportions of folk heroes. Sometimes bandits even act the part, setting out like Robin Hood to right wrongs and establish justice. Sometimes they rise to the position of judges in villages, arbitrating local disputes. And some social bandits even become actual revolutionary leaders. Apparently several of the *lestai* took on that role in Judea later in the first century. Sometimes these romantic figures have even been viewed as messiahs, the hope for the liberation and salvation of the nation. A few of the Judean and Galilean bandits apparently viewed themselves as messiahs. But most of the Jewish bandits probably didn't have such grandiose dreams. Many were just violent men trying to make a living, and enjoying the fact that they were annoying Rome in the process.

The Sicarii. One group of bandits became specialists in assassinations. The *sicarii,* as they were called (from the Latin word *sica,* "dagger"), became active during the administration of the abominable Roman governor Felix (A.D. 52-60; *Ant.* 20.8.5-7 [160-78]). Their first victim was a high priest by the name of Jonathan. Jonathan, a thoroughgoing moderate, was hated by both Felix and the hard-line Jewish resistance. Apparently they conspired together in his assassination, and the *sicarii* escaped from the crime unpunished. Emboldened by this success, the group became a plague on Judea, taking to raiding and plundering villages like bands of desperadoes. When Felix curtailed their raids, they devoted themselves for a time to assassinating collaborators. They would slip into crowds on feast days, insinuate themselves into the presences of prominent figures, then slide their blades between their victims' ribs. The Jewish aristocracy lived in fear of the *sicarii,* but these criminals apparently garnered a fair amount of popular support. They grew to be a numerous and influential group, figuring prominently in the Great Revolt of A.D. 66-74.

Luke mentions this group in Acts 21:38. According to his account Paul caused a riot in Jerusalem when he took his Gentile companions into the temple. As the mob dragged Paul into the streets to stone him, word came to a Roman officer there that the city was in an uproar. Seeing the crowd trying to kill Paul, the officer concluded that Paul must have been an infamous *sicarii* leader who had led a band of four thousand men into the desert. The account reveals the prominence and the significance of the group—four thousand soldiers was no mean army in those days. Yet the *sicarii* apparently weren't very popular in Jerusalem at that time. The Roman had concluded that Paul was the assassin because the crowds were trying to kill him, not because they wanted to crown him.

The Zealots. There was also a more distinctly religious faction in the Jewish resistance. Josephus tells us that around A.D. 6 a man named Judas, from Galilee, formed a "fourth philosophy" among the Jews (the other three being the Pharisees, Sadducees and Essenes). In *Antiquities* 18.1.6 (23-25) he describes the group in this manner:

> But of the fourth sect of Jewish philosophy, Judas the Galilean was the author. These men agree in all other things with the Pharisaic notions; but they

have an inviolable attachment to liberty, and say that God is to be their only Ruler and Lord. They also do not value dying any kinds of death, nor indeed do they heed the deaths of their relations and friends, nor can any such fear make them call any man Lord. And since this immovable resolution of theirs is well known to a great many, I shall speak no further about that matter; nor am I afraid that any thing I have said of them should be disbelieved, but rather fear, that what I have said is beneath the resolution they show when they undergo pain. And it was in Gessius Florus's time that the nation began to grow mad with this distemper, who was our procurator, and who occasioned the Jews to go wild with it by the abuse of his authority, and to make them revolt from the Romans.

This sect arose in response to a Roman order for a census to be taken of the Jews. Judas the Galilean argued that such enrollment constituted nothing less than slavery. He assured the people that if they resisted the Romans, God would aid them in their struggle. A small uprising ensued, but it was quickly put down. Nonetheless, his sect continued on, existing in obscurity, bound by an oath that they would suffer death before they would acknowledge Rome's dominion. Josephus tells us that the group continued to spread treasonous ideas among the masses until the Jews erupted in actual revolt in A.D. 66.

Apparently, just before the outbreak of the revolt this fourth philosophy spawned a group known as the Zealots.[5] The term *zealot* had a long and distinguished history in Judaism. In Numbers 25:6-13, because Phineas, Aaron's grandson, "was zealous for his God" he killed an Israelite man and his Midianite lover, and so won God's favor. Much later, Mattathias the Hasmonean "burned with zeal" and rose up against the Greek oppressors, and summoned everyone who was "zealous for the law" to join him in revolt (1 Macc 2:24, 27). Zeal came to be identified as a stubborn adherence to God's law and exclusive loyalty to God's people in spite of opposition. The term didn't necessarily have political connotations. But religious zeal and political zeal could become closely intertwined, and the

---

[5]As many scholars have observed, Josephus never explicitly identifies the Zealots as his fourth philosophy. But I believe the evidence is clear enough that the groups are one and the same. Josephus says that the fourth philosophy became active in A.D. 6 and inspired the revolt, but he doesn't mention a "fourth philosophy" in his account of the outbreak of the revolt. Instead, the role of chief instigators has been assumed by the Zealots, who seem to appear out of nowhere. Josephus also takes special note of the way members of the fourth philosophy would endure terrible suffering, rather than call anyone "lord," and remarks that most people have been observers of their perseverance. Later, he tells us that the Zealots amazed everyone by the way they bore suffering rather than calling Caesar "lord" (*War* 7.10.1 [418-19]).

sect that was chiefly responsible for inciting the Great Revolt took for themselves the name "Zealot."

SIMON THE ZEALOT

Was one of Jesus' disciples a revolutionary? Simon is identified as "the Zealot" in Luke 6:15 and Acts 1:13, to distinguish him from Simon Peter. Many scholars conclude that this means he was a member of the Zealot resistance movement. But Josephus never applies the term *zealot* to any group existing before the outbreak of the Great Revolt in A.D. 66. The religious resistance, or fourth philosophy, may not have been known by the name Zealot in the time of Jesus. Besides, it seems unlikely that a Jewish freedom fighter would have endured Jesus' teachings about submitting to the government; nor would he have passively allowed Jesus to be captured. The epithet "Zealot" may have been an honorary title given to Simon by Jesus or the other disciples (like "Peter" and "Sons of Thunder"), or it might even have been his family name, earned by a courageous ancestor. Seeing Simon as a freedom fighter makes for interesting sermon fodder, but it's not the only possible interpretation of the title *Zealot*.

Josephus tells us that the group's beliefs were similar to those of the Pharisees. Like the Pharisees, they believed that God would intervene in human affairs. The courses of events weren't predetermined; prayer and piety could make a difference in this world. Like the Pharisees, Zealots also believed that human beings had a responsibility to work with God in bringing about his will on earth. Also like the Pharisees, the Zealots wouldn't have considered death to be a great disaster. They shared the belief that God would restore them to life again, honoring their piety and perseverance at the glorious resurrection of the dead.

Messianic Hopes

One of the most significant aspects of Jewish history and society in this period was a dramatic expansion of messianic expectations. Probably not since the days of the Antiochan persecution had Jewish hopes for the advent of God's "Chosen One" been so intense. This hope seems remarkable, considering how very different the circumstances now were from what they had been in the days of Judas Maccabees. The Jews weren't particularly oppressed; they were relatively prosperous; they were accorded a good deal of self-government. But many Jewish hearts still burned with a sense of destiny, one that the Romans had frustrated. Like the Old Testament prophet Habakkuk, the pious wondered how God could allow a wicked people to rule over a more righteous nation. God was allowing the Romans to spread their pagan cults throughout the lands they conquered. Wouldn't it be better if the Jews were the conquerors with the power to spread their beliefs in the Lord? Certainly, such a situation couldn't continue indefinitely. God had a plan for his people. And the time was ripe to bring that plan to fruition.

So some of the Jews harassed Roman soldiers, merchants and Jewish collaborators; but other practical souls recognized the futility of such endeavors. The Jews had no chance of expelling the Romans from their land by mere human endeavor. Only a supernatural intervention by God Almighty would break the yoke of the oppressors and restore the Jewish nation to its rightful place in the world. A chosen deliverer—promised by the prophets of old—was the only hope for a restored Jewish commonwealth. So, while the sages searched the Scriptures for clues about when and how the Messiah would come, warlords imagined that they themselves might be the chosen deliverer. The expectations ranged wildly, from the mundane to the bizarre. But each messianic hope was founded on the basis of biblical prophecy. The Jews of this age were not enamored with new revelations but with the explication of ancient revelations.

The Davidic king. The term *messiah* derives from the Hebrew word *mashach*, "to smear, anoint." The nominative (noun) form, *mashiach*, means "anointed one." The word was used most often in the Old Testament to designate kings or high priests. Kings and priests were literally anointed with an oily balm as a sign of their office. It would be smeared on their heads and allowed to melt down their faces. (In the hot, dry Near Eastern climate, such treatment was considered quite pleasant. Ancient Egyptian friezes depict gatherings of nobles at play, each with a cone of fragrant lard sitting on his or her head—the ancient equivalent of party favors.) The term *messiah* could also be used symbolically of anyone who enjoyed divine favor. In Psalm 105:15 it's used as a synonym for "prophet" in a reference to the patriarchs Abraham, Isaac and Jacob. But the most frequent

use of the phrase "God's anointed" or "the anointed one" is as a designation of the king of Israel.

The notion of a coming "super king" was based on the promises that God
made to King David. According to 2 Samuel 7:11-16, God promised David
that his dynasty would be established forever, and there would always be a
descendant of David ruling over Israel. After Israel divided into two kingdoms (921 B.C.), David's descendants continued to rule in the southern kingdom until the Babylonians did away with the monarchy. But even before the
Babylonian exile, Isaiah and other prophets had begun to express hope that
God would raise up a "branch of David"—a messiah—who could reunite
the kingdom and lead God's people into righteousness (Is 9:1-7; 11:1-10; Jer
23:5-6; Amos 9:11-12). After the destruction of Jerusalem these hopes became
even more intense. Ezekiel predicted that God would restore the nation and
put David over them to lead the people in the ways of the Lord (Ezek 37:24-
28). In Zechariah 3:8 the prophet predicted the coming of the Lord's servant,
"the Branch" (i.e., the Branch of David), and may have expected a new dynasty to begin with Governor Zerubbabel. Later passages from the book of
Zechariah proclaimed the coming of a Davidic king who would rule from
"sea to sea" (Zech 9:10) and whose heirs would lead the Jews like the angel
of the Lord going before the nation (Zech 12:8). The coming of a new David
(or the establishment of a new Davidic dynasty) was clearly a focus for
much Jewish nationalism in the days after Jerusalem's destruction.

After decades of Persian rule, the burning hope for a Davidic king may
have diminished. Judah, primarily led by its high priests in those days,
seemed to be faring well. Why would they have wanted to return to the
days of warfare and apostasy typical of the monarchic period? In Ezra and
Nehemiah we read nothing about the messianic promises. Even Malachi,
who speaks fervently about the "day of the Lord" (i.e., the day when God
would execute judgment on the earth), never mentions the coming of a
new king. Ecclesiastes and Ben Sirach show no interest in messianic promises. The book of Daniel speaks of the coming of an "anointed ruler"
(*nagid,* Dan 9:25 NIV—probably a high priest), but it never promises an
anointed king *(melek).*[6] Daniel doesn't mention or even allude to God's
promises to David or the prophecies that foretold a new Davidic kingdom.
Rather, Daniel emphasized the coming of the kingdom of God (Dan 2:44-

---

[6]Daniel 11:22 uses the same term, *nagid,* as a title for the high priest. Rarely does the word
mean "king," and it is never used in messianic prophecies.

45; 7:27), which would be established without human agency. The prophet tells us explicitly that it's the archangel Michael who will deliver God's people from oppression (Dan 10:20—11:1; 12:1). Certainly, Daniel was aware of the older messianic prophecies. Perhaps the author emphasized a spiritual kingdom rather than physical kingdom so that his readers would put their trust in God, rather than seeking a human deliverer.

THE MESSIANIC PROPHET

According to Deuteronomy 18:14-22, God had promised through Moses that he would send Israel a "prophet like [Moses]" to lead the people into righteousness. From its context the original statement appears to speak not of a single prophet but of the whole line of true prophets who would teach the Word of God. But in later generations this prophecy was understood to refer to a single figure who would come and exercise a unique office, like that of Moses. Malachi might be referring to that prophecy in his prediction that God would send Elijah before the day of judgment (Mal 4:5). Some interpreters clearly linked Malachi and Deuteronomy together and predicted the coming of "a prophet like Moses" before the appearance of the Messiah (see Jn 1:21). Some of the Dead Sea Scrolls take this approach, predicting the coming of an anointed messenger who teaches the law and heralds the messianic deliverer (e.g., 1QS 9.11; 4Q174 3.12; 4Q175 1.1-8; 11QMelch 18-25). The Gospel writers, however, took a different tack: Elijah is John the Baptist (Mt 11:14), but the "prophet like Moses" is none other than Jesus himself, who appears as lawgiver and prophet par excellence (Mt 5—7; Jn 1:17; Acts 3:22).

The Hasmonean Dynasty certainly did little to encourage expectations of a coming "son of David." The Hasmoneans weren't from the line of David; they weren't even of the tribe of Judah—they were from Levi, as were all the priests. Yet 1 Maccabees describes Simon's reign in terms lifted from Old Testament messianic prophecies: "All the people sat under their own vines and fig trees, and there was none to make them afraid" (1 Macc

CHRONOMESSIANISM

Jewish messianic expectations ran high in the first century of the
Roman Empire. One factor encouraging these notions was "chro-
nomessianism," the belief that the Scriptures predicted the time of
the Messiah's coming. One favorite text was the book of Daniel,
whose prediction of a mighty, world-dominating kingdom seemed
to have been fulfilled in the Roman Empire. Since Daniel predicted
that the kingdom of God would be established during the reign of
this fourth kingdom, surely the coming of Messiah was near.

More precise calculations were based on Daniel's "seventy
weeks" prophecy. Daniel 9:24-27 states that God had decreed "seventy weeks" for the completion of Judah's punishment. The period
commences with "the time the word went out to restore and rebuild Jerusalem." Technically, that would have been 538 B.C., the
time of Cyrus's decree to allow the rebuilding of the temple, but it
could be interpreted in other ways—a "heavenly" decree, or the
decree to rebuild the wall issued around 450 B.C. The prophecy
states that an anointed leader would come seven weeks after the
decree. The city would then remain standing for sixty-two weeks.
But after the sixty-two weeks, a prince would "cut off" an anointed
one, and the city would be destroyed. For a final week the city
would be desolate, until God brought about the prince's end.

Originally, the prophecy may have referred to the removal of
the high priest by Antiochus Epiphanes and his persecution of the
Jews. Each day of the week would equal a year on the prophetic
timeline. "Seventy weeks," then, would be 490 years. Later interpreters read the prophecy as a timetable for the appearance of the
Messiah. They were probably uncertain of exactly when the rebuilding decree had been issued, but they could make educated
guesses. It was also possible to read Daniel 9:25 to mean that there
would be not seven weeks until the coming of the "anointed one"
but 69 weeks. So these interpreters would have been anticipating

the coming of Messiah around 483 years after the rebuilding of Jerusalem. Even without a precise chronology, they could have guessed that the period would elapse sometime in the late first century B.C. to first century A.D.

Evidence for such an interpretation in the period is scant, but it's not absent. A fragmentary text from Qumran Cave 11, the *Melchizedek Document*, predicts the coming of a "day of atonement" after ten jubilees (forty-nine-year periods). These 490 years must have been inspired by their understanding of Daniel's seventy weeks. The *Damascus Document* also seems to make use of this chronology. According to this text, it was 390 years after Nebuchadnezzar had sent the Jews into exile that the sectarian group was formed. Twenty years later God sent them their Righteous Teacher. The text also says that forty years after the Teacher's death, God would destroy all the group's enemies. Adding these numbers together and providing another forty years for the Teacher's work, we arrive at a figure of 490 years from the time of the exile to the time of the end.

It's also possible that the Great Revolt of A.D. 66-74 was inspired by Daniel's prophecy. Josephus tells us that the rebels were inspired to fight by a biblical prophecy predicting that *at that time* a ruler would come forth from Judea to conquer the world (*War* 6.312ff.). Elsewhere, Josephus tells us that Daniel was unique among the prophets because he not only told us what would happen but when it would happen (*Ant.* 10.267).

Later Christian and Jewish interpreters seem to agree that Daniel 9 was fulfilled in the first century. For Christians, the fulfillment came in Jesus Christ. A late-first-century Jewish text called the *Seder Olam*, or "Order of the World," also makes use of Daniel's seventy-week chronology. This text dates the end of the period—the time when an anointed one would be "cut off"—to around A.D. 70, the time of the fall of Jerusalem.

14:12; cf. Mic 4:4; Zech 3:10). Possibly the Hasmonean propagandists wanted to give the impression that the promises made to King David were being fulfilled in the Hasmonean priest-kings. There was no more need to look for a messiah. The long-awaited kingdom had come.

This propaganda machine was so effective that major pseudepigrapha produced in the Hasmonean era have little to say about a Davidic monarch. The portions of *1 Enoch* that were written in the Hasmonean era predict the coming of a universal king, but nothing is revealed of his ancestry (see 1 Enoch 90). The book of *Jubilees* (usually considered pre-Hasmonean) has the old patriarch Jacob predict that anointed rulers will arise from the tribe of Levi (*Jubilees* 31:15), but he predicts only a single great prince—the original David—coming from the tribe of Judah (*Jubilees* 31:18). The Greek *Testaments of the Twelve Patriarchs* (portions of which probably originated in the second century B.C.) speak a little about a coming ruler from the tribe of Judah—the Branch of God (chap. 24). But since this text has been retouched by a Christian copyist, sorting out the original Jewish ideas is difficult.[7] What's more significant is that the *Testament* gives much more attention to the coming of an ideal priest from the tribe of Levi, who will reign "like a king" over the earth (chap. 18). It is in *this* figure, not in the messiah from Judah, that Isaiah's prophecies about the messianic kingdom are to be fulfilled.[8]

So it seems then that the Hasmonean dynasty encouraged a shift in Jewish perspectives on the Messiah. But the shift was only temporary. Alexander Janneus's immorality, the civil wars between Aristobulus II and Hyrcanus II, and the final collapse of the dynasty demonstrated clearly that the messianic age hadn't arrived yet. With the fall of the Hasmoneans and the stripping of power from the high priesthood (especially under King Herod), there was a resurgence of interest in God's promises to David. The *Psalms of Solomon* are one of the most articulate witnesses to the thinking of the day. The Hasmoneans had never received a promise from God. They had usurped the throne that rightfully belonged to a descendant of King David. And now God would repay them by exterminat-

---

[7]Aramaic versions of the *Testament of Levi* have been discovered in a ruined synagogue in Cairo and among the Dead Sea Scrolls. The relationship between these texts and the Greek text are uncertain. But in the Aramaic versions Judah's role is minimized, implying that Judah's position in the Greek versions may have been magnified from his role in the original.

[8]In the *Testament of Levi* 18.5 there are allusions to Is 44:23; 11:9; in 18.7 there's an allusion to Is 11:2.

ing their whole lineage and bringing in his true, Davidic Messiah.

The Dead Sea Scrolls also spoke of the coming Davidic king. In the latter days a prince would appear who would lead the sons of light in their battle against the sons of darkness. This figure is identified by several titles, including "the Prince of the Congregation" and the "Messiah of Israel." But in several texts he's called "the Branch of David," an obvious reference to Isaiah's prophecy about the coming messianic king.[9] In some of the Dead Sea Scrolls (perhaps earlier texts?) he seems to play second fiddle to a figure called "the Messiah of Aaron," the messianic priest who interprets the laws and leads the Community in worship. But the Branch of David's ultimate destiny is to judge and rule over the Community and all the nations of the world. He leads the sons of light in their final conflict and personally executes the Roman ruler (4Q285).

Later texts further demonstrate the importance of the Davidic messiah in New Testament times. The apocalyptic *4 Ezra,* written near the end of the first century A.D., records a symbolic vision of a monstrous eagle and a talking lion (chaps. 11-12). An angel tells Ezra that the eagle represents the "fourth kingdom" that appeared in a vision of the prophet Daniel. In Daniel 7 there's recorded a vision of four animals representing different kingdoms: a winged lion, a bear, a leopard and another creature. The fourth beast isn't identified as any particular animal but merely as a unique and terrible creature. For the author of *4 Ezra* that animal could only have been an eagle, the symbol of the Roman Empire. The talking lion is explicitly identified as the Messiah, the descendant of David. He's destined to slay the eagle, judge the nations of the world and destroy them. Through his appearance, God's people will be delivered from their oppression.

Most of these warrior-king messianic expectations involved a figure who was totally mortal, possessing no supernatural powers. It was simply the fact that God was his patron that made him unconquerable. Some of the bandits who took on the role of kings probably thought of themselves as fulfilling the Davidic promises. Whether they were actually descended from David or not was irrelevant—they could easily understand the passages to be fulfilled in a figurative rather than literal descent. A few un-

---

[9]For example, the collection of messianic prophecies and interpretations called 4QFlorilegium, the *Commentary on Isaiah* (4QpIsa), 4QPBless, and a *War Scroll* fragment identified as 4Q285.

likely victories may have convinced these warlords that God was on their side, and they were all but guaranteed a full, glorious victory over the Roman oppressors.

The Son of Man. The Davidic warlord was certainly one of the most prominent messianic expectations of the late Second Temple Period, but it was hardly the only expectation. There were also more supernatural ideas afoot. A powerful stream of speculation was inspired by the vision recorded in Daniel 7. After the four terrible animals arise from the earth, Daniel sees "one like a son of man" (NIV) descend from heaven and receive eternal kingship (Dan 7:13-14). The phrase "son of man" is simply an idiomatic way of saying "human being" (or "mortal" as in Ezekiel 2:1; 3:1, 3, 4, 10, 17 NRSV). Probably, that's how Daniel used the phrase as well: in contrast to the animal-like figures who had appeared earlier in his vision, representing earthly powers, he now saw a human figure. Scholars have debated endlessly the original significance of the figure—whether he represents an angel, an individual or perhaps a nation (i.e., Israel). But the most likely explanation to me is that this "son of man" originally represented the kingdom of God, with its divine origins and glorious destiny. The kingdoms of this world were base, animalistic things compared to the splendor of the kingdom of God.

In the hands of Daniel's interpreters the "son of man" became a supernatural deliverer. Probably the earliest surviving example of this exegesis comes from the *Similitudes of Enoch* (37-71).[10] In these visions Enoch sees "the Son of Man" in heaven, standing before God. He existed from ancient times, hidden away in heaven until the day of his appearance. This son of man has been chosen by God to remove kings from their thrones and liberate the poor from oppression. He makes miraculous warfare, and in his presence gold, silver and metal weapons all melt away. Through him the dead will be resurrected. The righteous will enjoy eternal joy, while the wicked will be eternally destroyed. Even the angels will be judged by the son of man; thus no evil will exist in all heaven or earth after his appearance. Earth will be miraculously transformed so that only good things will exist. These visions depict a figure whose significance goes far beyond the

---

[10]This text is notoriously hard to date, but the lack of any clear allusions to the Roman Empire indicates to me that the text was produced before 63 B.C. The fact that no copy of the Similitudes has been found among the Dead Sea Scrolls may simply be an accident of preservation, or perhaps the people who collected the Scrolls rejected its lofty view of the Messiah.

nationalistic visions of the *Psalms of Solomon* or the Dead Sea Scrolls. He's truly a cosmic messiah, whose advent will bring about the consummation of human history.

Except for the New Testament, no other surviving texts from the first century A.D. use "son of man" as a messianic title. But there are other texts whose messianic concepts seem to have been inspired by Daniel's son of man. We've already seen how *4 Ezra* talks about the coming of the Davidic Messiah. Chapter 13 of that text recounts a vision in which "something like the shape of a man" comes up out of the sea and flies with the clouds of heaven. He has been hidden for ages but will be revealed at the end of time. This figure will take his stand on Mount Zion and judge the nations by the words of God's law. Clearly, *4 Ezra* drew on Daniel's son of man vision and probably on *1 Enoch* as well. So even though the title isn't used, we have evidence here that the tradition of a son of man/messiah persisted until the end of the first century, when *4 Ezra* was apparently written.

We can trace the messianic "son of man" idea further still, into rabbinic literature of the centuries after Jesus. There were two primary understandings of Daniel's son of man among the rabbis: a collective understanding (in which the son of man is interpreted as a symbol of Israel), and the messianic interpretation. According to some of the rabbis the Messiah would actually descend from heaven, perhaps literally coming with the clouds—understanding the symbolic son of man imagery as a literal vision of the future (e.g., *B. Tal. Sanhedrin* 96b-97a, 98a). Both Judaism and Christianity shared a central notion that the Messiah would originate in heaven, and in both cases, a principal source of the idea was Daniel 7.

Son of God. We often think of the title "Son of God" as unique to Christianity, but it's actually widely attested in ancient times. The most ancient religious texts ever discovered speak of kings as the "sons of the gods." In Sumer, the first civilization, kings circulated stories about how the gods had impregnated their mothers, resulting in their birth and accounting for their splendor. These weren't ancient, legendary kings, as in the ancient Greek myths—several historical figures also claimed divine parentage. There was also a notion of divine adoption: Mesopotamian kings were said to have been "born" into the gods' family on the day of their enthronement. In Egypt, all the pharaohs were known as the "sons of god," or even simply "the god on earth." During their lifetimes they were the incarnation of the sun god Re; after death, they became the underworld god Osiris. The Greeks, even before they had come to the East, had adopted the idea of divine kingship. We've already talked about the cults of Philip and Alexander the Great. We've seen too how Antiochus Epiphanes took his godhood very seriously, trying to force the Jews to worship him. Apparently, the Romans got the notion of the emperor's divinity from the East as well. "Son of god" was an official title of all the Caesars after Augustus.

From the historical narratives in the Bible, it might seem as if the Israelites utterly rejected the notion that their kings were in any way identified with the divinity. The Israelite monarchs were obviously such fallible fellows that one would be hard pressed to mistake any of them for a "son of God"! But we can't project our modern concepts of what it would mean to be "God's son" on ancient Israel. We sometimes read the word *son* too literally: in our thinking a son is a male, biological offspring or an adopted heir. But in ancient Near Eastern languages the word for "son" was used much more broadly than we use the term today. "Son" in ancient Hebrew meant not only a biological offspring, but it could also mean a descendant (as in the phrase "the sons of Abraham"), or it could mean a subordinate (as in the description of angels as "sons of God" in Gen 6:2; Job 1:6 and other passages) or even a disciple (as in the phrase "sons of the prophets," 2 Kings 2:3, 5; Amos 7:14). So the notion that the king was the son of a god didn't imply to the ancients that the king shared the god's moral and spiritual nature. In most cases it probably meant that he acted as the god's regent on earth, receiving through his "adoption" the authority to act on the god's behalf.

The Old Testament occasionally uses language that implies such a relationship between the Lord and the king—and sometimes, it might even imply more. In 2 Samuel 7:14 God tells King David that when his son Solomon becomes king, "I will be a father to him, and he shall be a son to me." In Psalm 2:7 God says to the king, "You are my son; today I have begotten you." In Psalm 45:6-7, the king of Israel is told:

> Your throne, O God, endures forever and ever.
>   Your royal scepter is a scepter of equity;
>   you love righteousness and hate wickedness.
> Therefore God, your God, has anointed you
>   with the oil of gladness beyond your companions.

Christians recognize the ultimate fulfillment of such verses in Jesus Christ. But the more difficult question is what these assertions meant to the ancient Israelites. Did they believe that all their kings were somehow adopted by God? Or did these verses express their ideal of kingship—that the king would live in such close fellowship with God that he would act as God's representative on earth? The royal chronicles show that the biblical authors had no illusions about their kings being morally perfect or endowed with supernatural abilities. Yet those kings were criticized precisely because they fell short of the ideal that the king would live in close communion with the Lord, executing God's will on the earth. At his ideal best, the king of Israel would have been the image of God on earth.

So it would seem natural that the Messiah, the king par excellence, would have a special relationship with God. There are a few surviving Second Temple Period texts that call the Messiah the Son of God. *First Enoch* 105:2 speaks of him in this manner. There also seem to be a couple of references in the Dead Sea Scrolls that speak of the Messiah as the Son of God. One text directly applies God's words to David (2 Sam 7:13-14), "I will be a father to him, and he shall be a son to me," to the Messiah (4Q174 "Florilegium," 3.10-11). Another may speak of God fathering the Messiah (1QSa 2.11-12). In *4 Ezra* the phrase "my son, the Messiah" appears often, although some scholars see this designation as a Christian interpolation. Even so, there's good evidence that the identification of the Messiah as God's Son wasn't a Christian innovation. It's interesting to note that according to the Gospels, when Jesus was tried by the high priest he was asked, "Tell us if you are the Messiah, the Son of God" (Mt 26:63).

But how would the Messiah become the "Son of God"? Would he be born into the world as God's Son, or would he be "adopted" by God at his coronation?[11] There's nothing in the surviving literature that tells us how the Jews of the Second Temple Period expected the Messiah to be born. They weren't necessarily expecting him to come into the world in some unusual fashion. The ancient Israelite kings were all born in the natural way, and yet they were (apparently) called the sons of God. The Roman emperors, too, rarely claimed to have been conceived in any fashion but the normal way; yet they also could claim to be sons of god. Being God's son wouldn't necessarily have implied to ancient peoples a miraculous conception. So the title could simply be an honorific one: all God's people are children of God, but the Messiah would be the Son of God par excellence.

On the other hand, *1 Enoch* and *4 Ezra* seem to associate the Messiah's supernatural powers with his divine origins. The Messiah would be able

---

[11]Some ancient Christian heretics espoused a teaching called "adoptionism," believing that Jesus did not become the Son of God until his baptism.

to exercise uncanny abilities because he wasn't your typical human. He already existed in heaven, hidden until the proper time, when God would send him to earth. These texts imply that it wasn't the Messiah's earthly birth that made him the Son of God, no matter what form that earthly birth might have taken. Rather, it was his eternal, unique relationship with God the Father.

Jesus and Jewish Messianism

This brief survey demonstrates the diversity in Jewish expectations in the time of Jesus. Simplistic characterizations that "the Jews were seeking a military messiah, and Jesus came preaching peace," don't do justice to the facts. The situation was far more complex than that. Jesus obviously struck a responsive cord in many Jewish people of his day; but others couldn't quite figure out what to make of him.

Jesus as Son of Man. Clearly, Jesus didn't stand dramatically outside the messianic expectations of his time. Most of the terminology that the New Testament uses for Jesus' role already appears in the intertestamental Jewish literature. That's certainly true of the term that Jesus usually uses to refer to himself: "Son of Man." We've considered at length the importance of the phrase in Jewish apocalyptic. But when Jesus calls himself the "son of man," the significance of his usage isn't always clear. Usually, he seems to be using the phrase to emphasize his humility, as in Matthew 8:20, "the Son of Man has nowhere to lay his head." But in a few instances Jesus makes clear reference to the vision in Daniel 7. One case is his eschatological discourse (Mt 24 and parallel passages), where he says that after a time of great tribulation, all people will see the Son of Man coming with the clouds of heaven in power and splendor (Mt 24:30). But would this Son of Man be Jesus himself? According to the Gospels, Jesus didn't make the identification clear until his trial. The high priest asked him if he was the Messiah, the Son of God. This time Jesus answered:

> I am. And
> "you will see the Son of Man
> seated at the right hand of the Power,"
> and "coming with the clouds of heaven." (Mk 14:62)

So here Jesus identified the Messiah with the Son of Man—and identified both with himself. To the high priest his statement was a blasphemy worthy of death. The high priest apparently understood Daniel 7 in the same way that *1 Enoch* understood the text. He considered the Son of Man to be a divine or semidivine figure, far above a mere human king. Otherwise, Jesus' answer could never have been interpreted as blasphemy.

THE HISTORICAL JESUS?

Perhaps the most vexing question in New Testament studies is the relationship between the historical Jesus and the Jesus of the Gospel accounts. The Gospels preserve the works and words of Jesus, but they also include the theological reflection of the church. They weren't simply biographies but teaching tools as well. All scholars recognize this fact. But there's great disagreement on how much the Gospels reflect the "authentic" words of Jesus, and how much of their content would best be called "interpretation" of Jesus' teachings. Did Jesus actually call himself the Son of Man? Was he truly regarded as the Messiah? In this section we will work with the assumption that the Gospels are a generally accurate record of Jesus' ideas, and that the church didn't simply invent a Jesus to embody its theological notions. In any event, the Gospel traditions will give us an accurate picture of how the first-century Christians understood the concept of the "messiah."

Jesus and Old Testament expectations. Two terms that the Gospels use to designate Jesus originated in the traditional Old Testament messianic expectations. One is the title *Messiah*, translated into Greek as *Christ*. The New Testament is the oldest extant corpus that actually uses the term *Messiah* as a title.[12] "Jesus is the Christ" (or "Jesus is the Messiah") is one of the most important confessions of faith in the New Testament.[13] But according to the Gospels, Jesus rarely identified himself as Messiah. Rather, this title was most often used by Jesus' fellow Jews. According to the Synoptic Gospels, Jesus repeatedly warned people not to let the cat out of the bag—they

---

[12]See, for example, Mt 1:16-18. No intertestamental Jewish literature uses "the Messiah" as a title, preferring constructions like "your Anointed One," or "the Lord's Anointed." In later Jewish literature "the Messiah" appears quite frequently as a title.

[13]See Mt 16:16 and parallels; Jn 11:27; Acts 18:5; 1 Jn 5:1.

weren't to spread word that he was the Messiah.[14] This "messianic secret," as it's called, has led some scholars to conclude that Jesus never really claimed to be the Messiah during his lifetime. They argue that the "messianic secret" was the early church's explanation for why Jesus wasn't actually hailed as the Messiah until after his death. But such skepticism is probably unwarranted. The Romans wouldn't have executed Jesus for performing miracles or even for saying he was the Son of Man. But the title Messiah was loaded with ominous political connotations. It was precisely because he claimed to be the Messiah that he was executed. Most likely he avoided using the term because of the misperceptions it would generate. He was indeed the Messiah, but not the kind of Messiah that most Jews had in mind. He would most surely conquer the world—but not until *after* his resurrection.

The other term with deep Old Testament roots is "Son of David." Interestingly enough, the Gospels use this phrase just like they use "Messiah." The Gospel traditions often assert that Jesus was a descendant of David, and on several occasions he's actually called Son of David.[15] But Jesus never calls *himself* Son of David. Like the title Messiah, the phrase "son of David" was often filled with nationalistic or militant connotations. Jesus probably consciously avoided using it. But to the church the identification of Jesus as David's descendant added weight to its claims that he was the legitimate Messiah of Israel.

Jesus as Son of God. Another messianic title used in the Gospels is "Son of God." Again, it's not Jesus' typical self-designation. This phrase is usually found on the lips of angels, demons and even God himself. Only those with some kind of supernatural insight could perceive that the humble carpenter from Nazareth was actually the Son of God. In the early church, however, this title eventually became the most important of all. In the Apostles' Creed we confess that "We believe in Jesus Christ, the only begotten Son of God." The next two affirmations explore the nature of Jesus' sonship: "Who was conceived by the Holy Spirit; born of the virgin Mary." Unlike the Roman Emperor, who would be granted divinity at his death, Jesus was divine by his very nature. The Jewish apocalypticists had never gone into detail about how the preexistent Son of Man would become the Jews' Messiah. Probably, they simply expected him to descend from

---

[14]Mt 8:4; 9:30; 17:9; Mk 1:44; 3:12; 5:43; 7:36; 8:30.
[15]Mt 1:1-17; 9:27; 15:22; 21:9; Mk 10:47-48; Lk 3:23-38.

heaven on a cloud. But the virgin birth expressed a belief that was absent in both Jewish and Roman royal ideology. Jesus wasn't the Son of God in some spiritual or social sense but in a biological sense as well.

THE SON OF GOD IN RABBINIC JUDAISM

Not surprisingly, rabbinic Judaism dropped the notion of the Messiah as Son of God. The Christians had "ruined" it for them. But they didn't abandon the notion that the Messiah would have supernatural origins and a unique relationship with God. Later rabbis continued to identify the Messiah with Daniel's "son of man" and developed elaborate stories about his heavenly preexistence and his earthly incarnation. In the rabbinic *Pesikta Rabbati* 33 we read, "At the beginning of the creation of the world the king Messiah was born, who arose in God's thoughts before the world was made." In another passage from the same text, Satan sees a light shining under God's throne and asks what the light might be. God responds that it's none other than the Messiah, hidden there until the time of his revelation.

Even so, most of the rabbis avoided the idea that the Messiah was actually divine. When the second-century Rabbi Akiba suggested that the "thrones" set up in Daniel 7:9 were for both God and the Messiah, his comrades rebuffed him. In their opinion he was suggesting that the Messiah was somehow God's equal—an opinion dangerously similar to that of the Christians (*B. Tal. Hagigah* 14a; *Sanhedrin* 38b).

Jesus' vicarious death. It's clear then that the Gospels' understanding of Jesus' person and work brought together several contemporary messianic expectations. It harmonized some of those ideas and enriched others with new, deeper understandings. But Jesus went beyond contemporary thought with the notion of his vicarious death—his suffering on behalf of sinful humanity. That the Messiah had to suffer and die for his people was hitherto unknown in Judaism. The message comes through most clearly in the enacted symbolism of the Lord's Supper (Mt 26:17-30; Mk 14:12-26; Lk 22:7-20). Here, Jesus compares the bread and wine of the Passover feast to his body that would be broken and his blood that would be shed for his followers. In the Epistles of Paul and John and the Epistle to the Hebrews the idea of Christ's atoning sacrifice is developed into a full-blown theology of grace. The Messiah had to die not simply because the prophets had said he would, but because he was the Lamb of God, who would take away the sins of the world (Jn 1:29).

Several centuries after Jesus, the Jewish rabbis would recognize the messianic import of such passages as Isaiah 53 ("the Suffering Servant") and develop their own idea of a messiah who would suffer for the sins of Israel. According to some rabbinic legends the Messiah accepted the suffering of Israel on himself so that Israel's pains wouldn't become unbearable (see *Pesikta Rabbati* 161a-b). Some texts describe him as a leper and others as a beggar (cf. *B. Tal. Sanhedrin* 98a). In one strand of tradition, the "messiah son of Joseph," who precedes the Messiah son of David, actually suffers death at the hands of his enemies to purge the sins of the nation (*B. Tal. Sukkoth* 52a; *Y. Tal. Sukkoth* 55b). We can't say for certain that Jesus anticipated the rabbis by several centuries. It's possible that the notion of a suffering messiah was part of Jewish messianic expectations of his day, but the idea didn't make its way into any of the literature that has survived to our day.

Jesus as messianic priest. Since Jesus offered himself as the perfect sacrifice, it was only natural that the church came to regard him as the ultimate high priest. Neither the Gospel writers nor the apostle Paul make the connection. Perhaps they were reluctant to draw parallels between Jesus, who was from the tribe of Judah, with the high priests, who came from the tribe of Levi. But the author of the Epistle to the Hebrews has no qualms about explicitly identifying Jesus as our "great high priest" (Heb 4:14). In several chapters we're given a systematic presentation of Christ's spiritual priesthood. For the author of Hebrews, the Levitical priesthood is irrelevant to the question of Christ's priestly role. The Levitical priests, in his view, were failures. They could only buy forgiveness for a year at a time, and they couldn't make anyone righteous in the process. It was an imperfect system for an imperfect nation. Instead, the author of Hebrews compares Jesus to Melchizedek, the priest-king of Salem (Heb 5:6-10; 7:1-26; see Gen 14:18-20). Hebrews draws on contemporary Jewish legends about Melchizedek. According to those legends Melchizedek was an eternal priest with no parents, no beginning and no end (see Ps 110:4). Jesus was made a high priest of the same type, serving perpetually in heaven, making atonement for the people of God.

The book of Hebrews brings a perspective to Jesus' ministry that's different from that of any other New Testament book. But it's not unique in Jewish literature. One of the Dead Sea Scrolls (11QMelchizedek) also draws from the Melchizedek legend. In this tantalizing fragmentary text Melchizedek is named as a heavenly advocate for the people of God. He'll deliver the children of light from the power of the devil, atone for their sins, judge the wicked spirits and establish the kingdom of God. The text is too fragmentary to determine whether or not the author of the scroll expected Melchizedek to become incarnate, or if he would simply carry out his ministry in heaven. But the surviving text is sufficient testimony to the existence of a tradition about the heavenly high priest Melchizedek. The author of the book of Hebrews was obviously aware of that tradition and used it to help his Jewish audience understand the priestly ministry of Christ.

From this brief treatment it's apparent that there was no essential conflict between the Jesus of the Gospels and the messiahs of Jewish speculation. The primary issues that led to Jesus' rejection by most Jews were probably his disdain for Pharisaic interpretations of the law, his ignoble death and the fact that most Jews were looking for a political liberator rather than a spiritual Messiah. But even after the church began to proclaim Jesus' death and resurrection, Jewish Christianity still fell well within the boundaries of Jewish orthodoxy. Those first Christians observed the laws and traditions of their forefathers; they rejected idolatry; they provided charity to Jews in need. Why then were Christians persecuted in first-century Palestine? Why did Jews and Christians drift apart and eventually become two separate religions? Why does such animosity exist against Jewish Christians even in our own day? Technically speaking, such questions lie beyond the purview of a study on intertestamental Judaism. But the bases of these attitudes were laid during the closing decades of the Second Temple Period. The irreparable breach between the church and rabbinic Judaism was caused by events that I will summarize in the epilogue.

For Further Reading

The volume of scholarly literature on Jewish resistance and messianism is vast. I've selected here a few collections of essays and some of the most recent, helpful or influential texts.

Caragounis, Chrys C. *The Son of Man: Vision and Interpretation*. Tübingen: J. C. B. Mohr, 1986. Not one of the most influential studies, but one of the most recent book-length treatments.

Charlesworth, James H. ed. *The Messiah: Developments in Earliest Judaism and Christianity*. Philadelphia: Fortress, 1992. Contains essays by both Christian and Jewish scholars.

Collins, John J. *The Scepter and the Star: The Messiahs of the Dead Sea Scrolls and Other Ancient Literature*. New York: Doubleday, 1995. An excellent recent study.

Gray, Rebecca. *Prophetic Figures in Late Second Temple Jewish Palestine: The Evidence from Josephus*. New York and Oxford: Oxford University Press, 1993. Somewhat controversial, but good surveys of issues and bibliography.

Hengel, Martin. *The Zealots: Investigation into the Jewish Freedom Movement in the Period from Herod I until 70 A.D.* Translated by David Smith. Edinburgh: T & T Clark, 1989. Defines Zealots more broadly than I would, but excellent collection of source material.

Horsley, Richard A., and John S. Hanson, *Bandits, Prophets, and Messiahs: Popular Movements at the Time of Jesus*. San Francisco: Harper and Row, 1985. Sociological approach to the subject.

Neusner, Jacob, William S. Green, and Ernest Frerichs, eds. *Judaisms and their Messiahs at the Turn of the Christian Era*. Cambridge: Cambridge University Press, 1987. A collection of essays by respected scholars.

Patai, Raphael, *The Messiah Texts: Jewish Legends of Three Thousand Years*. Detroit: Wayne State University Press, 1979. A fascinating anthology, arranged topically.

Epilogue
Anno Domini

W e've completed our survey of the intertestamental period, and we've moved well within the realm of New Testament times. But we haven't quite finished our story yet. One of the most pivotal events in the formation of Jewish and Christian beliefs occurred a few decades after the time of Jesus. It was an event so monumental that Jesus himself looked forward to it as "the end of the age." According to Matthew 24:1-3, Jesus told his disciples that the end would come with the destruction of Herod's temple. With that cataclysmic event an old era would draw to a close, and a new era would begin. Theologically, it was a milestone of immense significance. And historically, too, the fall of the temple represents a watershed: it marks the end of the Second Temple Period. So to conclude this survey of Second Temple Jewish history, I'll briefly chronicle the circumstances surrounding that most critical event.

Early Governors

In chapter nine I recounted the fates of Herod's sons. Archelaus, who was appointed the ethnarch of Judea, was deposed in A.D. 6. Judea came under the rule of Roman praefects, or governors. These were men drawn from the "equestrian" ranks of Roman society, one level below the nobility. (Territories administered in this manner were generally considered less important or less troublesome than those with higher-ranking governors.) Some of these governors were quite competent and compassionate. Most of them, however, were neither. Between A.D. 6 and A.D. 41 Judea was administered by six or seven different governors. We don't know many details about their administrations, with one exception: Pontius Pilate (A.D. 26-36).[1] Pilate was reputedly a cruel, greedy, insensitive man. He managed to offend the Jews before he ever passed a judicial decision. In view of the Jews' extreme sensitivity about images, the Roman governors had always instructed their troops to lower their standards—which were emblazoned with images of patron animals—before they entered Jerusalem. But Pilate ignored the convention and came into the city with his standards held high. His soldiers posted the offensive banners right in front of the temple. When a crowd of Jews gathered swearing they would rather die than permit the sacrilege to remain, he grudgingly removed them. Pilate further offended the Jews by appropriating temple funds to build an aqueduct. Anyone who protested the action was beaten into submission. He also insulted his subjects by placing votive shields with the emperor's name engraved on them in the temple itself. He was officially reprimanded by Rome on several occasions, which probably accounts for his uncharacteristic reticence in the matter of Jesus' trial. The last straw came a few years after Jesus' death. In A.D. 35 a prophet promised to produce the lost temple vessels on Mt. Gerizim in Samaria. He gathered a huge crowd of Samaritans to witness the miracle. Pilate, however, suspected that the gathering would erupt in rebellion, so he ordered his soldiers to attack the group and kill its leaders. The Samaritans lodged a formal protest with the governor of Coele-Syria, and Pilate was recalled to Rome.

Relations between the Jews and Romans were further strained by the Roman Emperor Caligula.[2] The mad monarch actually believed his own press releases and insisted on being worshiped as a god. Most of the empire humored him, but not the Jews. They stubbornly insisted that they were exempted from participating in the state cult. Caligula wasn't pleased—and in his wrath another scoundrel saw an opportunity for self-promotion. The governor of Egypt, who was already being investigated for corruption, thought he might get back into the emperor's favor if he initiated a persecution of the Jews. The year A.D. 38 was a bad one for the Jewish residents of Alexandria: synagogues were burned, citizenship was revoked and they were beaten and driven from their homes. But by the

---

[1] *Ant.* 18.3.1-2 (55-62), 18.4.1-2 (85-89); *War* 1.9.2-4 (169-77).
[2] *Ant.* 18.8.1-9 (257-309), 19.1.1-14 (1-113); *War* 1.10.1-5 (184-203).

end of the year the governor had been deposed and the persecution ended.

Meanwhile, the Jews of Judea were having their own problems with Caligula. In that same year, A.D. 38, Caligula had an altar erected for the imperial cult in Jamnia, a predominantly Jewish city on the coast. But the Jewish residents wouldn't endure such an insult, and they destroyed the offending structure. Caligula couldn't take such insolence lying down. He retaliated by ordering the governor of Syria, Publius Petronius, to erect a statue of the emperor in the Jerusalem temple.

What was the governor to do? Petronius was a just and thoughtful man, and he had no desire to carry out the ridiculous order. But knowing how cruel the emperor could be, he seemed to have no choice. The governor sent word to the Jewish leaders informing them of the emperor's order and implored them to accept Caligula's image without trouble. But a Jewish crowd descended on his headquarters in Ptolemais and begged the governor to reconsider. Petronius tried to be stern, ordering them to return home and prepare to receive the statue. After all, it was just a statue—what harm would it do? But the men, women and children fell on their knees and bared their necks before the Roman magistrate, saying they would rather be executed than to see their temple desecrated in such a manner. Petronius was deeply moved. Knowing that he was risking his career, he sent a message to Caligula, asking him to reconsider his order. At the same time Herod the Great's grandson, Herod Agrippa (now king of Philip's old realm), was also imploring the emperor to abandon the plan. Since Agrippa and Caligula had been boyhood friends, Agrippa's opinion carried much weight in Rome. So Caligula relented of his plan—for a while. But it wasn't long before he had a change of heart. How dare the Jews, and even one of his own officers, question his judgment? He sent a letter to Petronius ordering him to kill himself and to turn over the governorship to someone who would set up his image in the temple without delay. But fortunately for both Petronius and the Jews, Caligula was assassinated before the letter reached Ptolemais. The dead emperor never enjoyed the pleasure of humiliating his stubborn subjects.

King Agrippa and the Later Governors

The residents of Judea enjoyed a brief respite from Roman governors in A.D. 41. After Caligula's death, the crafty Herod Agrippa was very helpful in getting Claudius installed as emperor. The emperor rewarded Agrippa by adding Judea to his realm. So once again a Herodian king ruled over

Judea. But Agrippa was more than just a Herodian: he was also a Hasmonean, being the grandson of Herod's beloved wife Mariamne. This fact wasn't lost on the residents of Judea. They considered him the legitimate heir to the throne. According to a rabbinic legend, at the Feast of Tabernacles in A.D. 41 Agrippa was called on to read publicly from the book of Deuteronomy. When he reached the place that says, "You are not permitted to put a foreigner over you, one who is not one of your brethren" (Deut 17:15, author's translation), Agrippa began to weep.[3] But the Jews called out, "You are our brother! You are our brother!" (*M. Sotah* 7.8).

Agrippa was apparently well liked in Judea, and he acted with the utmost piety and good will toward his subjects. But that good will didn't extend equally to all within his realm. Agrippa initiated a persecution of the Christians as a way of demonstrating his solidarity with his orthodox Jewish subjects. James the son of Zebedee was a casualty of his zeal, and Peter almost fell under his hand. But the persecution didn't last long. Agrippa's prosperous reign was cut short in A.D. 44. Both the New Testament and Josephus agree that his demise came about as a divine punishment. While Agrippa was appearing at a public gathering at Caesarea, the pagan citizens of the area hailed him as a god. Acts 12:22 attributes their adoration to his eloquent speech. Josephus tells us that Agrippa was dressed in a silver robe that flashed like fire in the sun (*Ant.* 19.8.2 [343-52]). He obviously made quite an impression. Agrippa gladly accepted the worship of the crowds, so an angel of the Lord struck him with severe stomach pains. He died soon after, in great agony (Acts 12:23). His son, Agrippa II (Acts 25—26), received a kingdom of his own in A.D. 50 comprising territories northwest of Galilee and some areas of Galilee itself. He was also given responsibility for administering temple affairs. Judea, however, was never incorporated into his realm.

With Herod Agrippa's passing, Judea once again came under the administration of Roman governors. During this period graft and incompetence came to be the rule. The Jews chafed under the corrupt leadership, and riots started to become more frequent. The governor Felix (A.D. 52-60), before whom the apostle Paul presented his case (Acts 24), was a scandalous character.[4] His many illegal dealings incited the Jews to rebel fre-

---

[3]According to the Mishnah, it was the custom to read the book of Deuteronomy at the Feast of Tabernacles at the beginning of each sabbatical (i.e., eighth) year.
[4]*Ant.* 20.7.1-8.9 (137-82); *War* 1.12.8-13.7 (247-70).

quently. Scores of Judeans fled to the desert—some to prepare for war and others to await the kingdom of God. But Felix made no distinctions between the two. Whenever he discovered such pilgrim bands, he massacred them. During his administration a prophet known as "the Egyptian" appeared (cf. Acts 21:38), who promised to make the walls of Jerusalem collapse. Felix killed many of his followers, but the leader himself escaped. It was during Felix's tenure that the *sicarii* first began their seditious activities, assassinating anyone who might be considered a "collaborator." Jerusalem was being terrorized both by foreign oppressors and native rabble-rousers.

Because of his crimes Felix was recalled to Rome in A.D. 62. During the months before his replacement arrived, a wave of anarchy descended on the city. The high priest Ananus (son of the high priest Annas of the Gospels) used his position to secure the execution of his political rivals—including James the brother of Jesus (*Ant.* 20.9.1 [200]). Ananus was deposed by King Agrippa II after a tenure of only three months. When Porcius Festus (Acts 25—26) arrived to administer Judea, Jerusalem was a veritable powder keg.[5] Festus was a fair man, and he tried his best to pacify the Jews. But by now the tide of violence was becoming unstoppable. Festus died after only two years in office, and he was replaced by the abominable Albinus.[6] Josephus tells us that there was no wickedness that Albinus wouldn't entertain, but his principal vice appears to have been greed. He plundered both public and private funds to fill his purse. He made money from both the Roman partisans and the rebels. The Roman soldiers would round up the bandits, but then Albinus would take bribes from their comrades and release the criminals back on to the streets. With such a fine example to inspire him, the high priest Ananias also got in on the act, stealing the tithes meant for the support of the entire priesthood. So during the administration of Albinus, priests were starving, bandits were running rampant and the citizens of Jerusalem were growing ever more discontent. After two years' service, Albinus was recalled to Rome, and Gessius Florus came to pluck the province of its few remaining feathers.[7]

Like his predecessor, Florus had no qualms about robbing the people he was charged with protecting. But he surpassed Albinus's greed, plunder-

---

[5]*Ant.* 20.8.9-11 (182-96); *War* 2.14.1 (271).
[6]*Ant.* 20.9.2-5 (204-15); *War* 2.14.1 (272-76).
[7]*Ant.* 20.11.1 (252-58); *War* 2.14.2ff.

ing whole cities and doing nothing to maintain law and order in his realm. In A.D. 66 he ordered his soldiers to loot the temple treasuries in broad daylight. A crowd of Jews gathered to watch the Roman soldiers carry away the public funds and even the private trusts that were held in the temple's vaults. One of the spectators decided to have some fun with the situation—he began to pass baskets, collecting money for "poor Governor Florus." Unfortunately, Florus didn't think the joke was funny. He brought in his troops, sacked the city and crucified many of its leading citizens. Convinced he had taught Jerusalem a lesson, he marched his army back into the city the next day to collect whatever scraps they'd missed before. The chief priests persuaded some of the Jews to come forward and salute the soldiers, but the soldiers refused to acknowledge their greeting. Angered at being snubbed, some of the crowd began to hurl insults at the soldiers. Florus ordered his troops to attack them. But this time the mob had a numerical advantage. They overwhelmed the Roman troops and took control of the temple mount. Florus could see he was outnumbered and in no position to enforce his will on the city. He fled to Caesarea, leaving a cohort of Roman troops and the native leaders to restore order in Jerusalem.

But Jerusalem would not be pacified. Even appeals from King Agrippa II had no effect. The mob was taking control of the city. A daily sacrifice offered on behalf of the emperor ceased. Judea was now officially in revolt.

The Course of the Revolt

Josephus gives us lengthy—and somewhat contradictory—reports on the course of the Great Revolt in his autobiography and in *The Jewish War*. We needn't concern ourselves with the details here. But in brief, the Jews managed a few early victories over some small Roman forces. Encouraged by these triumphs they became more committed than ever to the cause of freedom. In Jerusalem a revolutionary council was assembled to prepare for the inevitable Roman response. This council assigned various tasks to some of Jerusalem's most prominent citizens. The current high priest, the politically moderate Ananus, was in charge of preparing Jerusalem's defenses. Flavius Josephus was put in charge of war efforts in Galilee. Although a young man, Josephus had a crucial assignment: Galilee would undoubtedly be the Jews' first line of defense.

Meanwhile, the Romans had taken the Revolt seriously. They appointed Vespasian, an experienced general, to go and quell the violence. He raised an army of 60,000 men and proceeded to Galilee. Josephus claims to have mustered an army of 100,000 citizen-soldiers and writes with pride about how well trained and disciplined they were. But the Galilean militia proved to have no stomach for a fight. Most of them deserted when news came of Vespasian's arrival. Josephus took the remainder of his army to the city of Jotapata and fortified it for a siege. The town held out stubbornly against the Roman onslaught, but eventually Vespasian's son Titus managed to scale the wall and open the city gates. Josephus fled with some of his troops and hid in a cave outside the city. After his soldiers had committed suicide, Josephus surrendered to Vespasian. He began to work with the Romans, trying to persuade the revolutionaries to give up the fight.

Vespasian took the rest of Galilee with little effort. Only a few cities resisted. The last holdout was Gischala, headquarters of one of the most adamant revolutionaries, a man named John. John abandoned his city and took his small army to Jerusalem, where he was welcomed with open arms. With John gone, Gischala opened its gates to the Romans. By the end of A.D. 67 all of Galilee was back under Roman control.

John of Gischala and his compatriots—who called themselves the Zealots—felt that the Jerusalem leadership was mismanaging the war effort. They took over the city and began to run it as tyrants. Anyone with connections to the old Jerusalem aristocracy was now considered an enemy of the people. The former leaders, including Ananus the high priest, were forced to take refuge in the inner courts of the temple. A new high priest was chosen by lot from among the citizens of Jerusalem. He was utterly unqualified for the job, but he met the chief criterion: he wasn't an aristocrat. John enlisted the aid of Idumean soldiers to help him take control of the city. A reign of terror ensued; anyone suspected of pro-Roman sympathies was arrested and executed. The Jewish aristocracy was suffering desperately. Not even the former high priest was spared. The Idumeans stormed the temple and slaughtered everyone who had taken refuge inside, including Ananus. Josephus saw this particular execution as the sin that sealed the fate of Jerusalem.

The Roman general Vespasian allowed these events to run their course. He proceeded throughout Palestine, subduing cities in Perea, Idumea and in Judea itself. In about a year most of the realm was once again at peace— with the exception of the capital city and a few scattered fortresses. Vespasian was about to turn his attention to Jerusalem when news arrived that the Emperor Nero had died, and Galba had been proclaimed emperor in his place. The general was making his plans to pay his respects to his new lord when news came that Galba had been assassinated. Otho had been named emperor—but not without protests. Vespasian bided his time, waiting to see if Rome would erupt in civil war.

Then a new bandit, Simon bar-Giora, appeared in Judea, pretending to be the Messiah. He began to amass followers, raiding cities and carrying off loot. After nearly a year of inactivity, Vespasian was forced to reassert himself. He subdued the cities that had aligned themselves with Simon and stationed troops in prominent locations throughout Judea. Simon's plundering activities were thwarted; but it didn't really matter. The bandit-messiah had bigger fish to fry. Some leaders in Jerusalem, chafing under the cruelty of John and his Zealots, had invited Simon to come and depose the tyrant. In the spring of A.D. 69 Simon entered Jerusalem like a liberating king. But those who had hoped he would be their deliverer were sadly mistaken. In fact, the city now found itself with not one cruel tyrant, but two.

Roman politics still prevented Vespasian from moving against Jerusalem. News arrived that the legions in Germany had replaced Otho with their general, Vitellius. But the legions in the East had their own candidate in mind: Vespasian himself. On July 1, A.D. 69, the legions of Egypt declared Vespasian emperor. Diverted once again from the revolt, Vespasian set about consolidating his support in Syria and Egypt. In December of 69 Vitellius was assassinated. Vespasian was now the undisputed emperor (and he proved to be a very competent one, indeed). He turned over the Jewish war to his son Titus as he made preparations to assume his new role in Rome.

Meanwhile, Jerusalem had become a battlefield. Simon and John were locked in constant conflict, and another faction had broken off from the Zealots and allied itself with a fellow named Eleazar. This group seized control of the inner temple courts. The three factions fought constantly against one another and continued their effort to ferret out any remaining members of the Jewish upper classes. They were even foolish enough to burn the stores of grain in Jerusalem—not realizing they condemned their own citizens to hunger during the inevitable siege. As the Roman army began setting up camp outside the city, Jerusalem was preparing to celebrate Passover. The temple gates had to be opened to admit celebrants, leaving Eleazar's group vulnerable. John seized the opportunity, smuggled his men into the temple and massacred Eleazar's party. Not even the Passover

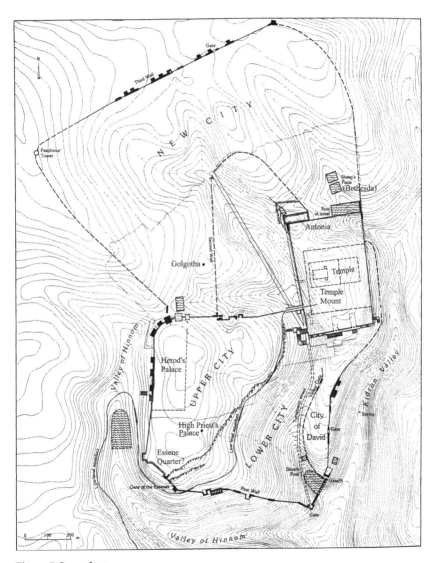

Figure 7. Jerusalem

day was spared from violence.

As General Titus began his assault on the north wall of Jerusalem, John and Simon struck a truce. They began working together to fortify Jerusalem against the invaders. The city was well designed, divided into various sections that were protected by stout walls. Near the center of the city, the temple mount was a fortress in itself, surrounded by thick ramparts. The great citadel, the Antonia (once called the Akra) was north of the temple, but nearby. The southwest part of the city was located on a hill and was called the "upper city." This area too was fortified. So taking the city wasn't merely a matter of breaching one wall but several. John had set up his headquarters in the Antonia, while Simon was ensconced in the upper city. Coming in from the north it took the Romans nearly a month to penetrate as far as the Antonia. They set up siege works outside the fortress's wall, but the Jews burned them. John proved a more capable leader at this point than many would have imagined, and he held out admirably. But eventually the Antonia was taken. John escaped to the upper city, while the Antonia was razed to the ground.

Many Jews had taken refuge in the temple courts. Titus attempted to batter down its walls, but Herod had built well. The sturdy structures refused to yield to the battering rams. There was, however, another access route available to Titus: the temple gates were primarily wooden. The Roman general ordered them burned. Soon the temple courts lay open to the frustrated Roman soldiers. Josephus tells us that Titus had hoped to spare the temple itself (although a recently discovered text throws some doubt on that assertion). The burning gates and the heat of battle incited his men to wanton destruction. The temple was set afire, and the innocent citizens who had taken refuge there, hoping for some divine deliverance, perished in the flames. The destruction was complete on the ninth day of the month of Ab (July-August), which the Jews had commemorated as the day on which the first temple had been destroyed by Nebuchadnezzar.

After the Antonia and temple mount were taken, the conquest of the upper city was no great undertaking. After a short siege the walls of this last stronghold were breached, and the two tyrants were captured. By now most of Jerusalem lay in ruins. Only the stalwart towers of Herod's palace and a section of the city wall remained standing. The site became the headquarters of a Roman legion, which burned pagan sacrifices in the place where the temple had stood. John and Simon were taken to Rome. John, considered the true leader of the revolt, was sentenced to life imprisonment. Simon, who had claimed to be a king, was led through the streets of Rome in the victory procession and then beheaded.

With the destruction of Jerusalem in A.D. 70 the Great Revolt was essentially over. But there still remained some rebel fortresses in the frontier, garrisoned by groups of *sicarii* who had taken control of them early in the war. It wasn't until A.D. 74 that the Romans took Masada, the last of these enclaves. This virtually impregnable stronghold resisted the Romans bravely. But with limited supplies and no hopes of reinforcement, it was clear that the rebels couldn't hold out forever. Seeing the end approaching swiftly, the Jews decided that they would rather die at their own hands and rob the Romans of their victory. Each man was instructed to kill his family and then himself. When the Romans finally breached Masada's defenses, they found the fortress eerily silent. The dead lay scattered. Only two women and five children, hidden in a cistern during the carnage, escaped to tell the story of the freedom-fighters' suicide pact.

Modern excavators at Masada have found many artifacts from the rebel's last days. Numerous skeletons were unearthed there. Discarded weapons have been recovered. Potsherds inscribed with Jewish names may have been the very lots used by the defenders to decide the order in which they would die. Manuscripts have been found there as well. One of the most poignant artifacts was a parchment copy of Ezekiel 37—the vision of the "valley of dry bones." In the vision, the prophet was shown a valley full of scattered bones. God directed Ezekiel to prophesy to the bones, and at his command they assembled themselves into skeletons, flesh grew on them, and they came to life. God told Ezekiel that he would do the same for Israel, raising the ruined nation to life once again. This passage of Scripture was deliberately buried by Masada's defenders so it could be found by future generations. What did it mean to the freedom fighters? Was it a last act of defiance—a testimony that they were sure their nation would be restored? Or was it a proclamation of faith in the resurrection: that even though they would die, yet they would live again? Or perhaps the text had some significance to them that from our vantage point we can't even begin to guess.

The Social Aftermath of the Revolt

The effects of the Great Revolt on Jewish society were profound. Jerusalem's remains were garrisoned with Roman troops, so the site could no longer serve as a place of religious pilgrimage or a focus for nationalistic hopes. Also the "House of Hewn Stone," meeting place for the Sanhedrin, no longer existed. The body that had for centuries administered justice among the people was dispersed. The Sanhedrin had played an especially important role in deciding religious controversies and judging cases that involved violations of the biblical laws. Who would judge Jewish religious conflicts now? The high priesthood, the other traditional pillar of authority, was gutted of its influence. With the temple in ruins, sacrifices had to cease. The high priest's public role was gone, and the office passed into obscurity. Undoubtedly the priesthood remained an honorable position for many years after the Revolt, but its political clout was largely eliminated.

Another group that suffered during the Revolt was the Sadducees. Always closely associated with the aristocracy, the rebels would surely have targeted the Sadducees for execution. With the Sanhedrin gone and the priesthood on the wane, the Sadducees—who had close ties with both institutions—lost their ability to influence Jewish political and religious life. Within a few generations, the Sadducees became extinct.

The Pharisees, however, were in a unique position to fill the power void. For a century or so they'd been the acknowledged leaders in Jewish religious affairs. Unlike the Sadducees, they weren't so bound to the temple as the center of their faith. In fact, the Pharisees had already been emphasizing that piety wasn't so much a matter of performing proper sacrifices as of obedience to the will of God. Before the destruction of the temple one of the teachers of the law says to Jesus, " 'To love [God] with all the heart, and with all the understanding, and with all the strength,' and 'to love one's neighbor as one's self'—this is much more important than all whole burnt offerings and sacrifices" (Mk 12:33). So the Pharisees didn't have to invent a whole new theology based on the destruction of the temple. Of course, they fully expected the temple to be rebuilt and sacrifices to resume. But until that day came, they assured their fellow Jews that they could still atone for their sins through the practice of mitzvoth—good works. The Pharisees and their descendants, the sages, devoted much energy to explicating the law and helping the people toward a precise understanding of their religious obligations. Only when Israel was righteous, the rabbis argued, would God send his Messiah and restore the nation—and the temple.

The Pharisees set up a "school" (that is, a center of study) in the town of Jamnia. To a people groping for direction the Pharisees spoke with hope and certainty. They urged the Jews to maintain their faith and their traditions in spite of the apparent cataclysm that had struck their land. Perhaps the Pharisees originally intended merely to guide their people in religious matters, but their leadership soon extended to civil matters as well. They even established an unofficial Sanhedrin. Of course, they didn't have any authority to pass laws or execute offenders. They depended almost wholly on their persuasive powers to bring order to Jewish society. And they weren't without competition: there were still Zealots afoot who would stir up anti-Roman sentiment at the drop of a hat. But the Pharisees and the rabbis who followed were developing a powerful presence in Judea. Eventually, they would rise beyond the status of simply one Jewish sect among many. Rabbinic Judaism became, in some sense, normative Judaism, and their unofficial authority would eventually be recognized by the Romans. By the third century A.D. the Roman emperors were dealing with the "patriarch," as the head of the rabbis came to be known, as the main civil authority of the Jews.

Jewish-Christian Relations

Usually, the Great Revolt is considered a watershed event in Jewish-Christian relations. It's difficult to assess the immediate effects of the temple's destruction on the relationship between Jews and Christians because most of our sources come from decades and centuries following the event. But the temple's fall certainly became the focal point of much Christian rhetoric in later times. Probably the Great Revolt didn't cause an immediate breech between Christians and Jews, but it certainly was a major factor contributing to the parting of the ways.

In the decades following Jesus' ascension, relations between Christians and Jews had been strained at times. According to Acts 2:47 the early Christian community enjoyed general good favor with the people of Jerusalem. A couple decades later the execution of James the brother of Jesus was met with great disfavor among the Jews (*Ant.* 20.9.1 [20-203]). So the Christians weren't universally hated. But there's a darker side to that picture. The incident may reveal something of the spirit of the times: the early Christians seemed to have enjoyed sympathy from the masses, while the Jewish leadership was hostile. Given the fact that the Christians were probably repudiating the temple sacrifices along with their proclamation of the resurrection, it's no wonder they would have earned the wrath of the priests and Sadducees. Jewish sects in this era weren't above persecuting those they opposed, as incidents in the days of Alexandra Salome and the experiences of the Dead Sea Community's "Teacher of Righteousness" demonstrate.

Relationships between the Christians and Pharisees weren't always amicable either. The Pharisees, who believed they had a lock on the religious sentiments of the masses, viewed the Christians as dangerous competition. We must not think that they were motivated simply by jealousy. In their eyes the Christians were leading the people astray from true faith of God. The Pharisees (like the Dead Sea Scrolls Community) believed that if the Jews failed to observe the laws scrupulously, God would punish the entire nation. And some Christians were advocating a major relaxation of the law. Paul especially "pushed the envelope" by insisting that Gentiles were to be included as equal partners in God's covenant without the requirements of circumcision or purity laws. Paul's method of recruiting converts among the God-fearers (Gentile admirers) in the Diaspora communities and drawing them away from the synagogues must have been especially galling. Indeed, in Rome a series of riots broke out over the very issue of Gentile proselytism, prompting the emperor Claudius to expel many Jews (and Christians) from Rome.[8] In Palestine the Pharisaic leaders were probably willing to endure the Jewish Christian community in Jerusalem, but Paul and the Gentile Christians weren't at all to their liking.

Relations between Christians and Jews were soured even more in the days of Emperor Nero. By then Christianity already had spread to the Roman Empire. Many slaves were becoming converts, and the Roman aristocracy was becoming nervous. This new religion represented a foreign innovation—which to the conservative Romans was reason enough to dislike it. Christianity spoke of freedom and human worth. It made people happy who should have been miserable. It caused people to break family ties, to abandon their ancestral gods and to adopt strange new customs. And Christians refused to worship the emperor. Wild stories circulated about secret Christian rites and barbaric practices. So when Rome caught fire in A.D. 64, and rumor had it that Nero himself might have been responsible, the emperor found the Christians a convenient scapegoat. He initiated a persecution so cruel and bloody that it actually generated some sympathy for the Christians.

---

[8]The Roman historian Suetonius, in his biography of Claudius (25.4), records that Claudius expelled the Jews who continued to riot at the instigation of "Chrestus," taken by most scholars to mean Christ. The incident is alluded to in Acts 18:2.

The Jews were exempted from this punishment. Apparently, by this time the Romans had learned to make a clear distinction between Jews and Christians. Perhaps during the trial of the apostle Paul in Rome, the nature and beliefs of this new faith had become a matter of public inquiry. Earlier, a group of Jews in Greece had tried to convince a Roman official that Paul preached a faith that was "contrary to the law"—apparently the law of Rome, since they don't say "our law" and since the Roman official would have cared nothing about the laws of the Jews (Acts 18:12-13). This group argued that Christianity was an illegal religion, outside the protection of the law. If Christianity were a Jewish sect, then the same laws that Julius Caesar had passed for the protection of Judaism would protect the Christians as well. But some Jewish leaders were insisting that it wasn't so— Christianity was *not* a Jewish sect but a new religion in its own right. Not all Jews shared this sentiment: Josephus, near the end of the first century A.D., still seems to regard the Christians as a Jewish sect (*Ant.* 18.3.3 [63-64]). But the Romans saw matters otherwise. Christianity was kicked out from under Judaism's protective umbrella and became fair game for Roman persecution. Such persecution was generally sporadic and rarely widespread, but the threat of it hung over the church for three centuries.

The Great Revolt added several more logs to the fire of Jewish-Christian animosity. The Jewish Christians, refusing to take part in revolt, were branded as traitors to their own people. They had many reasons for refusing to participate: Jesus had taught pacifism; Paul had taught submission to the government; and the messianic overtones of the Revolt would have repelled the Christians (since their Messiah had already come). The church historian Eusebius tells us that the Christians fled Jerusalem and settled in Pella, a city of the Decapolis, before the siege began. A prophetic oracle had warned them of Jerusalem's impending destruction.[9] There's certainly a kernel of history in the account, but many Christians had probably left Jerusalem before the Revolt began, seeking climates more favorable for their faith. In any case, the Christians very likely didn't suffer as greatly as many of their countrymen did.

The fall of the temple must have generated a good deal of animosity. To some of the Jews the fact that the Christians had predicted the temple's destruction, and in fact welcomed it, must have made them seem somehow *responsible* for the tragedy. Christian writers wasted no time in milking the

---

[9]Eusebius *Ecclesiastical History* 3.5, 2-3.

disaster for its apologetic value. They argued that the temple's fall justified their assertions that Jesus' death had made animal sacrifices obsolete. Now, only the sacrifice of Jesus could atone for Israel's sins and the sins of all humanity. Later church fathers claimed that Jerusalem's destruction was a divine punishment, because the Jews had rejected Jesus. It was the clearest evidence that God had abandoned the Jews. Of course, Jewish sages disagreed. They were certain that the Messiah would soon come, the temple would be rebuilt, and the priesthood would be restored to its proper place in Jewish society. Until then, God had made a way for the Jews to deal with sin and guilt: through the practice of *mitzvoth*—good works. It seemed very different from the church's central message, which stressed that "a person is justified not by the works of the law but through faith in Jesus Christ" (Gal 2:16).

We can say with some certainty that not all Jews and Christians hated one another. Throughout the first three centuries A.D., Jews and Christians intermingled freely, and Christians would even attend Jewish synagogue services (much to the consternation of their pastors). But the leadership of the two religions was growing further and further apart. The rabbinic sages following the Great Revolt resented Christianity and the way it appealed not only to Gentiles but to Jews as well. Talmudic tradition states that the rabbis of Jamnia added a curse to the synagogue service, pronouncing doom and damnation to the *minim*—the sectarians, which especially meant the Christians. Anyone who refused to say the curse was put out of the synagogue.[10] Apparently, Christians of the second century were still seeking to make converts in the Jewish synagogues, and the rabbis used this curse to expose possible proselytizers.

The animosity wasn't all one-sided. In the second century A.D. Christianity was experiencing its greatest growth among the Gentiles. Unfortunately, these Gentile converts brought an unseemly aspect of Greco-Roman culture to their faith: a virulent anti-Jewish sentiment. This hatred wasn't generated by religious differences. We've already observed that the Hellenistic world had a long-standing dislike for the Jews. But in the first century A.D., as Judaism was spreading throughout the Mediterranean world, some of the rhetoric became especially acerbic. Roman politicians and rhetoricians especially resented the ways that the masses

---

[10]*B. Tal. Berakhot* 28b. Many scholars believe this curse, one of the "Eighteen Benedictions," originated in the second century A.D., not the first, as the Talmud states.

were adopting Jewish customs like sabbath observance. The famous Latin satirist Horace made mocking caricatures of Jews in his plays. The Roman writers Seneca, Juvenal and especially Tacitus spoke with unbridled passion about the pernicious spread of Judaism throughout the realm, and called for their nation to reject or suppress the fast-growing faith. The Great Revolt encouraged some Romans to give free rein to their animosity. And in the second century A.D., more fuel was added to the fire: the Jews of Egypt, Cyrene and other regions rose up in bloody revolts in A.D. 115, wreaking terrifying violence on any Gentiles they could get their hands on. The carnage on the isle of Cyprus was so great that a law was passed that any Jew who stepped foot on the island would be executed. Then in A.D. 132 Judea once again erupted in revolt. This time a messianic figure named Simon bar Kosiba (nicknamed bar Kokhbah, "Son of the Star") led a well-organized campaign for Jewish independence. His forces inflicted heavy losses on the Roman legions before the revolt was crushed in A.D. 135. All this violence turned Gentile opinions of the Jews from mere distaste to bitter hatred. It inspired the Roman emperor Hadrian to begin a bloody persecution of the Palestinian Jews that lasted for several years.

Even after the third century A.D., when the Jewish revolutionary zeal was spent, the Gentile antipathy remained. And among the leaders of the church this hatred was institutionalized and "sanctified" with theological rationale. The Jews were "Christ-killers." They were under a curse. According to Augustine (A.D. 354-430) the Jews had been utterly rejected by God, and the church was now God's only chosen people. Bishop Ambrose (A.D. 340-397) encouraged his followers to burn synagogues. John Chrysostum (A.D. 347-407) portrayed Jews as veritable devils. Their synagogues were nothing more than "houses of prostitution" and "dwellings of demons." Those who should have loved and honored the Jews became their chief enemies. After the Emperor Constantine embraced Christianity in the early fourth century A.D. (and it was made the only legal religion by Theodosius in A.D. 380), anti-Judaism became an imperial policy.

The most tragic victims of this state of affairs were the Jewish Christians. Several church fathers poured vitriolic condemnation on those who worshiped Jesus and still observed Jewish traditions. Rejected by their ethnic brothers and sisters as traitors and rejected by their spiritual brothers and sisters as apostates, the "Nazarenes," as they were called, were persecuted by both Jews and Christians. This community could have served as a vital link between the Judaism and Christianity, fostering compassion and dialogue on both sides. Instead, they were increasingly marginalized, until the Muslims extinguished the last communities of Jewish Christians in the seventh century A.D.

Conclusion

Undoubtedly, one of the factors that has permitted the survival of anti-Semitism into our own day is that we've forgotten the Jewish roots of our faith. For centuries the church talked as if its faith had sprung from the ground or fallen from heaven instead of being nurtured in a Jewish milieu. The Old Testament was *our* book because the Jews had forfeited their rights to it. Its sole purpose was to point the way to Jesus. Some Protestants argued that for four hundred years God didn't speak to his people at all, and then suddenly he spoke a new revelation through Jesus and the apostles. God rejected Judaism and all it had stood for in favor of a new chosen people—the church.

In the last century or so there's been a renewed appreciation for the "Jewishness" of Christianity. The discovery of ancient apocalypses and the Dead Sea Scrolls has thrown new light on the origins of many core Christian affirmations. What we can recognize now, as never before, is that Christians and Jews share many common traditions. The ideas of the incarnation, the atonement and the kingdom of God can all be found in Jewish literature written before the coming of Jesus. The core teachings of Christian ethics—love of God and neighbors—were very much at home in the Jewish teachings of Jesus' day. We can no longer maintain the notion that Jesus stood radically outside the Judaism of his day. His message wasn't the *antithesis* of the Law and the Prophets; it was their *consummation*.

No doubt that by the end of the first century A.D. some significant differences had developed between Christianity and Judaism. Judaism was already placing its emphasis on proper performance of the laws and rituals, while Christianity was emphasizing proper beliefs. Judaism seems to have always been inherently less theological than Christianity—a distinction that continues to this very day. In part this difference arises from the greater impact of Greek thought on Christianity: the Hellenistic mindset prompted the church to systematic inquiry and classification of matters of the faith. Yet, fundamentally, Christianity and Judaism aren't diametrically opposed to each other even in this matter. The rabbis always contended for the importance of faith in the Lord. One couldn't be a Jew without adhering to the basic confession of faith, "Hear, O Israel! The LORD our God, the LORD is One!" (Deut 6:4 NIV). This article of belief was considered more important than any observance of the law. On the other hand, the Christian Scriptures firmly proclaim, "So faith by itself, if it has no works, is dead" (Jas 2:17). According to the New Testament, belief in Christ without good works is really no faith at all.

So Christianity and rabbinic Judaism weren't fundamentally that far apart. How could they have been? After all, they shared common Scriptures, a common history and a wealth of intertestamental literature that shaped the beliefs of both faiths. It's been our subsequent histories more than our doctrines that have kept us at odds with one another. But perhaps in the secret counsels of God, we may yet share a common destiny. It was the apostle Paul who wrote, "All Israel will be saved. . . . [F]or the gifts and calling of God are irrevocable" (Rom 11:26, 29). Perhaps there will come a day when all the deep wounds will be healed, and all God's people shall again be one.

For Further Reading

Avi-Yonah, Michael. *The Jews Under Roman and Byzantine Rule.* New York: Schocken, 1984. An interesting account of Jewish society from the Bar Kokhba revolt until the Byzantine era.

Evans, Craig A., and Donald A. Hagner, eds. *Anti-Semitism and Early Christianity: Issues of Polemic and Faith.* Minneapolis: Fortress, 1993.

Keith, Graham. *Hated Without a Cause? A Survey of Anti-Semitism.* London: Paternoster, 1997.

Mendels, Doron. *The Rise and Fall of Jewish Nationalism.* New York: Doubleday, 1992. An overview of Jewish national icons and ideals from Hellenistic times through the Bar Kokhba revolt.

Price, Jonathan J. *Jerusalem Under Siege.* Leiden: E. J. Brill, 1992. Book-length account of the Great Revolt and its causes.

Schürer, Emil. *A History of the Jewish People in the Age of Jesus Christ.* Edited by Geza Vermes, Fergus Millar and Matthew Black. Vol. 1, §§18-20. Edinburgh: T & T Clark, 1973.

Skaursaune, Oskar. *In the Shadow of the Temple: Jewish Influences on Early Christianity.* Downers Grove: InterVarsity Press, 2002. Argues for more extensive interaction and influence between Judaism and Christianity in the second to third centuries A.D. than most scholars would.

A Compendium
of Jewish History

c. 2000 B.C.	God calls a Semitic nomad named Abram to become the father of the Israelite race. He is promised the land of Canaan as his inheritance.
c. 1800-1400 B.C.	The Israelites move to Egypt, and become slaves there.
c. 1400 or 1280 B.C.	God directs Moses to lead the Israelites out of Egyptian bondage. Moses receives the laws from God.
c. 1250-1200 B.C.	The Israelites conquer Canaan.
c. 1200-1000 B.C.	Israel is ruled by charismatic leaders called "judges."
c. 1020 B.C.	The Israelites demand a king. God gives them Saul, the first Israelite monarch.
c. 1000-922 B.C.	God chooses David to replace Saul as king. David secures the kingdom against internal and external enemies. He is succeeded by his son Solomon. Israel enjoys a golden age.
c. 952 B.C.	Solomon constructs a glorious temple in Jerusalem.
922 B.C.	Solomon's successor, Rehoboam, incites civil war in Israel. The nation splits in two: Israel to the north, Judah to the south.
922-722 B.C.	Two Israelite kingdoms exist. Israel is ruled by a succession of several dynasties, while Judah is ruled by descendants of David.
722 B.C.	Israel, the northern kingdom, is destroyed by the Assyrians. Much of the native population is deported, and the region is repopulated by people of

	diverse ethnic backgrounds. These people become known as the Samaritans.
622 B.C.	King Josiah of Judah institutes a sweeping religious reform that centralizes all worship of the Lord in the Jerusalem temple, eliminating sacrifice at local shrines.
597 B.C.	Babylon conquers Judah, and places a vassal king on the throne.
587/6 B.C.	Judah rebels against Babylon, prompting the Babylonian king Nebuchadnezzar the Great to destroy Jerusalem and its temple. Leading Judean citizens are taken to Babylon as exiles.
538 B.C.	King Cyrus of Persia conquers Babylon, and issues a decree allowing the exiles to return to their homeland. Judah remains a Persian vassal, without a king.
515 B.C.	The Jews complete a new temple in Jerusalem, thus beginning the Second Temple Period.
c. 458-425 B.C.	Ezra and Nehemiah minister in Jerusalem. They are empowered by the Persian king to impose the "laws of the ancestors" on the people of Judah.
332 B.C.	The Macedonian king Alexander the Great conquers the East, and encourages the spread of Greek culture among people of Asia.
325-200 B.C.	Judea is under the rule of the Ptolemies, the Macedonian monarchs of Egypt.
323 B.C.	Alexander the Great dies, and his kingdom is divided among his generals. Egypt is ruled by the Ptolemies, and western Asia is ruled by the Seleucids.
200 B.C.	The Seleucid kingdom, based in Syria, takes Judah from the Egyptians, and adds it to its own kingdom.
167 B.C.	The Seleucid monarch Antiochus IV Epiphanes attempts to force the Jews to adopt Greek culture and religion. He desecrates the temple and persecutes the Jews.
164 B.C.	Jewish rebels, led by the Hasmonean family, retake the temple and secure an end to the persecution.

140 B.C.	The Jews succeed in winning independence from the Seleucid state.
140-63 B.C.	Judea is ruled by the Hasmonean Dynasty.
63 B.C.	The Romans conquer Judea, and it becomes part of a Roman province.
63-37 B.C.	Judea is administered by its high priest and governors.
37-6 B.C.	Herod the Great is king of Judea, which remains a vassal state of Rome.
6 B.C.-A.D. **41**	Judea is governed by Herod's son Archelaus until A.D. 4, when he is replaced with a succession of Roman governors. Galilee and the north Transjordan region are governed by Herod's other sons.
A.D. **41-44**	Herod Agrippa is king of Judea and vassal of Rome.
A.D. **44-66**	Judea is ruled by Roman governors.
A.D. **66**	Judea and Galilee revolt against Roman rule.
A.D. **70**	The Romans conquer Jerusalem, and the second temple is destroyed.
A.D. **74**	The Romans conquer the last Jewish strongholds, and the revolt is brought to an end.

Glossary and Pronunciation Guide

Most pronunciations will be self-explanatory, but vowels require some clarification:

Short "a," as in "can," is represented by the vowel alone. Long "a" sound, as in "day," is written "ay." Short "e" as in "pet" is represented by the vowel alone. Long "e" sound, as in "peat," is written "ee." Short "i," as in "tip," is represented by the vowel alone. Long "i" sound, as in "die," is written "ie." Short "o" sound, as in "sod," is represented by the vowel alone. Long "o," as in "toe," is written "oe." Short "u" sound, as in "put," is represented by the vowel alone. Long "u" sound is represented "oo." The shewah sound, or "semi-vowel," is represented as "uh." An asterisk before a term indicates that the term is also in the glossary.

Aemilius Scaurus (ee-MEE-lee-uss SKOW-russ). Roman general and governor of Coele-Syria.

Ahura Mazda (uh-HER-rah MAHZ-duh). Good god of the Zoroastrian duality.

Agrippa (uh-GRIP-puh). **1.** Roman general and friend of *Herod the Great, died 12 B.C. **2.** Agrippa I, grandson of Herod the Great and king of Judea, A.D. 37-44. **3.** Agrippa II, son of Agrippa I and Jewish king (though not of Judea), ruled c. A.D. 50-93

Alcimus (al-KI-muss). Jewish high priest, contemporary of Judas Hasmonai.

Alexander. 1. Alexander the Great, Macedonian king, died c. 323 B.C. **2.** Alexander Balas (BAL-ass), usurper of *Seleucid throne (150-145 B.C.) **3.** Son of *Aristobulus II, died c. 49 B.C. **4.** Son of *Herod the Great and *Mariamne, executed 7 B.C.

Alexander Janneus (jan-NEE-uss). *Hasmonean priest-king, 103-76 B.C.

Alexandra (al-eck-SAN-druh). Daughter of *Hyrcanus II, mother of *Mariamne.

Alexandra Salome (SAH-loe-may). *Hasmonean queen (76-67 B.C).

Angra Mainyu (AHN-gruh mah-EEN-you). The evil god in the Zoroastrian duality.

Antigonus (an-TI-goe-nuss). **1.** Successor of *Alexander the Great; died 302 B.C. **2.** Son of *Aristobulus II, ruled as *Hasmonean king (40-37 B.C.).

Antiochus (an-TEE-uh-cuss). Name of several *Seleucid rulers, including (among others): **1.** Antiochus I Soter (SOE-ter; 281-261 B.C.) **2.** Antiochus II Theos (THEE-oss; 261-246 B.C.) **3.** Antiochus III the Great (223-187 B.C.) **4.** Antiochus IV Epiphanes (eh-PIFF-uh-neez), who initiated the persecution of the Jews (175-164 B.C.) **5.** Antiochus V Eupator (you-PAY-tor *or* YOU-pa-tor; 164-162 B.C.) **6.** Antiochus VII Sidetes (si-DAY-tees; 139-129 B.C.) **7.** Antiochus VIII Grypus (GRIE-puss; 125-113, 111-96 B.C.).

Antipater (an-TI-puh-ter). **1.** Father of *Herod the Great. **2.** Son of Herod the Great and Doris.

apocalypse, apocalyptic (uh-POCK-uh-lips; uh-pock-uh-LIP-tick). A genre of Jewish literature characterized by symbolic imagery that usually purports to foretell the future. Apocalyptic literature is often characterized by a strong dichotomy between the course of the present age, and the course of events in the "end times."

Apocrypha (uh-POCK-ri-fuh). The collection of Jewish texts included in the Greek versions of the Old Testament but omitted from the version accepted by the rabbis as authoritative. Various apocryphal books are still included in Catholic and Orthodox editions of the Bible but omitted from Protestant versions. Also called "deuterocanonical."

Aramaic (air-uh-MAY-ick). Semitic language adopted as the official tongue of the Babylonian and western Persian empires. It was widely spoken by the Jews in the Second Temple Period.

Aretas (AIR-e-tass). Name borne by several *Nabatean kings.

Aristeas (air-iss-TAY-uss). Subject of pseudepigraphic letter which relates a legendary account of the translation of the *Septuagint.

Aristobulus (uh-riss-toe-BYOO-luss *or* air-riss-TAH-buh-luss). **1.** Aristobulus I (104-103 B.C.), *Hasmonean priest-king. **2.** Aristobulus II (67-63 B.C.), Hasmonean priest-king. **3.** Aristobulus III, son of Alexander Hasmoneus (son of Aristobulus II), who served briefly as high priest (35 B.C.) **4.** Aristobulus IV, son of *Herod the Great and *Mariamne, executed c. 7 B.C.

Artaxerxes (ar-tuh-ZERK-sees). Persian emperor from 465 to 425 B.C.

Azazel (A-zuh-zell). Biblical demon (?) identified as a fallen angel in *1 Enoch.*

Babylonian exile. Period from the destruction of Jerusalem and the removal of its leading citizens to Babylon in 586 B.C. until the time when King Cyrus of Persia allowed the Jews to return to Jerusalem in 538 B.C.

Bacchides. (BACK-ki-dees) Seleucid governor of Coele-Syria, killed Judas Maccabees in battle.

B.C.E. "Before Common Era" (= B.C.). This nomenclature is used in many academic texts.

Belial (bee-LIE-al). Literally, "worthlessness." Used as a title for the devil in the Dead Sea Scrolls and other Jewish literature.

Caligula (cuh-LIG-you-luh). Roman emperor, A.D. 12-41.

Cambyses (kam-BIE-sees). Persian emperor, 529-522 B.C.

canon (KA-nun). An authoritative list; especially, a list of books which are considered authoritative Scripture.

C.E. "Common Era" (= A.D.). This nomenclature is used in many academic texts.

Coele-Syria (SEE-luh SEER-ee-uh). A term used by the *Seleucids and Romans for the large administrative district that contained most of Palestine and Samaria, including Judea.

Darius (duh-RIE-ess *or* DARE-ee-uss). **1.** Darius I, emperor of Persia (522-486 B.C.). **2.** Darius II, emperor of Persia (423-404 B.C.). **3.** Darius III, emperor of Persia (336-331 B.C.).

Demetrius (duh-MEE-tree-uss). Name of several *Seleucid monarchs, including: **1.** Demetrius I Soter (SOE-ter, "savior"; 162-150 B.C.). **2.** Demetrius II Nicator (ni-KAY-tor, "victor"; 145-139, 129-125 B.C.). **3.** Demetrius III Eukairos (YOU-kie-ross; "well-timed"; 95-88 B.C.)

Diadochi (die-A-doe-kee). Successors to the empire of *Alexander the Great.

Elephantine (EL-uh-fan-teen). Island near Aswan, Egypt; site of an ancient Jewish military colony.

Enoch (EE-nock). Biblical patriarch who was "translated" to heaven (Gen 5:21-24). Subject of several *pseudepigrapha.

Epaminondas (eh-pa-mi-NON-dass). Theban general and statesman, 410-362 B.C.

eschatology (es-kuh-TAH-luh-jee). Literally, "study of the end" (from the Greek). It refers to the theological beliefs of a people concerning events that will transpire at the end of the world.

Essenes (ESS-seens). One of the major Jewish sects of the late *Second Temple Period, described by both *Josephus and *Philo of Alexandria. The Essenes lived in communes and believed in predestination and eternal life.

exegesis (eks-eh-JEE-sis). Biblical interpretation.

fourth philosophy. A Jewish sect described by *Josephus whose beliefs were similar to those of the Pharisees, except that they refused to acknowledge the legitimacy of Roman rule.

Gabinius (ga-BIN-ee-uss). Roman general and governor of *Coele-Syria during the high priesthood of *Hyrcanus II.

Great Revolt. A Jewish uprising against Roman rule that began with a riot in Jerusalem in about A.D. 66 and ended with the conquest of Masada in A.D. 74.

Haggadah (hah-GA-dah *or* hah-guh-DAH). Jewish biblical interpretation designed to derive devotional or theological insights from the text.

halakhah (hah-LAH-kah *or* hah-luh-KAH). Jewish biblical interpretation designed to derive legal principles from the text.

Hasidim (hah-si-DEEM). "Pious Ones"; a Jewish resistance group active before and during the Antiochan Persecution (167 B.C.) that opposed the adoption of Greek customs by the Jews.

Hasmonean (has-moe-NEE-an). The name of the family that initiated a successful revolt against *Antiochus Epiphanes and the *Seleucid Empire in 167 B.C.

Hellenistic. Referring to the Greek-inspired culture disseminated through the ancient Mediterranean world by *Alexander the Great and his successors.

Herod (HAIR-ud). **1.** Herod the Great, king of Judea and other territories (37-4 B.C.). **2.** Herod Antipas, son of Herod the Great and ruler of Galilee (4 B.C.- A.D. 39).

Hyrcanus (HER-can-uss *or* her-CANE-uss). **1.** A member of the Tobiad family who had *Ptolemaic sympathies. **2.** John Hyrcanus, *Hasmonean high priest, 135-104 B.C. **3.** Hyrcanus II, Hasmonean high priest, 63-40 B.C.

Idumean (i-doo-MEE-an). A resident of Idumea, a region located to the south of Judea. The Idumeans were probably descendants of the biblical Edomites and were so regarded by the Jews.

intercalation (in-ter-kuh-LAY-shun). The addition of a month to the Jewish liturgical year performed twice every seven years so that the lunar-based liturgical year would align more closely with the 365-day solar year.

Jamnia (JAHM-nee-ah). Center of rabbinic Judaism after the destruction of Jerusalem in A.D. 70 up through the Bar Kokhba Revolt in A.D. 132-135.

Jason. Brother of *Onias III, appointed high priest by *Antiochus Epiphanes in 174 B.C. to promote the Hellenization of Judea.

John of Gischala (gis-KAH-la). Leader of the Jewish revolt against Rome, A.D. 67-74.

Flavius Josephus (FLAY-vee-uss joe-SEE-fuss). Jewish historian who wrote at the end of the first century A.D. and early second century A.D.

Khirbet Qumran (KER-bit koom-RON). The ruins *(khirbeh)* near the Wadi (seasonal river) Qumran where many of the Dead Sea Scrolls were found and where most scholars believe at least some of them were written.

Lysias (LISS-ee-ass). Seleucid general under *Antiochus V.

Maccabee (MACK-uh-bee). "Hammerer"; the epithet given to Judas the Hasmonean, leader of the Hasmonean Revolt.

Mariamne (mare-ee-AHM-nay). Daughter of *Hyrcanus II, wife of *Herod the Great.

Masoretic (mass-or-RET-ick). Relating to the Masorah, or "tradition." The term refers to a medieval Jewish scribal tradition concerning the proper reading and pronunciation of the Hebrew Bible (Old Testament). Modern Old Testament translations are based on the "Masoretic Text" (as opposed to, e.g., the *Septuagint).

Mastema (mass-tay-MAH). Designation for the devil in some Jewish texts.

Melchizedek (mell-KIZZ-zuh-deck). Ancient biblical priest and king, contemporary of Abraham (see Gen 14:18-20).

memra (mem-RAH). Aramaic, "word" or "speaking." Usually the Word of the Lord, conceived in some rabbinic literature as an intermediary between God and creation.

Menelaus (meh-nuh-LAY-uss). Usurper of the Jewish high priesthood in the days of *Antiochus Epiphanes.

Midrash (MID-rahsh). Homiletical Jewish biblical interpretation. Specifically, "midrash" refers to a form where a text is quoted in full or in part, illuminating passages are added and an interpretation is given that brings out a "deeper meaning" of the text.

Mishnah (MISH-nah). The collection of rabbinic legal traditions compiled in the early third century A.D. The Mishnah is arranged according to topic (e.g., "Sabbath," "Women," "Washings," etc.).

Nabatea (nab-buh-TEE-uh). Arabic kingdom located to the southeast of Judea.

Nabonidus (nah-boe-NIE-duss). Babylonian king, ruled 556-539 B.C.

Nebuchadnezzar (neb-buh-kad-NEZZ-zer). Babylonian king, ruled 605-552 B.C. Destroyed the Jerusalem temple in 586 B.C.

Nephilim (ne-fill-LEEM). Giants born to human women from unions with angelic beings (see Gen 6:4).

Onias (oe-NIE-uss). **1.** Onias II, Jewish high priest who withheld tribute from the *Ptolemies c. 220 B.C. **2.** Onias III, high priest deposed by his brother *Jason c. 174 B.C. **3.** Jewish saint killed by crowd of Jerusalemites in 63 B.C.

Osiris (oe-SIE-riss). Egyptian god of the underworld.

Palestine. Literally, "the land of the Philistines." The name given to the former land of Israel by the Romans in the second century A.D.

Pentateuch (PEN-tuh-took). The "Books of Moses," first five books of the Old Testament.

Pesher (PAY-shur). Form of prophetic interpretation used in the Dead Sea Scrolls. A prophetic verse is quoted, then a contemporary or eschatological application is provided. Plural *pesharim* (pe-sha-REEM).

Phalanx (FAY-laynks). Military formation used successfully by *Alexander the Great.

Pharisee (FAIR-uh-see). The largest Jewish sect of the late *Second Temple Period. The Pharisees adhered to oral tradition and believed in limited free will and the resurrection of the dead.

Philip. 1. Macedonian king and father of *Alexander the Great; died 336 B.C. **2.** General of *Antiochus Epiphanes who attempted a coup in 162 B.C. **3.** Son of King *Herod the Great.

Philo of Alexandria (FIE-loe). Jewish philosopher, theologian and statesman, lived c. 20 B.C.-A.D. 40.

Pliny the Elder (PLI-nee). Roman scholar, A.D. 23-79.

Popillius Laenas (puh-PILL-ee-uss LEE-nuss). Roman general who opposed *Antiochus Epiphanes' invasion of Egypt.

pseudepigrapha (soo-duh-PIG-gra-fuh). "Falsely ascribed"; texts written in the name of an ancient sage or seer.

Ptolemy, Ptolemaic (TOLE-uh-mee, tole-uh-MAY-ick). **1.** Relating to the dynasty founded by Ptolemy, general and successor of *Alexander the Great. It was centered in Egypt. **2.** Throne name of every king of the Ptolemaic dynasty. **3.** Son-in-law of Simon Hashmonai, assassinated Simon around 134 B.C.

rabbinic Judaism. The predominant form of Judaism from about A.D. 200 forward. It espoused the legal teachings of the rabbis, or "great ones," and follows closely the theology of the *Pharisees.

rephaim (reh-fie-EEM). Hebrew, "those who sink down." Hebrew word for spirits of the dead.

Sadducee (SAD-you-see). One of the main Jewish sects, or schools of thought, in the late *Second Temple Period.

Salome (SA-loe-may). "peace." Sister of *Herod the Great.

Samaritan (suh-MARE-i-tan). A native of Samaria, the land located north of Judea whose religious beliefs were based on the teachings of the *Pentateuch.

Sanhedrin (san-HEE-drin). The Jewish senate.

satrap (SA-trap). The governor of a *satrapy* (SA-trap-ee), an administrative district in the Persian Empire.

scroll. A roll of parchment, papyrus or other material containing written texts. Scrolls were usually inscribed on one side, and sheets could be sewn together to accommodate a longer text.

Second Temple Period. The time of the second Jerusalem temple, 538 B.C.-A.D. 70.

Seleucid (suh-LOO-chid). Pertaining to the dynasty founded by Seleucus, general and successor of *Alexander the Great. It was centered in Syria, and its capital was Antioch.

Seleucus (suh-LOO-kuss). **1.** Seleucus I Nicator (ni-KAY-tor), first ruler of *Seleucid dynasty (304-281 B.C.). **2.** Seleucus II Callinicus (ka-LIN-i-kuss), Seleucid ruler (246-226 B.C.). **3.** Seleucus III Soter (SOE-ter), Seleucid ruler (226-223 B.C.). **4.** Seleucus IV Philopater, Seleucid ruler (187-175 B.C.).

Septuagint (sep-TOO-uh-jint *or* SEP-too-uh-jint). A Greek translation of the Hebrew Bible.

Sheol (shee-OLE). The Hebrew abode of the dead.

Sheshbazzar (SHESH-buh-zar). Jewish governor who led the first wave of repatriates from Babylon to Judea in 538 B.C.

Sicarii (si-CAR-ee-ee). "Dagger men"; Jewish assassins of the last decades of the Second Temple Period.

Soaemus (soe-EE-muss). Official of Herod the Great, executed on charges of committing adultery with Mariamne.

Talmud (TAL-mood). The authoritative text of *rabbinic Judaism. It consists of the *Mishnah and homiletical commentaries on the Mishnah known as the *gemara* ("completion").

Tannaitic (tan-nuh-IT-ick). Referring to the rabbis of the first two centuries A.D., prior to the completion of the *Mishnah.

Targum (TAR-goom). An Aramaic translation of the Old Testament. Many *targumin* contain "glosses," or expansions, of the biblical texts.

Tattenai (TAT-ten-eye). Late fifth century B.C. Persian governor of Abar-Nahara, the satrapy to which Judah belonged.

Tobiah (toe-BIE-uh). Judean sheik of Ammonite descent who opposed Nehemiah. His family was very influential in Judean politics in the early Hellenistic period.

Torah (tore-RAH). "Law"; the *Pentateuch, or first five books of the Hebrew Bible.

Tryphon (TRY-fon). *Seleucid general under *Alexander Balas; briefly seized the throne in c. 142 B.C.; assassinated Jonathan Hashmonai around 143 B.C.

Vespasian (vess-PAY-zee-an). Roman general and later emperor, ruled A.D. 69-79.

Xerxes (ZERK-sees). King of the Persia Empire, 486-465 B.C.

Zealots. Jewish resistance faction of the *Great Revolt, probably related to Josephus's *fourth philosophy.

Zerubbabel (zuh-ROO-buh-bull). Jewish governor of Judah who completed the Second temple.

Zoroaster (ZOR-uh-was-ter). Persian prophet and founder of Zoroastrianism.

Subject Index

Abar-Nahara, 55, 72, 336
agora, 228
Agrippa I, 265, 280, 309-10, 328-29
Agrippa II, 310-12, 329
Akra, 135, 148, 150, 155, 157, 187-88, 206, 269, 316
Albinus, 311
Alcimus, 151, 153-54, 329
Alexander (son of Aristobulus II), 152, 155-57, 191, 249-51, 329, 336
Alexander Janneus, 178-80, 199, 201-4, 206, 209, 211, 225, 281, 294, 329-30
Alexander the Great, 18, 106-9, 111-16, 119, 122-23, 213-14, 218, 235-36, 244, 266, 298, 327, 329-32, 334-36
Alexandria, 41, 108, 119, 121, 223-24, 252, 257, 308
angels, 27, 30, 76-80, 82, 86, 88, 91, 128, 169, 296, 298, 302
Animal Apocalypse, 28, 32, 88, 208
Antigonus (ruler of Judea), 194, 198, 250-51, 255, 257-61, 269, 330
Antigonus (successor of Alexander the Great), 114, 119, 330
Antioch, 120, 122, 126, 128, 132-33, 150, 156-57, 207, 222, 224, 251, 260, 335
Antiochus I Soter, 330
Antiochus III, 121-22, 126-27, 234, 330

Antiochus IV Epiphanes, 18, 21, 26, 110, 127-35, 137-38, 141, 146, 148-52, 155, 192, 200, 207-10, 218, 233, 266, 292, 298, 327, 330, 332-34
Antiochus VII Sidetes, 152, 188, 190-91, 330
Antipater (father of Herod the Great), 206, 251-55, 330
Antipater (son of Herod the Great), 271-73, 330
Antony, 247, 255-57, 259-60, 262-64, 269
Apion, 22, 40, 196, 215, 217, 227, 232-33
apocalypse, apocalyptic, 7, 28-29, 35, 241, 300, 302, 330
Apocrypha, 19, 23, 26, 34, 45-47, 90, 241, 330
Apollonius, 145, 156, 215
Apollonius Molon, 215
Aramaic, 19, 21, 26-27, 34, 42-43, 55, 59, 61, 65-66, 71-73, 88, 125, 174, 177, 217, 222, 224, 226-27, 234, 242, 294, 330, 333, 336
archaeology, 15-16, 47
archangels, 79
Aretas, 202, 330
Aretas III, 206, 330
Aristeas, Letter of, 22, 30-31, 222, 330
Aristobulus I, 196-99, 206, 211, 330
Aristobulus II, 203-8, 211, 250-51, 255, 281, 294, 329-30
Aristobulus III, 262-63, 271-72, 330
Aristotle, 106, 214, 237, 244
Artaxerxes, 59, 61, 196, 331
assimilation, 67, 243
astrology, 217, 236-37
Athens, 104-5, 213, 216, 243-44

Augustine, 244, 323
Augustus. *See* Octavian
Azazel, 80, 88-89, 331
Baal Shemayin, 125, 217
Babylonian exile, 69-70, 78, 81, 87, 91, 97, 161, 183, 186, 290, 331
Babylonians, 37, 48, 51, 57, 65, 72, 77, 85, 94, 183, 214, 235-36, 279, 290
Bacchides, 151-54, 331
bandits, 253-54, 260, 283, 285-86, 295, 311
Bar Kokhba, 325, 333
2 Baruch, 31, 280
Behistun (Bisitun), 66
Belial, 9, 88, 90, 180, 331
Ben Sira, 33-34, 91, 95, 226, 241, 290
Beth-Zechariah, 150
Beth-Zur, 147, 149-50, 158
calendar, 182-84, 208
Caligula, 266, 276, 308-9, 331
canon, canonization, 19-25, 32-33, 100, 331
Cassius, 255-56
Christianity, 19, 22, 40, 73, 91, 164-65, 173, 175, 178, 184, 209, 243-44, 281, 297, 305-6, 320-25
Cicero, 215
circumcision, 130-31, 231, 281, 320
Claudius, 309, 320
Cleopatra III, 199, 200, 247
Cleopatra VII, 252-53, 256-57, 259, 262-65
Community Rule, 33-34, 88, 284
Cyrus the Great, 49, 107
Damascus Document, 33-34, 178-79, 293
Daniel, book of, 18-19, 21, 23, 28, 32, 35, 73, 76, 78-79, 90, 99, 139, 143, 170, 208, 227, 280, 290-93, 295-97, 300, 303

225-26, 228, 231-33, 243-
44, 255, 257, 275, 280, 285,
305-6, 313, 320, 331, 334
Parthia, 120, 150, 191, 258
Paul, 24-25, 93, 97, 131, 169,
216, 223-24, 231, 240, 243,
256, 276, 281-82, 286, 304,
310, 320-21, 325
Pella, 321
Pentateuch, 63, 111, 171,
224, 227, 334-36
people of the land, 54, 58,
69-70, 72, 138
Perdiccas, 113-14
Persia, Persians, 18, 49, 54,
69, 73-74, 76, 78, 82, 85,
102, 104-5, 109, 112, 139,
149, 189, 221, 223, 327,
331, 336
personification, 241
pesher, 37
phalanx, 106
Pharisees, 14, 19, 27, 38, 91,
144, 160-73, 177-78, 180,
185, 195-96, 200-201, 203-
6, 270, 281, 284, 286, 288,
318-20, 332, 334-35
Phasaelus, 256-58
Philip of Macedon, 106,
113, 298, 309, 334
Philip (Seleucid general),
149-51, 334
Philip (son of Herod the
Great), 272, 274, 276, 334
Philo of Alexandria, 23, 41,
163, 173, 217-18, 224, 231,
234, 236, 238, 280, 332, 334
philosophy, 41, 74, 242-44
among the Jews, 238-39,
242
characteristic of the
Greeks, 105, 163, 169,
216-17,
Phoenicia, 118, 120-22, 145,
199, 217-18, 223
Phrygia, 114
Plato, 169, 216, 238, 242
Pliny the Elder, 176, 334

polis, 122, 123, 125, 130
Pollio, 269-70
Pompey, 207-8, 247-52
Pontius Pilate, 162, 308
Popillius Laenas, 134, 334
Prometheus, 80
prophecy, 18, 23, 29, 37, 56-
58, 196-97, 201, 289, 291-
93, 295
Psalms of Solomon, 31, 209,
280, 284, 294, 297
pseudepigrapha, 18, 27-29,
32, 37, 90, 294, 331, 334
Ptolemy (son-in-law of Simon Hashmonai), 114-16,
119, 126, 189-90, 334-35
Ptolemy I Soter, 115, 118,
334-35
Ptolemy II Philadelphus,
116, 118, 120, 123, 222-24,
334-35
Ptolemy III Uergetes, 120-
21, 233, 334-35
Ptolemy IV Philopator, 121-
22, 334-35
Ptolemy V Epiphanes, 116,
122, 334-35
Ptolemy VI, 133, 156-57,
334-35
Ptolemy IX Lathyrus, 199,
334-35
Ptolemy XII, 252, 334-35
Ptolemy XIII, 251-52, 334-
35
Qumran, 33-34, 36, 46, 176,
178, 185, 293, 333
rabbinic literature, 42, 44,
163, 165, 171-74, 234, 241-
42, 333
Raphael, 79, 306
resurrection of the dead, 8,
27, 32, 91, 96, 143, 161,
166, 169-71, 173, 288, 334
Revelation, book of, 20, 25,
28, 90, 282
Rome, 22, 112, 127-29, 134,
151-52, 207-8, 223, 230,
239, 245-51, 253, 256, 271-

72, 274, 277, 285-87, 314,
316-17, 320-21
as allies of the Jews, 152,
158
conquest of Judea, 28,
37-40, 175, 249-50, 259-
60
end of the republic, 246-
47
management of Judea,
31, 208, 263-66, 279-83,
308-9, 311
sabbath observance, 143-
44, 184, 323
sacrifices, 48, 53-54, 63, 67,
78, 111-12, 117, 130, 135,
174-75, 178, 182-84, 208,
215, 217, 234, 316, 318,
319, 322
Sadducees, 8, 14, 19, 27, 91,
95, 160-67, 169-73, 177-78,
185, 195-96, 203-4, 206,
220, 281, 286, 318-19
Salome, 199-200, 203, 205,
209, 211, 264, 271-72, 281,
319, 330, 335
Samaritans, 54, 56, 58, 63-
64, 108, 110-11, 145, 170,
192, 195, 249, 277, 308, 327
Sameas, 254, 269-70
Sanhedrin, 42, 59, 154, 163,
169, 204-5, 232, 234-35,
254-55, 269-70, 274, 276-
77, 297, 303-4, 318-19, 335
Satan, 82-83, 86-87, 89-90,
303
satrap, 55-56, 59, 66, 108,
114, 335
Scaurus, 207, 249, 329
scribe, 21, 28-29, 61-62
Scythopolis, 123, 225
Sebaste, 267, 272
Seleucids, 119-22, 125-28,
135, 145-47, 152, 158-59,
161, 187, 194, 214, 327, 331
Seleucus I, 114-15, 119-22,
335
Seleucus II, 120-21

Scripture Index